International Max Planck Research School (IMPRS)
for Maritime Affairs
at the University of Hamburg

For further volumes:
http://www.springer.com/series/6888

Hamburg Studies on Maritime Affairs
Volume 20

Edited by

Chen-Ju Chen

Fisheries Subsidies under International Law

Springer

Chen-Ju Chen
No. 137, Singjhong First Road
80243 Kaohsiung
Taiwan R.O.C.
crystalchenju@gmail.com

Dissertation zur Erlangung der Doktorwürde
an der Fakultät für Rechtswisseschaft der Universität Hamburg
Vorgelegt von: Chen-Ju Chen
Erstgutachter: Prof. Dr. Dr. h.c. Rüdiger Wolfrum
Zweitgutachter: Prof. Dr. Dr. h.c. Peter Ehlers
Tag der mündlichen Prüfung: 30. Juni 2010

ISSN 1614-2462 e-ISSN 1867-9587
ISBN 978-3-642-15692-2 e-ISBN 978-3-642-15693-9
DOI 10.1007/978-3-642-15693-9
Springer Heidelberg Dordrecht London New York

Library of Congress Control Number: 2010936900

Cover design: WMXDesign GmbH, Heidelberg

Printed on acid-free paper

Springer is part of Springer Science+Business Media (www.springer.com)

To my parents, Pey-Der Chen and Li-Chu Tsai

Preface

Even though fisheries subsidies have been around for centuries, these remain a relatively new subject in international law.

I wish to acknowledge and express my appreciation to all those who played a major role in the conception, development and successful completion of this dissertation.

First, I would like to express my gratitude to Prof. Dr. Rüdiger Wolfrum who acted as my doctoral supervisor and provided helpful suggestions and guidance in the development and formation of this dissertation. I also wish to thank Prof. Dr. Peter Ehlers who acted as the second reviewer. Of special note is Prof. Dr. Rainer Lagoni who was always there to provide assistance and encouragement whenever needed. Inexhaustible assistance was provided by the staffs of the International Max Plank Research School for Maritime Affairs and those at the libraries of the Heidelberg Max Planck Institute for Comparative Public Law and International Law and the Hamburg Max Planck Institute for Comparative and International Private Law. The seminars organized by Prof. Dr. Ehlers and Prof. Dr. Lagoni and the various projects coordinated by the International Max Planck Research School gave me a greater and deeper insight and understanding in maritime affairs. The full scholarships granted by the International Max Planck Research School ensured that I had all the necessary resources during my stay in Hamburg to complete my research without financial concerns.

I am indebted to Dr. Cornelius Hammer (Director General of the Federal Research Centre for Fisheries), Director Jean-Francois Pulvenis de Séligny M. and Dr. Rebecca Metzer (Fisheries and Aquaculture Economics and Policy Division, Fisheries and Aquaculture Department, Food and Agriculture Organization of the United Nations) for their assistance and support.

My most heartfelt gratitude and appreciation go to my parents and younger brother who were always there for me with love and encouragement throughout my extended absence from home.

Special thanks to my friends, Dr. Bui Anh, Dr. Necip Kagan Kocaoglu, Beatrice Schütte and Angelika Sitz, who helped me accomplish this study in a number of different ways. Finally, I wish to express special recognition for Luis Franco who helped me in the final stages of this study and; without whose help, brainstorming and challenging observations, I could have not completed this study.

Hamburg, July 2010 Chen-Ju Chen

Preface

Table of Contents

Abbreviations

AB	Appellate Body
ACP	African, Caribbean and Pacific
AD	Antidumping Agreement
AoA	Agreement on Agriculture
APEC	Asia-Pacific Economic Cooperation
Bridges Trade BioRes	Bridges Trade and Biological Resources
CAC	Codex Alimentarius Commission
CBD	Convention on Biological Diversity
CCAMLR	Commission for the Conservation of Antarctic Marine Living Resources
CCSBT	Commission for the Conservation of Southern Bluefin Tuna
CFP	Common Fisheries Policy
CITES	Convention on International Trade in Endangered Species of Wild Fauna and Flora
COFI(FAO)	Committee on Fisheries
COP	Conference of the Parties (to the CBD)
CPC	Contracting Party, Cooperating Non-Contracting Party, Entity or Fishing Entity
CRN	Central Registry of Notifications
CTE	Committee on Trade and Environment
DG	Directorate-General
DSB	Dispute Settlement Body
DSM	Dispute Settlement Mechanism
DSU	Dispute Settlement Understanding
DWF	Distant Water Fleet
DWFN	Distant Water Fishing Nation
EAFRD	European Agricultural Fund for Rural Development
EAGF	European Agricultural Guarantee Fund
EAGGF	European Agriculture Guidance and Guarantee Fund
EC	European Communities
EDB	Environmental Data Base
EEZ	Exclusive Economic Zone

EFF	European Fisheries Fund
ERDF	European Regional Development Fund
ESF	European Social Fund
EU	European Union
FAA	Fisheries Access Agreement
FAO	Food and Agriculture Organization of the United Nations
FIFG	Fisheries Instrument for Fisheries Guidance
FIRMS	Fishery Resources Monitoring System
FOC	Flags of Convenience
FPA	Fisheries Partnership Agreement
GATT	General Agreement on Tariffs and Trade
GFCM	General Fisheries Commission for the Mediterranean
GFT	Government Financial Transfer
HSVAR	High Seas Vessel Authorization Records
IATTC	Inter-American Tropical Tuna Commission
ICCAT	International Commission for the Conservation of Atlantic Tunas
ICES	International Council for the Exploration of the Seas
ICNAF	International Commission for the Northwest Atlantic Fisheries
ICSEAF	International Commission for the Southeast Atlantic Fisheries
ICTSD	International Centre for Trade and Sustainable Development
IEC	International Electrotechnical Commission
IGO	Intergovernmental Organization
IMF	International Monetary Fund
IOTC	Indian Ocean Tuna Commission
IPHC	International Pacific Halibut Commission
IPOA	International Plan of Action
ISO	International Organization for Standardization
ITO	International Trade Organization
ITQ	Individual Transferable Quota
ITU	International Telecommunications Union
IUU	Illegal, Unreported and Unregulated (Fishing)
LDC	Least-developed Country
LVFO	Lake Victoria Fisheries Organization
MAGP	Multi-Annual Guidance Programme
MCS	Monitoring, Control and Surveillance

MEA	Multilateral Environmental Agreement
MOU	Memorandum of Understanding
MSC	Marine Stewardship Council
MSY	Maximum Sustainable Yield
NAFO	Northwest Atlantic Fisheries Organization
NASCO	North Atlantic Salmon Conservation Organization
NGAG	Negotiating Group on Agriculture
NPOA	National Plan of Action
NRBPs	Negotiating Group on Natural Resource Based Products
NSP	National Strategic Plan
OECD	Organisation for Economic Co-operation and Development
OIML	International Organization of Legal Metrology
OJ	Official Journal (of the European Communities)
PGE	Permanent Group of Experts
PGFE	Permanent Group of Fisheries Experts
R&D	Research and Development
RFMO	Regional Fisheries Management Organization
RPOA	Regional Plan of Action
S&D	Special and Differential (Treatment)
SBSTTA	(CBD's) Subsidiary Body on Scientific, Technical and Technological Advice
SCM	(Agreement on) Subsidies and Countervailing Measures
SEAFDEC	Southeast Asian Fisheries Development Center
SME	Small and Medium-sized Enterprise
SPS	(Agreement on the Application of) Sanitary and Phytosanitary Measures
SVE	Small, Vulnerable Economy
TAC	Total Allowable Catch
TBT	(Agreement on)Technical Barriers to Trade
TPRM	Trade Policy Review Mechanism
TRIMs	(Agreement on) Trade-Related Investment Measures
TRIPS	(Agreement on) Trade-Related Aspects of Intellectual Property Rights
UN	United Nations
UNCLOS	United Nations Convention on the Law of the Sea
UNEP	United Nations Environment Programme

VMS	Vessel Monitoring System
WCO	World Customs Organization
WCPFC	Western and Central Pacific Fisheries Commission
WECAFC	Western Central Atlantic Fisheries Commission
WHO	World Health Organization
WSSD	World Summit on Sustainable Development
WTO	World Trade Organization
WWF	World Wildlife Fund

Introduction

The practice of governments providing financial assistance to sectors of the economy or directly to private companies in order to protect infant industries or encourage economic development in a given region has been in existence for many centuries. Scotland, for example, was already providing fisheries subsidies to herring and whale fisheries in the eighteenth century. Governments assist fishing industries in order to promote economic growth in coastal areas, help fishing industries modernize fleets, and more recently encourage these industries to move in a more responsible and environmentally friendly direction.

Fisheries subsidies are currently estimated to be between USD 15-20 billion annually, which represents approximately twenty percent of the revenues of global fisheries.[1] The majority of fisheries subsidies are granted by a handful of economically powerful nations in a wide variety of forms, including direct government payments to the fishing industries, tax waivers and deferrals, government loans and loan guarantees, and general programmes that affect fisheries.

Most fisheries subsidies have negative impacts on trade, the environment and sustainable development. On the trade front, fisheries subsidies can go against the efforts by the world community to liberalize international trade in fish and fish products. By giving an unfair competitive advantage to the exports of the subsidizing countries, this may result in negatively impacting the domestic fishing industries in the importing countries. In addition, the fishing industries of other exporting countries are put at a disadvantage when trying to compete in countries where subsidized products are imported. This includes the subsidizer's own domestic market which is protected against imports from non-subsidizers by being able to price its products below the prices of the potential imports. On the environmental and sustainable development fronts, subsidies can encourage the fishing industry to overfish and deplete fish stocks beyond sustainable levels, altering the ecological balance with perhaps irremediable consequences and eventually affecting the livelihood of the fishermen themselves by reducing fishing opportunities.

---

1 *Matteo Milazzo*, "Subsidies in World Fisheries: A Reexamination", World Bank Technical Paper No. 406 (Washington, D.C.: World Back, 1998); *WWF*, "Hard Facts, Hidden Problems: A review of Current Data on Fishing Subsidies" (Washington, D.C. and Gland: WWF, 2001); *R. Sumaila and D. Pauly*, "Catching More Bait: A Bottom-up Re-Estimate of Global Fisheries Subsidies" (Vancouver: University of British Columbia Fisheries Centre, 2006). However, due to the lack of data availability and comparability, these studies have been subject to some controversy.

C.-J. Chen, *Fisheries Subsidies under International Law*, Hamburg Studies on Maritime Affairs 20, DOI 10.1007/978-3-642-15693-9_1, © Springer-Verlag Berlin Heidelberg 2010

Because of the unique nature of the negative impacts of fisheries subsidies, the existing subsidies regulations, i.e. the General Agreement on Tariffs and Trade (GATT) and the Agreement on Subsidies and Countervailing Measures (SCM Agreement), which focus on the impact of subsidies on market and price distortions, fail to adequately address fisheries subsidies issues. An attempt was made to incorporate fisheries issues in the Uruguay Round Negotiations as part of the Agreement on Agriculture, but this was ultimately abandoned due to lack of consensus among Members of the World Trade Organization (WTO).

Fisheries issues remained largely disregarded until a Special Session of the United Nations General Assembly, dubbed the Earth Summit Agenda 21,[2] in 1997, which recognized the urgent need to prevent and eliminate overfishing and overcapacity and to make international trade and environmental policies mutually supportive of sustainable development. It further called for governments to consider the impact of subsidies on fishery conservation and management and to adopt appropriate action.[3] This was the first time that any action was taken on fisheries subsidies at the United Nations (UN) level.

The Food and Agriculture Organization of the United Nations (FAO) then developed some provisions which take into account that subsidies may lead to overcapacity and illegal, unreported and unregulated (IUU) fishing. However, due to their voluntary legal nature and reliance on a model of unilateral action by fishing nations, these were not sufficient to regulate fisheries subsidies effectively.

Given this background, there has been global interest in the necessity for enforceable fisheries subsidies regulations. Several WTO Members proposed to work on fisheries subsidies regulations within the WTO framework. In 2001, the Doha Ministerial Conference responded to this proposal by calling on Members to clarify and improve the SCM provisions to cover fisheries subsidies while taking into account the special needs of developing countries and the environment. Implicit in the Doha Ministerial Declaration was the recognition that a global dialogue would benefit all the fishing industries of WTO Members and would lead to a sustainable fish population for other smaller, developing, non-WTO Members.[4]

By launching negotiations based on concerns for fisheries conservation and sustainable development, and not merely traditional trade concerns, the WTO took a concrete step towards realizing the goal in the preamble to the Marrakesh Agreement establishing the WTO (WTO Agreement) which states that its goals include "the optimal use of the world's resources in accordance with the principles of sustainable development, seeking both to protect and preserve the environment

---

2 Earth Summit Agenda 21 was adopted by more than 178 governments at the United Nations Conference on Environment and Development (UNCED) held in Rio de Janeiro, Brazil, 3 to 14 June 1992. It was a comprehensive plan of action to be taken globally, nationally and locally by organizations of the UN system, governments and major groups in every area in which mankind affects the environment.

3 *UN* Doc. No. A/RES/S-19/2, "Resolution Adopted by the General Assembly" (19 September 1997), paras. 36(e) and (f).

4 *Derek J. Dostal*, "Global Fisheries Subsidies: Will the WTO Reel in Effective Regulations?", University Pennsylvania Journal of International Economic Law, Vol. 26, No. 4, pp. 815-839 (2005), at 828.

and to enhance the means for doing so."[5] By improving fisheries subsidies regulations to eliminate the negative impact of fisheries subsidies, the WTO has the opportunity to demonstrate that trade liberalization can benefit the environment and contribute to sustainable development and that trade liberalization and environmental protection can and should be complementary goals.

The WTO negotiations culminated in the legal draft on fisheries subsidies to be annexed to the SCM Agreement, circulated by the Chairman of the Negotiating Group on Rules in November 2007. Responding to the mandates of the WTO Ministerial Conferences, this legal text (Chair's text) includes a list of prohibited fisheries subsidies, the general exceptions to the prohibited fisheries subsidies, special and differential (S&D) treatment of developing country Members and the requirements for effective fisheries management systems as well as the notifications and surveillance procedures. Since then, the discussions at the WTO have focused on the provisions of the Chair's text, in particular on how to make them more enforceable.

Based on this background, this study seeks to determine whether the new fisheries subsidies regulations adequately address the shortcomings in the existing regulations as well as their impact on WTO Members.

The study is divided into four main parts as follows:

First, the study introduces the background of fisheries subsidies, including definition, classification and impacts. It then looks into the international fisheries instruments which contain principles for managing fisheries and provisions on fisheries subsidies. It further examines the current subsidies regulations within the GATT/WTO framework to understand to what extent that they can be applied to fisheries subsidies (Chapter 1).

Second, the study follows the path of the negotiations in the WTO through the submissions of Members in order to fully understand the complexity of the issues and the different positions taken by Members. Similarly, the mandates of the Doha and Hong Kong Ministerial Declarations which provide direction to the negotiations are also examined (Chapter 2).

Third, the study assesses how effective the proposed regulations are in meeting the diverse interests of the stakeholders by examining the Chair's text. It evaluates how well the Chair's text responds to the proposals made by Members during the negotiations, how it reacts to the input provided by interested international organizations and to what extent it adheres to the mandates of the Ministerial Declarations. The issues range from the scope of prohibited and non-prohibited fisheries subsidies, the effectiveness of the S&D treatment of developing country Members, the criteria established for subsidies to the fishing industries, the extent to which cooperation between the WTO and other competent international organizations

---

5 *Alice L. Mattice*, "The Fisheries Subsidies Negotiations in the World Trade Organization: a "Win-Win" for Trade, the Environment and Sustainable Development", Golden Gate University Law Review, Vol. 34, pp. 573 *et seq* (2005), at 574-575; Preamble to the Marrakesh Agreement Establishing the World Trade Organization, para. 1.

with fisheries expertise is used to administer and enforce the regulations, and the effectiveness of the transparency and surveillance provisions (Chapter 3).

Finally, the study looks at the procedures and legislation that the European Union (EU) has in place in order to manage fisheries subsidies and capacity through its structural policies. It further compares these provisions with the WTO Chair's text to understand how the proposed regulations would impact the EU (Chapter 4).

Chapter 1: Fisheries Subsidies and Current Regulations under International Law

I. Introduction

Due to the negative impact that fisheries subsidies have on trade, the environment and sustainable development, there is an urgent need to regulate fisheries subsidies. However, current legal frameworks are ineffective at regulating fisheries subsidies. Depletion of fish stocks can lead to permanent changes in the dynamics of the marine ecosystem as well as to the extinction of some fish species and the economic devastation of the communities whose livelihoods depend on healthy fisheries. These resources are non-renewable if not properly managed. In spite of work done by intergovernmental organizations on this front, progress to date has been insufficient to control fisheries subsidies. This Chapter looks into the nature of fisheries subsidies. It then examines to what extent current regulations under international law can be applied to fisheries subsidies and demonstrates why new legislation is required.

II. Background of Fisheries Subsidies Issues

A. Magnitude of Global Fisheries Subsidies

Subsidies to the fisheries sector in both developed and developing countries have existed for hundreds of years. In the late eighteenth century, fisheries subsidies already existed for herring and whale fisheries in Scotland. In the nineteenth century, several other North Atlantic fishing nations and Japan felt compelled to subsidize fishing, due to the fear that other nations with more modern fleets would otherwise grab their share of the fish harvested from international waters. By the middle of the twentieth century, governments that could afford it were supporting commercial fishing by various means, including helping with the conversion of fishing fleets to powered ships, and replacing oar and sail vessels, as well as through direct capital grants, loans and assistance for major port improvements.[6]

---

6 *Ronald P. Steenblik*, "Previous Multilateral Efforts to Discipline Subsidies to Natural Resource Based Industries" (Paris: OECD, 1998), at 19.

C.-J. Chen, *Fisheries Subsidies under International Law*, Hamburg Studies on Maritime Affairs 20, DOI 10.1007/978-3-642-15693-9_2,

There have been several significant intergovernmental efforts to quantify fisheries subsidies. A World Bank study estimated environmentally harmful global fisheries subsidies between USD 15-20 billion, depending on the low and high estimates for the various subsidy categories.[7] Similarly, the United Nations Environment Programme (*UNEP) and the* World Wildlife Fund (WWF) estimated that the actual level of global fisheries subsidies is at least USD 15 billion,[8] which amounts to 20 percent of the total value of global fish catches. More than 90 percent of global fisheries subsidies are provided by a few countries.[9] It is estimated that governments of the Organization for Economic Co-operation and Development (OECD) spend USD 6 billion on financial transfers,[10] of which one third is destined for research, management and enforcement, another third for fisheries infrastructure and another third in various other forms.[11]

The actual level of fisheries subsidies differs from what governments officially report to the international organizations. The reasons include the failure of most governments to comply with WTO legal obligations of notification requirements;[12] inadequate cooperation from governments with data collection efforts; failure to account fully for important classes of subsidies from which fishing enterprises directly benefit, including certain shipbuilding subsidies, subsidies to the fish-processing sector and payments under government-to-government fishing access agreements; underreporting of off-budget subsidies; and failure to account sufficiently for subsidies granted by sub-national governments, i.e. national, regional and local governments.[13] As most international mechanisms face these

---

7 *Matteo Milazzo, supra* note 1, at 74. This estimate is based on World Bank research in 1998. The World Bank conducted this study on subsidies in world fisheries with the intention of avoiding lending money for projects that may increase capacity or effort in marine capture fisheries.

8 *UNEP*, "A UNEP Update, United Nations Environment Programme, Division of Technology, Industry and Economics, Economics and Trade Branch" (Geneva: UNEP, 2004), at 1; *WWF, supra* note 1, at 24.

9 *Matteo Milazzo, supra* note 1, at 73-77. The countries include Japan, the EU, the United States, Canada, Russia, Korea, Indonesia, Taiwan, Norway and China.

10 *OECD*, "Policy Brief: Subsidies: a Way towards Sustainable Fisheries?" (Paris: OECD, 2005), at 1; *Ola Flaaten and Paul Wallis*, "Government Financial Transfers to Fishing Industries in OECD Countries" (Paris: OECD, 2000), at 5, stating that the figure was approximately USD 6.3 billion in 1997 and USD 6.0 billion in 1999.

11 *OECD*, "Review of Fisheries and Transition to Responsible Fisheries" (Paris: OECD, 2000). The various other forms consist of payments for access to other countries' waters, payments for vessel decommissioning and license retirement, transfers for investment and modernization, transfers for income support and unemployment insurance, and other cost-reducing transfers and direct payments.

12 Article 25 of the SCM Agreement.

13 *WWF, supra* note 1, at 15-23; *Anonymous*, "Scope for Market Liberalization in the OECD Fisheries Sector" (Paris: OECD, 2003), para. 24; *Carl-Christian Schmidt*, "Globalisation, Industry Structure, Market Power and Impact on Fish Trade, Opportunities and Challenges for Developed (OECD) Countries" (Paris: OECD, 2004), at 14.

difficulties in estimating the nature and size of fisheries subsidies, it is likely that the actual amount has been underestimated.

From an economic perspective, there are three potential justifications for subsidies. First of all, the infant-industry concept, whereby a government provides seed capital to develop a domestic industry if this is to take hold in the face of existing foreign competition. Second, a large and important firm may encounter temporary financial difficulties which may spill over and damage other sectors of the economy. By temporarily offering subsidy protection, the government might protect the entire economy. Third, subsidies can be used to provide incentives for firms to behave in environmentally friendly ways. Fishing vessel and license buyback programmes may fall into this category.[14] Other reasons for the implementation of subsidies, rarely justified by economists unless tied to one of the arguments stated above, are to provide an industry with a long-term advantage in the international marketplace and to permanently assure a reasonable level of employment in a geographical area. For instance, Norway has a policy of subsidizing the northern part of the country to sustain the physical presence of a population there and to maintain the fishing culture.[15]

B. Definition of Fisheries Subsidies

1. Definition by International Organizations

Fisheries subsidies are subsidies to the fisheries sector. Financial support, economic assistance, government financial transfers, government grants and state aid[16] are the most commonly used names for government payments to certain enterprises or sectors.[17] The range of possible definitions is extensive, from the narrow "government financial transfers to an industry, through payments to work-

---

14 *FAO* Doc. FAO Fisheries Technical Paper No. 437, "Introducing Fisheries Subsidies" (Rome: FAO, 2003), at 6-9.

15 *Ibid.*, at 9.

16 The use of different names and definitions can partially be explained by the purposes for which the various analyses of subsidies have been undertaken. These names do not cover the same definitions and have been used in rather different contexts over the years. *Anthony Cox and Carl-Christian Schmidt*, "Subsidies in the OECD Fisheries Sector: a Review of Recent Analysis and Future Directions" (Paris: OECD, 2002), paras. 6-7; *Anne Tallontire*, "Trade Issues Background Paper: The Impact of Subsidies on Trade in Fisheries Products" (Rome: FAO, 2004), at 4. These names are used interchangeably in this study.

17 *Anthony Cox*, "Overview of Approaches for Assessing Subsidies", in *OECD*, "Subsidy Reform and Sustainable Development, Economic, Environmental and Social Aspects", pp. 25-40 (Paris: OECD, 2006), at 25; *OECD*, "Environmentally Harmful Subsidies: Challenges for Reform" (Paris: OECD, 2005), at 16.

ers or to firms at the most conventional level"[18] to the broad "government action or inaction that modifies (by increasing or decreasing) the potential profits earned by a firm in the short, medium and long term."[19] Discussions of subsidies in international trade began by drawing the distinction between "export subsidies" and "domestic," "production" or "general" subsidies.[20] Subsidies granted to products for export purposes have been viewed as particularly harmful.[21]

Many studies by international organizations have been involved in defining fisheries subsidies, including the FAO and OECD. FAO developed the "Guide for Identifying, Assessing and Reporting on Subsidies in the Fisheries Sector" (the Guide)[22] to deal with all types of subsidies, from those that are easy to quantify to those that are difficult to assess with respect to their costs to the provider, as well

[18] *FAO* Doc. FAO Fisheries Technical Paper No. 437, at 2-3, illustrating that funds do not need to be passed directly from government to the industry for the government policy to constitute a subsidy.

[19] *Ibid.*, at 3; *W.E. Schrank and W.R. Keithly, Jr.*, "The Concept of Subsidies", Marine Resource Economics, Vol. XIV, pp. 151 *et seq* (1999), at 163.

[20] *S. Alessandrini*, "Subsidies, Strategic Trade Policies and the GATT", in *Jacques H. J. Bourgeois* (ed), "Subsidies and International Trade, a European Lawyer's Perspective", pp. 5-19 (Bruges: College of Europe, Kluwer Law and Taxation Publishers, 1991), at 5; *John H. Jackson*, "The World Trade System: Law and Policy of International Economic Relations" (2ed., Cambridge: The MIT Press, 1997), at 280-281, also emphasizing that economically, a distinction should be drawn between domestic and export subsidies, on the assumption that the latter distort international trade. Another distinction is drawn between specific and general subsidies, on the assumption that only the former distort competition and affect trade, while the latter apply uniformly across the economy and do not favour certain enterprises or industries.

[21] *John Barcelo*, "Subsidies, Countervailing Duties, and Antidumping after the Tokyo Round", Cornell International Law Journal, Vol. 13, pp. 257 *et seq* (1980), at 282-285. For example, it has been argued that because export subsidies are such an obvious attempt to impose burdens which are more political or producer-oriented than they are economic in a broader sense on other countries, perhaps an injury test should not even be a criterion for responding with countervailing duties in such cases. If this logic is followed, it might even be argued that an importing country should have the obligation to counter export subsidies by imposing countervailing duties on the products concerned. On the other hand, domestic or production subsidies are subsidies that are granted for the benefit of products, regardless of whether those products are exported or not. These are clearly the most perplexing, because they involve a vast range and number of government policies, many of which are perfectly justifiable as exercises of sovereign activity within a country.

[22] The Guide was a technical tool developed in 2002 as the first step of the FAO towards an improved understanding of the qualitative and quantitative effects of subsidies. The Guide provides guidance for assessing the costs to the provider and the benefits to the recipients, but it does not offer any methodology for evaluating whether subsidies have impacts on social, economic, trade or other characteristics of the economies in which they are used. *FAO* Doc. FAO Fisheries Technical Paper No. 438, "Guide for Identifying, Assessing and Reporting on Subsidies in the Fisheries Sector" (Rome: FAO, 2004).

as in determining the value to the recipient.[23] The Guide defines fisheries subsidies as government actions or inactions beyond normal practices that, by increasing or decreasing them, modify the potential profits of the fisheries industry in the short, medium or long term.[24] It considers that subsidies include regulatory interventions, interventions by third-country governments and profit-decreasing subsidies. The Guide constitutes an excellent support document for subsidy studies.

In 1993, the members of the Expert Group of the OECD Committee for Fisheries were of the opinion that the concept of assistance to the fishing industry should be defined as government interventions or the lack thereof which distort the allocation of resources in that country relative to an efficient allocation.[25] In recent OECD studies, government financial transfers (GFTs) are defined as the monetary value of interventions associated with fishery policies, whether they are from central, regional or local governments.[26] In general, a subsidy is a result of a government action that confers an advantage to consumers or producers, in order to supplement their income or lower their costs.[27] OECD analysts working on subsidies to marine capture fisheries seem for the moment to have adopted the GFT as the default measure, even if difficulties remain in assessing their size, due to the fact that some transfers are not posted as expenditure or because the amounts involved are relatively small.[28] These intergovernmental agencies have a diverse membership, with each member country having its own perspectives and interests, and tend to take a liberal view of subsidies: subsidies are what each member nation considers them to be.[29]

---

23 *FAO* Doc. No. COFI/2003/8, "Conclusions and Recommendations of the FAO Expert Consultation on Identifying, Assessing and Reporting on Subsidies in the Fishing Industry" (Rome: FAO, 2003), para. 4.

24 *FAO* Doc. FAO Fisheries Technical Paper No. 438, at 7-8, adding that "government" here means government and public bodies other than the ones in the country where the subsidy as such exists, including contributions from public and international development aid and cooperation institutions, and actions or inactions by non-fishery government agencies and organizations. "Fisheries industry" refers to all productive sub-sectors of the fisheries and aquaculture sector, i.e. all types of input industry, including transport and other support services: capture fisheries, aquaculture, processing and marketing. The term "potential profits" means the overall profitability of the industry. Although subsidies affect profits in the short, medium and long term, the Guide focuses on the more direct short-term financial effects.

25 *OECD* Doc. No. AGR/FI(93)11/REV1, "Economic Assistance to the Fishing Industry Observations and Finding" (Paris: OECD, 1993), para. 76, implying that the lack of efficient management of fish resources, restrictions on free trade in fish, fish products and fishing services, as well as on migration of fishermen and on foreign investment in the fishing industry, constitute assistance.

26 *Anthony Cox*, "OECD Work on Defining and Measuring Subsidies in Fisheries" (Paris: OECD, 2003), para. 4.

27 *Anthony Cox*, *supra* note 17, at 25; *Ronald P. Steenblik*, *supra* note 6, at 1.

28 *OECD*, *supra* note 17, at 16.

29 *FAO* Doc. FAO Fisheries Technical Paper No. 437, at 3.

2. Definition by the WTO

The term “subsidy” appeared for the first time in the Havana Charter[30] and was provisionally adopted in the General Agreement on Tariffs and Trade (GATT). The definition of subsidies was not agreed until the adoption of the Agreement on Subsidies and Countervailing Measures (SCM Agreement). The WTO offers a precise definition of subsidies under Article 1 of the SCM Agreement. Even though subsidies have been used as strategic trade policies in industrial countries since the eighteenth century, the term “subsidies” was one of the most frequently used and infrequently defined in the whole vocabulary of international trade regulations until the SCM Agreement.

The definition of subsidies under the SCM Agreement is given as the legal standing to justify countervailing duties and other disciplines against Members that violate the SCM Agreement. Serving as the only internationally agreed legal definition of subsidies, it is the starting point for many of the sectoral definitions used in practice.[31] This study focuses on the definition under the SCM Agreement for fisheries subsidies.

Article 1 of the SCM Agreement provides that a subsidy exists when there is a “financial contribution” by a “government or any public body within the territory of a Member”[32] that confers a “benefit.”[33] Accordingly, a subsidy is deemed to exist when a benefit is conferred on an industry as a result of (1) a direct transfer by the government of funds (e.g. grants, loans and equity infusion) or potential direct transfers of funds or liabilities (e.g. loan guarantees); (2) foregone or uncollected government revenues (e.g. fiscal incentives such as tax credits); (3) when the government provides goods or services other than general infrastructure or purchases goods; (4) when the government makes payments to a funding mechanism or to a private body to carry out any of the functions described above; or (5) when there is any form of income or price support in the context of Article XVI of GATT 1994.

---

30 *Gustavo E. Luengo Hernandez de Madrid*, “Regulation of Subsidies and State Aids in WTO and EC Law” (The Hague: Kluwer Law International, 2007), at 36. The purpose of the Havana Charter is to establish an International Trade Organization (ITO) which together with other multilateral institutions such as the World Bank and the International Monetary Fund, would contribute to stabilizing the economic, political and social situation following World War II. However, the establishment of ITO failed and GATT 1947 was founded.

31 *Anthony Cox*, *supra* note 17, at 25-26, explaining that the OECD also occasionally follows the definition under the SCM Agreement.

32 The subsidy may be provided by state-owned companies within the territory of a Member.

33 *WTO* Doc. No. WT/DS70/AB/RW, “Report of the Appellate Body, Canada-Measures Affecting the Export of Civilian Aircraft” (21 July 2000), para. 9.96.

C. Categorization of Fisheries Subsidies

A basic understanding of the fisheries subsidies programmes is helpful for examining the nature and impact of these and developing effective policies and regulations. Several instruments have classified the various types of fisheries subsidies based on their research. The main studies by the FAO and OECD can serve to illustrate the various categories of fisheries subsidies.

The FAO divides fisheries subsidies into six basic categories: (1) direct government payments to the fishing industry; (2) service and indirect financial transfers; (3) implicit payments to or charges against the industry; (4) general programmes that affect fisheries; (5) regulations; (6) lack of government intervention.[34] Further details of these six categories can be found in Table I of Attachment I. The OECD, on the other hand, divides fisheries subsidies into five basic categories: (1) direct payments; (2) cost-reducing transfers; (3) general services; (4) market-price support; (5) cost recovery.[35] Further details of these five categories can be found in Table II of Attachment I. The categorization of fisheries subsidies of the FAO is broader than that of the OECD.[36]

D. Impact of Fisheries Subsidies

The following section analyzes the various impacts of the different types of fisheries subsidies on trade, the environment and sustainable development.

1. Impact on Trade

In general, there are at least three impacts of subsidies on trade, including (1) enhancing the exportability of products to an importing country, (2) enhancing the exports of the subsidizing country to a third country, thereby adversely affecting the exports of another country, and (3) restricting imports into the subsidizing country.[37] All of these impacts violate the liberalization of international trade. The

---

34 *FAO* Doc. FAO Fisheries Technical Paper No. 437, at 11-13; *FAO* Doc. FAO Fisheries Technical Paper No. 438, at 15-17; *FAO* Doc. FAO Fisheries Report No. 638, "Report of the Expert Consultation on Economic Incentives and Responsible Fisheries - Rome, 28 November-1 December 2000" (Rome: FAO, 2000), paras. 33-36; *FAO*, "The State of World Fisheries and Aquaculture 2002" (Rome: FAO, 2002), at 93-95.

35 *Anthony Cox and Carl-Christian Schmidt*, *supra* note 16, paras. 12-21; *Anthony Cox*, *supra* note 26, paras. 6-11.

36 *OECD*, "Financial Support to Fisheries, Implications for Sustainable Development" (Paris: OECD, 2006), at 20-21.

37 To be more illustrative, the three effects of subsidies are (1) Subsidies of Country A can enhance the exportability of products to an importing Country B. Country B may wish to respond with countervailing duties. (2) Subsidies from Country A can enhance the export of its products to a third Country C, where they compete with

exact consequences of fisheries subsidies depend on how they are implemented and how they interact with other government policies. Subsidies may distort the efficient allocation of resources and the pattern of international trade.[38] Normally, without effectively restricting catches, fisheries subsidies enable fishermen to increase fish supplies to domestic and world markets, thus influencing trade flows and prices.

2. Impact on the Environment

Even though some international organizations, such as the FAO,[39] have found it difficult to prove the relationship that subsidies cause overcapacity and that overcapacity causes overfishing, it should be clear that overfishing could not take

similar products that are exported from Country B. In such a case, Country B does not have easy recourse to a response. Its own countervailing duties are not effective. It may not wish to competitively subsidize its exports. Thus, it must somehow induce the importing country, in this case Country C to respond to the subsidized imports. Country C, however, may be quite happy to receive such subsidized goods. Consequently, Country B's grievance against Country A may have to be aided by some other techniques, such as recourse to an international forum, such as the GATT. (3) A third effect of subsidies can be to restrain imports into the subsidizing country. Thus, if Country A subsidizes its bicycles even when all of those bicycles are sold in its home market, one effect is to make it harder for other countries such as B or C to export bicycles to Country A. The subsidy in this situation has become an import barrier, and economists can demonstrate that the effect is in some ways similar to a tariff. Once again, countervailing duties will not provide a remedy, because the country that is "harmed" is not receiving subsidized imports. *John H. Jackson, supra* note 20, at 280-281.

38 *Anonymous*, "Measuring Assistance to the Fishing Industry: Some Conceptual Issues, Submitted by the Australian Authorities" (Paris: OECD, 2001), at 1.

39 For example, the Guide explains that it is difficult to identify and assign reasonable values to subsidies from regulations and lack of government intervention, especially with regard to the industry value, since they affect the conditions under which the firm operates and are not directed to one distinguishable recipient or group of recipients. *FAO* Doc. FAO Fisheries Technical Paper No. 438, at 43-44. However, the Guide has been considered too theoretical. *FAO* Doc. FAO Fisheries Report No. 702, "Report of the Twenty-fifth Session of the Committee on Fisheries, Rome, 24-28 February 2003" (Rome: FAO, 2003), para. 72; *FAO* Doc. FAO Fisheries Report No. 752, "Report of the Technical Consultation on the Use of Subsidies in the Fisheries Sector" (Rome: FAO, 2004), paras. 10-15; *UNEP*, "UNEP Workshop on Fisheries Subsidies and Sustainable Fisheries Management, Geneva, 26-27 April 2004, Summary of the Chairs" (Geneva: UNEP, 2004), at 3-5; *WTO* Doc. No. TN/RL/W/161, "Communication from New Zealand, Fisheries Subsidies: UNEP Workshop on Fisheries Subsidies and Sustainable Fisheries Management" (8 June 2004), at 4-6; *WTO* Doc. No. WT/CTE/W/236, "Contribution by UNEP, UNEP Workshop on Fisheries Subsidies and Sustainable Fisheries Management, Geneva, 26-27 April 2004, Summary of the Chair" (17 June 2004), paras. 19 and 28.

place without overcapacity, and it is highly likely that overcapacity has been assisted by fisheries subsidies, in particular those subsidies for the construction and modernization of fishing fleets. Other studies, however, based on qualitative analysis, have concluded that fisheries subsidies have negative impact on the environment as detailed below.

a. Impact on Fisheries Resources

At a UNEP technical workshop in 2001, the consensus was that improperly designed fisheries subsidies programmes are among the direct causes of fisheries over-exploitation, particularly in the absence of effective management regimes. UNEP developed a matrix approach for assessing the impact of fisheries subsidies on fisheries resources under various management and bio-economic conditions.[40] It can serve as an analytical basis for designing new or improved fisheries subsidies regulations that will help protect fisheries resources, although there are difficulties in translating a matrix approach into clear and enforceable rules and obligations due to the complexity of the issues.[41]

The matrix approach is based on a framework of idealized fisheries management regimes including open access, catch control (with no property rights) and an effective management system (with catch control and property rights); and on the status of fisheries resources, including overcapacity, full capacity and less-than-full capacity.

In order to help further understanding of the conclusion of the matrix approach, relevant definitions should be made as follows:

(1) Fisheries management is the integrated process of information gathering, analysis, planning, decision making, allocation of resources and formulation and enforcement of fishery regulations by which the authority controls the present and future behaviours of the interested parties in the fishery, in order to ensure the continued productivity of the living resources.[42]

(2) Open access fisheries or common access fisheries can be defined as lacking any legal or regulatory framework. It is a condition of a fishery in which anyone who wishes to fish may do so. It means access to the fisheries resource is free to anyone who wants to use or harvest it because there is no ownership of the resource.[43]

---

40 *UNEP*, "Analyzing the Resource Impact of Fisheries Subsidies: A Matrix Approach" (Geneva: UNEP, 2004), at 4-18.

41 *UNEP*, "Chairman's Summary, UNEP Fisheries Subsidies Workshop Geneva, 12 February 2001" (Geneva: UNEP, 2001), at 4.

42 *FAO* Doc. FAO Fisheries Report No. 519 "Guidelines for responsible management of fisheries. Report of the Expert Consultation on Guidelines for Responsible Fisheries Management, Wellington, New Zealand, 23-27 January 1995" (Rome: FAO, 1995), at 54.

43 *Jon G. Sutinen,* NOAA Technical Memorandum NMFS-NE-158 "A framework for monitoring and assessing socioeconomics and governance of large marine ecosystems" (Massachusetts: National Marine Fisheries Service, 2000), at 28.

(3) In terms of fisheries, property right management is a claim to the benefit stream that some higher body, usually a government, will agree to protect through the assignment of duty to others who may covet, or somehow interfere with, the benefit stream.[44] Individual transferable quotas (ITQs) are usually applied to the property right management system. An ITQ is a right to harvest a particular amount of resources, that can be transferred, e.g. by sale, lease or will.[45]

(4) Before defining "capacity" or "overcapacity", the meaning of total allowable catch (TAC) should be clarified. TAC means the total catch allowed to be taken from a resource in a specified period as defined in the management plan.[46]

(5) On the basis of the FAO definition of fishing capacity,[47] the economic term "overcapacity" can be described in two ways. First, in input terms, "overcapacity" means there is more than the minimum fleet and effort required to produce a given TAC or given output (harvested catch) level. Thus, overcapacity can be measured to provide fishery managers with information on the ability of a fishing firm or industrial fleet to harvest the target level of capacity at its lowest cost for a given desired stock abundance level. It can be measured at the target levels as well as at economically efficient levels of production. Second, in output terms, overcapacity means the maximum harvest level that a fisherman or a fleet can produce with given levels of inputs which would exceed the desired level of harvesting or TAC.

(6) Based on the exploitation rate, which is the proportion of a fish population at the beginning of a given time period that is caught during that time period, the state of fish stocks can identified as under-exploited, intensively exploited, fully exploited, and over-exploited.[48]

(7) Overfishing means, in terms of biology, catching such a high proportion of one or all age classes in a fishery as to reduce yields and drive stock biomass,

---

44 *Ibid.*

45 *FAO* Fisheries Glossary, available at <www.fao.org/fi/glossary/default.asp> (last visited on 31 October 2009).

46 *Ibid.* The TAC may be allocated to the stakeholders (operating units such as countries, vessels, companies or individual fishermen) in the form of quotas as specific quantities or proportions. Quotas may or may not be transferable, inheritable and tradable.

47 Fishing capacity as defined by FAO is the amount of fish or fishing effort that can be produced in a period of time, e.g. a year or a fishing season, by a vessel or a fleet if fully utilized and for a given resource condition. It is the ability of a stock of input (capital) to produce output (measured as either effort or catch). It can be measured either in terms of input or in terms of output. In input terms, the economic definition of capacity can be considered as the minimum fleet and effort required to produce a given TAC or given output level. In output terms, capacity can be considered as the maximum harvest level that a fisherman or a fleet can produce with given levels of input, e.g. fuel, amount of fishing gear, ice, bait, engine horsepower and vessel size.

48 *FAO* Fisheries Glossary, *supra* note 45.

and spawning potential below safe levels. In a surplus production model, overfishing occurs when fishing levels are higher than those required for extracting the maximum sustainable yield (MSY) of a resource and when recruitment starts to decrease statistically. MSY is the highest theoretical equilibrium yield that can be continuously taken on average from a stock under existing environmental conditions without affecting significantly the reproduction process.[49]

(8) A stock would be considered "overfished" when exploited beyond an explicit limit beyond which its abundance is considered "too low" to ensure safe reproduction. In many fisheries fora the term "overfished" is used when biomass has been estimated to be below a limit biological reference point that is used as the signpost defining an "overfished condition".[50]

Based on this matrix, UNEP analyzed several basic types of fisheries subsidies under various management and bio-economic conditions, and presented their impacts on fisheries resources as follows:[51]

(1) Subsidies for fisheries infrastructure are expected to be harmful to fisheries resources except where incentives for ending overfishing are provided by an effective management system or where the fishery is clearly less than fully exploited.
(2) Subsidies for access to foreign countries' waters can be harmful to fisheries resources, unless the fisheries covered by the agreement are clearly under-exploited. Unfortunately, bilateral fisheries access agreements in the real world have almost always involved host-country fisheries in which capacity or exploitation levels are already high, and/or whose management controls are absent or weak.
(3) Subsidies for the decommissioning of vessels and license retirement are provided for fisheries that are already fully capitalized and usually overexploited in order to reduce capacity and pressure on stocks, as well as to increase the profitability of the fishermen. In most fisheries, the likelihood of actually reducing either capacity or effort through a decommissioning programme is low, and the danger of worsening the state of the fish stock is significantly greater.[52]
(4) Subsidies to capital costs are expected to be harmful in all instances,[53] unless an effective fisheries management system is in place. These can be harmful

49 *Ibid.*

50 *Ibid.*

51 *UNEP*, *supra* note 40, at 10-43.

52 *Ibid.* In addition, based on the OECD study, the available evidence suggests that most of these programmes fail and may actually increase overcapacity as they inject new capital into the fishery sector and are generally not introduced in conjunction with effective mechanisms to stop efforts increasing following the decommissioning.

53 *Ibid.* Subsidies to capital costs are those for investment and modernization, including government payments and tax incentives for building and modernizing fishing vessels, as well as loan guarantees and loan restructuring schemes. These subsidies

even in fisheries that are less than fully exploited, where subsidies to capital costs encourage the adoption of much more powerful fishing technologies, potentially causing an excess of fleet capacity well beyond a biologically sustainable level.

(5) Subsidies to variable costs provide an incentive to vessel owners to use more powerful and more fuel-consuming engines and are expected to be harmful unless effective management exists or the fishery is less than fully exploited. These subsidies are similar to subsidies to capital costs in their potential for harm.

(6) Subsidies to income particularly for fishing vessel owners could be harmful if the fishery is fully or overexploited and lacks economic incentives to eliminate overfishing or when open access prevails. Income subsidies in the form of "laying up" subsidies, payable to the vessel owner to compensate for temporarily retiring a vessel, are likely to have the effect of discouraging reductions in capacity that would otherwise be financially more attractive.

(7) Price support subsidies are expected to be harmful in most circumstances unless the fishery has appropriate economic incentives to eliminate incentives for overfishing, such as property rights or community-based management. Price supports have had a clear impact on levels of fishing effort, and can speed up the transition from a condition of less-than-full exploitation to over-exploitation.

Only subsidies to management services have not proved to be harmful to fishery resources.[54] Management services to the fisheries sector include setting fishing regulations, surveillance and enforcement of those regulations, stock assessments, and a wide range of research on fish habitats, fishing technology, market issues and other topics.[55] However, subsidies to research that clearly benefit only the fishing industry and are not for the general public are an exception, although these are likely to be marginal in their impact.[56]

According to this analysis, although properly designed fisheries subsidies can contribute to the achievement of sustainable fisheries, most subsidies are potentially harmful to fish stocks, particularly in the absence of effective management; certain fisheries subsidies could be harmful even under ideal management con-

often lead to increased fishing pressure and are widely provided, in particular the subsidies to vessel modernization.

54 Given that research, management and enforcement expenditure is essential for ensuring the management and research of publicly-owned fisheries resources and the enforcement of regulations, the OECD assumes that these programmes are benign in terms of the environment and economy; however, their effectiveness has not been tested as yet in OECD countries. *OECD*, *supra* note 10, at 6; *R. Sumaila and D. Pauly*, *supra* note 1, at 13.

55 *UNEP*, *supra* note 40, at 21.

56 *Ibid.*, at 43.

ditions.[57] Subsidies that contribute directly to increased fishing capacity or effort are among the most harmful, e.g. subsidies to capital costs or to operating costs.

b. Impact on the Ecosystem and Biodiversity

The environmental impact of fisheries subsidies can be large enough to cause damage to the whole ecosystem and biodiversity.[58] Over-exploitation resulting from fisheries subsidies reduces the gene pool and alters the ecological relationships between predators, symbionts, competitors and prey. The reduction or removal of one species shifts the balance of the ecosystem and affects the resilience of its stocks. When the ecosystem is disturbed strongly enough, the impact may be irreversible: some species currently over-exploited may lose their ecological niche and therefore may never be able to recover. Furthermore, subsidies have a serious impact on biodiversity by unintentionally promoting by-catches which are discarded and bottom trawling which damages the seabed habitat.

3. Impact on Sustainable Development

Sustainable development is defined as "development which meets the needs of current generations without compromising the ability of future generations to meet their own needs".[59] This concept supports strong economic and social development, in particular for people with a low standard of living. It can also be divided into three constituent parts, comprising environmental sustainability, economic sustainability and sociopolitical sustainability. The impact of fisheries subsidies on sustainable development is analyzed as follows:

The impact of fisheries subsidies on fisheries sustainability depends on management systems in place and their enforcement. Fisheries subsidies leading to increased effort and catches may also result in increased by-catches, the catching of non-targeted species.[60] It is argued that governments risk sending mixed sig-

---

57 *Ibid.*, at 47, adding that few if any fisheries are subject to management that is sufficiently "effective" to ensure that fisheries subsidies will not harm fisheries resources. Moreover, several types of fisheries subsidies can be expected to be harmful to fisheries resources under ideal management conditions, including subsidies to infrastructure, subsidies to access to foreign countries' waters, subsidies to capital costs, subsidies to variable costs and price support subsidies.

58 *OECD* Doc. No. Env/EPOC/GSP/BIO(2003)2/FINAL, "Perverse Incentives in Biodiversity Loss" (Paris: OECD, 2003), at 19-21; *Thorir Ibsen*, "Iceland's Proposal about Fisheries Subsidies", in *Myron H. Nordquist and John Norton Moore* (eds), "Current Fisheries Issues and the Food and Agriculture Organization of the United Nations", pp. 459-478 (The Hague: Nijhoff, 2000), at ***470.***

59 *UN* Doc. No. A/RES/42/187, "Report of the World Commission on Environment and Development" (11 December 1987).

60 It is estimated that fishermen discarded roughly six billion pounds of fish each year, roughly twenty-five percent of what they caught during the 1980s and the

nals to the industries by providing financial transfers that encourage increased fishing and at the same time offering transfers seeking to reduce by-catches.[61]

Moreover, the positive short term effects on profits can undermine economic sustainability in the long term, as reduced fish stocks ultimately lead to lower catches with higher costs and lower revenues. Even if governments decide to avoid this by imposing effort and catch control, ineffective enforcement may worsen the situation.

With regard to social sustainability, fisheries subsidies have been used in many countries to solve problems of regional development, community support and unemployment in fishing communities. Fisheries subsidies can be used to improve the education and skills of fishermen and increase their living standards. Subsidies for income support and unemployment insurance, including payments to stop fishing temporarily or to ensure income during bad weather, or because of the lack of alternative employment opportunities, may prevent adjustment away from unsustainable levels of fishing and increase community dependence on government support.[62] In the small-scale fisheries sector, the subsidy plays a rather important role in the contribution not only to the national economy, but also to the fishery trade, food security, social security and poverty alleviation and livelihood support to fishery-dependent communities. However, social policy tools rather than fisheries management tools or fisheries subsidies programmes should be the main mechanism for meeting social objectives. Moreover, the benefits of subsidies to small-scale fisheries concerning social sustainability will also be offset by the negative impact of subsidies on international trade and the environment.

In conclusion, although adequate information and data are still needed for further analysis as the FAO indicated, other studies demonstrate various negative impacts on trade, the environment and sustainable development. Eliminating fisheries subsidies together with effective fisheries management can ensure fisheries sustainability. Although effective fisheries management lies at the heart of almost all the policy challenges facing the fishery sector, even where effectively designed management systems are in place, anything less than perfect enforcement general may result in fisheries subsidies having negative impacts, such as undesirable economic, environmental and social effects.

III. International Fisheries Instruments

International law has extended to areas as diverse as international trade, human rights, environmental protection, etc. Given the nature of fisheries subsidies and different international legal regimes,[63] regulating fisheries subsidies at the global

early 1990s. *PEW Oceans Commission*, "America's Living Oceans: Charting a Course for Sea Change" (Virginia: PEW, 2003), at 43.

61 *OECD*, *supra* note 10, at 4.

62 *Ibid.*, at 4-6.

63 Stephen D. Krasner defined "regimes" as "sets of implicit or explicit principles, norms, rules, and decision-making procedures around which actors' expectations

level falls under the scopes of the international trade regime and the international fisheries regime. It can be seen as a phenomenon of "the fragmentation of international law" which results from the diversification and expansion of international law.[64] The fragmentation of international law is an age old issue, but has just recently emerged in the case of fisheries subsidies regulations.

This section looks into major international fisheries instruments in order to have a broader understanding of fisheries management instruments and to find out the subsidies-related provisions and decisions under these instruments. The next section will find out how the trade regime can be applied to fisheries subsidies.

A. *Current Fisheries Management Instruments*

1. UNCLOS and Fish Stock Agreement

The United Nations Convention on the Law of the Sea (UNCLOS)[65] establishes a regime for the conservation and management of fisheries resources on the basis of the maritime zones[66] or the types of fish stocks[67] that occur in these zones. Its fisheries provisions covers the conservation and utilization of the living resources in the Exclusive Economic Zones (EEZs),[68] in particular the optimum utilization of fisheries resources,[69] the conservation and management of the living resources of the high seas[70] and the protection and preservation of the marine environment.[71]

However, two issues remained open. First, the UNCLOS focuses on issues concerning the EEZ and does not adequately address the problem of high seas fishing.

---

converge in a given area of international relations", *Stephen D. Krasner*, "Structural causes and regime consequences: regimes as intervening variables," in *Stephen D. Krasner* (ed), "International Regimes", pp. 1-22 (United States: Cornell University Press, 1983).

64 The phenomenon of "the fragmentation of international law" attracted the attention of the International Law Commission that established a study group on the "fragmentation of international law." See further information at International Law Commission (ILC), *UN* Doc. No. A/CN.4/L.702, "Report of the Study Group, Fragmentation of International Law: Difficulties arising from the Diversification and Expansion of International Law: Conclusions" (18 July 2006); *UN* Doc. No. A/CN.4/L.682 and Corr.1, "Analytical Study finalized by the Chairman" (13 April 2006).

65 Adopted on 10 December 1982 and came into force on 16 November 1996. Available on-line at <www.un.org/Depts/los/convention_agreements/texts/unclos/unclos_e.pdf> (last visited on 31 August 2009).

66 Namely, internal waters, archipelagic waters, territorial seas, exclusive economic zones (EEZs), continental shelf areas and high seas.

67 Namely, straddling fish stocks, highly migratory species, marine mammals, anadromous stocks and catadromous species.

68 Part V, Articles 61-64 of the UNCLOS.

69 Articles 62.1 and 64.1 of the UNCLOS.

70 Part VII, Section 2 of the UNCLOS.

71 Part XII of the UNCLOS.

Second, some States reflag their vessels to register them with non-member States that offer flags of convenience (FOCs) in order to avoid the application of high seas conservation and management measures determined by regional fisheries organizations.

Responding to the first issue, the Agreement for the Implementation of the Provisions of the United Nations Convention on the Law of the Sea of 10 December 1982 relating to the Conservation and Management of Straddling Fish Stocks and Highly Migratory Fish Stocks (Fish Stocks Agreement) was adopted in 1995.[72] It facilitates the implementation of certain provisions of the UNCLOS concerning the conservation and management of straddling fish stocks and highly migratory fish stocks.[73] The implementation of the Fish Stocks Agreement relies on both States and sub-regional or regional fisheries management organizations (RFMOs) or arrangements. States, either directly or through RFMOs, are obliged to pursue cooperation to ensure the effective conservation and management of straddling fish stocks and highly migratory fish stocks.[74]

2. FAO Compliance Agreement and Other Instruments

Concerning the second issue and high sea fisheries, the FAO was requested to draft relevant agreements by the Declaration of Cancún in May 1992.[75] The call for an agreement was reiterated by Agenda 21, which was adopted in the United Nations Conference on Environment and Development (UNCED) in June 1992.[76] It was also supported by the FAO Technical Consultation on High Seas Fishing

72 Adopted on 4 August 1995 and entered into force on 11 December 2001. Available on-line at <http://daccessdds.un.org/doc/UNDOC/GEN/N95/274/67/PDF/N9527467.pdf?OpenElement> (last visited on 31 August 2009).

73 Articles 116-119 of the UNCLOS.

74 Article 8.1 of the Fish Stock Agreement.

75 Declaration of Cancún was adopted in the International Conference on Responsible Fishing. It also called on the UN to declare the next ten years the "Decade of Responsible Fishing" to ensure concerted efforts towards sustainable fisheries practices. The principles embodied in this Declaration reflected the problems concerning the conservation and management of the fisheries resources both within the EEZs and on the high seas as well as those related to the environment. See further information available on-line at <http://legal.icsf.net/icsflegal/uploads/pdf/instruments/res0201.pdf> (last visited on 31 August 2009).

76 Agenda 21 addressed the pressing problems of the early 1990s and aimed at preparing the world for the challenges of the following century. It is subdivided into 4 sections and 40 chapters. It contains chapters relevant for fisheries and provides the objectives, guidelines and plans for the conservation and management of fisheries resources, in particular those of the high seas. See further information available on-line at <www.fao.org/fishery/topic/14841/en> (last visited on 21 August 2009).

held in September 1992.[77] Hence, the FAO began to negotiate these fisheries issues under Article XIV of the FAO Constitution.[78]

Given this background, the FAO Agreement to Promote Compliance with International Conservation and Management Measures by Fishing Vessels on the High Seas (Compliance Agreement)[79] was adopted in 1993. It sets out the responsibility of flag States[80] and requires them to maintain detailed records on all their vessels authorized to fish on the high seas and to make all such information available to the FAO.[81]

Later, the FAO Code of Conduct for Responsible Fisheries was adopted by the FAO Conference in November 1995.[82] It reflects to a large extent the principles and international standards of behaviour for responsible practices with a view to ensuring the effective conservation, management and development of living aquatic resources, with due respect for the ecosystem and biodiversity. It also contains provisions that have been given binding effect by means of other obligatory legal instruments[83]: as an example, the Compliance Agreement is an integral component of the Code of Conduct. Given this background, even though its application is voluntary,[84] it has been considered to be not merely a non-binding instrument.[85] The Code of Conduct also provides substantive provisions on fisheries

---

77 *FAO* Doc. FAO Fisheries Report No. 484, "Report of the Technical Consultation on High Sea Fishing" (Rome: FAO, 1992). The objective of the Consultation was to obtain scientific and technical information that might be used for the proper management of high seas fisheries. It also addressed the issues of statistics, research, management (responsible fishing practices and new concepts and techniques), institutions, participation of developing countries in high seas fishing and the legal framework.

78 Article XIV of the FAO Constitution states that "in this Constitution the term "agriculture" and its derivatives include fisheries, marine products, forestry, and primary forestry products." Available on-line at <www.fao.org/docrep/x5584E/x5584e0i.htm> (last visited on 31 August 2009).

79 Adopted by the FAO Conference on 24 November 1993 and came into force on 24 April 2003. Available on-line at <www.fao.org/legal/treaties/012t-e.htm> (last visited on 31 August 2009).

80 Article III of the Compliance Agreement.

81 Articles IV and V of the Compliance Agreement.

82 Available on-line at <www.fao.org/docrep/005/v9878e/v9878e00.HTM> (last visited on 31 August 2009).

83 Preface of the Code of Conduct.

84 Article 1.1 of the Code of Conduct.

85 Scholars have considered the Code of Conduct different from normal soft-law documents, because it covers general principles of fisheries law. It is implemented and used by the FAO as an instrument to generate new international norms, so it is not a normal non-binding instrument. It is considered to "reflect international minimum standards" as provided in the Fish Stock Agreement and may be applied by the International Tribunal for the Law of the Sea. *Rüdiger Wolfrum*, "The Role of the International Tribunal for the Law of the Sea," in *Myron H. Nordquist and John Norton Moore* (eds), "Current Fisheries Issues and the Food and Agriculture Organization of the United Nations", pp. 369-385 (The Hague: Kluwer Law International, 2000); *Rüdiger Wolfrum*, "Introduction", in *Rüdiger Wolfrum and Volker*

management, fishing operations, aquaculture developments, integration of fisheries into coastal area management, post-harvest practice and trade, and fisheries research.[86] It also places great emphasis on the regional and sub-regional fisheries organizations for its implementation.[87]

In order to facilitate and reinforce the implementation of the Code of Conduct, the FAO prepares technical guidelines which have no formal legal status and are intended to be flexible and capable of evolving as circumstances change or as new information becomes available. The FAO has also concluded four voluntary international plans of action (IPOAs) within the framework of the Code of Conduct. These IPOAs specifically target the reduction of the incidental catch of seabirds in longline fisheries; the conservation and management of sharks; the management of fishing capacity (IPOA-Capacity);[88] the prevention, deterrence and elimination of illegal, unreported and unregulated fishing (IPOA-IUU).[89] Each IPOA calls upon governments to implement national plans of action in accordance with agreed international measures.

3. Other Conventions and Declarations

Another instrument, from the perspective of marine biodiversity, is the Convention on Biological Diversity (CBD)[90], which was ratified in 1995 as a follow up to UNCED. It complements UNCLOS in relation to the conservation and sustainable use of marine biodiversity. Its three objectives are (1) the conservation of biological diversity, (2) the sustainable use of its components and (3) the fair and equita-

Röben (eds), "Developments of International Law in Treaty Making", pp. 1-13 (Berlin: Springer, 2005), at 6. One considered that the Code of Conduct has also acquired the customary international law status. *Maria Gavouneli*, "Functional Jurisdiction in the Law of the Sea" (Leiden: Martinus Nijhoff, 2007), at 108. Further information on the Code of Conduct, see *Gerald Moore*, "The Code of Conduct for Responsible Fisheries", in *Ellen Hey* (ed), "Development in International Fisheries Law", pp. 85-105 (The Hague: Kluwer Law International, 1999), at 91-95; *Jürgen Friedrich*, "Legal Challenges of Nonbinding Instruments: The Case of the FAO Code of Conduct for Responsible Fisheries", German Law Journal, Vol. 109, No. 11, pp. 1539-1564 (2008).

86 Articles 6-12 of the Code of Conduct.

87 Article 7.1.5 of the Code of Conduct.

88 *FAO*, "International Plan of Action for Reducing Incidental Catch of Seabirds in Longline Fisheries. International Plan of Action for the Conservation and Management of Sharks. International Plan of Action for the Management of Fishing Capacity" (Rome: FAO, 1999). These IPOAs were adopted by the FAO Committee on Fisheries (COFI) in February 1999 and endorsed by the FAO Council at the session in June 1999.

89 *FAO*, "International Plan of Action to Prevent, Deter and Eliminate Illegal, Unreported and Unregulated Fishing" (Rome: FAO, 2001). This IPOA was adopted by the FAO COFI in March 2001 and endorsed by the FAO Council in June 2001.

90 See further information on the CBD available on-line at <www.cbd.int> (last visited on 31 August 2009).

ble sharing of the benefits arising out of the utilization of genetic resources. These are to be achieved by appropriate access to genetic resources, by appropriate transfer of relevant technologies, taking into account all rights over those resources and to technologies, and by appropriate funding.[91]

Other declarations important to fisheries conservation and management include the 1995 Jakarta Mandate on Marine and Coastal Biological Diversity which addresses the conservation and sustainable use of marine and coastal biodiversity,[92] the 2001 Reykjavik Declaration on Responsible Fisheries in the Marine Ecosystem which is the first to formally adopt the ecosystem approach into responsible fisheries,[93] and the 2002 Plan of Implementation of the World Summit on Sustainable Development (WSSD), which urges States to implement fisheries instruments in order to achieve sustainable fisheries and restore depleted fish stocks not later than 2015.[94] The role of the FAO is expressly recognized and reference is made to the Code of Conduct and its IPOAs and technical guidelines.[95]

Based on these instruments, several basic elements of the effectiveness of fisheries management have been developed, namely (1) international cooperation;[96]

---

91 Section A of the CBD.

92 The Jakarta Mandate represents a global consensus on the importance of marine and coastal biological diversity and is a part of the Ministerial Statement on the implementation of the CBD, as adopted by the Conference of the Parties (COP) at its second meeting held in Jakarta in November 1995. Marine and coastal protected areas were one of the five thematic issues identified within the Jakarta Mandate. See further information available on-line at <www.cbd.int/marine/about.shtml> (last visited on 31 August 2009).

93 The Reykjavik Conference on Responsible Fisheries in the Marine Ecosystem was held in Reykjavik, Iceland in October 2001. The objectives of the Conference were to gather and review the best available knowledge on the marine ecosystem issues, to identify means by which ecosystem considerations can be included in capture fisheries management, and to identify future challenges and relevant strategies. See further information availaböe on-line at <ftp://ftp.fao.org/fi/DOCUMENT/reykjavik/y2198t00_dec.pdf> (last visited on 31 August 2009).

94 Paragraph 31(a) of the Plan of Implementation of the World Summit on Sustainable Development (WSSD), stating that "to achieve sustainable fisheries, it is necessary at all levels to maintain or restore stocks to levels that can produce the maximum sustainable yield with the aim of achieving these goals for depleted stocks on an urgent basis and where possible not later than 2015." The WSSD took place in Johannesburg, South Africa from 26 August to 4 September 2002. It agreed to the Plan of Implementation, which extensively treated issues related to fisheries. *UN Department of Economic and Social Affairs, Division for Sustainable Development*, "Plan of Implementation of the World Summit on Sustainable Development" (2002). Available on-line at <www.un.org/esa/sustdev/document s/WSSD_POI_PD/English/WSSD_PlanImpl.pdf> (last visited on 31 August 2009).

95 Paragraphs 31(c) and (d) of the Plan of Implementation of the WSSD.

96 It refers to cooperation through regional fisheries organizations and arrangements. Relevant provisions: Articles 64 and 118 of the UNCLOS; Articles 8.3 and 14 of the Fish Stock Agreement; Article V of the Compliance Agreement.

(2) strengthening the responsibility of flag States;[97] (3) strengthening the effectiveness of regional fisheries organizations and arrangements;[98] (4) consistency or compatibility;[99] (5) large marine ecosystem;[100] (6) long-term sustainability;[101] (7) optimum utilization of fisheries resources;[102] (8) the precautionary approach to fisheries management.[103]

The principles of fisheries management developed in these instruments should be taken into consideration in global, regional and national fisheries subsidies regulations and policies.

B. Subsidies-related Provisions

Among the instruments discussed above, few provisions and declarations are related to subsidies. Before looking into the provisions, there is a decision of the CBD which is noteworthy. At the early stage of the CBD, its Subsidiary Body on Scientific, Technical and Technological Advice (SBSTTA)[104] recommended making explicit reference to fishery subsidies and reviewing the role of govern-

---

97 It refers to more effective enforcement by flag States of conservation and management measures. Relevant provisions: Article 117 of the UNCLOS; Articles 5 and 19 of the Fish Stock Agreement; Article 8.2 of the Code of Conduct. Some parallel provisions develop the responsibilities of coastal States and port States.

98 It means strengthening regional fisheries organizations and arrangements in order to improve their effectiveness in establishing and implementing conservation and management measures. Relevant provisions: Article 13 of the Fish Stock Agreement; Article 7 of the Code of Conduct.

99 It refers to the fact that the domestic laws and regulations shall be consistent with the international fisheries instruments. Relevant provisions: Article 62 of the UNCLOS; Article 7.2 of the Fish Stock Agreement; Article 8.2.6 of the Code of Conduct.

100 It recognizes the complexity of the marine ecosystem and the interconnections among component parts, not limiting management measures to only specific stocks. Relevant provisions: Article 194 of the UNCLOS; Article 2 of the CBD.

101 It refers to the ability of a stock to persist in the long term. Relevant provisions: Articles 63.2, 64 and 111 of the UNCLOS, Articles 5 and 10 of the Fish Stock Agreement, Articles 6.3 and 7 of the Code of Conduct.

102 It usually refers to maximum sustainable yield (MSY). Relevant provisions: Articles 61.3, 62.1 and 64.1 of the UNCLOS; Articles 5 and 7 of the Fish Stock Agreement; Articles 7.1 and 12.1 of the Code of Conduct. However, scholars have questioned whether MSY is appropriate. *R.R. Churchill and A.V. Lowe*, "The Law of the Sea" (2ed., Manchester: Manchester University Press, 1988), at 226.

103 It is management according to the precautionary approach which exercises prudent foresight to avoid unacceptable or undesirable situations, taking into account that changes in fisheries systems are only slowly reversible, difficult to control, not well understood and subject to change in the environment and human values. Relevant provisions: Articles 5(c), 6.6 and 6.7 of the Fish Stock Agreement; Article 7.5 of the Code of Conduct.

104 Article 25 of the CBD.

ment subsidies in contributing to overcapacity.[105] However, the Conference of Parties (COP)[106] later decided that they should focus on pollution issues instead of fisheries issues.[107] Consequently, at the conventional level, there is no explicit provision regulating fisheries subsidies. Other provisions can be found in the IPOAs analyzed as follows:

1. International Plan of Action for the Management of Fishing Capacity

The International Plan of Action for the Management of Fishing Capacity (IPOA-Capacity)[108] developed by the FAO contains provisions related to subsidies. It recognizes the potential of subsidies for leading to overcapacity which is a problem that, among others, contributes substantially to overfishing and the degradation of fisheries resources.[109] Therefore, the following comments describe how capacity and subsidies are addressed in fisheries instruments.

The Fish Stock Agreement already requires that costal States and States fishing on the high seas shall take measures to prevent or eliminate excess fishing capacity.[110] The Code of Conduct emphasized that excess fishing capacity should be prevented and avoided[111] and that such management measures should promote economic conditions for responsible fisheries.[112] Based on the principles and objectives of the Code of Conduct, the IPOA-Capacity was progressively developed to manage excess fishing capacity.[113]

According to the IPOA-Capacity, a series of actions should be taken for fisheries requiring urgent measures, including the assessment and monitoring of fishing capacity, and the preparation and implementation of national plans.[114] When preparing and implementing national plans, States should assess the possible impact of all factors, including subsidies, which might contribute to excess fishing capacity and should distinguish between these and those which produce a positive

105 Para. 7 of the Recommendation I/8 of the SBSTTA.

106 The Conference of Parties (COP) is the governing body of the CBD and advances implementation of the CBD through the decisions it takes at its periodic meetings.

107 Annex to Decision II/10 of the COP.

108 *FAO*, *supra* note 88.

109 Para. 1 of the IPOA-Capacity.

110 Article 5(h) of the Fish Stock Agreement. Although Article 62.2 of the UNCLOS provides that the coastal State shall determine its capacity to harvest the living resources of the EEZ, it does not contain the idea of preventing or eliminating excess fishing capacity.

111 Articles 6.3 and 7.4.3 of the Code of Conduct.

112 Article 7.2.2 of the Code of Conduct.

113 It is an instrument that applies to all States whose fishermen engage in capture fisheries. Footnote 1 of the IPOA-Capacity, stating that the term "State" includes Members and non-Members of the FAO and also applies *mutatis mutandis* to "fishing entities" other than States.

114 Part III of the IPOA-Capacity.

effect or are neutral.[115] States should also reduce and progressively eliminate all factors, including subsidies, which directly or indirectly contribute to excessive fishing capacity and undermine the sustainability of marine living resources.[116]

In order to achieve the goal of capacity reduction, the IPOA-Capacity also provides four major strategies, namely (1) the conduct of national, regional and global assessments of capacity, (2) the preparation and implementation of national plans to manage capacity, (3) the strengthening of RFMOs and other mechanisms for improved management of fishing capacity; and (4) immediate actions for international fisheries.[117]

Given these obligations to assess and manage capacity, on the regional level, regional fishery bodies and similar organizations continue their work to implement the IPOA-Capacity.[118] Until November 2009, only two RFMOs had submitted their Regional Plans of Action for the Management of Fishing Capacity (RPOA-Capacity), namely Lake Victoria Fisheries Organization (LVFO) and Inter-American Tropic Tuna Commission (IATTC).

At the national level, some States have developed or plan to develop National Plans of Action for the Management of Fishing Capacity (NPOA-Capacity) and some have incorporated capacity considerations into their day-to-day fisheries management systems.[119] Until November 2009, only three countries had submitted their NPOA-Capacity to the FAO, namely the United States, Namibia and Indonesia.

Because States should report to the FAO on the assessment, development and implementation of their plans for the management of fishing capacity,[120] the FAO is to collect all relevant information and data which might serve as a basis for further analysis aimed at identifying factors contributing to overcapacity, e.g. lack of input and output control, unsustainable fisheries management methods and subsidies which contribute to overcapacity.[121] FAO also provides pertinent assis-

---

115 Para. 25 of the IPOA-Capacity.

116 Para. 26 of the IPOA-Capacity.

117 Para. 8 of the IPOA-Capacity.

118 Such as Commission for the Conservation of Antarctic Marinc Living Resources (CCAMLR), Pacific Islands Forum Fisheries Agency (FFA), General Fisheries Commission for the Mediterranean (GFCM), Inter-American Tropical Tuna Commission (IATTC), International Commission for the Conservation of Atlantic Tunas (ICCAT), Indian Ocean Tuna Commission (IOTC), Northwest Atlantic Fisheries Organization (NAFO) and the Southeast Asian Fisheries Development Center (SEAFDEC).

119 *FAO*, Fisheries and Aquaculture Department, Key Issues, Fishing Capacity, available on-line at <www.fao.org/fishery/topic/2898/en> (last visited on 31 August 2008), adding that preliminary assessments of capacity on the fishery level have been undertaken by around three quarters of States responding to a 2004 FAO survey, and all of the major producers responding to the survey had undertaken preliminary assessments of capacity.

120 Para. 44 of the IPOA-Capacity.

121 Para. 45 of the IPOA-Capacity.

tance to States in the implementation of their NPOA-Capacity and reports biennially on the implementation of the IPOA-Capacity.[122]

In recent practice, preliminary assessments of capacity have been undertaken, but very few fisheries appear to have been the object of formal capacity assessments and in this sense the practice of capacity assessment lags far behind the practice of stock assessment.

2. International Plan of Action for IUU Fishing

Illegal, unreported and unregulated (IUU)[123] fishing accounts for a large part of global fishing[124] and has negative impact on targeted fish stocks and the wider marine ecosystem.[125] IUU fishing is also encouraged by fisheries subsidies which reduce operational and capital costs.[126] The international fisheries instruments are not able to effectively combat IUU fishing, due to a lack of political will, policy priorities, a lack of capacity for governing and resources for ratifying or acceding to and implementing these instruments.[127] Therefore, the FAO adopted and endorsed the International Plan of Action to Prevent, Deter and Eliminate Illegal,

122 Paras. 45-48 of the IPOA-Capacity.

123 This terminology was first formally mentioned in the CCAMLR meeting in October 1997.

124 *David J. Doulman*, "A General Overview of Some Aspects of Illegal, Unreported and Unregulated Fishing", in *FAO* Doc. Fisheries Report No. 666, "Report of and Papers Presented at the Expert Consultation on Illegal, Unreported and Unregulated Fishing" (Rome: FAO, 2001), para. 9. In some important fisheries, IUU fishing accounts for up to 30 percent of the global catch, and in one instance it has been suggested that IUU catches could be as high as three times the permitted catch level. It occurs in both small-scale and industrial fisheries, in marine and inland-water fisheries, as well as in zones of national jurisdiction and on the high seas. See further information at *U. R. Sumaila, J. Alder and H. Keith*, "The Cost of Being Apprehended for Fishing Illegally: Empirical Evidence and Policy Implications", in *OECD*, "Fish Piracy Combating Illegal, Unreported and Unregulated Fishing", pp. 201-230 (Paris: OECD, 2004), at 201 and 222.

125 It is because IUU fishermen often ignore the regulations designed to protect the marine environment, such as restrictions on the harvest of juveniles, closed spawning grounds and gear modifications required to reduce the by-catch of non-targeted species.

126 Other factors that encourage IUU fishing may include the existence of excess fleet capacity, flags of convenience (FOC), strong market demand for particular fish species and products, ineffective national fishery administration, inadequate sanctions, inappropriate regional fisheries management regimes and ineffective fisheries monitoring, control and surveillance (MCS), including the lack of a vessel monitoring system (VMS). *FAO* Doc. FAO Fisheries Report No. 722, "Report of the Expert Consultation on Fishing Vessels Operating under Open Registries and Their Impact on Illegal, Unreported and Unregulated Fishing" (Rome: FAO, 2004), at 25.

127 *Olav Schram Stokke and Davor Vidas*, "Regulating IUU Fishing or Combating IUU Operations", in *OECD*, *supra* note 124, pp. 19-48, at 22.

Unreported and Unregulated Fishing (IPOA-IUU). The IPOA-IUU defines IUU fishing as follows: (1) Illegal fishing is fishing activities conducted by vessels of States that are parties to a RFMO but operate in violation of its rules, or operate in a State's waters without permission or in contravention of its laws and regulations. (2) Unreported fishing is fishing activities which have not been reported or have been misreported to relevant national authorities or RFMOs. (3) Unregulated fishing is fishing activities conducted by vessels without nationality or flying the flag of States which are not parties to relevant RFMOs and which therefore consider themselves not bound by their rules.[128]

It also provides the measures to prevent, deter and eliminate IUU fishing. It calls on States, as far as possible in their national law, to avoid granting economic support, including subsidies, to companies, vessels or persons that are involved in IUU fishing.[129] In order to prevent IUU fishermen from benefiting financially from their illegal activity and to reduce the volume of IUU-caught fish being transhipped, landed and laundered, the IPOA-IUU also provides trade restrictions on IUU fishing.[130] The FAO also collects information and data that might serve as a basis for analyzing how subsidies contribute to IUU fishing.[131] Until November 2009, several countries had submitted their NPOA and RPOA to the FAO.[132]

These IPOAs, due to their voluntary legal nature and reliance on a model of unilateral action by fishing nations, are regarded as an ineffective international instrument.[133] Current fisheries instruments are insufficient to provide the legal basis to regulate fisheries subsidies effectively. In the next section, the study investigates how current WTO regulations can be applied to fisheries subsidies.

IV. Subsidies Regulations within the GATT/WTO Framework

A. *Multilateral Subsidies Regulations within the GATT/WTO Framework*

Since there is no regulation directly applicable to fisheries subsidies within the trade regime, this type of subsidy falls under the general subsidy regulations within the GATT/WTO framework. In order to understand to what extent the

---

128 Para. 3 of the IPOA-IUU.

129 Para. 23 of the IPOA-IUU.

130 Paras. 65-76 of the IPOA-IUU. These trade restrictions should comply with the WTO agreements and be used after prior consultation with interested States.

131 Para. 88 of the IPOA-IUU.

132 They include twelve countries and two organizations: European Commission and LVFO. See further information available on-line at <www.fao.org/fishery/ipoa-iuu/npoa/en> (last visited 31 August 2009).

133 *David K. Schorr*, "Fisheries Subsidies and the WTO", in *Gary P. Sampson and Bradnee Chambers* (eds), "Trade, Environment and the Millennium", pp. 175-206 (2ed., Tokyo: United Nations University Press, 2002), at 182-183.

existing regulations can be applied to fisheries subsidies, the following section looks at how these evolved from GATT to the current SCM Agreement.

1. GATT Subsidies Provisions

GATT, originally intended as a temporary instrument, became by default the primary legal framework governing international trade. Before entry into force of the WTO agreements, the basic rules on subsidies were to be found in the provisions of Article XVI of GATT 1947.[134]

GATT rules used the term "subsidy" without defining it. Article XVI of GATT 1947 had two sections: Section A concerning subsidies in general and Section B concerning export subsidies.

Section A of Article XVI required subsidizing contracting parties to fulfil two obligations.

First, any contracting party, granting or maintaining any subsidy which operates directly or indirectly to increase exports of any product from, or to reduce imports of any product into its territory, should notify the counterparts of their subsidies programmes in writing with the following information: (i) the extent and nature of the subsidization, (ii) the estimated effect of the subsidization on the quantity of the affected product or products imported into or exported from its territory, and (iii) the circumstances making the subsidization necessary.[135] However, this provision was rarely applied in practice, since the contracting parties were unwilling to give information about their subsidies to others. The general practice was that in most cases a contracting party discovered another contracting party's subsidy and challenged it under the general mechanisms established in GATT 1947.[136]

Second, if "serious prejudice" to the interest of any other contracting party was caused or threatened by subsidies which were aimed directly or indirectly at increasing exports of any product from, or at reducing imports of any products into the territories of the contracting parties, the party granting the subsidy had an

---

[134] Even after entry into force of the WTO agreements, the discussion of general subsidies rules should still begin with Article XVI of GATT 1994, which is an update of GATT 1947. In the *Brazil-Desiccated Coconut* dispute, the panel made it clear that, as was also confirmed by the Appellate Body (AB), the SCM Agreement did not supersede Article XVI of GATT 1994 as the basis for the WTO disciplines of countervailing measures. *WTO* Doc. No. WT/DS22/R, "Report of the Panel, Brazil-Measures Affecting Desiccated Coconut" (17 October 1996), para. 227; *WTO* Doc. No. WT/DS22/AB/R, "Report of the Appellate Body, Brazil-Measures Affecting Desiccated Coconut" (21 February 1997), at 14; *Marc Benitah*, "The Law of Subsidies under the GATT/WTO System" (The Hague: Kluwer Law International, 2001), at 155-156.

[135] Article XVI.1 of the GATT 1947.

[136] *Gustavo E. Luengo Hernandez de Madrid, supra* note 30, at 199.

obligation to consult with the other contracting party or parties regarding the possibility of limiting the subsidies.[137]

Under Section B of Article XVI, contracting parties should seek to avoid using subsidies for the export of "primary products", but were not actually forbidden to do so. This provision further stipulated that such subsidies should not be applied in a manner which would result in the subsidizing contracting party having more than an equitable share of world export trade in that product.[138] "Primary products" here were defined as any farm, forest or fishery products, or any mineral, in its natural form or which has undergone such processing as was customarily required to prepare it for marketing in substantial volume for international trade.[139]

2. Tokyo Round Subsidies Code

The Tokyo Round Negotiations, which took place from 1973 to 1979 with 120 participating countries, continued GATT's efforts to progressively reduce tariffs. It also had the goal of establishing new guidelines and mechanisms for trade management. Participants in the negotiations fell into two major groups. On one side were countries, led by the United States, which had become frustrated by what they saw as a growing use of subsidies for domestic production by their trade competitors. On the other side were those, led by the European Communities, which were alarmed by the rapid increase in the number of countervailing duty actions filed in the United States. The contracting parties finally issued the *"Agreement on Interpretation and Application of Articles VI, XVI and XXIII of the GATT"* (Subsidies Code)[140] to clarify the regulations of the GATT 1947. It was a so-called "two-track solution": in return for other countries reducing their subsidy practices, the United States would adopt an injury test to restrict the reach of its countervailing duty laws.[141] However, the Subsidies Code was a temporary fix and was signed by only one-third of GATT's contracting parties.[142]

The Subsidies Code tightened the subsidies provisions under Article XVI of the GATT 1947. With respect to export subsidies, it distinguished between primary and non-primary products. The Subsidies Code prohibited signatories from using

137 Article XVI.1 of the GATT 1947.

138 Article XVI.3 of the GATT 1947; *Pierre Didier,* "WTO Trade Instruments in EU Law" (London: Cameron May, 1999), at 248.

139 The Note Ad Article XVI of the GATT 1947, Section B, para. 2.

140 Agreement on Interpretation and Application of Articles VI, XVI and XXIII of the GATT (Subsidies Code) is one of the series of Agreements on non-tariff barriers emerging from the negotiations on interpretations of GATT rules. Articles VI, XVI and XXII of the GATT 1947 are the main regulations for regulating serious prejudice caused by subsidies.

141 *Robert O'Brien*, "Subsidies Regulation and State Transformation in North America, the GATT and the EU" (New York: St. Martin's Press, 1997), at 113.

142 *Richard H. Snape*, "International Regulation of Subsidies", World Economy, Vol. 14, pp.139-164 (1991), at 150.

subsidies for non-primary products.[143] Signatories also agreed not to grant subsidies for certain primary products in a manner which would result in the signatory granting such subsidy gaining more than an equitable share of world export trade.[144] The Subsidies Code noted that for the purposes of the Agreement "certain primary products" meant any farm, forestry or fishery products. In contrast to GATT 1947, mineral products were not covered by the Subsidies Code.[145]

3. Uruguay Round Negotiations on Subsidies and Countervailing Duties

The 1986 Punta del Este Decision[146], which launched the Uruguay Round Negotiations, introduced a new subsidy regime for agricultural and non-agricultural products. One of the objectives of the Negotiating Group on Agriculture (NGAG) was the improvement of the competitive environment by tightening disciplines on the use of all direct and indirect subsidies and other measures affecting agricultural trade directly or indirectly.[147] The Negotiating Group on Subsidies and Countervailing Measures on the other hand was set up to improve relevant provisions in GATT.[148]

The United States proposed to include fisheries in the discussion of NGAG. Other countries, however, did not support this approach.[149] Because the negotiations to include fisheries subsidies failed, the Agreement on Agriculture (AoA) covers most primary products (HS Chapters 1 to 24) with the exception of fish and fish products.[150] The preamble to the AoA states that its long-term objective is to provide for substantial progressive reductions in agricultural support and protec-

143 Article 9.1 of the Subsidies Code.

144 Article 10.1 of the Subsidies Code.

145 Interpretative Note 29 to the Subsidies Code.

146 General Agreement on Tariffs and Trade Punta del Este Declaration, Ministerial Declaration of 20 September 1986, available on-line at <www.sice.oas.org/trade/Punta_e.asp> (last visited on 31 March 2008).

147 *Ibid.*, stating that negotiations shall aim to achieve greater liberalization of trade in agriculture and bring all measures affecting import access and export competition under strengthened and more operationally effective GATT rules and disciplines. They should take into account the general principles governing the negotiations by improving the competitive environment through increased disciplines on the use of all direct and indirect subsidies and other measures affecting agricultural trade directly or indirectly, including the phased reduction of their negative effects and dealing with their causes.

148 *Ibid.*, stating that negotiations on subsidies and countervailing measures shall be based on a review of Articles VI and XVI and the MTN Agreement on subsidies and countervailing measures with the objective of improving GATT disciplines relating to all subsidies and countervailing measures that affect international trade.

149 *Ronald P. Steenblik*, *supra* note 6, at 21-22.

150 Article 1 of Annex 1 of the AoA.

tion over an agreed period of time, in order to avoid restrictions and distortions in world agricultural markets.[151]

4. WTO Agreement on Subsidies and Countervailing Measures

Providing greater uniformity and certainty in its implementation, the Agreement on Subsidies and Countervailing Measures (SCM) elaborates on the provisions relating to subsidies and countervailing measures in the GATT 1947 and in the Tokyo Round Negotiations. The SCM Agreement imposes disciplines to ensure that subsidies do not adversely affect the interests of WTO Members. There are also disciplines on countervailing measures aimed at ensuring that these do not unjustifiably impede trade and that these provide relief for products adversely affected by subsidies.[152] The following section examines the most important disciplines under the SCM Agreement.

a. Structure of the SCM Agreement

The SCM Agreement can be divided into several parts as follows:[153]

(1) Part I sets out the definition of a subsidy by identifying elements required for a subsidy to exist and introduces the concept of specificity.
(2) Parts II, III and IV categorize subsidies according to whether they are prohibited, actionable or non-actionable, and introduce the traffic light analogy for identification. Remedies are outlined for each of these three types of subsidy.
(3) Part V deals with the application of Article VI GATT and sets out the investigation and evidence procedures which must be followed before countervailing measures can be imposed. There are also important substantive provisions for the determination of injury, the definition of domestic industry and the calculation of the amount of a subsidy in terms of the benefit to the recipient.
(4) Parts VI and VII provide for the creation of a Committee on Subsidies and Countervailing Measures (SCM Committee) and the notification and surveillance procedures aimed at strengthening the subsidies rules under the SCM Agreement.
(5) Part VIII sets out detailed provisions to take into account the special situation of developing countries. These special provisions allow least-developed and developing country Members to grant otherwise prohibited subsidies to their exports for specific periods of time.
(6) Parts IX, X and XI deal with transitional arrangements, dispute settlement and final provisions. These provisions refer to Articles XXII and XXIII of the

---

151 Preamble of the AoA.

152 Part V of the SCM Agreement.

153 *Konstantinos Adamantopoulos and Maria J. Pereyra-Friedrichsen*, "EU Anti-Subsidy Law & Practice" (Bembridge: Palladian Law Publishing, 2001), at 10-11.

GATT as well as the Dispute Settlement Understanding (DSU) for the settlement of disputes arising under the SCM Agreement.[154]

(7) The SCM Agreement also includes seven annexes, among which there is an illustrative list of export subsidies, various guidelines such as on the consumption of inputs in the production process and the criteria for the determination of the substitution drawback systems as export subsidies. Procedures for developing information concerning serious prejudice, instructions for the calculation of the total *ad valorem* subsidization, and procedures for on-the-spot verifications are also included in the annexes.

b. Requirement of Specificity

Article 1 requires that a subsidy shall be "specific" to an enterprise or industry or group of enterprises or industries in order to be subject to the SCM Agreement. The basic principle is that a subsidy that distorts the allocation of resources within an economy should be subject to discipline. Where a subsidy is widely available within an economy, such a distortion in the allocation of resources is presumed not to occur. Thus, only "specific" subsidies are subject to the SCM Agreement. Under the scope of Article 2, there are four types of "specificity": enterprise-specificity[155], industry-specificity[156], regional specificity[157] and prohibited specificity[158]. If a subsidy does not meet any of these requirements, there are other explicit circumstances under which specificity can be assumed.[159]

c. Traffic Light Classification

The SCM Agreement classifies specific subsidies in three types: prohibited subsidies (red light), actionable subsidies (amber light) and non-actionable subsidies (green light) with a "traffic light" approach.

---

[154] Article 30 of the SCM Agreement.

[155] Enterprise-specificity is that a government targets a particular company or companies for subsidization and is regulated under Article 2.1 of the SCM Agreement.

[156] Industry-specificity is that a government targets a particular sector or sectors for subsidization and is regulated under Article 2.1 of the SCM Agreement.

[157] Regional specificity is that a government targets producers in specified parts of its territory for subsidization and is regulated under Article 2.2 of the SCM Agreement.

[158] Prohibited specificity is that a government targets export goods or goods using domestic inputs for subsidization and is regulated under Article 2.3 of the SCM Agreement.

[159] Article 2.1(c) of the SCM Agreement. Such circumstances include the following: use of a subsidy programme by a limited number of certain enterprises, predominant use by certain enterprises, the granting of disproportionately large amounts of subsidy to certain enterprises, and the manner in which discretion has been exercised by the granting authority in the decision to grant a subsidy.

(1) Red Light: Prohibited Subsidies

Subsidies which are designed to affect trade directly and, therefore, "most likely" to have adverse effects on the interests of other Members are prohibited. Article 3 of the SCM Agreement prohibits subsidies which are granted contingent on export performance (export subsidies) and subsidies which are granted contingent on the use of domestic in preference to imported products (domestic content subsidies).[160] The scope of these prohibitions is relatively narrow. They are subject to an accelerated dispute settlement procedure and the Member found to grant or maintain such a subsidy must withdraw it without delay.[161]

(2) Amber Light: Actionable Subsidies

Part III (Articles 5 to 7) of the SCM Agreement regulates actionable subsidies. Except for prohibited subsidies and non-actionable subsidies, all other subsidies are actionable. Most subsidies fall into this category. If subsidies have "adverse effects" on the interests of other Members, action can be taken against them. "Adverse effects" are deemed to exist when any of the following three conditions is met:

(a) injury to the domestic industry of another Member;
(b) nullification or impairment of benefits accruing under GATT 1994;[162] or
(c) serious prejudice to the interests of another Member.[163] Serious prejudice is deemed to exist when subsidies exceed five percent of the *ad valorem* of a product; or when subsidies are intended to cover operating losses sustained by an industry or enterprise (except for one-time restructuring measures); or when subsidies directly forgive debts.[164]

These can be challenged through the dispute settlement procedure or by countervailing measures. If the subsidizing Member does not take appropriate steps to remove the adverse effects or withdraw the subsidy, the complaining Member can be granted authorization by the Dispute Settlement Body to take countermeasures commensurate with the degree and nature of the adverse effects determined to exist.[165] However, a complaining Member usually finds it difficult to demonstrate the adverse effects arising from these subsidies.

---

160 Article 3.1(a) and (b) of the SCM Agreement.

161 Article 4 of the SCM Agreement.

162 Nullification or impairment arises most typically where the improved market access presumed to flow from a bound tariff reduction is undercut by subsidization.

163 Article 5 of the SCM Agreement.

164 For detailed information as to the calculation of the total *ad valorem* subsidization, see Annex IV of the SCM Agreement. It is noteworthy that according to Article 31, the provisions of Article 6.1 should apply for a period of five years, beginning with the date of entry into force of the WTO Agreement. This required renewal of Article 6.1 did not occur.

165 Article 7.9 of the SCM Agreement.

(3) Green Light: Non-Actionable Subsidies

Under certain circumstances, subsidies for research, social and environmental reasons can be justified. Part IV (Articles 8 to 9) of the SCM Agreement regulates non-actionable subsidies, including non-specific subsidies and subsidies which are (a) granted for research activities conducted by firms or by higher education or research establishments on a contract basis with firms; (b) granted to disadvantaged regions within the territory of a Member pursuant to a general framework of regional development and non-specific within eligible regions; and (c) granted to promote adaptation of existing facilities to new environmental requirements.[166] The term "existing facilities" means facilities which have been in operation for at least two years at the time when new environmental requirements are imposed.[167]

Moreover, these subsidies must be notified in advance of their implementation to the SCM Committee with yearly updates.[168] If a Member believes that a notified programme does not satisfy the criteria of Article 8 or that the conditions set out in a notified programme have been violated, that Member may request binding arbitration.[169]

This category has no longer any legal effect because its applicability expired at the end of 1999,[170] and no renewal has been made under Article 31 of the SCM Agreement. Some Members consider that Article 8 should not be extended unless the Members agree to improve the requirements and the quality of notifications.[171]

d. Notification and Surveillance Instruments

On the basis of Article XVI.1 of GATT 1994, the notification and surveillance instruments for subsidies programmes have been incorporated in the WTO framework under Part VII of the SCM Agreement. Members are required to notify any specific subsidy granted or maintained within their territories.[172] Any Member may request information on the nature and extent of any subsidy granted or maintained by another Member. These provisions also apply to non-actionable subsidy programmes.[173]

166 Article 8.2 of the SCM Agreement.

167 Interpretative Note 33 to the SCM Agreement.

168 Article 8.3 of the SCM Agreement.

169 Article 8.5 of the SCM Agreement.

170 Articles 8 and 31 of the SCM Agreement.

171 *Paul C. Rosenthal and Robert T.C. Vermylen*, "Review of Key Substantive Agreements: Panel II E: Antidumping Agreement (AD) and Agreement on Subsidies and Countervailing Measures (SCM): the WTO Antidumping and Subsidies Agreements: Did the United States Achieve Its Objectives During the Uruguay Round?", Law and Policy in International Business, Vol. 31, pp. 871 *et seq* (2000), at 896.

172 As of July 31 1997, 76 Members had submitted a new and full notification regarding specific subsidies. *WTO*, "WTO Annual Report 1997" (Geneva: WTO, 1997), at 108.

173 Article 8.3 of the SCM Agreement. However, until the end of 1997 no notification on non-actionable subsidies had been made.

(1) Institutions

Under Article 24 of the SCM Agreement, the SCM Committee has been established as a consultation forum designed to play a role at each step of the proceedings. In practice, the SCM Committee meet not less than twice a year to enable Members to consult on any matter relating to the operation and objectives of the SCM Agreement and make declarations on issues related to the SCM Agreement or specific subsidies.[174] In general, the SCM Committee does not usually interpret the provisions of the SCM Agreement, but rather limits itself to expressing the opinions of certain Members concerning the operability of the SCM Agreement. It is only in the case of non-actionable subsidies that such a committee plays a more active role by authorizing the Member requesting consultation to adopt the appropriate countermeasures.[175]

Moreover, the SCM Committee should establish a Permanent Group of Experts (PGE) which may be requested to assist a panel in deciding disputes as provided for in Article 4.5,[176] and to give an advisory opinion on the existence and nature of any subsidy, especially on subsidy programmes brought up by Members.[177]

(2) Notifications and Surveillance

Article 25 of the SCM Agreement sets up the obligation and requirement for WTO Members to submit their notifications of subsidies.[178] Members ought to notify all subsidies as defined in Article 1 of the SCM Agreement that meet the specificity criteria and are granted or maintained within their territories.[179] Unlike non-actionable subsidies, which are required to be notified in advance of their implementation, the question of whether the notification of other subsidies should take place before or after they are granted is not mentioned under Article 25 of the SCM Agreement. Moreover, the information to be provided in the notification should be sufficient to enable other Members to evaluate the trade effects and to understand the operation of the notified subsidy programmes.[180] The notification system makes the subsidies programmes of each Member more transparent and more specific as to the notified subsidies and the information provided is communicated in a written document. Members who consider that there are no measures in their

---

174 Article 24.1 of the SCM Agreement.

175 Article 9.4 of the SCM Agreement. Also *Gustavo E. Luengo Hernandez de Madrid*, *supra* note 30, at 200-201.

176 Article 4.5 of the SCM Agreement.

177 Articles 24.3 and 24.5 of the SCM Agreement.

178 *Gustavo E. Luengo Hernandez de Madrid*, *supra* note 30, at 199, adding that such notifications, except for those expressly mentioned as confidential by the subsidizing Member, are public, and notifications of subsidies according to Article 25 of the ASCM have the signature G/SCM/N* under WTO document database.

179 Article 25.2 of the SCM Agreement. This does not exclude possible subsidies granted by sub-national entities.

180 Article 25.3 of the SCM Agreement. Such information includes the form and the amount of the subsidy, the subsidy's policy objective or purpose, its duration, statistical data permitting an assessment of the trade effects of the subsidy, etc.

territories requiring notification under Article XVI.1 of the GATT 1994 and the SCM Agreement must inform the Secretariat accordingly in writing.[181]

However, the information contained in these notifications is usually not sufficient to see whether the subsidies conform with the SCM Agreement.[182] In the event that a Member does not notify the subsidies programmes or appropriately respond to another's request for information, the matter can be brought to the attention of the SCM Committee.[183] Members must also notify of all preliminary or final actions taken with respect to countervailing duties as well as their legislation on the subject.[184]

Although Members generally provide notifications of their subsidies, the objective of improving transparency is not fully achieved in practice. Due to the volume of notifications and delays from the submissions of many Members, it is difficult to examine these notifications in detail.[185] Notification of a measure does not prejudge either its legal status under the GATT 1994 or the SCM Agreement.[186] This implies that the SCM Agreement does not include sanctions or negative consequences for a Member who fails to notify a subsidy.

To summarize, this system of notification and surveillance has improved transparency and compliance of WTO Members. However, given the insufficient information contained in the notifications and the limited powers that the SCM Committee has in practice, this system has not been very effective.

(3) Notifications on Subsidies to the Fisheries Sector

In principle, notification of fisheries subsidies under the SCM Agreement could be an important source of data and could enhance transparency and government accountability regarding the granting of subsidies.[187] On the basis of all notifications on all types of subsidies submitted to the SCM Committee from 1 January 1995, the CTE conducted a survey and came up with the following four broad categories which could potentially impact the fisheries sector:[188] (a) subsidies to the harvest-

181 Article 25.6 of the SCM Agreement.

182 *Gustavo E. Luengo Hernandez de Madrid*, *supra* note 30, at 200.

183 Articles 25.9 and 25.10 of the SCM Agreement.

184 Articles 25.11 and 25.12 of the SCM Agreement.

185 *WTO* Doc. No. G/SCM/W/421, "Communication from the European Community to the Committee on Subsidies and Countervailing Measures, Frequency of Article 25 Subsidy Notifications" (30 March 1999), para. 2.

186 Article 25.7 of the SCM Agreement.

187 *UNEP*, *supra* note 41, at 4.

188 *WTO* Doc. No. WT/CTE/W/80, "Note by the Secretariat to the Committee on Trade and Environment, GATT/WTO Rules on Subsidies and Aids Granted in the Fishing Industry" (9 March 1998); *WTO* Doc. No. WT/CTE/W/80/Add.1, "Note by the Secretariat to the Committee on Trade and Environment, GATT/WTO Rules on Subsidies and Aids Granted in the Fishing Industry, Addendum" (21 September 1999); *WTO* Doc. No. WT/CTE/W/80/Add.2, "Note by the Secretariat to the Committee on Trade and Environment, GATT/WTO Rules on Subsidies and Aids Granted in the Fishing Industry, Update of Notifications under the SCM Agreement, Addendum" (1 June 2001).

ing sector; (b) subsidies to the shipbuilding industry;[189] (c) subsidies to the processing industry; (d) various other subsidies, in particular those related to research and development (R&D) or marketing. Subsidies to aquaculture and infrastructure are not identified. The purpose of this compilation was to illustrate the types of subsidies notified by WTO Members and to show that the notification mechanism of the SCM Agreement represents a source of transparency in this sector.[190] From September 1999 to April 2001, only a few Members provided notifications on subsidies programmes in the fisheries sector.[191] From this survey, it is apparent that the notifications from developing country Members are mostly absent.[192]

e. Special Regime Applicable to Developing and Least-developed Countries

Since WTO Members recognize that subsidies may play an important role in economic development programmes of developing country Members,[193] Part VIII of the SCM Agreement allows a more flexible approach for these Members. Some subsidies can be viewed as an adequate instrument for encouraging the economic development of certain Members, considering the importance that these have on the welfare of developing country Members and the limited effects that these have on trade distortion.[194]

Under Article 27 of the SCM Agreement, exceptions regarding subsidies granted by developing country Members have been established. For example, the SCM Agreement grants developing country Members referred to in Annex VII[195]

---

189 With respect to subsidies to the shipbuilding industry, there is no clear indication as to whether these subsidies include fishing vessels. *WTO* Doc. No. WT/CTE/W/80 (9 March 1998), at 12.

190 *Ibid.*, para. 32.

191 *WTO* Doc. No. WT/CTE/W/80/Add.2 (1 June 2001).

192 The Members which submitted notifications include the European Communities (for Belgium, Denmark, Finland, Germany, Italy, Ireland, Latvia, the Netherlands, Portugal, Slovenia, Spain, Sweden, and the United Kingdom), Japan, Korea, and Norway.

193 Article 27.1 of the SCM Agreement. Also *Gustavo E. Luengo Hernandez de Madrid*, *supra* note 30, at 201, illustrating that exceptions to the general regime of regulating subsidies had already been included in Article 14 of the 1979 Subsidies Code. The exceptions made in trade for developing countries could be applied retrospectively to the GATT 1947, where such countries were not subject to the principle of reciprocity in tariff reductions. See Article XXXVI:8 of the GATT.

194 *Gustavo E. Luengo Hernandez de Madrid*, *supra* note 30, at 201, illustrating that in these cases, the global welfare that results from the development of those countries prevails over the distorting effects that their subsidies may cause in trade flows. Moreover, since these countries' economies are weak, their governments cannot grant a large number of subsidies. The effects on trade distortion is considered limited.

195 According to Annex VII of the SCM Agreement, these countries are the least-developed countries designated as such by the United Nations and the following

full exemption from the prohibition of export subsidies.[196] In addition, exemption from the prohibition of domestic content subsidies[197] is granted for eight years from the date of entry into force of the SCM Agreement. Other developing country Members (not included in Annex VII) are granted exemption from the prohibition of export subsidies for eight years and from the prohibition of domestic content subsidies for five years.[198] During this period of time, these Members should work towards eliminating such export subsidies in a progressive manner.[199] The eight year transition period provided for this group of developing country Members can be extended subject to approval by the SCM Committee.[200] Developing country Members which reach "export competitiveness" in any given product must phase out their export subsidies for such products within two years.[201] For actionable subsidies, the presumption of serious prejudice[202] does not apply to those granted by developing country Members.[203]

Many developing country Members have been dissatisfied with the special and differential (S&D) treatment granted to them by Article 27 of the SCM Agreement, because they seldom benefit from these provisions. First, given the fact that these exceptions principally refer to subsidies for industrial products and that the production and export of industrial products by developing country Members does not represent a large share of total global trade, the impact of the exceptions is not very significant in practice.[204] Second, it restricts the right of developing countries to use subsidies as a developmental policy instrument because it requires the phasing out of subsidies. The phase-out period is considered too short. Even if

---

developing countries shall be subject to the provisions which are applicable to other developing country Members according to Article 27.2(b) when GNP per capita has reached USD 1,000 per year: Bolivia, Cameroon, Congo, Côte d'Ivoire, Egypt, Philippines, Ghana, Guatemala, Guyana, India, Indonesia, Kenya, Morocco, Nicaragua, Nigeria, Pakistan, Dominican Republic, Senegal, Sri Lanka and Zimbabwe.

196 Article 3.1(a) of the SCM Agreement.

197 Article 3.1(b) of the SCM Agreement.

198 Articles 27.2 and 27.3 of the SCM Agreement.

199 Article 27.4 of the SCM Agreement.

200 The eight year transition period ended on 1 January 2003, although it was extended for 19 developing countries until the end of 2006. This provision has been considered as a truly mandatory provision, which uses linguistically concrete and enforceable commitments. The language under Article 27.2 was the subject of a WTO dispute involving Brazilian aircraft, in which the panel confirmed that eight years was eight years. *WTO* Doc. No. WT/DS46/R, "WTO Report of the Panel, Brazil—Export Financing Programme for Aircraft" (14 April 1999), paras. 4.157, 7.49-7.51.

201 Articles 27.5 and 27.6 of the SCM Agreement. "Export competitiveness" in a product exists if a developing country Member's exports of that product have reached a share of at least 3.25 percent in world trade of that product for two consecutive calendar years.

202 Article 6.1 of the SCM Agreement.

203 Article 27.8 of the SCM Agreement.

204 *Gustavo E. Luengo Hernandez de Madrid*, *supra* note 30, at 204.

extensions are to be granted, complex application procedures need to be followed.[205] Many developing country Members were still unable to face competition when the phase-out periods ended.[206] Additional time and support are required. Third, due to the fact that Article 6.1 was not renewed,[207] the provision exempting developing country Members from the presumption of serious prejudice is no longer effective.

5. Remedies under WTO Law

Under the SCM Agreement, there are two types of remedy available for a Member who reasonably believes that its interests are adversely affected by the use of a prohibited or actionable subsidy by another Member. The remedies are as follows:

(1) A unilateral remedy is the imposition of countervailing measures against subsidized imports from other WTO Members after an investigation. If a Member determines that subsidized imports cause "material injury"[208] to its domestic industry, it can impose countervailing measures, following the substantive and procedural requirements under Part V (Articles 10 to 23) of the SCM Agreement.
(2) A multilateral remedy is, namely, the recourse to the WTO dispute settlement mechanism (DSM) in order to secure the withdrawal of the subsidies or the removal of their adverse effects. If a Member considers that a prohibited subsidy is being used or that an actionable subsidy results in adverse effects, it can initiate a dispute settlement procedure before the DSB.

It should be noted that multilateral procedures against prohibited or actionable subsidies and national procedures for adopting countervailing duties can be invoked parallel to each other and carried out simultaneously.[209] However, only one form can be applied to remedy the effects that a subsidy has on the domestic market of the importing Member: either (1) a countervailing duty from Part V, or (2) a retaliatory measure in accordance with Articles 4 (for prohibited subsidies) and 7 (for actionable subsidies) of the SCM Agreement. Additionally, non-actionable subsidies are not subject either to dispute settlement or to countervailing measures. WTO Members should also avoid overlapping anti-dumping duties and counter-

---

205 *WTO* Doc. No. WT/MIN(01)/17, "Implementation-Related Issues and Concerns, Ministerial Conference, Fourth Session, Doha, 9-14 November 2001" (20 November 2001), paras. 10.5-10.6, referring the procedures for extensions under Article 27.4 to *WTO* Doc. No. G/SCM/39, "Procedures for Extensions under Article 27.4 for Certain Developing Country Members" (20 November 2001).

206 *Frank J. Garcia*, "Beyond Special and Differential Treatment", Boston College International and Comparative Law Review, Vol. 27, pp. 291 *et seq* (2004), at 306.

207 Articles 6.1 and 31 of the SCM Agreement.

208 Article 15 of the SCM Agreement.

209 Interpretative Note 35 to the SCM Agreement.

vailing duties applied against another WTO Member's measure, since the accumulation of these duties against imports of the same product is not permitted.[210]

The procedure for the adoption of countervailing duties is characterized by its transparency and clarity. The predictability of countervailing duties being adopted has improved, and as a result Members know the reasons why another Member imposes countervailing duties. Members can reach a compromise via consultations,[211] and individuals can use the domestic procedures of the importing Members for appeal.[212] The number of countervailing duties adopted by Members continues to fall.

The DSM, which is one of the major achievements of the Uruguay Round negotiations, was established to ensure compliance with WTO law. Rulings by the DSB are legally binding upon WTO Members, unlike the pre-Uruguay Round system, where the GATT contracting parties found to be in breach of GATT provisions frequently ignored the GATT panel rulings.[213] Furthermore, the DSM has been considered more efficient, effective and respected than the former GATT resolution procedure, which was more a diplomatic than a legal process.[214] The main drawback of the DSM, nonetheless, is the lack of direct access by individuals. The DSM is exclusively reserved for WTO Members.[215] The only recourse for private parties is to persuade their governments to take up their case. However, the interests of a particular national industry may not coincide with the global interests of its government.

Regarding fisheries subsidies, there have so far been almost no cases of countervailing duties on wild-caught fish and fish products initiated and no fisheries subsidies cases brought to the DSB under the regulations established by the SCM Agreement. One case of relevance goes back to the GATT period: in that case, involving fresh Atlantic groundfish which had been exported from Canada to the United States in 1980's, the United States government considered that the Fishers Unemployment Insurance provided by the Canadian government was part

210 *Gustavo E. Luengo Hernandez de Madrid*, *supra* note 30, at 188.

211 Article 13 of the SCM Agreement.

212 Article 23 of the SCM Agreement.

213 *Konstantinos Adamantopoulos and Maria J. Pereyra-Friedrichsen*, *supra* note153, at 27.

214 However, the DSM has been considered ineffective recently. The recent dispute in the Airbus/Boeing case, thought to be the biggest and toughest case brought to the DSB, challenges the enforcement of the SCM Agreement and the competence of DSB, since both parties are likely to be found guilty of subsidization and neither side has a great incentive to give up its practices. *WTO* Doc. No. WT/DS316/1, "Request of Consultations by the United States, European Communities & Certain Member States-Measures Affecting Trade in Large Civil Aircraft" (12 October 2004); *WTO* Doc. No. WT/DS317/1 "Request for Consultations by the European Communities, United States-Measures Affecting Trade in Large Civil Aircraft" (12 October 2004). *Ryan E. Lee*, "Dogfight: Criticizing the Agreement on Subsidies and Countervailing Measures amidst the Largest Dispute in World Trade Organization History", North Carolina Journal of International Law and Commercial Regulation, Vol. 32, pp. 115 *et seq* (2007), at 158.

215 *Gustavo E. Luengo Hernandez de Madrid*, *supra* note 30, at 198.

of their general system of unemployment insurance and as such was not specific to fisheries. It was therefore exempt from the countervailing rules of GATT.[216]

B. Problems Applying Current Regulations to Fisheries Subsidies Cases

The SCM Agreement was created to deal with market distortions resulting from subsidies. Although fisheries subsidies can lead to the types of market distortions envisaged in the SCM Agreement, they can, however, because of their nature, have other negative impacts on trade, the environment and sustainable development not covered adequately by the SCM Agreement. The fishing industry is unique in the sense that its production in many instances depends on a fishing area shared by many countries/competitors. These areas have fisheries resources that are limited and which could be depleted if not fished in a responsible manner. This type of environmental impact, which can be aggravated by aggressive subsidization, is not covered by the SCM Agreement. In addition to the negative impact on the environment, the very nature of having a common production facility (fishing area) means that the irresponsible or subsidized behaviour of one participant in the common fishing area could have significant adverse effects on the catch of another country. With manufacturing industries, such as those envisaged in the SCM Agreement, this manner of direct impact on another country's production capacity does not exist. Hence no action could be taken against the subsidizer in this case. Disruptions of this type to the production output of another country alter trade flows and markets. Lastly, developing countries' ability to set up their own fishing fleets and, as a result, their ability to participate in the fishing industry can be impaired by distant water fleets from other countries whose governments have purchased access rights to the EEZs of developing countries. This developmental dimension is not considered in the SCM Agreement either.

Moreover, due to the great diversity of fish and fish products as well as the many different ways by which countries can support their fisheries sector and the unique nature of trade/market distortions described above, it is difficult to identify these to the extent required by thc SCM Agreement to prove either serious prejudice under Article 6 and material injury under Article 15 of the SCM Agreement.

The problems identified in the previous section are further aggravated by the notoriously poor quality of notifications for the fishing sector. The notification requirement of fisheries subsidies is manifestly disregarded 90 percent of the time.[217] The system in practice is ineffective in delivering reliable data on fisheries subsidies.[218] Furthermore, the information provided in the majority of these

---

216 *FAO* Doc. FAO Fisheries Technical Paper No. 437, at 33-34.

217 *WWF*, "Turning the Tide on Fishing Subsidies, Can the World Trade Organization Play a Positive Role?" (Washington, D.C. and Gland: WWF, 2002), at 10.

218 Some Members are unwilling to notify their programmes to the WTO, although this requirement seems sufficient to cover some types of subsidies.

notifications does not comply with the requirement in the WTO's standard questionnaire.[219]

Given that transparency is essential not only in the process of definition and categorization but also in supporting the implementation of current or future international commitments,[220] it is suggested that the notification requirement needs special attention with two goals in mind: namely, the legal consequences of the absence or inadequacy of notification as well as a detailed information list, giving the identity of subsidized enterprises, how subsidies are applied, the particular fisheries affected by a given subsidy and the amount of subsidies on a vessel, fleet and fishery basis.[221] Due to the lack of transparency in this sector, it is difficult to know accurate statistics and subsidies programmes in the fishery sector, and it obstructs any action of a Member against another Member if the subsidies programmes can only be estimated or must be calculated from doubtful data.

V. Conclusion

Fisheries subsidies, in their various forms, amount to a high percentage of the global fisheries trade and have negative impact on trade, the environment and development. Among the international fisheries instruments, the IPOAs developed by the FAO take into account the role of subsidies in building excess reduction and giving incentives to IUU fishing. However, the results to date show the ineffectiveness of existing fisheries instruments.

The WTO, with its pivotal role in international trade and its power to issue binding regulations for the international community, has the necessary expertise, legal framework and mechanisms to enact measures to control fisheries subsidies on a global scale. The SCM Agreement creates a series of multilateral and domestic remedial mechanisms to establish the legality of a subsidy that has an adverse effect on trade or on the markets of its Members and uses countervailing duties as a means of protection against the subsidized imports.

However, due to the unique nature of the fishing industry and great variety of fisheries subsidies, the current provisions of the SCM Agreement do not adequately cover fisheries subsidies. Hence, improved WTO disciplines, either as an amended SCM Agreement or as an agreement specifically designed for the fishing industry, *à la* the Agreement on Agriculture, need to be considered.

It has taken a great deal of effort, international negotiations and legislation: from GATT 1947, then the Subsidies Code in the Tokyo Round Negotiations to the SCM Agreement to reach the point where we are now. In Chapter 2, we look

219 *Tracey M. Price*, "Negotiating WTO Fisheries Subsidy Discipline: Can Subsidy Transparency and Classification Provide the Means Towards an End to the Race for Fish?", Tulane Journal of International and Comparative Law, Vol. 13, pp. 141 *et seq* (2005), at 166.

220 *UNEP*, *supra* note 41, at 4.

221 *WWF*, "What's the Catch?" (Washington, D.C. and Gland: WWF, 2005), at 8-9.

at the development of WTO negotiations on the new regulations resulting from the mandates of the Doha Ministerial Conference.

Chapter 2: Fisheries Subsidies Negotiations within the WTO Framework

Due to increased international awareness of the importance of fisheries subsidies, this issue has made its way into WTO negotiations and at a series of Ministerial Conferences in the past decade.[222] At first, the arguments among the WTO Members were on whether the existing SCM Agreement was sufficient for regulating fisheries subsidies or whether there was a need for new fisheries subsidies regulations within the WTO framework. The mandates of the Doha Ministerial Declaration and of the Hong Kong Ministerial Declaration firmly established that there was a need for new fisheries subsidies regulations. At first the debate was on whether the structure of fisheries subsidies regulations should be based on a top-down or bottom-up approach. The discussions then moved increasingly towards a more detailed scrutiny of the sub-categories of fisheries subsidies and more concrete legal texts. This Chapter examines the negotiations at different stages from the Uruguay Round Negotiations to the most recent status to understand the reasoning and positions of different Members.

I. Discussions on Fisheries Subsidies during the Uruguay Round Negotiations

During the Uruguay Round Negotiations, fisheries issues were discussed in the Negotiating Group on Natural Resource Based Products (NRBPs). However, submissions to this Negotiating Group could not reach a consensus on how to address fisheries issues, including tariffs, non-tariff measures, subsidies and access to resources. It was finally decided to negotiate fisheries issues along with other natural resource-based products as part of a broader negotiation, and fisheries issues were moved to the Market Access Group along with other negotiating sub-

---

[222] Ministerial Conferences, empowered to take decisions on all matters under any of the Multilateral Trade Agreements, are at the top of the hierarchy in the decision-making and negotiating process and are held at least once every two years with representatives of every WTO Member as required by the Marrakesh Agreement Establishing the World Trade Organization, the WTO's founding charter. However, a practice has developed in the recent past of mini-ministerials between the rich and powerful Members being held in advance of the biennial Ministerial meetings.

C.-J. Chen, *Fisheries Subsidies under International Law*, Hamburg Studies on Maritime Affairs 20, DOI 10.1007/978-3-642-15693-9_3, © Springer-Verlag Berlin Heidelberg 2010

jects. The insistence of the European Communities[223], Japan and Korea on linking access to resources with access to markets partly resulted in the failure of the work in the Negotiating Group on NRBPs. At the end of the Uruguay Round Negotiations, WTO Members left subsidies to the fisheries sector outside the regulations and reduction commitments of agricultural subsidies in the Agreement of Agriculture. Fisheries subsidies were then included under the scope of the SCM Agreement, which covers all goods except agricultural products.[224]

Hence, fisheries subsidies negotiations remain one of the issues that straddle both unfinished business from the end of the Uruguay Round Negotiations and the so-called 'new issues' in later negotiations. Concerns about unsustainable fisheries subsidies which undermine the viability of global fisheries as well as distort trade flows have created a connection between trade and environment issues.[225]

II. Discussions on Fisheries Subsidies before the Seattle Ministerial Conference

A. Establishing the Environmental Data Base on Fisheries Subsidies

Before fisheries subsidies discussions within the WTO framework started in the Committee on Trade and Environment (CTE)[226] in 1997, several subsidies programmes in the fishery sector of WTO Members could be found in the Environmental Data Base (EDB).[227] The EDB was established in 1996 in compliance with the requirements of various WTO regulations. This was required by the CTE to improve the transparency of trade measures used for environmental purposes and

223 Since 1 December 2009 "European Union" has been the official name in the WTO. Before that, "European Communities" was the official name in WTO business for legal reasons and that name continues to appear in older material.

224 *Gareth Porter*, "Fisheries Subsidies and Overfishing: Towards a Structured Discussion" (Geneva: UNEP, 2002), at 3-4.

225 *Roman Grynberg and Jan Yves Remy*, "Small Vulnerable Economy Issues and the WTO", in *Ivan Mbirimi, Bridget Chilala, and Roman Grynberg* (eds), "From Doha to Cancun: Delivering a Development Round", pp. 269-290 (London: Commonwealth Secretariat, 2003), at 283.

226 The Committee on Trade and Environment (CTE) was established by the WTO General Council in January 1995. It is a non-negotiating body created to explore the environmental implications of trade. Its mandate is set out in Annex I of the Marrakesh Ministerial Decision on Trade and Environment of 15 April 1994, with reference to a list of ten items. Under Item 6 of the work programmes at the CTE, several papers were submitted in response to a request by the Secretariat of the CTE and Members for factual background information and subsidies to the fisheries sector.

227 The Environmental Data Base (EDB) involves the manner with which diverse environment-related notifications are to be classified and catalogued.

environmental measures and requirements which can have significant trade effects.[228] Some environment-related fisheries subsidies were notified to the EDB.[229]

B. Discussions at the Committee on Trade and Environment

After the establishment of the WTO, the CTE began discussions on the role that subsidies play in the fisheries sector. In response to a request by Members of the CTE,[230] the Secretariat in its note indicated that subsidies in the fishery sector (which were considered as trade restrictions and distortions) assume a variety of forms and were primarily provided to reduce the operating and capital costs of

[228] These notifications can be divided into two groups, including those made in accordance with WTO provisions which either refer explicitly to the environment or are generally regarded as relating to environmental objectives and those not made in accordance with WTO provisions but reflect the broad-based, multi-sectoral and at times imprecise definition of environmental policies themselves. Regarding the first group of notifications, these WTO provisions include Annex 2, paragraph 12 of the AoA; Article 8.2(c) of the SCM Agreement; Articles 2 and 5 of the Agreement on Technical Barriers to Trade (TBT Agreement); Article XIV(b) of the General Agreement on Trade in Services; Article 27.2 of the Agreement on Trade-Related Aspects of Intellectual Property Rights (TRIPS Agreement); and measures taken pursuant to Article XX of the GATT. *WTO* Doc. No. WT/CTE/W/46, "Note by the Secretariat to the Committee on Trade and Environment, Provisions of the Multilateral Trading System with Respect to Transparency of Trade Measures Used for Environmental Purposes and Environmental Measures and Requirements Which Have Significant Trade Effects" (29 April 1997) , at 3.

[229] *Ibid.*, at 9. The notifications of environment-related fisheries subsidies under the SCM Agreement include a regional structural adjustment programme for fisheries and the aquaculture sector in which a secondary objective was the conservation of fisheries (*WTO* Doc. No. G/SCM/N/16/EEC, "Committee on Subsidies and Countervailing Measures - Subsidies - Updating Notifications pursuant to Article XVI.1 of the GATT 1994 and Article 25 of the Agreement *[...]* measures - European Communities" (2 April 1997)) and the inclusion in a Fisheries Fund of the objective of "protection and improvement of the environment" (*WTO* Doc. No. G/SCM/N/3/Hun/Suppl.1, "Committee on Subsidies and Countervailing Measures – Subsidies - Notification Pursuant to Article XVI.1 of the GATT 1994 and Article 25 of the Agreement on *[...]* measures - Hungary - Supplement" (14 June 1996)). Furthermore, the notifications made under the AoA include supports for the "conservation and responsible utilization of wild fisheries" as well as a list of assistance measures to promote the "conservation and responsible utilization of wild fisheries" (*WTO* Doc. No. G/AG/N/Aus/5, "Committee on Agriculture - Notification under Article 16.2 of the Agreement: Monitoring of the Follow-up to the Decision on Measures Concerning the Possible *[...]* developing Countries - Australia" (25 September 1996)).

[230] The Members were the United States and New Zealand.

harvesting.[231] Subsidies for reducing vessel fuel costs could lead to the loss of high-migration or straddling stocks by encouraging long-range harvesting. Subsidies for vessel construction would increase total fleet capacity. In view of the fact that global fisheries resources continue to undergo an alarming deterioration, whereby the extent of annual harvesting worldwide is undermining the sustainability of fisheries resources, the Secretariat also indicated that the reasons for fish stock declines are varied, including overcapacity and overfishing of fishing fleets, open access to fish resources as a result of the absence of property rights for fisheries resources, inappropriate fisheries management practices, marine pollution, fish by-catch mortality and increased ultra-violet radiation on marine food chains.[232]

The fisheries subsidies issue at the WTO negotiations was introduced formally by the United States in 1997.[233] Concerned that global fisheries resources had been overused, the United States was of the opinion that subsidies in the fishery sector not only promote overfishing and undermine the sustainability of fisheries resources, but also distort fish trade, leading to less efficient production. The majority of global fisheries subsidies have negative impact from a conservation standpoint, since they encourage the movement of additional capital into an economic sector that is already overcapitalized; promote overfishing by vessels already in existence in the fisheries; exacerbate and compound the already difficult problems of fisheries management; and represent a misallocation of government financial resources that could otherwise be employed more efficiently.[234]

With regard to trade distortion, the economic consequences of subsidization reflect the conservation effects in that they promote over-production and delay market-balancing adjustment. In this submission, the United States mentioned that fisheries subsidies not only promote a misallocation of economic resources and structural overcapacity by delaying the exit of players from the market, but also distort the market equilibrium and affect trade by shifting the burden of adjustment onto non-subsidized producers. Furthermore, subsidies can complicate the situation for developing countries to take full economic advantage of the fish resources in their own EEZs. Not to mention the fact that the problem of fisheries subsidies is more acute for developing countries whose economies are less diversified and more dependent on export earnings from their natural resources.[235]

---

231 *WTO* Doc. No. WT/CTE/W/67, "Note by the Secretariat to the Committee on Trade and Environment, Environmental Benefits of Removing Trade Restrictions and Distortions" (7 November 1997), para. 91.

232 *Ibid.*, para. 88, citing *UNEP*, "The Role of Trade Policies in the Fishing Sector: Summary Report, UNEP/WWF workshop on 'The Role of Trade Policies in the Fishing Sector'" (Geneva: UNEP, 1997); and *R. McLeod*, "Market Access Issues for the New Zealand Seafood Trade, New Zealand Fishing Industry Board" (1996).

233 *WTO* Doc. No. WT/CTE/W/51, "Submission by the United States to the Committee on Trade and Environment, Environmental and Trade Benefits of Removing Subsidies in the Fisheries Sector" (19 May 1997).

234 *Ibid.*, at 2.

235 *Ibid.*, at 3-4.

In 1999, Australia further suggested that improved transparency and greater monitoring and assessment of the size and various forms of fisheries subsidies should be the first step in addressing concerns about their impact on trade and the environment.[236] Moreover, it is necessary to assess whether existing WTO regulations are effective in limiting the negative impact and whether additional regulations are able to reduce the overall level of support and to ensure it is provided in less distorting forms.[237]

Meanwhile, in its submission to the CTE,[238] Iceland argued that the economies of the global marine fisheries are heavily distorted by the fisheries' common property problem as well as by direct and indirect government fisheries subsidies. The environmental effects of fisheries subsidies depend to a large extent on the fisheries management system. Providing subsidies to a common property fishery generally results in more economic waste and a greater risk of permanent damage to the ecosystem. However, providing subsidies to a property-rights-based fishery, i.e. a fishery where the common property problem has been substantially alleviated, may only amount to a non-distorting financial transfer to the holders of fishing property rights.[239] Furthermore, by applying economic models to analyze the environmental effects of fisheries subsidies, Iceland demonstrated that fisheries subsidies, irrespective of whether they exist as cost reductions or price supports, encourage increased fishing efforts and exacerbate the already serious common property problem of ocean fisheries.[240]

C. *Discussions at the General Council as Partial Preparation for the Seattle Ministerial Conference*

Besides its submissions to the CTE, Iceland also raised the issues at the General Council in preparations for the Seattle Ministerial Conference and proposed that the Members should agree to eliminate subsidies contributing to fisheries over-

---

236 *WTO* Doc. No. WT/CTE/W/105, "Submission by Australia to the Committee on Trade and Environment, Trade Liberalization and the Environment: A positive Agenda for Trade Reform" (2 February 1999).

237 *Ibid.*, para. 31.

238 Both in *WTO* Doc. No. WT/CTE/W/111, "Submission by Iceland to the Committee on Trade and Environment, On the Environmental Impact of Fisheries Subsidies" (11 March 1999), and *WTO* Doc. No. WT/CTE/W/103, "Submission by Iceland to the Committee on Trade and Environment, the Icelandic Fisheries Management System: a Market-Driven Sustainable Fisheries Regime" (25 January 1999). The latter submission outlined the Icelandic subsidy-free fisheries management system and concluded that no one single action could bring about the positive result of achieving sustainable development in fisheries as would the elimination of government subsidies. Also in *Thorir Ibsen*, "Sustainable Fisheries: the Linkages with Trade and Environment", Linkages Journal, Vol. 4., No. 2 (28 May 1999), available on-line at <www.iisd.ca/journal/ibsen.html> (last visited on 31 August 2008).

239 *WTO* Doc. No. WT/CTE/W/111 (11 March 1999), paras. 1 and 3.

240 *Ibid.*, para. 18.

capacity.[241] Iceland not only restated the problems of inadequate fisheries management regimes and fisheries subsidies, but also expressed a similar opinion to that in the submission by New Zealand,[242] regarding the importance of the fisheries subsidies issue for developing countries and the necessity to consult with the FAO regarding WTO actions in the field of fisheries subsidies.[243]

At the WTO High Level Symposium on Trade and Environment in March 1999, Australia, Iceland, New Zealand, the Philippines and the United States jointly submitted a statement on the need to eliminate environmentally damaging and trade-distorting subsidies in the fishery sector,[244] and urged Members to make an early commitment to progressively eliminating this kind of fisheries subsidies. It would represent a clear "win-win" achievement in the areas of trade, environment and sustainable development. New Zealand also suggested several steps to cope with the fisheries subsidies issue, including support for the implementation of the FAO IPOA-Capacity and an analysis of existing WTO regulations. Furthermore, WTO Members needed to reflect further on this issue, not only in the CTE but in the context of preparations for the Seattle Ministerial Conference.[245]

Afterwards, New Zealand proposed that a Work Programme should be initiated as part of the upcoming negotiations to develop WTO commitments and regulations directed at the elimination of subsidies that distort trade in fish products and impact negatively on the conservation and sustainability of global fish stocks. New Zealand also considered the Seattle Ministerial Conference as a great opportunity to address the fisheries subsidies situation, since the WTO had a clear mandate to address trade-distorting measures and the expertise for elaborating regulations in this area.[246]

---

241 *WTO* Doc. No. WT/GC/W/229, "Communication from Iceland to the General Council, Preparations for the 1999 Ministerial Conference: Fisheries Subsidies" (6 July 1999), para. 2. It was submitted by Iceland during the special session of the General Council on 7 July 1999 and gained support from almost twenty Members at the meeting.

242 *WTO* Doc. No. WT/CTE/W/121, "Submission by New Zealand to the Committee on Trade and Environment, Benefits of Eliminating Trade Distorting and Environmentally Damaging Subsidies in the Fisheries Sector" (28 June 1999).

243 *WTO* Doc. No. WT/GC/W/229 (6 July 1999), paras. 7-9, also see *WTO* Doc. No. WT/GC/W/303, "Communication from Australia, Iceland, New Zealand, Norway, Peru, Philippines and United States to the General Council, Preparations for the 1999 Ministerial Conference: Fisheries Subsidies" (6 August 1999). These submissions were submitted not only by developed countries, but also together by developing countries.

244 *WTO* Doc. No. WT/CTE/W/121 (28 June 1999), Annex 1.

245 *WTO* Doc. No. WT/GC/W/229 (6 July 1999).

246 *WTO* Doc. No. WT/GC/W/292, "Communication from New Zealand to the General Council, Preparations for the 1999 Ministerial Conference: Elimination of Trade Distorting and Environmentally Damaging Subsidies in the Fisheries Sector" (5 August 1999), paras. 2 and 9.

D. Arguments over Fisheries Subsidies Discussions

Although Australia, Iceland, New Zealand and the United States emphasized the negative impact of fisheries subsidies and called for the elimination of subsidies contributing to overcapacity and overfishing, Japan emphasized that in order to guarantee a sustainable utilization of fishery resources, it was inappropriate to single out the fisheries subsidies issue, because of the various factors which hinder sustainable utilization of fishery resources. It was also necessary to solve the problems resulting from other factors, which include ineffective and inadequate fisheries management, the lack of fishing capacity control, insufficient enforcement and IUU fishing activities, including the operations of flags of convenience (FOC) fleets that do not abide by international conservation rules.[247] Efforts to improve fishery management require technical expertise and should be conducted by the FAO.[248]

During this period of time, the fisheries subsidies issue came up initially at the CTE and then at the General Council, as a result of the submissions and efforts of several WTO Members. However, there was no consensus on whether there was a need for new fisheries subsidies regulations within the WTO framework.

III. Results on Fisheries Subsidies Negotiations at the Seattle Ministerial Conference

The matters negotiated at the Seattle Ministerial Conference in 1999 were very diverse, including tariffs, anti-dumping, subsidies, safeguards, investment measures, trade facilitation, electronic commerce, competition policy, fisheries, transparency in government procurement, technical assistance, capacity-building and other development issues, and intellectual property protection, as well as many other subjects — in addition to agriculture and services.[249] However, accompanied as it was by protest activities, the Seattle Ministerial Conference can only be considered as the launch-pad of the fisheries subsidies negotiations. Although the subsidies proposal suffered the same fate as at the Seattle Ministerial Conference, it was never rejected and indeed the issue of fisheries subsidies received broad-

---

[247] *WTO* Doc. No. WT/GC/W/221, "Communication from Japan to the General Council, Preparations for the 1999 Ministerial Conference: Negotiations on Forestry and Fishery Products" (28 June 1999), para. 28. Japan again explained the factors of depletion of fisheries resources in a further submission after the Seattle Ministerial Conference, *WTO* Doc. No. WT/CTE/W/173, "Submission by Japan to the Committee on Trade and Environment, Japan's Basic Position on the Fishery Subsidy Issue, Item 6" (23 October 2000).

[248] *WTO* Doc. No. WT/GC/W/221 (28 June 1999), para. 26.

[249] Seattle Ministerial Conference, the Third WTO Ministerial Conference was held in Seattle between 30 November and 3 December 1999, see further information available at <www.wto.org/english/thewto_e/minist_e/min99_e/min99_e.htm> (last visited on 20 January 2008).

based support.[250] Despite the failure of the Seattle Ministerial Conference to launch and set parameters for a new round of multilateral trade negotiations, during the preparation for the Seattle Ministerial Conference a Working Group in the area of fisheries subsidies had been established in order to identify any subsidy which might have adverse effects on trade, environment and sustainable development, as well as any subsidy which might have positive effects in these areas.[251]

IV. Negotiations on Fisheries Subsidies before the Doha Ministerial Conference

At this stage, the arguments focused on whether there was a need for new fisheries subsidies regulations under the WTO framework and how it could comply with the activities of other international organizations. The discussion finally resulted in the decision of the Doha Ministerial Declaration.

A. Members Call for New Fisheries Subsidies Rules within the WTO Framework

After the Seattle Ministerial Conference, Iceland proposed that the WTO Secretariat should conduct a factual study on the impact of fisheries subsidies in close cooperation with the FAO, RFMOs and other organizations, taking into consideration the importance of the fisheries sector for developing countries and least-developed countries. Iceland also proposed that the study should focus on the impact of fisheries subsidies on trade distortions, fisheries management, overcapacity and overfishing, as well as the marine environment.[252]

At the same time, New Zealand continued to study this area actively and encouraged other WTO Members to contribute with their own analyses as well as national experiences in order to deepen understanding among WTO Members of the issues underlying the discussion on fisheries subsidies.[253] New Zealand was of the opinion that the WTO had an essential role to play in this issue, given that, in the absence of concerted unilateral action by Members to reduce and eliminate fisheries subsidies with adverse effects, additional WTO rules in this area would need to be considered.[254]

---

250 *Thorir Ibsen,* supra note 58, at 473.

251 *WTO* Doc. No. WT/CTE/W/132, "Communication from Iceland to the Committee on Trade and Environment, Fisheries Subsidies and the Environment" (21 February 2000), para. 8.

252 *Ibid.,* paras. 9 and 10.

253 *WTO* Doc. No. WT/CTE/W/134, "Communication from New Zealand to the Committee on Trade and Environment, Subsidies in the Fisheries Sector: Update on Recent Work Conducted by New Zealand" (24 February 2000), para. 1.

254 *Ibid.*, para. 17.

The United States analyzed certain types of fisheries subsidies and their impacts, and added a new dimension to the analysis by identifying categories of fisheries subsidies that are environmentally harmful and trade-distorting.[255] According to the submission by the United States, fisheries subsidies that are environmentally harmful and trade-distorting are classified as follows:[256]

(1) Subsidies that reduce capital (fixed) and operating (variable) costs:
   (a) Domestic fisheries: government-funded commercially applicable research and development; government loans and loan refinancing at below market rates; government loan guarantees that facilitate below market rate loans; government forgiveness of government-funded loans; investment tax credits; income tax deferrals/accelerated depreciation allowances; exemption from national sales and fuel excise taxes; government-supported marine insurance at below market rates where such insurance is commercially available; government ownership/management of fishing enterprises if inconsistent with market terms; State trading if inconsistent with market terms and customary business practices; assistance to shipbuilding when the benefits accrue specifically to fishers.
   (b) International fisheries: government-funded foreign access payments; government assistance to foreign fishery joint ventures; government-supported fishing vessel exports; government-supported below market risk insurance for foreign fishery investments.

(2) Subsidies that support incomes and prices: domestic price support programmes; government purchases for above market remuneration; rebates of certain taxes on inputs if the finished product is exported; government-funded export subsidies; sector-specific income maintenance programmes; regional economic development, if effectively fisheries sector-specific.

From the viewpoint of cost/revenue impact, subsidies encourage overfishing and overcapacity, because they: (1) reduce fixed and variable costs; (2) enhance revenues and incomes; and (3) mitigate risks.[257] With reduced costs and risks and enhanced revenues, fishing vessels are likely to fish at an unsustainable level. These harmful subsidies tend to have the worst environmental effects in open-access fisheries, less negative effects in regulated open-access fisheries and the least negative effects in rights-based fisheries.[258] Moreover, the environmental effects may occur not only within the EEZ of the subsidizing coastal State, but also on the high seas and in the EEZs of other coastal States where the subsidizing country's fishing fleets operate.[259] Although the trade effects of fisheries subsidies were not carefully evaluated, the United States inferred that the trade impact is

---

255 *WTO* Doc. No. WT/CTE/W/154, "Communication from the United States to the Committee on Trade and Environment, Environmentally-Harmful and Trade-Distorting Subsidies in Fisheries" (4 July 2000).

256 *Ibid.*, at 4-5.

257 *Ibid.*, para. 8.

258 *Ibid.*, para. 9.

259 *Ibid.*, para. 10.

adverse, since the aggregate trade effect is usually to suppress prices.[260] The illustrative list of fisheries subsidies with negative impact in the submission by the United States subsequently stimulated a vigorous discussion.

B. Other Members Propose a Holistic Approach to Fisheries Subsidies

In spite of the fact that several Members urged the elimination of fisheries subsidies, e.g. New Zealand, Iceland, Australia, Argentina, Chile, Hong Kong China and Peru,[261] the other group of Members, led by Japan and Korea, considered that discussions in the CTE should await results of the ongoing work in other organizations, i.e. the Asia-Pacific Economic Cooperation (APEC), the FAO and the OECD, and stated that a comprehensive factual analysis of fisheries management and fisheries subsidies is important.[262] Korea also emphasized the importance of employment in the fisheries sector, while Japan asked for concrete examples of harmful fisheries subsidies.

Moreover, Japan indicated that there were other different factors for fishery depletion and suggested that the FAO should be requested to undertake technical work which the CTE could use on a case-by-case basis to examine under which circumstances certain subsidies have negative impact on fishery resources.[263] Commenting on the submission of the United States,[264] Japan argued that the categories proposed by the United States should not be addressed within the WTO, because the WTO, which focuses its discussion on international trade issues, could not be expected to be a good forum for conducting a technical work related to fisheries.[265] Japan added that trade-distorting fisheries subsidies could be regulated under the SCM Agreement, as long as the negative trade effects fall within the meaning of "adverse effects" stipulated in Article 5 of the SCM Agreement.[266]

Along with Japan, Tunisia, the European Communities, Canada and Norway agreed that the central issue for sustainable fisheries is sound fisheries management, which is the competence of the FAO, and that the CTE should request the

---

260 *Ibid.*, para. 16.

261 *WTO* Doc. No. PRESS/TE/033, "Trade and Environment Bulletin: CTE Holds Information Session with MEAs and Addresses the Relationship between the WTO and MEAs, the Export of Domestically Prohibited Good, the TRIPS Agreement and Fisheries Subsidies" (10 July 2000). Also see papers by Australia (*WTO* Doc. No. WT/CTE/W/105 (2 February 1999)); Iceland (*WTO* Doc. No. WT/CTE/W/103 (25 January 1999) and WT/CTE/W111 (11 March 1999)); New Zealand (*WTO* Doc. No. WT/CTE/W/121 (28 June 1999)); and the United States (*WTO* Doc. No. WT/CTE/W/154 (4 July 2000)).

262 *Ibid.*, at 8.

263 *WTO* Doc. No. WT/CTE/W/173 (23 October 2000), paras. 6 and 7.

264 *WTO* Doc. No. WT/CTE/W/154 (4 July 2000).

265 *WTO* Doc. No. WT/CTE/W/173 (23 October 2000), paras. 10 and 11.

266 *Ibid.*, para. 12.

FAO to pursue this work as a basis for its further study on fisheries subsidies.[267] The European Communities, reflecting on its fisheries management framework and making reference to its Green Paper on the future of the Common Fisheries Policy,[268] reiterated that the FAO should be the main forum for discussions on fisheries and the various aspects of fisheries management.[269] However, Iceland, later supported by Australia, Canada, Chile, New Zealand, Norway, Peru, the Philippines, Thailand, the United States and others, called on the WTO to address the aspect of sustainable fisheries management under its mandate, i.e. fisheries subsidies.[270]

Korea, on the basis of its national experience, stated that some fisheries subsidies play a positive role in conserving fisheries resources and improving the marine environment; therefore, the Members should not rush to conclusions on the effects of fisheries subsidies without fully considering all relevant factors.[271] A comprehensive approach, taking into account the socio-economic needs of the fishing industry and coastal communities, the unique domestic environment and development needs of countries, would lead to constructive discussions on fisheries subsidies in the CTE.[272] Korea added that it is necessary to start the discussion by building a consensus on the definition of fisheries subsidies.[273] The lack of such a definition would be confusing and misleading in the further discussion of fisheries subsidies.

C. Follow-up with Other Relevant International Organizations

At this time, the Secretariat of the CTE reviewed the work done in other international organizations, e.g. the FAO and UNEP, and proposed an overall picture of fisheries subsidies.[274] These organizations pursue activities on fisheries subsi-

---

267 *WTO* Doc. No. PRESS/TE/034, "Trade and Environment Bulletin: CTE Holds MEA Information Session and Discusses WTO-MEA Relationships, Services and the Environment, Relations with IGOs and NGOs, Fisheries subsidies and Liberalizing Environmental Services" (31 October 2000), at 8.

268 See *infra* Chapter 4 for analysis on the Common Fisheries Policy.

269 *WTO* Doc. No. PRESS/TE/036, "Trade and Environment Bulletin: UNEP and MEAs Participate in CTE Information Session on Compliance and Dispute Settlement. CTE Discussions WTO-MEA Relationship, Domestically Prohibited Goods, Biodiversity Convention and TRIPS Agreement, ECO-labelling, and Fisheries Subsidies Reform" (6 July 2001), at 7.

270 *WTO* Doc. No. PRESS/TE/034 (31 October 2000), at 8.

271 *WTO* Doc. No. WT/CTE/W/175, "Communication from Korea to the Committee on Trade and Environment, Utilization of Subsidies and their Positive Role in the Fisheries Sector" (24 October 2000), para. 20.

272 *Ibid.*

273 *Ibid.*, para. 18.

274 *WTO* Doc. No. WT/CTE/W/167, "Note by the Secretariat to the Committee on Trade and Environment, Environmental Benefits of Removing Restrictions and Distortions: the Fisheries Sector-Item 6 of the Work Programme" (16 October 2000), and *WTO* Doc. No. WT/CTE/W/167/Add.1, "Note by the Secretariat to the

dies and their work can complement and guide the ongoing discussions at the CTE on the nature, extent and implications of fisheries subsidies in the context of the transition to sustainable fisheries management.

As an example, the FAO compiles and disseminates information on fisheries subsidies at a global level. It reported on the results of its expert consultation on economic incentives and responsible fisheries in December 2000,[275] which was the first inter-agency meeting to collaborate on work on fisheries subsidies between the WTO and FAO. Its Sub-Committee on Fish Trade also committed itself to ensuring that future multilateral trade negotiations should be based on the SCM Agreement within the WTO framework.[276] The general consensus was that fisheries subsidies negotiations are the exclusive province of the WTO and that the role of the FAO and its Sub-Committees should be limited to the identification and discussion of trade problems at the request of Members.[277] Moreover, although the observer status of the FAO at the WTO does not allow for direct participation, its technical expertise may be called upon by the negotiating parties and can be of great value.

Since 1997, the UNEP has also been one of the leading intergovernmental bodies promoting international efforts to understand and respond to the problem of harmful fisheries subsidies. It analyzes the challenges, concerns and existing tools for addressing fisheries subsidies and provides options for moving forward.[278] It

Committee on Trade and Environment, Environmental Benefits of Removing Restrictions and Distortions: the Fisheries Sector-Item 6 of the Work Programme" (19 June 2001).

275 *WTO* Doc. No. WT/CTE/W/189, "Communication from the FAO to the Committee on Trade and Environment, Update of FAO Activities Related to Fisheries, Report of the Expert Consultation on Economic Incentives and Responsible Fisheries, 28 November-1 December 2000" (18 June 2001).

276 *FAO* Doc. COFI:FT/VII/2000/5, "Item 7.1 of the Provisional Agenda, Committee on Fisheries, Sub-Committee on Fish Trade, Seventh Session, Bremen, Germany, 22-25 March 2000, Implementation of World Trade Organization Agreements and Multilateral Trade Negotiations: Agreements on the Application of Sanitary and Phytosanitary Measures, Technical Barriers to Trade and on Subsidies and Countervailing Measures" (Rome: FAO, 2000), citing that the AoA contains regulations dealing with subsidies in the agricultural sector which are less stringent or allow more delay in implementation than the rules of the SCM Agreement.

277 *FAO* Doc. COFI:FT/VII/2000/6, "Item 7.2 of the Provisional Agenda, Committee on Fisheries, Sub-Committee on Fish Trade, Seventh Session, Bremen, Germany, 22-25 March 2000, Implementation of World Trade Organization Agreements and Multilateral Trade Negotiations: Ongoing Multilateral Trade Negotiations and FAO Training Programme" (Rome: FAO, 2000), para. 1.

278 *WTO* Doc. No. WT/CTE/W/187, "Communication from UNEP to the Committee on Trade and Environment, UNEP Fisheries Subsidies Workshop, Chairman's Summary" (15 March 2001). The options included creating an additional category for prohibited fisheries subsidies, adopting exceptions to prohibited subsidies, shifting the burden of proof of actionable subsidies, creating a non-actionable category for certain fisheries subsidies, allowing subsidies under specific policy condi-

also works closely with governments, other organizations, as well as RFMOs.[279] The UNEP technical workshop in 2001, with the goal of combining the objectives of minimizing trade distortions, protecting the environment and natural resources, and enhancing development opportunities for developing countries, suggested placing the fisheries subsidies issue on the agenda of the WTO Doha Ministerial Conference in order to negotiate stronger fisheries subsidies regulations.[280]

To facilitate CTE Members' understanding of the links between the multilateral environment and trade agendas, and of building awareness of the use of trade-related measures in multilateral environmental agreements (MEAs), the CTE held an Information Session with other MEA Secretariats. During the session, the Convention on Biological Diversity (CBD) called on the CTE to work on the potential "win-win" opportunities in trade and the environment which would result from eliminating trade restrictions and distortions in the fisheries sector.[281] More specifically, it concluded that there was a consensus that the WTO has the competence to realize these "win-win" opportunities by removing harmful subsidies.

D. Status of Negotiations before the Doha Ministerial Conference

Based on these observations, WTO Members could be roughly divided into two groups, regarding the question of whether it is appropriate to discuss the fisheries subsidies issue under the WTO negotiations. The "Friends of Fish" Members,[282] including Iceland, New Zealand, the United States, Australia, Chile, Peru and Norway, called for WTO action to deal with the fisheries subsidies issue. However, Japan, Korea and the European Communities emphasized the need to apply a holistic approach to fisheries issues in general and that subsidies should be considered in the context of the sustainable use of fisheries resources.

---

tions, emphasizing concerns for artisanal and small-scale fisheries, and emphasizing concerns for special needs of developing countries.

279 *UNEP*, *supra* note 8, at 1; *UNEP*, *supra* note 39, at 6-7, emphasizing that the UNEP has worked to encourage and support an increased role for RFMOs in the international discussion of fisheries subsidies and fisheries management. The UNEP also continues its active role in regular meetings of relevant secretaries of international organizations and RFMOs to pursue areas in which joint work may be of mutual benefit.

280 *UNEP*, *supra* note 41, at 5.

281 *WTO* Doc. No. PRESS/TE/033 (10 July 2000); *WTO* Doc. No. WT/CTE/W/149, "Communication from the CBD Secretariat to the Committee on Trade and Environment, Response of the Executive Secretary of the Convention on Biological Diversity (CBD) to the Chair of the CTE" (28 June 2000).

282 The "Friends of Fish" is an informal term referring to a group of WTO Members who have spoken for special WTO regulations on fisheries subsidies. At various times, active members of the "Friends of Fish" coalition have included Argentina, Australia, Chile, Ecuador, Iceland, New Zealand, Norway, the Philippines, Peru and the United States of America.

V. Outcome of the Fisheries Subsidies Issue at the Doha Ministerial Conference

The Doha Ministerial Conference in 2001 made a contribution to moving the negotiations forward. It envisaged negotiations lasting approximately three years from November 2001 to January 2005. The Doha Ministerial Declaration provided the mandate for negotiations on a range of subjects and other work, e.g. those on agriculture and services.

With regard to fisheries subsidies, paragraph 28 of the Doha Ministerial Declaration states that in the context of the Doha negotiations, participants shall aim to clarify and improve WTO disciplines on fisheries subsidies, taking into account the importance of this sector to developing countries.[283] Paragraph 31 of the Doha Ministerial Declaration also notes that fisheries subsidies form part of the negotiations on trade and the environment.[284] Negotiations on fisheries subsidies form part of a more extensive reform of the Anti-Dumping and SCM Agreements. After Doha, the negotiations have taken place in the Negotiating Group on Rules which reports to the WTO's Trade Negotiations Committee.

This mandate of the Doha Ministerial Declaration indicates that the negotiations on fisheries subsidies should reflect the interdisciplinary elements of the general subsidies negotiations and provide the fisheries subsidies negotiations with the qualitative parameters that they should meet. The elements and parameters include the following:[285] (1) Negotiations on new disciplines on fisheries subsidies should take place in the context of the broader negotiations on improving and clarifying, inter alia, the existing SCM Agreement; (2) the negotiations have to take into account the needs of developing and least-developed countries and the importance of the fisheries sector to these countries (through, for example, more operational special and differential (S&D) provisions in fisheries subsidies); and (3) the negotiations must be held with a view to enhancing the mutual supportiveness of trade and the environment.

This represents a considerable milestone for the WTO: for the first time, it purports to help conserve natural resources in pursuit of a "win-win" outcome which provides positive results for trade liberalization, environmental stewardship and sustainable development.[286] Since Doha, it has been considered that the WTO has

---

283 *WTO* Doc. No. WT/MIN(01)/DEC/1, "WTO Doha Ministerial Declaration" (20 November 2001), para. 28.

284 *Ibid.*, para. 31.

285 *Roman Grynberg*, "WTO Fisheries Subsidies Negotiations: Implications for Fisheries Access Arrangements and Sustainable Management", in *Ivan Mbirimi, Bridget Chilala, and Roman Grynberg* (eds), *supra* note 225, pp. 291-314, at 291; *Roman Grynberg*, "WTO Fisheries Subsidies Negotiations: Implication for Fisheries Access Arrangements and Sustainable Management", Marine Policy, Vol. 27, pp. 499-511 (2003), at 499; *UNEP*, "Reflecting Sustainable Development and Special and Differential Treatment for Developing Countries in the Context of New WTO Fisheries Subsidies Rules" (Geneva: UNEP, 2005), at 2.

286 *Alice L. Mattice*, *supra* note 5, at 574; *WWF*, *supra* note 217, at 1.

an unprecedented opportunity to help improve the environmental and economic health of the world's oceans by disciplining harmful fisheries subsidies.[287]

A few months after the Doha Ministerial Conference, the Johannesburg World Summit on Sustainable Development (WSSD) in 2002 listed the WTO fisheries subsidies negotiations as a top priority for achieving sustainable fisheries and reaffirmed the Doha mandate by requiring countries to eliminate subsidies that contribute to IUU fishing and overcapacity.[288]

However, the Doha Ministerial Declaration covers a diverse agenda and the negotiations at this stage were not very productive. Not only the lack of an auspicious political and economic environment for the negotiations, but also the limited progress made on issues of particular interest to developing countries[289] gave rise to a pessimistic assessment. The situation is also complicated by the lack of expertise and limited financial resources in developing countries, which means that they have difficulty in defending their interests in the negotiations.[290]

VI. Negotiations on Fisheries Subsidies before the Cancún Ministerial Conference

A. Contribution of the Committee on Trade and Environment

After Doha, the WTO's commitment to initiating negotiations on fisheries subsidies took place in the Negotiating Group on Rules, and some work on fisheries subsidies continued in the CTE. The Secretariat of the CTE continued to gather and analyze the information from Members as well as to update Members on the work in other intergovernmental fora and on the notifications to the SCM Committee.[291] During this time, several important submissions were made by the Members involved to the Negotiating Group on Rules and the CTE.

---

287 *UNEP*, "Incorporating Resource Impact into Fisheries Subsidies Disciplines: Issues and Options, a Discussion Paper" (Geneva: UNEP, 2004), at 1.

288 Para. 31(f) of Plan of Implementation of the WSSD, *supra* note 94, requiring countries to "eliminate subsidies that contribute to illegal, unreported and unregulated (IUU) fishing and to overcapacity, while completing the efforts undertaken by WTO to clarify and improve its disciplines on fisheries subsidies, taking into account the importance of this sector to developing countries."

289 The issues of particular interest to developing countries include agriculture, S&D treatment and access to medicine under the TRIPS Agreement.

290 *Pradeep Metha*, "Trade, Debt and Finance: A Complex Agenda for the WTO", in *Ivan Mbirimi, Bridget Chilala, and Roman Grynberg* (eds), *supra* note 225, pp. 315-334, at 331-334.

291 *WTO* Doc. No. PRESS/TE/038, "Trade and Environment Bulletin: WTO Committee on Trade and Environment Focuses on Market Access Issues, Fisheries Subsidies, Technical Cooperation and Capacity Building, and Its Mandate to Identify and Debate the Environmental and Developmental Aspects of WTO Negotiations (4 April 2002).

B. New Zealand Demonstrates the Need to Improve Fisheries Subsidies Disciplines

At this point, New Zealand analyzed the research paper on fisheries subsidies discussions in the CTE,[292] and together with other "Friends of Fish" Members, claimed that the provisions under the SCM Agreement are insufficient to regulate fisheries subsidies.[293] New Zealand stated that fisheries subsidies not only lead to the standard market distortions which can be addressed by the existing SCM regulations, but also distort access to fisheries resources and have negative impact on the environment and development.[294] Moreover, it continued that it is difficult to identify the sort of market distortions at which SCM regulations are directed, due to the heterogeneous nature of fish products and the economic structure of the fishing industry. Taking all these factors into account, it concluded that it is necessary to improve existing WTO regulations.[295]

Furthermore, New Zealand stated that the characteristics of fish products are the source of specific technical obstacles to the use of the "serious prejudice" and "determination of injury" provisions of the SCM Agreement.[296] First, because of the heterogeneity of fish products, products from distinct species can be in direct competition on the market; while superficially similar fish products from the same family can command different prices. As a result, it is difficult to determine a "like-product" to decide the existence of serious prejudice.[297] Moreover, as to the fact that fisheries subsidies are trade-distorting, the heterogeneity and diversity of fish products make it difficult to establish the unsubsidized reference prices which are necessary to demonstrate that the subsidies cause injuries to the domestic industry of another Member or serious prejudice to the interests of another Member.[298] It is essential to establish reference prices and quantify the price effects of a subsidy to demonstrate that it causes serious prejudice or injury. These impediments to the application of existing rules underline the need for specific measures to improve WTO regulations on fisheries subsidies.

---

[292] *WTO* Doc. No. WT/CTE/W/204, "Submission from New Zealand on Paragraph 32(i) of the Doha Declaration to the Committee on Trade and Environment, Fisheries Subsidies" (19 March 2002).

[293] *WTO* Doc. No. TN/RL/W/3, "Submission from Australia, Chile, Ecuador, Iceland, New Zealand, Peru, Philippines and the United States to the Negotiating Group on Rules, the Doha Mandate to Address Fisheries Subsidies: Issues" (24 April 2002).

[294] *Ibid.*, paras. 13-14.

[295] *Ibid.*. para. 16.

[296] *WTO* Doc. No. TN/RL/W/12, "Submission from New Zealand to the Negotiating Group on Rules, Fisheries Subsidies: Limitations of Existing Subsidy Disciplines" (4 July 20002).

[297] Article 6.3 of the SCM Agreement.

[298] Article 5 of the SCM Agreement: Adverse Effects; Article 6 of the SCM Agreement: Specific Prejudice; and Article 15 of the SCM Agreement: Definition of Injury.

C. United States Proposes New Approaches Regarding New Disciplines

The United States, a strong supporter of the WTO negotiations on fisheries subsidies, has supported attempts to clarify the connection between fisheries subsidies and adverse effects on trade and conservation.[299] The United States concluded that global fisheries subsidies amount to between 15 and 20 percent of aggregate dockside revenues, which was three to four times higher than the five percent threshold for presuming "serious prejudice" under Article 6.1 of the SCM Agreement.[300]

Furthermore, in order to encourage discussions among the Members and to accomplish the mandates of the Doha Ministerial Declaration, the United States identified key issues and methods for classifying fisheries subsidies in a "traffic light" approach, including the questions of whether to expand the category of prohibited ("red light") fisheries subsidies and whether to establish a presumptively harmful ("dark-amber") category under Article 6.1 of the SCM Agreement.[301] In detail, this proposal suggested that the expansion of prohibited subsidies category could expressly cover those fisheries subsidies that directly promote overcapacity and overfishing or that have other direct trade-distorting effects. With respect to the presumptively harmful category, subsidies exceeding a certain value of production could be presumed to cause "serious prejudice," but this presumption could be rebutted if certain environmental criteria were met, such as by stating that the subsidy was not used to fish in a fishery that was in an overfishing condition and that the subsidy did not result in overcapacity or overfishing.[302]

In addition, to make better data available for Members to assess and categorize subsidies, the Rules Group should consider improving the quality of notifications under the SCM Agreement by means of provisions for more detailed fishery-specific information or making notifications of fisheries subsidies under the SCM Agreement more complementary of existing fishery-related notification or information, e.g. on capacity, in other fisheries instruments.[303] Based on this proposal,

---

299 *WTO* Doc. No. TN/RL/W/21, "Communication from the United States to the Negotiating Group on Rules, Adverse Trade and Conservation Effects of Fisheries Subsidies" (15 October 2002). Also see *WTO* Doc. No. TN/RL/W/3 (24 April 2002).

300 *WTO* Doc. No. TN/RL/W/21 (15 October 2002), at 3.

301 *WTO* Doc. No. TN/RL/W/77, "Communication from the United States to the Negotiating Group on Rules, Possible Approaches to Improved Disciplines on Fisheries Subsidies" (19 March 2003), paras. 5 and 6.

302 However, this proposal could not convince some Members, such as Japan and Korea in their later submissions. *WTO* Doc. No. TN/RL/W/84, "Questions from Japan Concerning Papers on the Fisheries Subsidies Issue to the Negotiating Group on Rules" (30 April 2003); *WTO* Doc. No. TN/RL/W/97, "Korea's Comments on the Submission from the United States (TN/RL/W/77)" (5 May 2003).

303 *WTO* Doc. No. TN/RL/W/77 (19 March 2003), para. 7. This idea on improving notifications was also questioned by Japan in a later submission regarding the reason why this objective could not be achieved within the framework of the SCM Committee. *WTO* Doc. No. TN/RL/W/84 (30 April 2003).

the WTO dispute settlement mechanism could enforce environmental sustainability in the fisheries, which would constitute a fundamental change in the multilateral trading system.[304]

D. "Friends of Fish" Members Propose Possible Categorizations

In addition to the submission expressing the need for new fisheries subsidies regulations,[305] another submission of several "Friends of Fish" Members referred to different approaches to classification of fisheries subsidies programmes proposed by other international organizations recently, e.g. the APEC, OECD, FAO and UNEP, to indicate different views on the merits of various types of fisheries subsidies programmes.[306]

E. Chile Proposes New Disciplines

Considering fisheries resources as a classical example of the "tragedy of the commons," Chile put forward its proposal on improving fisheries subsidies regulations.[307] Because of the subsidies provided by other coastal countries, Chile was faced with the inability to export its fish products or export less than it could to markets which are supplied by the subsidized fleets. Chile also considered limited access to productive resources as a trade barrier.[308]

As a result, Chile proposed several provisions to be added to the SCM Agreement to improve the existing regulations. In the "red light" category, it proposed that all fisheries subsidies of a commercial nature[309] or directly promoting overcapacity and overfishing should be expressly prohibited. The remaining subsidies, falling into the "amber light" category, should not be prohibited, to the extent that they are sufficiently accredited and notified to the WTO. However, since subsidies affect trade, the subsidizing Member, who has not fully

---

304 *Roman Grynberg and Natallie Rochester*, "The Emerging Architecture of a World Trade Organization Fisheries Subsidies Agreement and the Interests of Developing Coastal States", Journal of World Trade, Vol. 39, No. 3, pp. 503-526 (2005), at 512.

305 *WTO* Doc. No. TN/RL/W/3 (24 April 2002).

306 *WTO* Doc. No. TN/RL/W/58, "Submission from Argentina, Chile, Iceland, New Zealand, Norway and Peru to the Negotiating Group on Rules, Subsidies in the Fisheries Sector: Possible Categorizations" (10 February 2003). However, this proposal was questioned in a later submission by Japan regarding the ground to proceed to the categorizations. *WTO* Doc. No. TN/RL/W/84 (30 April 2003).

307 *WTO* Doc. No. TN/RL/W/115, "Communication from Chile to the Negotiating Group on Rules, Possible Approaches to Improved Disciplines on Fisheries Subsidies" (10 June 2003).

308 *Ibid.*, paras. 2-7.

309 These subsidies are those directly geared towards lowering costs, increasing revenues or raising production (by enhancing capacity).

met its notification obligations or has failed to notify the programme, has the responsibility of demonstrating that the subsidy in question does not cause injury to the complaining Member. On the other hand, the complaining Member should provide evidence of the injury, taking into account the preservation of resources and social development of communities.[310] As with the approach submitted by the United States,[311] shifting the burden of proof is the method applied to balance the interests between subsidizing Members and complaining Members.

F. Japan Requires Further Reasons for New Disciplines

In response to the submission of the "Friends of Fish" Members[312] and to formally state its basic position, Japan submitted proposals to the Negotiating Group on Rules.[313] Japan's proposal can be summarized as follows:

First, Japan believed that, based on paragraph 28 of the Doha Ministerial Declaration, the Negotiating Group on Rules should deal with the fisheries subsidies issue as part of the overall clarification and improvement of the SCM Agreement in a cross-sectoral manner and from the viewpoint of trade distortion. It is essential to conduct negotiations aimed at clarifying and improving regulations under the SCM Agreement, while preserving the basic concepts, principles and effectiveness of the SCM Agreement and its instruments and objectives.[314]

Second, Japan considered that the reasons for the need for special fisheries subsidies regulations proposed by other Members still remained unclear. Japan emphasized that it is unnecessary to create a set of special fisheries subsidies regulations from the viewpoint of trade distortion.[315]

Third, efforts to correct the alleged trade distortion by applying the relevant existing provisions, such as the remedies provided under Part III of the SCM Agreement, should be made before moving to amend the SCM Agreement.[316]

---

310 *WTO* Doc. No. TN/RL/W/115 (10 June 2003), at 2, the proposed provisions to be added to the SCM Agreement.

311 *WTO* Doc. No. TN/RL/W/77 (19 March 2003).

312 *WTO* Doc. No. TN/RL/W/3 (24 April 2002).

313 *WTO* Doc. No. TN/RL/W/11, "Japan's Basic Position on the Fisheries Subsidies Issue to the Negotiating Group on Rules" (2 July 2002).

314 *WTO* Doc. No. TN/RL/W/11 (2 July 2002), para. 19; *WTO* Doc. No. TN/RL/W/52, "Japan's Contribution to Discussion on Fisheries Subsidies Issue to the Negotiating Group on Rules" (6 February 2003), para. 13.

315 *WTO* Doc. No. TN/MA/W/15/Add.1, "Communication from Japan to the Negotiating Group on Market Access, Market Access for Non-agricultural Products: Addendum-Japanese Proposal on Sustainable Development and the Trade of Forest and Fishery Products" (6 January 2003). In this addendum to a proposal on "Market Access for Non-Agricultural Products-Communication from Japan (TN/MA/W/15)", Japan addressed matters relevant to the fisheries sector, including the fisheries subsidies issue.

316 *WTO* Doc. No. TN/RL/W/11 (2 July 2002), para. 5.

Fourth, the issues regarding access limitation to fisheries resources should be regulated under the UNCLOS framework and relevant fisheries management arrangements.[317]

Fifth, Japan concluded that the WTO should examine how to address fisheries subsidies at the regular session of the CTE to deal with the problems of IUU fishing and overcapacity, the solution of which is considered to be necessary for achieving the sustainable development of fisheries at the WSSD.[318] The CTE's work should be based on the findings by international organizations with expertise in fisheries, such as the FAO.[319]

Sixth, Japan analyzed the studies made by the OECD, APEC and FAO and concluded that these theoretical analyses reached a common understanding that the "effects of subsidies on resources vary, depending on the status of resources and fishery management." Fisheries subsidies cannot be prohibited merely from the viewpoint of their negative impact on resources.[320]

G. Korea Requests More Proof on the Need for New Disciplines

Another Member, Korea, was not convinced by the arguments that the peculiarities of fisheries subsidies and the heterogeneity of fisheries products are of such a nature as to justify sectoral treatment for fisheries subsidies. It submitted another proposal to the Negotiating Group on Rules, supporting the viewpoint of Japan.[321] The standpoints of Korea could be listed as follows:

First, given that subsidies have not been proved to be fully responsible for fisheries depletion[322] and that the reliability of available fisheries information depends on its sources, it was premature to base the WTO discussions on the assumption that subsidies are responsible for fisheries depletion.[323]

---

317 *Ibid.*, paras. 7-9.

318 *WTO* Doc. No. TN/MA/W/15/Add.1 (6 January 2003), para. 16.

319 *WTO* Doc. No. TN/RL/W/52, "Japan's Contribution to Discussion on Fisheries Subsidies Issue to the Negotiating Group on Rules" (6 February 2003), paras. 13-15.

320 *WTO* Doc. No. WT/CTE/W/226, "Submission by Japan to the Committee on Trade and Environment, Analysis on the Relationship between Fisheries Subsidies and Over-Exploitation of Fisheries Resources" (24 April 2003), paras. 5-6.

321 *WTO* Doc. No. TN/RL/W/17, "Korea's Views on the Doha Development Agenda Discussions on Fisheries Subsidies to the Negotiating Group on Rules" (2 October 2002).

322 *Ibid.*, at 2, noting the WTO Secretariat submission said that the principal cause of stock depletion was inadequate management of fisheries resources (*WTO* Doc. No. WT/CTE/W/167 (16 October 2000), para. 15), and a study of the OECD concluded that the effect of transfers on resource sustainability was difficult to determine, as there are many influences on fish stock health that are difficult to disentangle (*OECD* Doc. No. AGR/FI(2000)10/FINAL, "Transition to Responsible Fisheries, Government Financial Transfers and Resource Sustainability: Case Studies" (3 October 2000)).

323 *WTO* Doc. No. TN/RL/W/17 (2 October 2002), at 2-3.

Second, in regard to the SCM Agreement, the proposal required more evidence to prove the need for the improved regulations under the WTO framework for the following reasons. (1) Responding to the statement of New Zealand that the heterogeneous nature of fish products caused difficulty in demonstrating the trade-distorting effects of fisheries subsidies under Part III of the SCM Agreement,[324] the proposal indicated that other types of products, e.g. wine products and clothing products (and the EC provides electronic products) were also heterogeneous products and disagreed with providing sectoral treatment to fisheries subsidies due to the heterogeneity of fish products.[325] (2) It also stated that the difficulty of seeking remedies under Part III was a structural issue of the SCM Agreement itself and not limited to fish products.[326] (3) Last but not least, the challenge of identifying a "like product" or a reference price did not stop the imposition of countervailing duties or anti-dumping duties against fish products. Examples given were the countervailing duty on fish products imposed by the United States on fresh Atlantic ground-fish from Canada in 1986 and the anti-dumping duty imposed by the United States on fresh and chilled Atlantic salmon from Norway.[327]

It considered that the SCM Agreement was the major cornerstone of the WTO framework and that the integrity of the SCM regime should be preserved.[328] Consequently, Korea was of the opinion that more convincing proof was required for the need for improved regulations under the WTO framework.

H. European Communities Address the Proposed Solution

From the outset of the fisheries subsidies negotiations in the wake of Doha, the European Communities remained uncharacteristically silent until it had completed its own internal reform of the Common Fisheries Policy. During its reform in 2002, the European Communities made a clear choice in adjusting the objectives of its fisheries policy to ensure sustainable development in environmental, economic and social terms.[329] After the internal European Communities discussion had been settled, the European Communities came out firmly in favour of enhanced disciplines in the sector.[330] It followed the discussion with great interest and suggested taking the process to the Negotiating Group on Rules further forward.

---

324 *WTO* Doc. No. TN/RL/W/12 (4 July 2002), paras. 3-6.

325 *WTO* Doc. No. TN/RL/W/17 (2 October 2002), at 5.

326 *Ibid.*, from the initiation to 2002, there was only a single case where a WTO dispute panel ruled that 'serious prejudice' existed under Part III of the SCM Agreement, *WTO* Doc. No. WT/DS54/55/59/64/R, "Indonesia-Certain Measures Affecting the Automobile Industry, complaints by the US, the EC and Japan" (Indonesia-Auto) (July 23, 1998).

327 *Ibid.*

328 *Ibid.*, at 6.

329 See *infra* Chapter 4 for analysis on the Common Fisheries Policy.

330 *Roman Grynberg and Natallie Rochester*, *supra* note 304, at 513.

The European Communities submitted its first formal proposal on fisheries subsidies to the Negotiating Group on Rules in 2003.[331] This submission contains two important issues, namely the categorizations of fisheries subsidies and the requirement of notifications.

First, it stated that the main pillars of fisheries subsidies regulations should be set out as: capacity-enhancing subsidies that should be prohibited and others that should be permitted and therefore non-actionable. The proposed solution is summarized as follows:[332]

(1) Prohibited fisheries subsidies to include:
  (a) subsidies for marine fishing fleet renewal (e.g. construction of vessels, increase in fishing capacity); and
  (b) subsidies for the permanent transfer of fishing vessels to third countries, including transfers through the creation of joint enterprises with third country partners.
(2) Permitted fisheries subsidies to include:
  (a) subsidies to support the retraining of fishermen, early retirement schemes and diversification;
  (b) limited subsidies for the modernization of fishing vessels to improve safety, product quality or working conditions or to promote more environmentally friendly fishing methods;
  (c) subsidies to fishermen and vessel owners who have to temporarily stop their fishing activity, when stoppages are due to unforeseeable circumstances such as natural disasters, or in the framework of tie-up schemes linked to permanent capacity reduction measures in the context of recovery plans for overexploited fish stocks; and
  (d) subsidies for the scrapping of vessels and the withdrawal of capacity.

Second, this submission also emphasized that increased transparency is *a conditio sine qua non* for dealing effectively with the problem of fisheries subsidies. The very low number and the quality of notifications result from the lack of information on fisheries subsidies and the bad record of affected Members. Therefore, it was suggested that the Secretariat of the SCM Committee should keep a "scoreboard" of notifications per member and per type of programme.[333] The scoreboard idea was supported by the submission of Chile emphasizing that notifications should be complementary to the existing notifications in other forums, e.g. the FAO, and particularly that the notification of subsidies in the amber category should be mandatory.[334]

---

331 *WTO* Doc. No. TN/RL/W/82, "Submission of the European Communities to the Negotiating Group on Rules, Fisheries Subsidies" (23 April 2003).

332 *Ibid.*, at 2-3.

333 *Ibid.*, at 4.

334 *WTO* Doc. No. TN/RL/W/115 (10 June 2003).

I. China as a Developing Country Addresses Certain Issues for Discussions

As a developing country having substantial interest in fishing, China submitted its proposal to the Negotiating Group on Rules. China stated that there is a need to determine the scope of fisheries subsidies, take into account the concerns about S&D treatment of developing country Members and provide for certain types of non-actionable subsidies.[335] With regard to the classification of fisheries subsidies, China proposed not only to discuss the classification method used for fisheries subsidies by the OECD and FAO, but also to establish a "green light" catalogue to support fisheries subsidies contributing to the fisheries conservation, trade liberalization and sustainable development.[336]

J. Small Vulnerable Coastal States Expect Exceptions

Several small vulnerable coastal States in the Pacific and Indian Oceans and in the Caribbean Sea also submitted a paper from the perspective of small vulnerable coastal States.[337] For them, the fisheries management issue was not an appropriate subject matter for the WTO and it should be best addressed in other more appropriate forums, e.g. the FAO. Moreover, fisheries activities in these small vulnerable coastal States fell into three separate categories, which included (1) revenues generation from access fees for distant water fleets; (2) domestic and foreign fishermen operating for export in the EEZ and the territorial sea to supply canneries, landing facilities and domestic processing facilities; and (3) artisanal fisheries within the EEZ and the territorial sea for the domestic and export market.[338]

Seeking S&D treatment in fisheries subsidies negotiations, the proposal expressed that with respect to the improvement of fisheries subsidies disciplines, Article 1 of the SCM Agreement should be clarified to explicitly exclude the following from being defined as subsidies: access fees and development assistance, fiscal incentives for domestication and development of fisheries, and artisanal fisheries.[339]

---

335 *WTO* Doc. No. TN/RL/W/9, "Proposal from the People's Republic of China on Fisheries Subsidies to the Negotiating Group on Rules" (20 June 2002).

336 *WTO* Doc. No. TN/RL/W/88, "Comments from the People's Republic of China on the United States Proposal on Fisheries Subsidies (TN/RL/W788) to the Negotiating Group on Rules" (1 May 2003).

337 *WTO* Doc. No. TN/RL/W/136, "Fisheries Subsidies, submitted by Antigua and Barbuda, Belize, Fuji Islands, Guyana, the Maldives, Papua New Guinea, Solomon Islands, St. Kitts and Nevis to the Negotiating Group on Rules" (14 July 2003).

338 *Ibid.*, at 1-3.

339 *Ibid.*, at 3.

K. Status of Negotiations before the Cancún Ministerial Conference

The establishment of a prohibited category of fisheries subsidies as a key discipline had been envisaged at this time by several Members, although some still questioned the need to discuss the fisheries subsidies issue within the Negotiating Group on Rules. Several possible approaches to defining an expanded red light category had also been suggested, including prohibiting subsidies that "directly promoted overcapacity and overfishing, or had other direct trade distorting effects,[340] prohibiting "capacity enhancing subsidies,"[341] and prohibiting "all fisheries subsidies of a commercial nature, directly geared towards lowering costs, increasing revenues, raising production (by enhancing capacity), or directly promoting overcapacity and overfishing."[342] The discussions on whether to apply a broader prohibited category and how broad it should be guided WTO negotiations later.

VII. Results on Fisheries Subsidies Negotiations at the Cancún Ministerial Conference

The Cancún Ministerial Conference in 2003 ended without the Members reaching a consensus to move forward in the Doha negotiations. It did not launch or conclude a round of negotiations, but it rather provided the necessary framework and political guidance to allow negotiators in Geneva to continue their work towards completion of the round by January 1, 2005.[343] This Conference split up into different focus groups, including one on "other issues" that concentrated on trade and the environment negotiations. In addition, the talks at this Conference focused on granting observer status to MEAs, ecolabelling and the relation between the Agreement on Trade-Related Aspects of Intellectual Property Rights (TRIPS Agreement), the CBD and the protection of traditional knowledge.[344] However, the potentially irreconcilable differences on issues, e.g. agriculture, meant that a consensus was not reached. The fact that no consensus was reached does not mean failure for the issues presented in the Doha Ministerial Declaration. In terms of trade and the environment, WTO Members should reach a consensus on clarifying the relationships

---

340 *WTO* Doc. No. TN/RL/W/77 (19 March 2003).

341 *WTO* Doc. No. TN/RL/W/82 (23 April 2003).

342 *WTO* Doc. No. TN/RL/W/115 (10 June 2003).

343 As the Chairperson and Mexican Foreign Minister Luis Ernesto Derbez stressed on Day 3 of the Conference. Further information is available on-line at <www.wto.org/english/thewto_e/minist_e/min03_e/min03_12sept_e.htm> (last visited on 20 January 2008).

344 The negotiations continued to expand and approached the consensus upon issues dealing with relationships between Article 27.3 of the TRIPS Agreement and paragraph 19 of the Doha Ministerial Declaration (relating to the patenting of plants and animals, the CBD and traditional knowledge).

between existing WTO rules and specific trade obligations set out in multilateral environmental agreements (MEAs); the information exchange between the WTO and MEA secretariats; the criteria for granting observer status to other international organizations; and the liberalization of trade in environmental goods and services.[345]

VIII. Negotiations on Fisheries Subsidies before the HK Ministerial Conference

Just before the Hong Kong Ministerial Conference the focus of the negotiations shifted from the issue of whether there was a need for specific regulations in the fisheries sector to the question of the nature and extent of such regulations.[346] Furthermore, the discussion was not merely bound to the ultimate structure of fisheries subsidies. Instead, more detailed discussions regarding the sub-categories of fisheries subsidies were made during the negotiations. In order to develop a common understanding of the definition and treatment of various sub-categories of fisheries subsidies, this phase of technical discussions was essential to ensure the production of clear and enforceable rules, irrespective of the ultimate structure of fisheries subsidies regulations.

A. Structure of Fisheries Subsidies Regulations

Two approaches were proposed for addressing the structure of fisheries subsidies regulations, mainly based on the question of whether there should be a broad ban on fisheries subsidies or not. There was a vigorous discussion between these two approaches, i.e. top-down and bottom-up approaches. The following sections examine the proposals of Members by dividing them into two groups.

---

[345] WTO Cancún 5th Ministerial Conference, "Briefing Notes -- Trade and Environment", see further information available on-line at <www.wto.org/english/the WTO_e/minist_e/min03_e/brief_e/brief14_e.htm> (last visited on January 20, 2008). Several possible ways of effectively incorporating environmental issues into international trade had been addressed by both environmentalists and trade advocators to change the current institutions. The proposals ranged from the creation of new international organizations to an international court of environmental law. Others had considered amendments to GATT to create specific exceptions for MEAs, while others had called for the expansion of the WTO or for the UN to police the environment. *Richard Skeen*, "Will the WTO Turn Green? The Implications of Injecting Environmental Issues Into the Multilateral Trading System", Georgetown International Environmental Law Review, Vol. 17, pp. 161 *et seq* (2004), at 194-195.

[346] *WTO* Doc. No. TN/RL/9, "Negotiating Group on Rules, Report by the Chairman to the Trade Negotiations" (25 June 2004), para. 8.

1. The Supporters of the "Top-Down" Approach

The so-called top-down approach, which concentrates on a broad prohibition together with a list of exceptions, was led by New Zealand and comprised a number of Members, including Argentina, Chile, Ecuador, Peru, the Philippines and the United States.

a. New Zealand

After supporting the broad prohibited category of fisheries subsidies, New Zealand proposed that an effective way to resolve the problem of overcapacity and overfishing through subsidies rules was to target programmes that have revenue or cost impacts for the industry.[347] In the opinion of New Zealand, the prohibition of subsidies that promoted overcapacity and overfishing was a common feature of initial proposals in the negotiations. However, to address overcapacity and overfishing or even "trade distortions" through subsidy rules was problematical.[348] Their proposal further stated that costs and revenues were among the factors of fisheries subsidies which could encourage overfishing and overcapacity and which could easily be quantified.[349] In order to respond to the difficulty of quantifying fishing capacity and effort, the cost/revenue impact test could be introduced to estimate how subsidies could lower the production costs and increase the revenues of the industry.[350]

An approach involving a broad prohibition of fisheries subsidies as the primary discipline would also have to be balanced with exceptions and transitional provisions, including S&D treatment provisions for developing countries. Hence, a list of exceptions would be useful for coping with the lack of transparency and reliable information in the fisheries sector.[351] Compared to the positive "green light" category, in the interests of effectiveness and avoiding circumvention, it would be preferable to start with primary disciplines that were comprehensive in their coverage, with only limited and defined exceptions.[352]

---

[347] *WTO* Doc. No. TN/RL/W/154, "Communication from New Zealand to the Negotiating Group on Rules, Fisheries Subsidies: Overcapacity and Overexploitation" (26 April 2004), paras. 5-7.

[348] *Ibid.*, para. 1.

[349] New Zealand was of the same opinion as the proposal of the United States (*WTO* Doc. No. WT/CTE/W/154 (4 July 2000), para. 8).

[350] *Roman Grynberg and Natallie Rochester*, *supra* note 304, at 514, adding that New Zealand also proposed that overcapacity which is based mainly on capital costs is an important but not the only contributing factor to overfishing.

[351] *WTO* Doc. No. TN/RL/W/154 (26 April 2004), paras. 9-11.

[352] *Ibid.*, para. 14.

b. "Friends of Fish" Members

Several "Friends of Fish" Members supported the submission of New Zealand in 2004[353] and emphasized that the top-down approach offered a simple, enforceable and flexible structure that would lead to greater transparency.[354] This proposal indicated that the following areas of fisheries subsidies needed to be considered as exceptions: (1) government expenditure for management frameworks, including those relating to surveillance, monitoring, enforcement and associated research; (2) government expenditure for general infrastructure; (3) certain fisheries-related social insurance programmes, e.g. job training to assist people in leaving the sector; (4) government expenditure for access; and (5) appropriately structured decommissioning subsidies.[355] Moreover, identifying other areas of concern, such as S&D treatment at an early stage would help the Negotiating Group on Rules accommodate the concerns in a targeted and effective way.[356]

c. United States

Several Members[357] expressed similar views to those of the United States,[358] proposing that the fundamental regulation applicable to the particularly harmful subsidies should be a prohibition. In order to guide the negotiations further, the United States submitted another paper to support the top-down approach with the following ideas.[359]

First, the United States agreed with the features of the top-down approach, i.e. simplicity, enforceability, transparency, etc.

Second, the United States criticized the fact that the "bottom-up" approach, contemplating a small number of prohibited subsidies and a large number of permitted subsidies, could potentially lead to a set of regulations weaker than the current rules.

Third, the top-down approach could provide sufficient flexibility to address appropriately the exceptional programmes. A thorough discussion on potential exceptions to the prohibition could also improve the transparency of the Members' subsidies programmes.

---

353 *WTO* Doc. No. TN/RL/W/154 (26 April 2004).

354 *WTO* Doc. No. TN/RL/W/166, "Communication from Argentina, Chile, Ecuador, New Zealand, Philippines, Peru to the Negotiating Group on Rules, Fisheries Subsidies" (2 November 2004), para. 8.

355 *Ibid.*, para. 11.

356 *Ibid.*, para. 13.

357 *WTO* Doc. No. TN/RL/W/82 (23 April 2003) of the European Communities; *WTO* Doc. No. TN/RL/W/115 (10 June 2003) of Chile; *WTO* Doc. No. TN/RL/W/154 (26 April 2004) of New Zealand.

358 *WTO* Doc. No. TN/RL/W/77 (19 March 2003).

359 *WTO* Doc. No. TN/RL/W/169, "Communication from the United States to the Negotiating Group on Rules, Additional Views on the Structure of the Fisheries Subsidies Negotiations" (13 December 2004).

Fourth, the exceptions were to remain actionable; hence, there would be the need to consider the possibility of clarification of the "serious prejudice" provisions under Article 6 of the SCM Agreement.[360]

2. The Supporters of the "Bottom-Up" Approach

The so-called bottom-up approach, mainly supported by Japan, Korea, Taiwan,[361] the European Communities[362] and some developing country Members, consists of a positive list of prohibited subsidies.

a. Japan

Japan strongly supported the bottom-up approach to the structure of fisheries subsidies regulations for the following reasons.

First, the absence of the agreed definition of "fisheries subsidies" led to serious uncertainty during the negotiation of a top-down approach.[363]

Second, a bottom-up approach would be the better alternative when attempting to balance five elements of the fisheries subsidies regulations required by the mandates of the Doha Ministerial Declaration[364] and the requirement of the WSSD, namely clarifying and improving WTO regulations, including the prohibition of subsidies related to IUU fishing and overcapacity (e.g., red category of subsidy); ensuring sustainable development (e.g., green category); taking into account the importance of the fisheries sector for developing countries; ensuring transparency; and encouraging cooperation with other international organizations.[365]

Third, to avoid the risk that subsidies for conservation and sustainable development, such as payments for capacity reduction or scientific research for aquatic resources, were roughly banned under the top-down approach, the bottom-up

---

360 Other relevant discussions in *WTO* Doc. No. TN/RL/W/3 (24 April 2002), paras. 9-11; *WTO* Doc. No. TN/RL/W/12 (4 July 2002); *WTO* Doc. No. TN/RL/W/115 (10 June 2003), paras. 4-7.

361 Taiwan uses the name "the Separate Customs Territory of Taiwan, Penghu, Kinmen and Matsu" as a WTO Member. In this study, the terms of Chinese Taipei and Taiwan are used interchangeably without prejudice.

362 *WTO* Doc. No. TN/RL/W/82 (23 April 2003).

363 *WTO* Doc. No. TN/RL/W/159, "Communication from Japan to the Negotiating Group on Rules, Fisheries Subsidies: Proposed Structure of the Discussion" (7 June 2004), para. 1.

364 Besides paragraph 28 of the Doha Ministerial Declaration, Japan also took other relevant paragraphs into consideration: paragraph 6, which reaffirmed the commitment to the objective of sustainable development and encouraged efforts to promote cooperation between the WTO and relevant international environmental and developmental organizations, especially the WSSD, and paragraph 10, which confirmed the collective responsibility for ensuring internal transparency.

365 *WTO* Doc. No. TN/RL/W/159 (7 June 2004), para. 6.

approach, taking into account the various roles of subsidies, would be the better alternative structure for the negotiation.[366]

Furthermore, taking into account the fisheries conservation and management concepts within the UNCLOS,[367] Japan proposed the following examples of prohibited and permitted subsidies to the Negotiating Group on Rules.[368]

First, Japan proposed establishing a classification of fisheries subsidies based on the principle of the "conservation and sustainable utilization of fisheries resource." Fisheries subsidies which promote the conservation and sustainable utilization of fisheries resources and which are provided within the framework of the conservation and the sustainable utilization of the fisheries resources and, therefore, are recognized to have no real adverse effects on the status of resources (although they have the potential to exacerbate the status of resources) should be permitted.[369]

Second, fisheries subsidies related to IUU fisheries and fishing vessel construction in poorly managed fisheries which are against the conservation and sustainable utilization of fisheries resources and encourage the fishing activities that exacerbate the status of the resources should be prohibited.[370]

Third, if the fisheries are properly managed and if subsidies do not result in an increase in total fishing capacity, the subsidies for vessel construction should be permitted, since they do not cause any deterioration in resources.[371] Properly managed fisheries here mean that the fisheries be managed in accordance with the UNCLOS, RFMOs and national regulations, i.e. when the fishing activities abide by their management regulations, in the case of the fisheries which target resources subject to the management of a RFMO, or when the fishing activities are managed under an effective resources management framework such as licensing and community-based management based on a proper evaluation of the resources.[372]

Fourth, subsidies aimed at the socio-economic stability and development of the local communities and without any direct relation to the conservation and sustain-

---

366 *Ibid.*, para. 8.

367 More specifically, in accordance with the UNCLOS framework, many nations have developed national fisheries management frameworks, e.g. total allowable catch systems, international fisheries management organizations have been established and regional fisheries management bodies have introduced international conservation and management measures.

368 *WTO* Doc. No. TN/RL/W/164, "Paper by Japan to the Negotiating Group on Rules, Proposal on Fisheries Subsidies" (27 September 2004), para. 1.

369 *Ibid.*, paras. 7 and 8.

370 *Ibid.*, paras. 9 and 10.

371 *Ibid.*, para. 13. Regarding this, some comments were made by various Members, including "the threshold or the standard of proper management is unclear" and "it is inappropriate for coastal countries to determine whether their own fisheries management is proper or not", see *WTO* Doc. No. TN/RL/W/201, "Paper from Japan to the Negotiating Group on Rules, Fisheries Subsidies, Subsidies for Vessel Construction and Modification" (6 March 2006), para. 5.

372 *WTO* Doc. No. TN/RL/W/164 (27 September 2004), para. 13.

able utilization of fisheries resources should not be considered as fisheries subsidies.[373]

Fifth, since the potential new regulations on fisheries subsidies would be a subset of the SCM Agreement, government payments and government support for general infrastructure fall outside the scope of the SCM Agreement and should, of course, fall outside the new regulations on fisheries subsidies. Japan also illustrated that general infrastructure to be, for instance, programmes for the construction of fishing ports, sewage facilities for the fishing communities and coastal protection facilities against storms and waves.[374]

To take every relevant element into consideration, the bottom-up approach would provide a holistic perspective for examining the effects of fisheries subsidies and identifying whether they should be prohibited or permitted.

b. Korea

Questioning the basis of New Zealand's proposal in April 2004,[375] Korea argued that there should not be any causal link between cost/revenue impacts of subsidies and overcapacity or overfishing.[376] According to Article 1.1 of the SCM Agreement, the "benefit" test was the same as considering cost/revenue impacts as New Zealand proposed. Hence, all the subsidies under the SCM Agreement have cost or revenue impacts on the recipients in a direct or indirect manner. Korea emphasized that in regulating subsidies it was important to identify the actual effects of subsidies programmes and that different types of fisheries should be taken into account, such as small-scale subsistence fisheries vs. large-scale commercial fisheries and traditional coastal fisheries vs. modernized distant water fisheries.[377]

c. Taiwan

A joint submission by Japan, Korea and Taiwan further underlined the demerits of the top-down approach as follows:[378]

First, that the top-down approach was fundamentally wrong, because it prohibited fisheries subsidies only because of their existence without any effect test and that it constituted an inadequate framework for new fisheries subsidies regulations.[379]

---

373 *Ibid.*, para. 14.
374 *Ibid.*, para. 15.
375 *WTO* Doc. No. TN/RL/W/154 (26 April 2004).
376 *WTO* Doc. No. TN/RL/W/160, "Questions and Comments from Korea on New Zealand's Communication on Fisheries Subsidies (TN/RL/W/154) to the Negotiating Group on Rules" (8 June 2004), para. 3.
377 *WTO* Doc. No. TN/RL/W/160 (8 June 2004), paras. 9-11.
378 *WTO* Doc. No. TN/RL/W/172, "Communication from Japan; the Republic of Korea; and the Separate Customs Territory of Taiwan, Penghu, Kinmen and Matsu to the Negotiating Group on Rules, Contribution to the Discussion on the Framework for the Disciplines on the Fisheries Subsidies" (22 February 2005), paras. 1-9.
379 *Ibid.*, para. 1.

Second, top-down supporting Members proposed to "start with a prohibition on subsidies that "benefit" the fishing industry".[380] This submission stated that a subsidy by definition confers "benefit" to the recipient. Given that fisheries subsidies are granted the same "prohibition" treatment as Article 3 of the SCM Agreement, an adverse effect test is necessary for deciding whether there is trade distortion, especially under the mandate of paragraph 28 of the Doha Ministerial Declaration.[381]

Third, that the top-down approach was not consistent with the basic principles of the current SCM Agreement, which takes a positive-list approach, prohibiting only two types of subsidies that severely distort trade under Article 3.

Fourth, that the top-down approach lacked flexibility for future policy needs, since the top-down approach unduly restricted policy tools needed for coping with a changing environment.

Fifth, that the top-down approach would lead to a race for exceptions as the negotiating Members would be forced to include their wish list in the exception box.

Sixth, that the top-down approach caused inequity with other sectors by eliminating the effect test regarding subsidies to the fisheries sector, while other sectors were disciplined on the basis of the adverse trade effect test.

Moreover, this submission suggested that a starting point of the discussion should be the expansion of prohibited subsidies based on an adverse effect test, given that several proposals, containing different formulations,[382] expanded the scope of prohibited subsidies.[383] It further suggested the following major issues for the future framework.

First, based on Articles 1 and 2 of the SCM Agreement, general infrastructure, e.g. construction of fishing ports, sewage facilities for the fishing communities and coastal protection facilities against storms and waves, should fall outside the scope of the new regulations.

Second, the following types of subsidies might be candidates for the prohibited subsidies, because they are deemed to cause serious harm directly to the fisheries resources: subsidies for the construction of new fishing vessels resulting in capacity enhancement; subsidies for fishing-vessel modification for capacity enhancement; subsidies for shipbuilding yards for fishing vessels; subsidies for overseas

---

380 *WTO* Doc. No. TN/RL/W/166 (2 November 2004), para. 9.

381 Paragraph 28 of the Doha Ministerial Declaration emphasized the preservation of the basic concepts, principles and effectiveness of the Agreements, including the Agreements on Implementation of Article VI of the GATT 1994 and the SCM Agreement, and their instruments and objectives.

382 *WTO* Doc. No. TN/RL/W/77 (19 March 2003) of the United States proposed the prohibition of fisheries subsidies that would "directly promote overcapacity or over-fishing" or that would "have other direct trade distorting effects"; *WTO* Doc. No. TN/RL/W/82 (23 April 2003) of the European Communities proposed the prohibition of fisheries subsidies that enhanced fishing capacity; *WTO* Doc. No. TN/RL/W/164 (27 September 2004) of Japan proposed the prohibition of fisheries subsidies that were related to "IUU fishery or construction of fishing vessels engaging in poorly managed fishery."

383 *WTO* Doc. No. TN/RL/W/172 (22 February 2005), para. 9.

transfers of fishing vessels to those that are not CPCs (contracting parties, cooperating non-contracting parties, entities or fishing entities) of RFMOs; and subsidies relating to IUU fishing.[384]

Third, the following government programmes with positive effects on fish stock recovery, social security, welfare and R&D should be permitted as non-actionable: fishing vessel decommissioning with vessel scrapping and withdrawal of fishing licenses; resource enhancement and protection of the environment (artificial reef, ocean ranching, fingerlings release, fishing ground clean-up, etc.); expenditure for fisheries resource management; R&D for sustainable fisheries (development of environmentally friendly fishing gear and technology, stock sampling and assessment, etc.); retraining of fishermen and early retirement schemes; and assistance for fishermen in terms of a social safety net (crew insurance, disaster relief, compensation for suspension of fishing activity, etc).[385]

B. Detailed Discussion on Sub-Categories of Fisheries Subsidies

Despite the argument on the structure of new regulations, several sub-categories of fisheries subsidies and other provisions, summarized below, were discussed in Members' submissions to the Negotiating Group on Rules. These discussions enriched the understanding of various types of subsidies programmes to the fisheries sector and provided Members with the opportunity of sharing their national experience and contemplating the context of potential regulations. Participation in these discussions on different types of subsidies did not prejudge Members' positions on the final structure of fisheries subsidies regulations, either the top-down or bottom-up approach.

1. Governmental Management Services

In order to move the discussion further, New Zealand tabled a more detailed proposal regarding management services.[386] Developing a common understanding with respect to the definition and treatment of various categories of fisheries subsidies required considerations of identification and discussion of subsidy categories as well as treatment under new regulations. New Zealand, therefore, initiated the discussion of fisheries subsidies to management services, which several Mem-

[384] *Ibid.*, para. 13. Japan further discussed these prohibited subsidies separately in its other submissions, including *WTO* Doc. No. TN/RL/GEN/47, "Paper from Japan to the Negotiating Group on Rules, IUU Fishing and Fisheries Subsidies" (10 June 2005), discussing two types prohibited fisheries subsidies: subsidies for overseas transfers of fishing vessels to non-CPCs of RFMOs and subsidies relating to IUU fishing; *WTO* Doc. No. TN/RL/W/201 (6 March 2006), discussing subsidies for vessel construction and modification.

[385] *Ibid.*, para. 14.

[386] *WTO* Doc. No. TN/RL/GEN/36, "Paper from New Zealand to the Negotiating Group on Rules, Fisheries Subsidies to Management Services" (23 March 2005).

bers had agreed should not be prohibited under new fisheries subsidies regulations.[387] In addition to sharing its national experience on management services programmes, New Zealand proposed three sub-categories to be incorporated in any list of permitted subsidies, including research to inform fisheries management decision makers; creating and implementing fisheries management systems; and enforcing fisheries management rules.[388] This proposal provided another issue for the negotiations.

2. Special Enforcement

The European Communities also reminded the Members of the issue of the implementation and enforcement of the subsidies regulations which had been drawn up within the WTO framework.[389] Given that the enforcement mechanisms applicable to WTO rules were insufficient and that the requirements of notifications and transparency were ineffective,[390] the European Communities shared its internal experience on how to administer and enforce these rules. The European Communities has put in place an elaborate internal State aid control system, based on four pillars, namely the principle of pre-notification and authorization, the principle of *ex post* surveillance, the incorporation of the rules and notification requirements into domestic law, and the exceptions to the general pre-authorization principle.[391] The enforcement system established in the Communities may not be ideal for the other WTO Members in the negotiations, but it can serve as a guideline for identifying an enforcement system for WTO Members.

There are two types of enforcement system, namely that implemented domestically ("the domestic control system") and that imposed at the WTO level ("the WTO control system"). The WTO control system should entail a rigorous and

387 Relevant proposals included *WTO* Doc. No. TN/RL/W/166 (2 November 2004) of Argentina, Chile, Ecuador, New Zealand, Philippines, Peru; *WTO* Doc. No. TN/RL/W/169 (13 December 2004) of the United States; and *WTO* Doc. No. TN/RL/W/172 (22 February 2005) of Japan, Korea and Taiwan.

388 *WTO* Doc. No. TN/RL/GEN/36 (23 March 2005), paras. 9-11.

389 *WTO* Doc. No. TN/RL/W/178, "Paper from the European Communities to the Negotiating Group on Rules, Fisheries Subsidies" (11 April 2005); *WTO* Doc. No. TN/RL/GEN/39, "Paper from the European Communities to the Negotiating Group on Rules, Paper on Fisheries" (12 May 2005).

390 *WTO* Doc. No. TN/RL/W/178 (11 April 2005), para. 3, stating that effective transparency could help distinguish distorting from "virtuous" subsidies. The difficulty, however, was that the effects of these harmful subsidies were not immediately apparent and thus difficult to detect. In the case of the fisheries sector, an economic effect resulting from fisheries subsidies took time to become visible.

391 *WTO* Doc. No. TN/RL/W/178 (11 April 2005), para. 4, stating that, based on this system, all aid to the fisheries sector, whether financed from the national or Community budget, should comply with the general rules as laid down in the Communities regulations governing the Structural Fund for Fisheries (Financial Instrument for Fisheries Guidance), in particular in relation to both the type and the allowed rates of aid.

continuous screening at the WTO level with requirements for both pre-notification and follow-up reporting of all subsidies given by all levels of governments.[392] The pre-notification mechanism already exists in other WTO agreements.[393] The domestic control system would rely essentially on an *ex post* monitoring system of subsidies to the fisheries sector.[394] An accurate and timely reporting system for non-prohibited subsidies given by all levels of governments should be established and be made readily accessible to the other WTO Members, i.e. by disclosing them on a known internet site.[395] Any subsidies not disclosed in due time in the domestic control system would be deemed prohibited. Moreover, not only should some forms of *de-minimis* rules be introduced, but there should also be a phase-in period of several years for developing countries to receive special help via an intensive programme on establishing a comprehensive system for transparency and enforcement which could be either WTO based or introduced as a domestic control system.[396]

3. Vessel Decommissioning and License Retirement

With respect to vessel decommissioning and license retirement, the so-called buy-back programmes, some Members proposed viewing them as included in a category of permitted subsidies,[397] or as candidates for exceptions to the prohibition.[398] A submission of the United States, therefore, proposed to define buybacks as government payments to vessel owners for the permanent retirement of vessels or withdrawal of licenses from a fishery.[399] These buyback programmes which aim at removing overcapacity in targeted fisheries may include both direct government assistance (grants) and loans to the fishing industry to finance the buyback. However, some of these programmes lead to the return of the removed overcapacity or even an increase in capacity.[400] The submission provided examples of the national

392 *Ibid.*, para. 5, explaining that the pre-notification to the WTO would have to be done in sufficient time for other Members to examine the proposed subsidy and subsidy scheme (programme) for its WTO compatibility, and that follow-up reporting could be yearly and include data on the amounts granted in that year. Any subsidy which was not notified or reported would be presumed prohibited.

393 Such as the TBT Agreement and the Agreement on Import Licensing Procedures.

394 *WTO* Doc. No. TN/RL/W/178 (11 April 2005), para. 5.

395 *Ibid.*

396 *Ibid.*, paras. 5 and 6.

397 *WTO* Doc. No. TN/RL/W/82 (23 April 2003); *WTO* Doc. No. TN/RL/W/172 (22 February 2005).

398 *WTO* Doc. No. TN/RL/W/166 (2 November 2004); *WTO* Doc. No. TN/RL/W/169 (13 December 2004).

399 *WTO* Doc. No. TN/RL/GEN/41, "Communication from the United States to the Negotiating Group on Rules, Fisheries Subsidies: Programmes for Decommissioning of Vessels and Licence Retirement" (13 May 2005), para. 4.

400 *Ibid.*, para. 5, explaining the reasons include (1) latent capacity or effort: the existence of inactive licences or unused vessels that could become active in the fishery after the buyback, as the fishery becomes more profitable; (2) leakage: the ability

experience of the United States[401] and concluded that buyback and similar programmes designed to permanently remove overcapacity from fisheries are strong candidates for an exception to the expanded prohibition of fisheries subsidies, provided that appropriate programme conditions are attached.[402] The conditions developed in the programmes of the United States can be instructive for the Negotiating Group on Rules to develop an understanding of such programme conditions.[403]

4. IUU Fishing

Japan proposed to prohibit subsidies related to IUU fishing[404] and provided detailed information on key issues and the current situation of IUU fisheries in order to prevent IUU fishing.[405] Japan identified that subsidies have been one of the factors that benefit IUU fishing[406] and that the most typical subsidies which might benefit IUU fisheries would be subsidies for overseas transfers of fishing vessels to non-CPCs of RFMOs.[407] This type of subsidy should be considered prohibited unless an appropriate bilateral arrangement between exporting and importing countries exists.[408] Moreover, provided that there should be other types of fisheries

of vessels, gear, financial resources and human capital to move from the fishery subject to the buyback to other fisheries, which may sometimes also suffer from overcapacity; (3) capital stuffing: the use of profits generated by a fishery after a buyback programme to invest in capital improvements that enhance the gear or power of remaining vessels, thereby potentially increasing overcapacity; (4) perverse incentives: increased effort in anticipation of compensation through a buyback programme.

401 *Ibid.*, para. 7 and Addendum, providing three examples of recent federal buyback programmes of the United States, i.e. the Bering Sea Pollock fishery, the Pacific Coast Groundfish fishery and the Bering Sea and Aleutian Islands Crab fishery.

402 *Ibid.*, para. 12.

403 *Ibid.*, para. 13, illustrating that under the US Sustainable Fisheries Act of 1996, buybacks are authorized only when they occur in conjunction with programme features designed to prevent the replacement of fishing capacity removed from the targeted fishery. Based on the US Sustainable Fisheries Act of 1996 and other relevant legislation, general principles for constructing buyback programmes have been set out, when allowing fisheries managers the flexibility to develop specific requirements for particular fisheries.

404 *WTO* Doc. No. TN/RL/W/172 (22 February 2005), para. 13 (v).

405 *WTO* Doc. No. TN/RL/GEN/47 (10 June 2005).

406 *Ibid.*, para. 11.

407 *Ibid.*, paras. 4, 9 and 10, explaining that because a vessel may be re-flagged to a non-CPC in order to operate freely, regardless of the ever-tightening international management measures, and to avoid the decreasing TACs set by RFMOs, the most serious problems related to IUU fisheries are caused by FOC operations on the high seas, which are conducted by vessels temporarily re-flagged to non-CPCs which possess neither the ability nor the will to manage those vessels while the virtual owners of those vessels live in other countries.

408 *Ibid.*, para. 15.

subsidies which are indirectly beneficial to IUU operations, information from Members on how to design fisheries subsidies in order not to facilitate or contribute to IUU fisheries should be shared in the Negotiating Group on Rules for further consideration of this issue.[409]

5. Aquaculture

New Zealand addressed the scope of aquaculture fisheries and whether WTO fisheries subsidies regulations should be developed to cover aquaculture.[410] Aquaculture has become more and more important, since aquaculture fisheries production has increased at a greater rate than wild capture production in recent years.[411] Some examples of aquaculture subsidies have also been notified by WTO Members.[412]

New Zealand stated that the nature of aquaculture fishery production, in a controlled environment and generally within the territorial waters of a State, means that subsidies to these fisheries are more amenable to existing SCM regulations. New Zealand encouraged Members to consider the issues regarding subsidies to aquaculture fisheries, such as those that distort trade and circumvent existing SCM regulations, which should be regulated.[413]

---

409 *Ibid.*, para. 16.

410 *WTO* Doc. No. TN/RL/GEN/54, "Submission from Australia, Ecuador and New Zealand to the Negotiating Group on Rules, Contribution to the Discussion on the Framework for Disciplines on Fisheries Subsidies-Aquaculture" (1 July 2005).

411 *Ibid.*, at 2.

412 *Ibid.*, at 3, illustrating subsidies for inland hatching fisheries to mitigate the environmental effects of dam construction (*WTO* Doc. No. G/SCM/N/95/USA, "Submission from the United States to the Committee on Subsidies and Countervailing Measures, New and Full Notification Pursuant to Article XVI:1 of the GATT 1994 and Article 25 of the Agreement on Subsidies and Countervailing Measures" (31 October 2003)); subsidies for land improvement, acquisition of land and agricultural mechanization (*WTO* Doc. No. G/SCM/N/95/JPN, "Submission from Japan to the Committee on Subsidies and Countervailing Measures, New and Full Notification Pursuant to Article XVI:1 of the GATT 1994 and Article 25 of the SCM Agreement" (4 September 2003)); subsidies to assist with the implementation of programmes for the promotion of sustainable fisheries to ensure the stable, safe and efficient supply of food to people (*WTO* Doc. No. G/SCM/N/95/JPN (4 September 2003)); subsidies to both regional governments and non-governmental organizations for the promotion of aquaculture to assist with the sustainable management of fisheries resources (*WTO* Doc. No. G/SCM/N/95/JPN (4 September 2003)); and subsidies for the development of commercial fisheries for marketing and aquaculture research for non-salmon species (*WTO* Doc. No. G/SCM/N/95/CAN, "Submission from Canada to the Committee on Subsidies and Countervailing Measures, New and Full Notification Pursuant to Article XVI:1 of the GATT 1994 and Article 25 of the Agreement on Subsidies and Countervailing Measures" (30 March 2004)).

413 *Ibid.*, at 5.

6. Fisheries Infrastructure

Given the fact that fisheries infrastructure accounts for a substantial proportion of government expenditure on global fisheries, particularly in developed countries, New Zealand initiated a dialogue on the category of "subsidies to fisheries infrastructure."[414] Government provision of "general infrastructure" is excluded from the definition of a subsidy under Article 1.1 of the SCM Agreement. New Zealand was of the opinion that the new fisheries subsidies regulations should also be consistent with the existing SCM Agreement and that general infrastructure should not be included in the new regulations.[415] Moreover, there should be another consideration regarding the requirement of specificity under Article 2 of the SCM Agreement that only infrastructure specific to the fisheries should be included in the new regulations.[416]

New Zealand divided subsidies to fisheries infrastructure into those to "capital infrastructure" and those to "operational infrastructure". Capital infrastructure is associated with the indirect costs of production, e.g. ports, storage and transport infrastructure. Operational infrastructure is associated with the direct and variable costs of production, e.g. bait services, fuel, ice and at-sea fishing support services. Subsidies to "operational infrastructure" should be prohibited under the new regulations.[417] In cases of subsidies to capital infrastructure, New Zealand referred to the existing subsidy classifications in fisheries subsidies literature[418] and proposed that these subsidies could be broken down into three non-exhaustive subcategories as follows.

First, subsidies to fishing-port facilities: further discussion and detailed information is needed before reaching a consensus, since the information available on this type of activity under the WTO subsidies notifications is limited.

---

414 *WTO* Doc. No. TN/RL/GEN/70, "Paper from New Zealand to the Negotiating Group on Rules, Subsidies to Fisheries Infrastructure" (14 October 2005).

415 *WTO* Doc. No. TN/RL/GEN/70 (14 October 2005), paras. 4 and 11.

416 *Ibid.*, footnote 4.

417 *WTO* Doc. No. TN/RL/GEN/70 (14 October 2005), para. 19; *WTO* Doc. NO. TN/RL/W/154 (26 April 2004).

418 *UNEP*, *supra* note 40, identifying three common types of fisheries infrastructure, including harbour facilities and moorage; fishing port infrastructure enhancement; and support to producer organizations. Also see *OECD*, "Environmental Aspects of Fisheries Subsidies", Background Paper Prepared for the OECD Technical Expert Meeting on Environmentally Harmful Subsidies, Paris, 3-4 November (Paris: OECD, 2003); *OECD*, "Transition to Responsible Fisheries: Economic and Policy Implications" (Paris: OECD, 2000), identifying the following types of programmes within the category of "fisheries infrastructure expenditure": support for building port facilities for commercial fishermen; reduced charges for the use of government-provided infrastructure; support for improving fishing villages; regional development grants; support for enhancing the fisheries community environment; fisheries-enhancement expenditure; support for artificial reefs; aid for restocking of fish resources; and expenditure on exploratory fishing.

Second, subsidies to the development of fishing communities: since they are important for social policies, they can be considered as a suitable candidate for exemption from any prohibited category of fisheries subsidies.

Third, subsidies to processing facilities for fisheries products: since these could have an indirect effect on fishing capacity by reducing the costs and/or increasing the revenues associated with fishing, they should be considered as not exempt from any prohibited category of fisheries subsidies.[419]

Moreover, subsidies for conservation and for research and development should not be prohibited under this proposal.[420] Subsidies for conservation could include support for artificial reefs, aid for restocking fisheries resources and fisheries enhancement expenditure.

7. Artisanal and Small-Scale Fisheries

Artisanal and small-scale fisheries are generally characterized by low input levels, high labour-capital ratios and usually support a subsistence standard of living. These fisheries are important to both developing countries and developed countries. Several submissions and remarks were made on the need for special consideration for these fisheries.[421]

The paper from Korea to the Negotiating Group on Rules suggested that subsidies provided to small-scale fisheries should be categorized as a green subsidy in the context of a social safety net.[422] The paper also recognized the difficulties arising from the lack of an authoritative definition of small-scale fisheries components.[423] It illustrated various definitions of small-scale fisheries under different international bodies[424] and suggested that a combination of socio-economic and

419 *WTO* Doc. No. TN/RL/GEN/70 (14 October 2005), paras. 10-18.

420 *WTO* Doc. No. TN/RL/GEN/70 (14 October 2005), para. 20. One of the conservation subsidies, artificial reefs, has been considered in the context of subsidies to "resource enhancement and protection of environment", and treated as non-actionable by Japan, Korea and Taiwan in *WTO* Doc. No. TN/RL/W/172 (22 February 2005).

421 *WTO* Doc. No. TN/RL/W/77 (19 March 2003) of the United States, *WTO* Doc. No. TN/RL/W/172 (22 February 2005) of Japan, Korea and Taiwan, and *infra* discussions on *WTO* Doc. No. TN/RL/GEN/56 (4 July 2005) of Brazil, *WTO* Doc. No. TN/RL/GEN/57/Rev.2 (13 September 2005) of several small vulnerable coastal States.

422 *WTO* Doc. No. TN/RL/GEN/92, "Paper from the Republic of Korea to the Negotiating Group on Rules, Fisheries Subsidies: Small-Scale Fisheries" (18 November 2005), para. 2.

423 Even the FAO cannot provide a specific definition, not to mention that it is inappropriate for the WTO simply to adopt and apply the FAO definition due to the fundamentally different purposes of the WTO and FAO.

424 *WTO* Doc. No. TN/RL/GEN/92 (18 November 2005), paras. 5-8, illustrating the studies on small-scale fisheries by international organizations such as the FAO, OECD and WTO, which use different terms, e.g. artisanal fisheries, family fishing and aboriginal fisheries, to indicate small-scale fisheries.

technical considerations would be useful for explaining what small-scale fisheries are. It also emphasized the need for an agreement on a simple and standard criterion for small-scale fisheries.[425]

Besides sharing Korea's national experience of small-scale fisheries legislation,[426] it suggested that Members should take sufficient care in avoiding an adverse impact of such special considerations on fisheries resources, and the rules for these considerations should be clear, definite and accompanied by a transparency scheme in order to guarantee the fair and effective functioning of the regulations and to prevent circumvention.[427]

C. Concerns from Small Vulnerable Coastal States

Similar to the paper previously submitted by small vulnerable coastal States in the Pacific and Indian Ocean and in the Caribbean,[428] a group of these Members proposed approaches to fisheries subsidies regulations.[429] The issues contained in this proposal can be summarized as follows.

First, it reaffirmed the commitments made in the WSSD in Johannesburg to replenish fish stocks to sustainable levels by 2015.[430]

Second, it recognized the efforts of relevant international organizations to increase the human and institutional resources of developing countries to implement sustainable fisheries management strategies at national and regional levels in accordance with the UNCLOS. These efforts through multilateral agencies and donor-assisted programmes should continue as a priority.[431]

Third, since the measures developed in the Negotiating Group on Rules might not adequately address environmental concerns,[432] it suggested strengthening

---

425 *Ibid.*, paras. 10-12.

426 *Ibid.*, paras. 13-16.

427 *Ibid.*, para. 23.

428 *WTO* Doc. No. TN/RL/W/136 (14 July 2003).

429 The original submission was made by Fiji, Papua New Guinea and the Solomon Islands, and subsequently joined by other like-minded small vulnerable coastal Members. *WTO* Doc. No. TN/RL/GEN/57, "Paper from Fiji, Papua New Guinea and the Solomon Islands to the Negotiating Group on Rules, WTO Fisheries Subsidies Disciplines Architecture on Fisheries Subsidies Disciplines" (7 July 2005), *WTO* Doc. No. TN/RL/GEN/57/Rev.1, "Paper from Fiji, Jamaica, Papua New Guinea, and the Solomon Islands to the Negotiating Group on Rules, WTO Fisheries Subsidies Disciplines Architecture on Fisheries Subsidies Disciplines" (4 August 2005), and *WTO* Doc. No. TN/RL/GEN/57/Rev.2, "Paper from Antigua and Barbuda, Barbados, Dominican Republic, Fiji, Grenada, Guyana, Jamaica, Papua New Guinea, St, Kitts and Nevis, St. Lucia, Solomon Islands, and Trinidad and Tobago to the Negotiating Group on Rules, WTO Fisheries Subsidies Disciplines Architecture on Fisheries Subsidies Disciplines" (13 September 2005).

430 Paragraph 31(a) of Plan of Implementation of the WSSD, *supra* note 94.

431 *WTO* Doc. No. TN/RL/GEN/57/Rev.2 (13 September 2005), paras. 4-5.

432 *Ibid.*, para. 8, in cases of the "traffic light" approach, it might not serve to promote the conservation of fish stocks, because even if a dispute has been brought to the

regional and national fisheries bodies, and identifying and rehabilitating endangered species, e.g. those employed by the FAO and MEAs are more responsive to the problem of threatened fisheries species.

Fourth, it also expressed concerns that the information used in examining the relationship between subsidies and fisheries depletion was based mainly on data for more advanced countries with large-scale industrial fleets.[433]

Fifth, a top-down approach should address the goal of sustainable development of the fisheries sector in developing coastal States and appropriate exceptions should be made to allow for the realization of development objectives.[434]

Sixth, as for S&D treatment of developing countries, it suggested some examples which should not be subject to subsidies regulations, including any development assistance to developing coastal States; assistance to artisanal or small-scale fisheries; access fees in fisheries access agreements; and fiscal incentives.[435]

D. Proposals of Brazil

Showing stronger concern for the fisheries issues of developing countries, in March 2005 Brazil presented its position on and contribution to fisheries subsidies regulations under the SCM Agreement.[436] In its proposal, Brazil defined fisheries subsidies, excluding the public service of fisheries management, and classified fisheries subsidies, based on their design and effects, in a red box (prohibited subsidies) and a green box (non-actionable subsidies) consisting of an exhaustive list.[437] S&D treatment of developing countries and transitional periods were also taken into account.

Following its proposal in March 2005, Brazil submitted another paper to introduce following major changes and improvements and incorporate comments made by Members as well as to further develop some of the suggestions that had been put forward.[438] The submission revised the original definition of fisheries subsidies in the March proposal to exclude aquaculture subsidies by defining fisheries subsidies as all "capture" fisheries subsidies programmes, except for inland fish-

---

Dispute Settlement Body, fisheries resources could continue to be depleted during litigation. Moreover, even if a general prohibition or "top-down" approach were adopted, it might still be difficult to explicitly address overcapacity and overfishing under WTO rules.

433 *Ibid.*, para. 9.

434 *Ibid.*, paras. 12-13.

435 *Ibid.*, paras. 14-16.

436 *WTO* Doc. No. TN/RL/W/176, "Paper from Brazil to the Negotiating Group on Rules, Contribution to the Discussion on the Framework for Disciplines on Fisheries Subsidies" (31 March 2005).

437 *Ibid.*, para. 21.

438 *WTO* Doc. No. TN/RL/GEN/56, "Paper from Brazil to the Negotiating Group on Rules, Contribution to the Discussion on the Framework for Disciplines on Fisheries Subsidies" (4 July 2005), para. 1.

eries.[439] It considered artisanal fisheries non-actionable.[440] If any vessel and/or company of a Member were found to be engaged in IUU fishing according to any RFMO, "serious prejudice" under Article 5(c) of the SCM Agreement would be deemed to exist regarding all non-actionable subsidies granted by that Member.[441] To improve the quality of notifications and transparency, it suggested requiring detailed reporting about the actual uses of the subsidies.[442] Concerning the challenges that the small vulnerable coastal Members face as well as S&D treatment for developing country Members, "serious prejudice" of Article 5(c) of the SCM Agreement should be deemed to exist only in certain cases.[443]

In a later submission by Brazil, these ideas were tentatively translated into a legal draft as the first attempt to develop possible legal language for the future disciplines and attached as Annex VIII to the SCM Agreement.[444] This submission, due to its form, moved the negotiations forward and provided a milestone for more concrete fisheries subsidies disciplines under the SCM Agreement.

---

439 *Ibid.*, para. 2 (i), defining that except for inland fisheries, all capture fisheries subsidies programmes should be included in the definition of "fisheries subsidies".

440 *Ibid.*, para. 2 (ii)(a)(2), citing that subsidies to artisanal fishing are to be considered non-actionable if: granted to fisheries activities performed on an in-shore basis with non-automatic net-retriever devices; granted to activities carried out on an individual basis (including, but not necessarily, family members); the basic scope of the activities encompasses both family livelihood and a small profit trade; and there is no employer-employee relationship in the activities carried out.

441 *Ibid.*, para. 2 (ii).

442 *Ibid.*, para. 4, suggesting that the notification should include information regarding the identification of fisheries in which subsidized fishing takes place under a given subsidies programme; about the status of the fisheries in question; about subsidy amounts on a per-vessel, per-fleet and per-fishery basis; and a specific description of how subsidies are actually applied; whether the fishery is under management by a RFMO, the nature of the monitoring, the quantitative limits applicable to the Member and the RFMO website; and the identification of specific enterprises receiving subsidies.

443 *Ibid.*, para. 5 (ii), illustrating the cases are (a) subsidies benefiting any vessel and/or company not operating under the rules and/or limits established by a RFMO for a Member; (b) any vessel and/or company found to be engaged in IUU fishing according to any RFMO. In this situation, serious prejudice shall be deemed to exist regarding all actionable subsidies granted by the developing country Member; (c) subsidies granted to any vessel and/or company involved with the exploitation of fisheries "patently at risk"; (d) subsidies granted to a fleet or an enterprise to cover operating losses.

444 *WTO* Doc. No. TN/RL/GEN/79, "Paper from Brazil to the Negotiating Group on Rules, Further Contribution to the Discussion on the Framework for Disciplines on Fisheries Subsidies" (16 November 2005), para. 1. The Annex is composed of 7 articles, including Article 1: definitions and coverage; Article 2: non-actionable subsidies; Article 3: prohibited subsidies; Article 4: prevention of circumvention; Article 5: special and differential treatment of developing country Members; Article 6: notification; and Article 7: transitional provisions. The alternative of an amendment or annex approach does not reflect the choice of a top-down or bottom-up approach.

E. Status of Negotiations before the Hong Kong Ministerial Conference

Shortly before the Hong Kong Ministerial Conference took place in December 2005, a submission from several Members supporting the top-down approach urged further movement on fisheries subsidies disciplines.[445] Based on a suggested work plan from the submission of several Members in November 2004,[446] there were a number of detailed contributions on sub-categories of fisheries subsidies, including governmental management services,[447] special enforcement,[448] vessel decommissioning and license retirement,[449] IUU fishing,[450] aquaculture,[451] fisheries infrastructure[452] and artisanal and small-scale fisheries.[453] These contributions provided a strong basis for eventually reaching a common understanding of the definitions and treatment of various categories of fisheries subsidies as well as for related discussions on the nature and extent of regulations that would be needed.[454] This submission further suggested other noteworthy areas, e.g. conservation subsidies, regional development programmes, fisheries-related social insurance programmes and research and development programmes.[455] In order to accelerate the text-based outcome for the new regulations, it reaffirmed the principles for guiding the development of the new regulations in line with a broad-based prohibition,[456] and emphasized the need to return to the discussion on the structure of the regulations.

---

445 *WTO* Doc. No. TN/RL/W/196, "Paper from Brazil; Chile; Colombia; Ecuador; Iceland; New Zealand; Pakistan; Peru and the United States to the Negotiating Group on Rules, Fisheries Subsidies" (22 November 2005).

446 *WTO* Doc. No. TN/RL/W/166 (2 November 2004).

447 *WTO* Doc. No. TN/RL/GEN/36 (23 March 2005).

448 *WTO* Doc. No. TN/RL/GEN/39 (12 May 2005).

449 *WTO* Doc. No. TN/RL/GEN/41 (13 May 2005).

450 *WTO* Doc. No. TN/RL/GEN/47 (10 June 2005).

451 *WTO* Doc. No. TN/RL/GEN/54 (1 July 2005).

452 *WTO* Doc. No. TN/RL/GEN/70 (14 October 2005).

453 *WTO* Doc. No. TN/RL/GEN/92 (18 November 2005).

454 *WTO* Doc. No. TN/RL/W/196 (22 November 2005), para. 8.

455 *Ibid.*, para. 11.

456 *Ibid.*, paras. 14-15, illustrating that the principles for guiding the development of the new regulations included simplicity and enforceability, transparency, flexibility and responsiveness, consistency with the mandates of the Doha Ministerial Declaration and S&D treatment of developing countries. On the basis of these principles, these Members continued to support strongly the concept of a broad-based prohibition as the best means for delivering on the Doha Ministerial Declaration.

IX. Results on Fisheries Subsidies Negotiations at the HK Ministerial Conference

The shift of the discussion from whether to regulate fisheries subsidies under a bottom-up or top-down approach to one on sub-categories and S&D treatment paved the way for a breakthrough agreement at the "mid-round" WTO Ministerial Conference in Hong Kong in December 2005.

The issue of fisheries subsidies and a possible restructuring of the applicable agreements of the WTO were on the agenda of this Ministerial Conference.[457] In the Hong Kong Ministerial Declaration, Ministers issued a negotiating mandate that called for an enforceable ban on fisheries subsidies that "contribute to overcapacity and overfishing." The commitment to a strong environmental outcome on fisheries subsidies made headlines around the world and moved the talks to a new level of intensity. Whereas the debate on fisheries subsidies had first centred on the Doha negotiating mandate, the focus quickly shifted to the scope and strength of an eventual ban on some types of fisheries subsidies.

Annex D of the Hong Kong Ministerial Declaration reaffirmed the intention of clarifying the existing rules and stated that Ministers: (1) *recall* Members' commitment at Doha to enhance the mutual supportiveness of trade and environment, (2) *note* that there is a broad agreement that the Group should strengthen disciplines on subsidies in the fisheries sector, also by prohibiting certain forms of fisheries subsidies that contribute to overcapacity and over-fishing, and (3) *call on* participants promptly to undertake further detailed work to, *inter alia*, establish the nature and extent of those disciplines, including transparency and enforceability. Appropriate and effective S&D treatment for developing and least-developed Members should be an integral part of the fisheries subsidies negotiations, taking into account the importance of this sector for developing priorities, poverty reduction, and livelihood and food security concerns.[458]

Concerning developing and least-developed country Members, it reaffirmed Members' commitment to the Work Programme on Small Economies and urged Members to adopt specific measures that would facilitate the fuller integration of small, vulnerable economies into the multilateral trading system, without creating a sub-category of WTO Members.[459]

However, it did not lay down when a decision on fisheries issues should be expected. In spite of the fact that the discussion had been in progress for several years and different proposals had been made to change the SCM Agreement, the Hong Kong Ministerial Declaration did not include any specific decisions on fisheries issues. However, it did emphasize the concerns regarding S&D treatment of developing countries, taking into consideration the importance of the fisheries

[457] WTO Hong Kong 6th Ministerial Conference, Ministerial Declaration, adopted on 18 December, further information available on-line at <www.wto.org/english/thewto_e/minist_e/min05_e/final_text_e.htm> (last visited on January 20, 2008).

[458] *Ibid.*, Annex D, para. 9.

[459] *Ibid.*, para. 41.

sector for development priorities, poverty reduction, and livelihood and food security concerns.

X. Negotiations on Fisheries Subsidies after the Hong Kong Ministerial Conference

Following the Hong Kong Ministerial Conference, technical proposals on a range of fisheries subsidies topics were submitted by various WTO delegations, with these submissions revealing convergence on some points and conflict on others. Furthermore, Members were required to submit their text-based proposals, so that the work of the Negotiating Group on Rules could be intensified and the planned time-frame could be met. Since then, legal drafts have been proposed by several Members leading the negotiations.

However, on July 28, 2006, the General Council of the WTO indefinitely recommended suspending the Doha Round Negotiations as Members had failed to reconcile differences in their positions on key issues, i.e. farm tariffs and agricultural subsidies.[460] In spite of this, the Negotiating Group on Rules continued to work on fisheries subsidies, using the constructive submissions provided by Members which addressed particularly difficult issues such as S&D treatment and sustainability criteria.[461] The legal text of fisheries subsidies regulations drafted by the Chairman of the Negotiating Group on Rules in late 2007 moved the negotiations further forward.

A. Legal Drafts Submitted Prior to the Chair's Text in November 2007

Although the discussion stalled in 2006, it progressed from a more conceptual phase to a phase where it was more focused on convergence. In early 2007, the negotiation was revived by a Norwegian proposal which introduced the criterion of using the length of fishing vessels to classify small-scale fisheries. Several other Members also submitted their legal drafts on fisheries subsidies, including Argentina, Brazil,[462] Taiwan, the European Communities, Indonesia, Japan, Korea, New Zealand and the United States.

---

460 *WTO News–General Council*, "*General Council Supports Suspension of Trade Talks, Task Force Submits "Aid for Trade" Recommendations"* (July 27-28, 2006).

461 *WTO* Doc. No. TN/RL/21, "Report by the Chairman to the Trade Negotiations Committee to the Negotiating Group on Rules, Negotiating Group on Rules" (27 July 2007), para. 3.

462 After the first submission of a legal draft to the *WTO* Doc. No. TN/RL/GEN/79 (16 November 2005), Brazil has revised it several times. The study concentrates on its latest submissions in 2007.

1. New Zealand

New Zealand submitted a paper as a contribution to the negotiations, based on the broad prohibition of fisheries subsidies.[463] The submission adopted an amendment approach, consisting of proposed amendments to the SCM Agreement, with an exhaustive list of non-prohibited fisheries subsidies and product coverage for fisheries subsidies.[464] It proposed to broadly prohibit subsidies to fisheries for the harvesting, processing, transporting, marketing or selling of fish and fish products under the proposed Article 3.1 of the SCM Agreement.

Consequently, New Zealand elaborated its suggested exhaustive list of non-prohibited fisheries subsidies under the proposed Annex VIII in a later submission.[465] According to this proposed exhaustive list of exemptions from prohibition, there should not be an overall increase in capacity.[466] General infrastructure subsidies were not covered under the prohibition and fisheries infrastructure subsidies were proposed to be treated as non-prohibited, but remained actionable and subject to enhanced transparency provisions.[467] Moreover, both artisanal fishing and access payments should be considered non-prohibited, but subject to transparency provisions under proposed Article 25. Regarding access payments, the new regulations would focus only on the subsidies provided by fishing nations to their long distance fishing fleets for access to the fishing resources of developing countries.[468]

2. Japan, Korea and Taiwan

Japan, Korea and Taiwan also submitted a legal draft based on the bottom-up approach.[469] In the draft, the fisheries subsidies which should be prohibited or non-actionable were separately listed under Articles 3 and 8 of the SCM Agree-

463 *WTO* Doc. No. TN/RL/W/196 (22 November 2005), paras. 14-15.

464 *WTO* Doc. No. TN/RL/GEN/100, "Paper from New Zealand to the Negotiating Group on Rules, Fisheries Subsidies Framework for Disciplines" (3 March 2006).

465 *WTO* Doc. No. TN/RL/GEN/141, "Paper from New Zealand to the Negotiating Group on Rules, Fisheries Subsidies Exhaustive List of Non-Prohibited Fisheries Subsidies" (6 June 2006).

466 *Ibid.*, para. 1.

467 *Ibid.*, para. 2.

468 *Ibid.*, para. 3.

469 *WTO* Doc. No. TN/RL/GEN/114, "Communication from Japan; the Republic of Korea; and the Separate Customs Territory of Taiwan, Penghu, Kinmen and Matsu to the Negotiating Group on Rules, Fisheries Subsidies Framework for Disciplines" (21 April 2006); *WTO* Doc. No. TN/RL/GEN/114/Rev.1, "Communication from Japan; the Republic of Korea; and the Separate Customs Territory of Taiwan, Penghu, Kinmen and Matsu to the Negotiating Group on Rules, Fisheries Subsidies Framework for Disciplines, Revised" (2 June 2006).

ment. Basically, subsidies, except under certain conditions of the Annex VIII,[470] for the construction and modification of fishing vessels, subsidies for shipbuilding yards, subsidises for overseas transfers of fishing vessels to non-participants of RFMOs and subsidies relating to IUU fishing should be prohibited.[471] The following subsidies should be non-actionable: subsidies for the decommissioning of fishing vessels; subsidies for fisheries stock enhancement and marine environment protection; subsidies for research and development for sustainable fisheries; subsidies for unemployment relief, early retirement or re-education, retraining and alternative employment assistance for fishermen; subsidies for a social safety net for fishermen; subsidies for small-scale and artisanal fisheries; and subsidies for access fees.[472]

In 2007, Japan, Korea and Taiwan, on the basis of their previous legal draft in 2006,[473] submitted another revised legal draft based on the annex approach.[474] This proposal was the most developed legal draft of these three Members and the major points contained in this proposal can be summarized as follows.

First, it reaffirmed the bottom-up approach and the need to reconsider the structure of fisheries subsidies regulations in compliance with the basic concepts, principles and effectiveness of the SCM Agreement and its instruments and objectives.[475]

Second, it emphasized that the top-down approach seriously undermines policy flexibility, because the top-down approach denies the chance for further policy developments when the fisheries' environment changes and policy needs arise.[476]

Third, due to the uncertainties of global fisheries and fish stocks, it should be inappropriate to provide explicitly some specific "sustainability criteria" in the new regulations as a condition for granting subsidies.

---

470 *WTO* Doc. No. TN/RL/GEN/114 (21 April 2006), Annex VIII. The proposed Annex VIII (Conditions for Vessel Construction and Modification Subsidies referred to in Sub-Paragraph (i) and (ii) of Paragraph 1(c) of Article 3) basically aimed at avoiding an increase in certain criteria, including gross tonnage, volume of fish hold and engine power. In the legal draft in April 2006, in the case of fishing-vessel construction, the subsidies could be considered non-prohibited on the condition that the gross tonnage of the newly constructed vessel was reduced by more than 20% of the sum of the gross tonnage of the vessels to be withdrawn. However, in the later legal draft in June 2006 (*WTO* Doc. No. TN/RL/GEN/114/Rev.1 (2 June 2006)), the benchmark was raised so that "each of the following items of the new vessel is reduced by at least 50% of (the sum of) that of the vessels to be withdrawn: (i) gross tonnage, (ii) volume of fish hold, and (iii) engine power."

471 *WTO* Doc. No. TN/RL/GEN/114 (21 April 2006), the proposed Article 3.1.(c).

472 *Ibid.*, the proposed Article 8.1.

473 *WTO* Doc. No. TN/RL/GEN/114 (21 April 2006); *WTO* Doc. No. TN/RL/GEN/114/Rev.1 (2 June 2006).

474 *WTO* Doc. No. TN/RL/GEN/114/Rev.2, "Communication from Japan; the Republic of Korea; and the Separate Customs Territory of Taiwan, Penghu, Kinmen and Matsu to the Negotiating Group on Rules, Fisheries Subsidies: Framework for Disciplines" (5 June 2007).

475 *Ibid.*, at 3.

476 *Ibid.*

Fourth, it highlighted the need for the notification and review process to be effective. In order to overcome the problems that the non-binding FAO instruments may not be a good reference for binding WTO regulations and that fisheries resources may not continue to be sustainable during the same period of time as the life of the subsidized vessels, the proposal strengthened the provisions of the "notification, enquiry point and peer-view".[477] Based on this provision, peer-view of the notifications and reports from the enquiry points, the SCM Committee should set up an *ad hoc* group of fishery experts. However, the opinion of this group of experts should not be binding, as the Committee is not directly responsible for fishery resource management.[478]

Fifth, it would be inappropriate to formulate a universally applicable definition for a sector as dynamic and diverse as small-scale fisheries, so the proposal listed the characteristics of small-scale fisheries across the world.[479] It also emphasized that the provisions for small-scale fisheries should apply to all Members, since small-scale fisheries may also exist in developed countries.[480]

Sixth, it underlined that some of the developing country Members had built up more advanced and more competitive distant water fishing fleets than developed country Members. Therefore, it stated, with regard to S&D treatment, that prohibition and other obligations of certain forms of fisheries subsidies applicable to the high-seas area should be equally applied to all Members, since the UNCLOS does not distinguish between developing and developed countries in terms of rights and obligations relating to highly migratory species and straddling stocks.[481]

Seventh, taking the development dimension into consideration, several points were made in the text proposal as follows: subsidies for access fees should be regarded as "non-actionable" (Article 2); provisions for small-scale fisheries should be established and flexible treatment applied to small-scale fisheries in developing country Members (Article 2); less strict provisions should be applied to other fisheries solely operating in the EEZ of developing country Members, taking into account the potential for development in such waters; as for subsidies granted by developing country Members for high-seas fishing, the same treatment should be applied as to developed country Members; and technical assistance for notification by developing country Members can be sought (Article 4.3).[482]

---

477 *WTO* Doc. No. TN/RL/GEN/114/Rev.2 (5 June 2007), the proposed Annex [VIII] to the Agreement on Subsidies and Countervailing Measures, Article 3-Notifications, Enquiry Point and Peer-Review.

478 *Ibid.*, at 8.

479 *Ibid.*, at 4, interpreting that small-scale fisheries can be characterized as (i) inshore or near-shore fishing operations, (ii) labour intensive, (iii) targeting multiple species by the use of a large range of different fishing techniques, and (iv) supplying products to local and domestic markets while export-oriented production has increased in the last one to two decades.

480 *Ibid.*

481 *Ibid.*

482 *Ibid.*, at 9.

3. United States

The United States also proposed a text in three areas,[483] including (1) appropriate conditions to be attached to vessel-capacity reduction (buyback) programmes, which were proposed as a potential exception to a broad prohibition; (2) provisions for the periodic review by the SCM Committee of the effectiveness of new fisheries subsidies regulations, including an appropriate role for intergovernmental organizations with fisheries expertise; and (3) provisions for the appropriate involvement of fisheries experts in addressing technical and scientific questions that could arise in dispute settlement proceedings under new fisheries subsidies regulations.[484] This proposed text could be adapted equally to an annex approach or an amendment to the SCM Agreement. With regard to buyback programmes, in addition to a detailed discussion by the United States in May 2005,[485] there was a general consensus that these programmes should be carefully structured so that the removed capacity would not be replaced.[486] The proposal reaffirmed that exceptions to a prohibition should remain actionable under the other relevant WTO rules.[487]

When the negotiations resumed in 2007, based on the substantial convergence on the scope of the exceptions to prohibition of the legal texts drafted by New Zealand and Brazil,[488] the United States also offered its proposed regulations to the Negotiating Group on Rules.[489] This proposal contained the following points.

First, the existence of fisheries subsidies should comply with the elements under Article 1 and the requirement of specificity under Article 2 of the SCM Agreement.

Second, it recognized the ineffectiveness of current rules on "serious prejudice" under Article 6 of the SCM Agreement in the fisheries sector and proposed two customized criteria, namely that the effect of the subsidy is either (a) to increase

---

483 *WTO* Doc. No. TN/RL/GEN/127, "Communication from the United States to the Negotiating Group on Rules, Fisheries Subsidies" (24 April 2006).

484 The provisions regarding fisheries expertise are adapted from Article 11 of the SPS Agreement.

485 *WTO* Doc. No. TN/RL/GEN/41 (13 May 2005).

486 Under the top-down approach, these programmes have been considered as an exception to the prohibition if appropriate conditions are defined, in *WTO* Doc. No. TN/RL/GEN/100 (3 March 2006), Annex VIII, p. 1(b) and *WTO* Doc. No. TN/RL/GEN/79/Rev.1, "Paper from Brazil to the Negotiating Group on Rules, Possible Disciplines on Fisheries Subsidies, Revision" (21 February 2006), Art. 2.1(b). Under the bottom-up approach, other Members also acknowledge the need to develop appropriate conditions for these programmes, in *WTO* Doc. No. TN/RL/W/172 (22 February 2005), para. 14(i) and *WTO* Doc. No. TN/RL/W/82 (23 April 2003), at 3.

487 *WTO* Doc. No. TN/RL/GEN/127 (24 April 2006).

488 *WTO* Doc. No. TN/RL/GEN/141 (6 June 2006) of New Zealand; *WTO* Doc. No. TN/RL/GEN/79 (16 November 2005) of Brazil.

489 *WTO* Doc. No. TN/RL/GEN/145, "Proposal from the United States to the Negotiating Group on Rules, Fisheries Subsidies: Proposed New Disciplines" (22 March 2007).

the capacity of the subsidizing Member to produce the "like product"; or (b) to increase the subsidizing Member's relative share of the "like product" as compared to non-subsidized production over a representative period.[490]

Third, subsidies to aquaculture would be covered in the existing SCM Agreement instead of the new fisheries subsidies regulations.[491]

Fourth, to avoid loopholes and to retain Members' rights under the existing SCM Agreement, exceptions to the prohibition should remain actionable.[492]

Fifth, to improve transparency, it proposed that each Member should establish an inquiry point to respond to reasonable enquiries from other Members and interested parties concerning its fisheries management system, including measures in place to address fishing capacity and effort and the biological status of managed fish stocks.[493]

Sixth, regarding consultations and dispute settlement, it proposed that the existing provision on expertise in Article 13 of the Dispute Settlement Understanding could be adequate, or Members should determine whether there was a need for an explicit provision. It considered that the FAO and other international organizations, instead of providing expert opinions by themselves as organizations, could be requested to provide assistance in identifying the appropriate experts.[494] The issues regarding the dispute settlement mechanism and the check point in the enforcement system were initially raised in the proposal, meaning that the control system and the dispute settlement system could be the subject of further detailed discussions.

4. European Communities

Following the principle that the new regulations should be simple, transparent and enforceable, the European Communities also submitted its text-based proposal to the Negotiating Group on Rules.[495] The submission contained the following major points.

First, it reiterated the importance of an effective transparency and enforcement mechanism, which could be achieved through the WTO control system or domestic enforcement system.[496]

Second, applying an annex approach to address these articles, it considered the following subsidies as prohibited subsidies: those for the construction of new

---

490 *Ibid.*, paras. 5 and 6.

491 *Ibid.*, at 8, the proposed Annex [VIII] to the Agreement on Subsidies and Countervailing Measures, Annotation of Article 1 and footnote 1.

492 *Ibid.*, para. 6.

493 *Ibid.*, para. 8. This kind of mechanism has also worked well in Article 10.1 of the TBT Agreement.

494 *Ibid.*, at 12, the proposed Annex [VIII] to the Agreement on Subsidies and Countervailing Measures, Annotation of Article 10.

495 *WTO* Doc. No. TN/RL/GEN/134, "Submission from the European Communities to the Negotiating Group on Rules, Fisheries Subsidies" (24 April 2006).

496 *WTO* Doc. No. TN/RL/W/178 (11 April 2005).

fishing vessels, for the renovation of existing fishing vessels and for the permanent transfer of fishing vessels to other countries.[497]

Third, it considered the following two types of subsidies as permitted: (a) subsidies contingent upon a reduction in fishing capacity or that are provided for the specific purpose of mitigating the negative social and economic consequences of reductions in capacity; (b) subject to no increase in capacity, subsidies granted in the context of conservation measures, for product development, for the modernization of vessels including improved working conditions and safety on board, and subsidies that promote more environmentally friendly fishing operations.[498]

Fourth, the provision of a periodic review regarding the lists of prohibited subsidies and permitted subsidies had also been taken into account.[499]

Fifth, based on its internal experience, the submission highlighted the prerequisites of notifications under the proposed Article 5 pursuant to the transparency and effectiveness of the control system.[500]

Sixth, concerning S&D treatment of developing country Members, it proposed as long as such Member did not increase its fishing capacity, to an extent that it was an impediment to the sustainable exploitation of fisheries resources worldwide.[501]

5. Norway

To bring the discussion substantially further in terms of scope and ambition for fisheries subsidies regulations, Norway submitted a legal draft.[502] The negotiations did not resume until the submission of this proposal at the beginning of 2007. This submission contained several major points as follows.

First, it summarized the status of negotiations as follows:[503] (1) that there were still fundamental conceptual differences between the top-down and bottom-up approaches, although during the discussions on the necessary exceptions the differences had in fact become smaller; (2) that there was no consensus on a general prohibition of all forms of fisheries subsidies; (3) that no one had attempted to define what the fisheries sector was; however, many Members considered that inland fisheries and aquaculture fisheries should be exempted; (4) that Members also recognized that there is a difference between inshore fisheries[504] and fisheries on the high seas which are usually large-scale; (5) that there was no consensus on other types of government support to the processing industry, either in the form of

497 *WTO* Doc. No. TN/RL/GEN/134 (24 April 2006), para. 2.
498 *Ibid.*, the proposed Annex Article 3.
499 *Ibid.*, the proposed Annex Article 4.
500 *Ibid.*, the proposed Annex Article 5.
501 *Ibid.*, the proposed Annex Article 6.
502 *WTO* Doc. No. TN/RL/GEN/144, "Proposal by Norway to the Negotiating Group on Rules, Fisheries Subsidies" (26 January 2007).
503 *Ibid.*, at 1.
504 Subsistence, artisanal, small-scale, etc.

price support for fish products or support for building warehouses and freezing facilities.

Second, it considered that although access payments should be considered permissible for developing countries, it is still necessary for the fishing industry of developed countries to reimburse their governments for financing such access agreements.[505]

Third, it proposed focusing not only on subsidies for the building of fishing vessels but also on subsidies for the acquisition, maintenance, repairing or upgrading of fishing vessels, including any technical or electronic equipment on board the vessel.[506]

Fourth, in order to deal with the structure of new regulations and the ambiguous definitions of different types of fisheries, it proposed a definition of fishing vessels. It defined fishing vessels as any vessels used for the purpose of the commercial exploitation of fisheries resources, including processing vessels and vessels engaged in transhipment. Fishing vessels can be classified as large and small, and it assumed that most damage is caused by large vessels. The distinction between large and small vessels should be based on the length of fishing vessels - at 15 meters.[507] This parameter, though crude, is simple, workable and can be applied to all Members, developing and developed alike.

Fifth, some developing country Members preferred to have the "policy space" for financing the build-up of fishing capacity, but some called for strict regulations. Since half of global fish trade was generated by developing countries and seven of the global top ten producers were developing countries, developing country Members should not be granted full exemption from the regulations.[508] It proposed that developing countries might subsidize fishing vessels up to 20 meters in length, provided that they fulfilled certain conditions relating to the scope of operation of the vessels.[509] If the programmes were related to capacity build-up linked to under-utilized fish stocks for development purposes, the developing countries should be allowed to subsidize fishing vessels up to 28 meters in length.[510]

505 *WTO* Doc. No. TN/RL/GEN/144 (26 January 2007), at 1.

506 *Ibid.*, at 2, explaining that, based on an OECD study, 70 percent of governmental transfers are used to finance either biological research and fisheries management systems or measures financing infrastructure, and the remaining 30 percent of governmental transfers are subsidies for the building of fishing vessels. *Anthony Cox and Carl-Christian Schmidt*, *supra* note 16.

507 *Ibid.*, the proposed Annex [VIII]-Fisheries Subsidies, Article 1.1. Other Members might not agree with this parameter, since they were using different systems: gross tonnage of vessel, volume of fishing hold, engine power, etc. For example, Japan suggested four criteria to define "capacity", including number of vessels, individual gross tonnage, volume of fish hold and engine power, *WTO* Doc. No. TN/RL/GEN/47 (10 June 2005).

508 *Ibid.*, at 2.

509 *Ibid.*, the proposed Annex [VIII]-Fisheries Subsidies, Article 2.

510 *Ibid.*, the proposed Annex [VIII]-Fisheries Subsidies, Article 3.

Sixth, any fisheries management plan should be notified and subject to the questions and discussion in the SCM Committee. In terms of the status of fisheries resources, it should be approved by an independent institution, e.g. a biological research institute or an RFMO.[511]

Seventh, it recognized some exceptions, but these remained actionable, since the proposed regulations were to form an additional element to the existing SCM Agreement.[512]

In this proposal, the criterion adopted on the length of fishing vessels was an attempt to make a breakthrough in the negotiations.

6. Brazil

During this period of time, Brazil revised its legal draft on the basis of its previous submission.[513] This version of its proposed legal draft contained the following major provisions.

First, it defined fisheries subsidies as subsidies given to or on behalf of any firm and/or person linked in fact or in law, directly or indirectly to harvesting activities of capture fisheries. The public service of fisheries management, inland fisheries and aquaculture were excluded.[514]

Second, based on the top-down approach, it proposed that all fisheries subsidies be prohibited, except those treated as exceptions, including subsidies for a social safety net for fishermen; subsidies for fisheries research; subsidies related to fisheries stock enhancement; subsidies aimed at improving vessel and crew safety; subsidies for vessel capacity reduction programmes; other subsidies indirectly liked to the harvesting activities of capture fisheries; subsidies for compensating for natural or environmental disasters.[515]

---

511 *Ibid.*, at 3-4, illustrating that besides the FAO, the scientific/biological bodies of RFMOs and other scientific and biological organizations, such as the Advisory Committee for Fisheries Management of the International Council for the Exploration of the Seas (ICES) are capable of assessing whether there are under-utilized stocks in any particular part of the ocean.

512 *Ibid.*, at 4-5.

513 *WTO* Doc. No. TN/RL/GEN/79/Rev.1 (21 February 2006); *WTO* Doc. No. TN/RL/GEN/79/Rev.2 (21 April 2006); *WTO* Doc. No. TN/RL/GEN/79/Rev.3, "Paper from Brazil to the Negotiating Group on Rules, Possible Disciplines on Fisheries Subsidies, Revision" (2 June 2006); *WTO* Doc. No. TN/RL/GEN/79/Rev.4, "Paper from Brazil to the Negotiating Group on Rules, Possible Disciplines on Fisheries Subsidies, Revision" (13 March 2007).

514 *WTO* Doc. No. TN/RL/GEN/79/Rev.4 (13 March 2007), the proposed Annex VIII to the Agreement on Subsidies and Countervailing Measures, Article 1 (Definition and coverage).

515 *WTO* Doc. No. TN/RL/GEN/79/Rev.4 (13 March 2007), the proposed Annex VIII to the Agreement on Subsidies and Countervailing Measures, Articles 1 (Prohibition) and 2 (Exceptions).

Third, developing country Members should be allowed to grant or maintain fisheries subsidies to fishing activities related to the subsistence and livelihood of the fishermen and their families; fishing vessel construction, repair and modernization or gear acquisition or improvement; and operational costs for fishing activities.[516]

Fourth, granting or maintaining fisheries subsidies should not cause "fisheries adverse effects" on the interests of other Members.[517] In brief, this provision laid out specific fisheries adverse effects on the fisheries sector in order to set an effective criterion for ensuring that the exceptions and S&D provisions do not cause overfishing. Each Member should establish and make operational their fisheries management systems, based on international practices and the best scientific information available.

Fifth, it considered that choosing "capacity" as the sole parameter for verifying the occurrence of fisheries adverse effects, as it did in the first version of the legal text, is controversial and imprecise, due to there being little consensus among specialists in the matter and no direct relation between a vessel's physical features and overfishing.[518] Therefore, it suggested two dimensions aimed at capturing not only the fishing potential of each fleet in terms of capacity, but especially the volume actually fished in terms of production.[519]

7. Indonesia

Supporting the top-down approach, Indonesia also submitted its legal draft on fisheries subsidies regulations from the perspective of a developing country.[520] The following major issues were included in its first legal draft.

First, with regard to technical assistance and fisheries expertise for developing countries in certain areas, it emphasized that developed countries should provide not only technical assistance for fisheries management but also assistance for full participation in RFMOs adjacent to their EEZs, including RFMO scientific and research programme activities.[521]

516 *WTO* Doc. No. TN/RL/GEN/79/Rev.4 (13 March 2007), the proposed Annex VIII to the Agreement on Subsidies and Countervailing Measures, Article 4 (Special and Differential Treatment of Developing Country Members).

517 *Ibid.*, the proposed Annex VIII to the Agreement on Subsidies and Countervailing Measures, Article 5 (Fishery Adverse Effects).

518 The capacity of a fleet (physical: aggregate gross tonnage, volume of fish hold, engine power, etc; and productive: autonomy of the vessel, number of times that it goes to sea, etc) should be a static and potential parameter that has nothing to do directly with the sustainability of its activities.

519 *WTO* Doc. No. TN/RL/GEN/79/Rev.4 (13 March 2007), at 2-3.

520 *WTO* Doc. No. TN/RL/GEN/150, "Proposal from the Republic of Indonesia to the Negotiating Group on Rules, Fisheries Subsidies: Proposed New Disciplines" (2 July 2007).

521 *Ibid.*, paras. 4 and 5.

Second, concerning the definition of artisanal and small-scale fisheries, it defined artisanal fishing as primarily subsistence fishing close to the shore with certain specified engine-size to tonnage ratios and primarily operated by individuals or families, and small-scale fishing includes fisheries operating within 12 nautical miles and to a depth of 20 meters.[522] These should receive S&D treatment.

Third, with an archipelago of over 17,000 islands, it proposed not exempting archipelagic waters from the agreement so as to conserve and protect the archipelagic marine environment and to protect and develop archipelagic waters as a unit.[523]

Fourth, fisheries experts should be explicitly engaged for matters arising under this agreement, e.g. the measuring of adverse effects on fisheries resources.[524]

Subsequently, Indonesia submitted a revised legal draft,[525] using an approach which sought to bring together the "top-down" and "bottom-up" approaches by defining fisheries subsidies as "actionable" with a conditional exception on non-actionable subsidies.[526] It consisted of several major points.

First, the word "prohibited" is used differently in the SCM Agreement and applied only to export subsidies or import substitution subsidies. It is not used as a generic term for a subsidy that is subject to regulations as it is used in fisheries subsidies negotiations.

Second, subsidies which fall within the scope of the exceptions[527] or which are held to be S&D treatment[528] are deemed to be non-actionable.

Third, fisheries subsidies resulting in adverse effects on the interests of other Members as defined in the existing SCM Agreement and in adverse effects on fishery resources outlined in the proposed Annex Article 6 are deemed to be actionable under existing multilateral dispute settlement proceedings or domestic-track countervailing duty proceedings.[529]

Fourth, the concept of "adverse effect to fishery resources"[530] is considered as an alternative, additional condition for applying subsidy remedies, when there is

---

[522] *Ibid.*, para. 6.

[523] *Ibid.*, para. 7.

[524] *Ibid.*, para. 9.

[525] *WTO* Doc. No. TN/RL/GEN/150/Rev.1, "Revised Proposal from the Republic of Indonesia to the Negotiating Group on Rules, Fisheries Subsidies: Proposed New Disciplines" (10 September 2007).

[526] *Ibid.*, para. 4.

[527] *Ibid.*, the proposed Annex [VIII] to the Agreement on Subsidies and Countervailing Measures, Article 3: Exceptions to Actionable Subsidies.

[528] *Ibid.*, the proposed Annex [VIII] to the Agreement on Subsidies and Countervailing Measures, Article 4: Special and Differential Treatment of Developing Country Members.

[529] *Ibid.*, the proposed Annex [VIII] to the Agreement on Subsidies and Countervailing Measures, Article 2: Fishery Subsidies Actionable.

[530] *Ibid.*, the proposed Annex [VIII] to the Agreement on Subsidies and Countervailing Measures, Article 6: Adverse Effects.

"injury" to a fishery sector.[531] Its structure is parallel to that of the existing SCM Agreement on "adverse effects",[532] "serious prejudice"[533] and "injury".[534]

Fifth, regarding technical assistance and fishery expertise, it made it clear that technical assistance to developing country Members should be on mutually agreed terms and conditions,[535] and addressed the role of fishery expertise both in the implementation of new fisheries subsidies regulations and in determining adverse effects on the fishery resource.

B. Submissions on Sub-Categories of Fisheries Subsidies

Besides the overall text-based proposals, there were still some submissions regarding sub-categories of fisheries subsidies in 2006, including subsidies for vessel construction and modification, and subsidies for social security and welfare payments.

1. Subsidies for Vessel Construction and Modification Proposed by Japan

Japan made a substantial contribution to the discussion, particularly through its proposals in 2004[536] as well as the joint proposal co-sponsored by Korea and Taiwan in February 2005.[537] The proposal made by Japan in March 2006 further examined two types of proposed prohibited subsidies from the joint proposal, i.e. subsidies for the "construction of new fishing vessels resulting in capacity enhancement" and for the "fishing vessel modification for capacity enhancement."[538] It defined "capacity enhancement" based on inputs, e.g. fishing capacity, instead of on outputs, e.g. fisheries production. It also applied the combination of four criteria, i.e. number of vessels, individual gross tonnage, volume of fish hold and engine power, to making the new regulations applicable to all types of fisheries and effectively preventing the expansion of fishing capacity while allowing necessary flexibility for policy makers.[539]

Regarding S&D treatment of developing country Members, since they have only a small fisheries industry and the impact on global fisheries resources is very

531 *Ibid.*, paras. 5 and 7.
532 Article 5 of the SCM Agreement.
533 Article 6 of the SCM Agreement.
534 Article 15 of the SCM Agreement.
535 *WTO* Doc. No. TN/RL/GEN/150/Rev.1 (10 September 2007), the proposed Annex [VIII] to the Agreement on Subsidies and Countervailing Measures, Article 4: Special and Differential Treatment of Developing country Members, paras. 4 and 7.
536 *WTO* Doc. No. TN/RL/W/159 (7 June 2004) and *WTO* Doc. No. TN/RL/W/164 (27 September 2004).
537 *WTO* Doc. No. TN/RL/W/172 (22 February 2005).
538 *WTO* Doc. No. TN/RL/W/201 (6 March 2006), para. 4.
539 *Ibid.*, paras. 9-11.

small or negligible, there should be an exemption from the application of prohibited subsidies and a longer transitional period.[540]

2. Subsidies for Social Security and Welfare Payments Proposed by Taiwan

In a paper by Taiwan,[541] it was suggested that the area of social security and welfare payments should be considered as non-actionable fisheries subsidies for socio-economic reasons.[542] These socio-economic considerations were related to the impact of uncontrollable natural forces on the fishing industry, the essential nature of the fishing industry for rural development, the preservation of culture and traditional lifestyles, and the importance of the fishing industry to the economic development of developing countries.[543] It also provided a non-exhaustive list of these types of subsidy, namely subsidies for the relief of natural disasters at sea; subsidies for the off-season; unemployment relief and early retirement fund; and subsidies for fishermen's re-education, re-training or alternative employment assistance.[544] In pursuit of environmental and sustainable fisheries management, it was necessary to consider these subsidies non-actionable in order to balance trade, environment and social security and welfare concerns.

C. Submissions on Special and Differential Treatment

Besides the continuous submissions of textual legal drafts on fisheries subsidies regulations, there was another trend after mid-2007 concerning S&D treatment with more concrete provisions, in particular from the perspective of developing and least-developed country Members.

1. India

In the submission from India on small-scale and artisanal fisheries,[545] S&D treatment of developing countries was addressed. This submission highlighted the importance of and need for S&D treatment regarding small-scale and artisanal fisheries under the new fisheries subsidies regulations, similar to the submissions

---

540 *Ibid.*, paras. 15-16.

541 *WTO* Doc. No. TN/RL/W/202, "Communication from the Separate Customs Territory of Taiwan, Penghu, Kinmen and Matsu to the Negotiating Group on Rules, Fisheries Subsidies for Social Security and Welfare" (6 March 2006).

542 *Ibid.*, para. 2.

543 *Ibid.*, para. 4.

544 *Ibid.*, para. 6.

545 *WTO* Doc. No. TN/RL/W/203, "Submission by India to the Negotiating Group on Rules, Small-scale, Artisanal Fisheries" (6 March 2006).

of other Members.[546] In view of the fact that the words "artisanal", "traditional" and "small-scale" were used interchangeably and in an overlapping manner in several discussions, and that the socio-economic conditions in different countries varied, it was useful to develop general characteristics applying to such category instead of developing a common definition.[547]

2. Argentina

With respect to provisions on S&D treatment under the legal text, Argentina, bearing in mind the development and environment dimensions, addressed its concerns and drafted a detailed regulation.[548] The submissions of Argentina reaffirmed that S&D treatment should grant developing country Member the policy flexibility to develop their national fishing capacity within sustainable limits. They contained the following major points.

First, only providing longer transition periods or establishing statistical criteria cannot accommodate the different needs and priorities of developing country Members. These provisions should be consistent with the priorities of development, poverty reduction and ensuring means of subsistence and improved food security for these Members.[549] Additional flexibility for least-developed countries

---

546 *WTO* Doc. No. TN/RL/W/77 (19 March 2003) of the United States, footnote 1, stating that subsidies to artisanal fisheries is not the intended focus of the new fisheries subsidies regulations; *WTO* Doc. No. TN/RL/GEN/56 (4 July 2005) of Brazil; *WTO* Doc. No. TN/RL/GEN/79 (16 November 2005), Brazil; *WTO* Doc. No. TN/RL/GEN/92 (18 November 2005), *WTO* Doc. No. TN/RL/GEN/57/Rev.2 (13 September 2005) of several small vulnerable coastal States.

547 *WTO* Doc. No. TN/RL/W/203 (6 March 2006), paras. 11-13. The general characteristics of these fisheries should be based on recognition of the following: they are traditional fisheries involving fishing households or small groups of fishworkers; the fishing vessel could vary from gleaning or a one-man canoe to up to 20 m, including trawlers, seiners or long-liners; they use relatively small fishing vessels, which may be non-motorized or use small outboard engines (up to 10 bhp); the fishing is confined to areas close to the shoreline; the use of fishing gear such as beach seine and gill nets, hook and line, and traps; the use of labour-intensive technologies; artisanal fisheries can be both subsistence and commercial, providing for local consumption or export as well. The general characteristics, differing from country to country, are composed of socio-economic and technical elements; therefore, they should be defined in an inclusive manner in order to account for such differences.

548 *WTO* Doc. No. TN/RL/GEN/138, "Paper from Argentina to the Negotiating Group on Rules, Fisheries Subsidies: Special and Differential Treatment" (1 June 2006); *WTO* Doc. No. TN/RL/GEN/138/Rev.1, "Paper from Argentina to the Negotiating Group on Rules, Fisheries Subsidies: Special and Differential Treatment, Revision" (26 January 2007); *WTO* Doc. No. TN/RL/W/211, "Paper from Argentina to the Negotiating Group on Rules, Fisheries Subsidies: Continuation of Work on Special and Differential Treatment" (19 June 2007).

549 *WTO* Doc. No. TN/RL/GEN/138 (1 June 2006), para. 4.

and technical assistance should also be considered under the notification provisions.[550]

Second, these provisions should avoid undue restrictions on developing countries and take into account the international obligations laid down in the UNCLOS and the standards developed in the Code of Conduct. In the earlier submission, it stated that developing country Members should "have" a national fisheries management system "in keeping with the FAO Code of Conduct for Responsible Fisheries" to be allowed to maintain or grant certain fisheries subsidies.[551] In the latter submission, developing country Members should "demonstrate" that they have this system "in line with the FAO Code of Conduct of Responsible Fisheries".[552] The relationship established between the national system and the Code of Conduct would be similar to the technical regulations and "relevant international standards" under the Agreement on Technical Barriers to Trade (TBT Agreement) as well as the sanitary or phytosanitary measures and "international standards, guidelines or recommendations" under the Agreement on the Application of Sanitary and Phytosanitary Measures (SPS Agreement). The national system should be "in harmony with" or "in conformity with" the Code of Conduct, i.e. it must follow the principal guidelines of the Code of Conduct in respect of good fishing practices.[553] If such principles or concepts are removed from the context, it would lead to re-wording or re-interpretation, a task clearly exceeding the specific sphere of WTO competence.[554] A developing country Member should demonstrate that its domestic legislation contains the required elements in line with the Code of Conduct and that it has an adequate system of monitoring, surveillance and penalties to ensure compliance with good fishing practices.[555]

Third, these provisions should be selective and limited in identifying certain subsidies programmes.[556] Developing countries were allowed to resort to programmes of fishing vessel construction and modernization and gear acquisition, and to programmes for supporting the operation of fishing fleets, e.g. supply of

---

550 *Ibid.*, Part IV: Proposed Legal Draft, Article X: Special and Differential Treatment, para. 5.

551 *Ibid.*, Part IV: Proposed Legal Draft, Article X: Special and Differential Treatment, para. 3.

552 *WTO* Doc. No. TN/RL/GEN/138/Rev.1 (26 January 2007), Article X: Special and Differential Treatment, para. 3(c).

553 *WTO* Doc. No. TN/RL/W/211 (19 June 2007), footnote 3, citing *UNEP* Doc., "Sustainability Criteria for Fisheries Subsidies" (2007), at 16, "the Code of Conduct represents a substantial and growing body of international norms of responsible fishing. The Code itself enjoys a breadth of support and an absence of dissent that is rare even for a "voluntary" agreement. Moreover, many of its core elements are replicated in binding international instruments, including UNCLOS, the Fish Stocks Convention and the Compliance Agreement."

554 *Ibid.*, para. 10.

555 *Ibid.*, paras. 11-12.

556 *WTO* Doc. No. TN/RL/GEN/138 (1 June 2006), para. 6.

fuel, bait or ice.[557] Moreover, following Brazil's definition of artisanal fishing,[558] these provisions were based on the idea that artisanal fishing should be unrestricted for developing countries.[559]

Fourth, the access-payment provisions agreed with the right of developing countries to receive payment for access to their fishing grounds or other rights, along with strict requirements on granting countries.[560] Government-to-government payments should not be deemed to be fisheries subsidies.[561]

Fifth, based on this structure, no specific institutional arrangement would be necessary, since the existing dispute settlement mechanism is adequate for verifying that the national decision has been made in accordance with recognized international methods and on the basis of the scientific information available.[562]

Sixth, in the case of migratory stocks, it suggested that the option was to exclude them from S&D treatment, when the intention of subsidizing fisheries to catch migratory stocks was to exploit these species.[563]

3. Brazil

Brazil responded to the call of the Chairman of the Negotiating Group on Rules on S&D treatment through a submission in June 2007 with two major issues.[564]

First, besides being of the opinion that more flexibility should be granted to developing countries, this submission also favoured the approach of a fisheries management system in dealing with limits for S&D treatment. In other words, the flexibility should be granted under the scope of a national fisheries management system in the developing country Member.

---

[557] *WTO* Doc. No. TN/RL/GEN/138 (1 June 2006), Part IV: Proposed Legal Draft, Article X: Special and Differential Treatment, para. 1.

[558] *WTO* Doc. No. TN/RL/GEN/79/Rev.2, "Paper from Brazil to the Negotiating Group on Rules, Possible Disciplines on Fisheries Subsidies, Revision" (21 April 2006), the proposed Annex VIII footnote 3, defining artisanal fisheries as the fishing activities related to the subsistence of the fisherman and his family. Those activities are performed on an in-shore basis with non-automatic net-retriever devices, provided that (a) the activities are carried out on an individual basis, including, but not necessarily, the family members; (b) the basic scope of the activities encompasses both family livelihood and a small profit trade; and (c) there is no major employer-employee relationship in the activities carried out. Artisanal fishing shall also include fishing activities related to traditional fishing communities."

[559] *WTO* Doc. No. TN/RL/GEN/138 (1 June 2006), para. 11, and Part IV: Proposed Legal Draft, Article X: Special and Differential Treatment, para. 1(c).

[560] *Ibid.*, para. 12.

[561] *WTO* Doc. No. TN/RL/GEN/138/Rev.1 (26 January 2007), para. 6.

[562] *WTO* Doc. No. TN/RL/W/211 (19 June 2007), para. 27, especially that the panels or the Appellate Body would not be to determine the existence of a surplus.

[563] *WTO* Doc. No. TN/RL/W/211 (19 June 2007), para. 32.

[564] *WTO* Doc. No. TN/RL/W/212, "Paper from Brazil to the Negotiating Group on Rules, Fisheries Subsidies: "Fisheries Adverse Effects" and "S&D" Treatment" (29 June 2007).

Second, regarding the importance of artisanal and small-scale fisheries to developing countries, it abandoned direct reference to the terms "artisanal" and "small-scale", since there was no consensus on the definitions, and the most appropriate criteria for characterizing "subsistence" and "livelihood" did not seem to be entirely clear to Members.[565] It considered that such criteria should be essentially related to the nature of the activities and how they were performed.[566] This avoided static parameters, such as the length of the vessels proposed by Norway. Non-mechanized artisanal and small-scale fisheries with negligible risk were less likely to harm the sustainability of the fisheries resources, so they could be considered as an exception to the general prohibition.[567]

Furthermore, Brazil and Argentina jointly proposed to use qualitative elements, i.e. certain subsidies could only be maintained or granted if the domestic fishing capacity was "reasonably lower" than necessary to harvest a "sustainable allowable catch".[568]

4. African, Caribbean and Pacific Group

Since many small developing countries had been particularly troubled by the proposal to regulate government financing of access agreements, the African, Caribbean and Pacific (ACP) Group, consisting mainly of small island and coastal States,[569] also addressed its concerns about access payments to developing countries.[570] The UNCLOS provides the legal basis and economic motivation for the

565 *Ibid.*, at 4.

566 *WTO* Doc. No. TN/RL/GEN/79/Rev.4 (13 March 2007), the proposed Annex VIII to the Agreement on Subsidies and Countervailing Measures, Article 4, para. 1(a) and footnote 7, stating that "developing country Members shall be allowed to grant or maintain fisheries subsidies for fishing activities related to the subsistence and livelihood of the fishermen and their families. These activities are performed on an in-shore basis with non-automatic net-retriever devices, provided that (a) the activities are carried out by fishermen, on an individual basis or organized in associations, including, but not necessarily, the family members; (b) the basic scope of the activities encompasses both family livelihood and a small profit trade; and (c) there is no major employer-employee relationship in the activities carried out."

567 *WTO* Doc. No. TN/RL/W/212 (29 June 2007), at 4.

568 *WTO* Doc. No. TN/RL/GEN/151, "Proposal from Argentina and Brazil to the Negotiating Group on Rules, Special and Differential Treatment" (17 September 2007), para. 2; *WTO* Doc. No. TN/RL/GEN/151/Rev.1, "Paper from Argentina and Brazil to the Negotiating Group on Rules, Fisheries Subsidies: Special and Differential Treatment and Fishery Adverse Effects, Revision" (26 November 2007), para. 5 and proposed Article X.2.

569 The ACP Group represents the African, Caribbean and Pacific Group of States, further information available on-line at <www.acpsec.org> (last visited on 25 March 2008).

570 *WTO* Doc. No. TN/RL/W/209, "Communication from the ACP Group to the Negotiating Group on Rules, Access Fees in Fisheries Subsidies Negotiations" (5 June 2007).

negotiation of Fisheries Access Agreements (FAAs)[571] between coastal States and distant water fishing nations (DWFNs) or their fleets.[572] The FAAs may come in two main forms, either government-to-government (whereby the DWFN government purchases fisheries access rights from the coastal State governments) or private-to-government (whereby the private sector of the DWFN purchases those fisheries access rights from the coastal State governments). Only the former falls into the scope of the new fisheries subsidies regulations. The submission of the ACP Group contained the following main points.

First, it stated that, according to the requirements for a subsidy to exist under the SCM Agreement,[573] the transfer of funds from a DWFN government to a coastal State government did not result in a subsidy that was specific to an enterprise or industry, and certainly not to one within the jurisdiction of the DWFN. Hence, this government-to-government transfer was not subject to current disciplines of the SCM Agreement.

Second, it expressed that there is controversy on the second level of transactions which deal with the further transfer of fishing rights from DWFN governments to their private fishing fleets and the possibility of their including a subsidy component, in particular when the DWFN government transfers those access rights to its private fishing fleet for less than the full amount of the access fees paid to the coastal State government.[574] No consensus was reached in the negotiations regarding the fact that what is required under the UNCLOS may be prohibited under the WTO regulations.[575] The ACP Group attached great importance to

---

571 *Ibid.*, para. 1, defining Fisheries Access Agreements (FAAs) as contractual arrangements whereby governments or private fishing fleets pay coastal States for access to fisheries resources within the coastal States' EEZs.

572 *Ibid.*, para. 1, referring to Article 62.4(a) of the UNCLOS, which states that where a coastal State does not have the capacity to harvest its determined entire allowable catch, "it shall, through agreements or other arrangements ... give other States access to the surplus of the allowable catch." These access agreements may be subject to terms and conditions including the "payment of fees and other forms of remuneration," commonly referred to as fishery access payments.

573 Articles 1.1 and 2 of the SCM Agreement.

574 *WTO* Doc. No. TN/RL/W/209 (5 June 2007), para. 3.

575 Several Members addressed the issue of access payments in the negotiations. Brazil proposed that "in case of a government-to-government payment for access by foreign vessels to fishing resources of a developing country's maritime jurisdiction or to quotas or any other rights established by any regional fishery management organization or arrangement (access rights), a fishery subsidy shall be deemed to exist if a benefit is conferred in the onward transfer of those access rights from the paying government" (*WTO* Doc. No. TN/RL/GEN/79/Rev.4 (13 March 2007)). Argentina proposed that a growing consensus that government-to-government payments are not deemed to be fisheries subsidies; however, it is understood that the general disciplines [on fisheries subsidies] should include the instances in which the transfer of such rights by a government to specific enterprises is not done in exchange for a fair trade price (*WTO* Doc. No. TN/RL/GEN/138/Rev.1 (26 January 2007)). However, in contrast, Argentina previously proposed that payments or other financial transfers received in direct or indirect exchange for access by for-

revenues from access payments for their economic development,[576] the indirect and positive impact of access payments on employment generation, value-addition (growth of upstream and downstream activities) and stimulating effects on the development of fishing efforts in these States. It therefore proposed that all transactions relating to fisheries access agreements, including the further transfer of fishing rights, should be excluded from regulations. Bringing any element of fisheries access arrangements into the scope of new regulations would have a bearing on the total amount of fishery access payments made at the government-to-government level.[577]

Third, reconsidering the requirements for a subsidy to exist, access payments result from a series of bilateral negotiations with the DWFNs, and therefore there is no "market" benchmark, which is the logical basis for determining the "financial contribution".[578] In addition, the interpretation of "benefit" under Article 1.1(b) of the SCM Agreement focuses on whether there is a benefit to a recipient rather than a cost to a government. It is difficult to examine the existence of a benefit from the amount paid in access payments from a DWFN government to the coastal State.[579] Therefore, the proposal of the ACP Group reaffirmed that the transactions of fisheries access fees should be exempted from the fisheries subsidies disciplines and the further transfer of DWFN rights should be considered non-prohibited and non-actionable.

---

eign vessels to fishing resources of a developing country's EEZ or any other rights established by a regional fisheries management organization shall be exempt from the prohibition on fisheries subsidies (*WTO* Doc. No. TN/RL/GEN/138 (1 June 2006)). Norway, instead of proposing a textual language, expressed its willingness to consider suggestions that make it necessary for the fishing industry of developed Members to reimburse their governments for the financing of such access agreements (*WTO* Doc. No. TN/RL/GEN/144 (26 January 2007)). The United States also proposed that fisheries subsidies disciplines do not cover government-to-government payments to obtain access for a Member's distant water fishing fleets to fisheries resources within the EEZ of another country. Under certain circumstances, the further transfer of those access rights to the Member's fishing fleet is covered by the proposed fisheries subsidies disciplines but is not prohibited (*WTO* Doc. No. TN/RL/GEN/145 (22 March 2007)).

576 *WTO* Doc. No. TN/RL/W/209 (5 June 2007), para. 8, illustrating that, according to a study commissioned by the International Centre for Trade and Sustainable Development (ICTSD), more than 25 percent of total government revenue is obtained from access fees in several Pacific island countries.

577 *Ibid.*

578 *Ibid.*, para. 9, citing Panel Report, *Canada – Measures Affecting the Export of Civilian Aircraft*, WT/DS70/R, adopted 20 August 1999, para. 9.112. Endorsed in Appellate Body Report, *Canada – Measures Affecting the Export of Civilian Aircraft*, WT/DS70/AB/R, adopted 20 August 1999, paras. 149-161.

579 *Ibid.*, para. 10, interpreting that it is not always easy to distinguish whether the amount paid in "access fees" by a DWFN government to the coastal State represents only the commercial rate for access to those fisheries or also includes a component of development assistance.

The ACP Group, together with India, stated the significance of artisanal and small-scale fishing to developing countries.[580] In line with the need for developing countries both to preserve policy space and to pursue development goals, the co-sponsors urged deeper involvement of the Members in the sufficient S&D provisions.

5. Small Vulnerable Economies

From the perspective of the small, vulnerable economies (SVEs), a bulk of small, vulnerable coastal Members jointly expressed their opinions on the new regulations. Their paper in 2007 contained the following major points.[581]

First, based on the mandates of the Doha Ministerial Declaration and Hong Kong Ministerial Declaration, it considered that these mandates give clear instruction and guidance to negotiations on S&D provisions, reflect the need for S&D treatment to be an integral component of the regulations and recognize that the fisheries sector is important to these Members for socio-economic reasons.[582]

Second, it expressed that S&D treatment is not only an instrument for assisting these Members to implement the emerging rules, but must also allow them the opportunity to take advantage of the natural resources in their maritime space and enhance their level of fishery productivity. SVE Members should also seek to minimize the environmental and ecological impacts.[583]

Third, it stated that due to the inability of these Members to enforce fisheries management regimes and the voluntary Code of Conduct,[584] it is necessary for developed country Members and international organizations to provide technical

[580] *WTO* Doc. No. TN/RL/W/217, "Communication from India and the ACP Group to the Negotiating Group on Rules, Joint Statement on Treatment of Artisanal and Small-scale Fisheries in Fisheries Subsidies Negotiations" (15 February 2008).

[581] *WTO* Doc. No. TN/RL/W/210, "Communication from Barbados, Cuba, Dominican Republic, El Salvador, Fiji, Guyana, Honduras, Mauritius, Nicaragua, Papua New Guinea, and Solomon Islands to the Negotiating Group on Rules, S&DT in the Fisheries Subsidies Negotiations: Views of the Small, Vulnerable Economies (SVEs)" (6 June 2007); *WTO* Doc. No. TN/RL/W/210/Rev.1, "Communication from Antigua and Barbuda, Barbados, Cuba, Dominican Republic, El Salvador, Fiji, Guyana, Honduras, Mauritius, Nicaragua, Papua New Guinea, and Solomon Islands to the Negotiating Group on Rules, S&DT in the Fisheries Subsidies Negotiations: Views of the Small, Vulnerable Economies (SVEs)" (18 June 2007); *WTO* Doc. No. TN/RL/W/210/Rev.2, "Communication from Antigua and Barbuda, Barbados, Cuba, Dominican Republic, El Salvador, Fiji, Guyana, Honduras, Jamaica, Mauritius, Nicaragua, Papua New Guinea, and Solomon Islands to the Negotiating Group on Rules, S&DT in the Fisheries Subsidies Negotiations: Views of the Small, Vulnerable Economies (SVEs)" (22 June 2007).

[582] *WTO* Doc. No. TN/RL/W/210/Rev.2 (22 June 2007), at 1.

[583] *Ibid.*, paras. A (ii)-(iv).

[584] Article 1 of the Code of Conduct states that the Code is voluntary.

and financial assistance to these Members to enhance their management plans and fulfil the environmental criteria.[585]

Fourth, since there was no consensus on the definition and treatment of artisanal and small-scale fisheries, it suggested that any definition based on physical attributes, e.g. the length of the vessels, should recognize the reality of these fisheries in the SVE Members, including the domestic definitions used by SVE Members, which allow a certain level of modernization, e.g. engine horsepower of up to 300hp, and the use of navigation and safety equipment and mechanized fishing gear, as improved technology becomes available.[586] Socio-economic considerations should also be taken into account, including the importance of this sector to employment, food security, poverty reduction and nutrition.[587]

Fifth, it also suggested other areas in the regulations where S&D treatment provisions should apply, namely appropriate flexibility for industrial and semi-industrial fishing for SVEs; a longer period of time to implement the agreement; and greater opportunity for consultation before any DSB cases.[588]

Furthermore, a later submission of these SVEs affirmed that fuel subsidies, usually provided by SVEs to their fishing industries, have negligible or no impact on overcapacity or overfishing and are more affordable and manageable than subsidies to capital costs. Moreover, SVEs are able to monitor and regulate these types of subsidy better than subsidies to capital costs.[589] Considering the impor-

---

585 *WTO* Doc. No. TN/RL/W/210/Rev.2 (22 June 2007), paras. B (ii) and (iii), emphasizing that the Code of Conduct, an appropriate guideline, is a voluntary instrument and should not be simply integrated in a WTO Agreement as a binding discipline.

586 *Ibid.*, para. C (iv).

587 *Ibid.*, para. C (v).

588 *Ibid.*, para. D (i).

589 *WTO* Doc. No. TN/RL/W/226, "Communication from Barbados, Cuba, El Salvador, Fiji, Honduras, Mauritius, Papua New Guinea and Tonga to the Negotiating Group on Rules, Small, Vulnerable Economies (SVEs)-Statement on Key Aspects of Article III of the Fisheries Subsidies Annex" (20 March 2008); *WTO* Doc. No. TN/RL/W/226/Rev.1, "Communication from Barbados, Cuba, Dominican Republic, El Salvador, Fiji, Honduras, Mauritius, Papua New Guinea and Tonga to the Negotiating Group on Rules, Small, Vulnerable Economies (SVEs)-Statement on Key Aspects of Article III of the Fisheries Subsidies Annex" (31 March 2008); *WTO* Doc. No. TN/RL/W/226/Rev.2, "Communication from Barbados, Cuba, Dominican Republic, El Salvador, Fiji, Honduras, Mauritius, Papua New Guinea, St. Vincent & the Grenadines, and Tonga to the Negotiating Group on Rules, Small, Vulnerable Economies (SVEs)-Statement on Key Aspects of Article III of the Fisheries Subsidies Annex" (24 April 2008); *WTO* Doc. No. TN/RL/W/226/Rev.3, "Communication from Barbados, Cuba, Dominican Republic, El Salvador, Fiji, Honduras, Jamaica, Mauritius, Papua New Guinea, St. Vincent & the Grenadines, and Tonga to the Negotiating Group on Rules, Small, Vulnerable Economies (SVEs)-Statement on Key Aspects of Article III of the Fisheries Subsidies Annex" (13 May 2008); *WTO* Doc. No. TN/RL/W/226/Rev.4, "Communication from Barbados, Cuba, Dominican Republic, El Salvador, Fiji, Honduras, Jamaica, Mauritius, Papua New Guinea, St. Lucia, St. Vincent & the Grenadines, and Tonga to the Negotiating Group on Rules, Small, Vulnerable Economies (SVEs)-Statement on

tance of fisheries to their national socio-economic development, the SVEs expected to have more policy flexibility in this respect.

D. Legal Text by the Chairman of the Negotiating Group on Rules

While the Doha Round Negotiations as a whole have been confronted with a series of challenges and delays with continuing divisions among the major players on agriculture and industrial tariffs, the fisheries subsidies talks most likely benefited from the delays in the general negotiations, which allowed continuing formal and informal dialogues on key issues.[590] As a result, the Chairman of the Negotiating Group on Rules, Ambassador Guillermo Valles Games, in late 2007 released the Chairman's draft of proposed WTO rules on fisheries subsidies, anti-dumping and countervailing measures (the Chair's text),[591] which was considered by delegates as a good starting point.[592] The Chair's text represents a substantial advance in the negotiations and a landmark in the efforts of the world community to get global fisheries back on a sustainable path.[593] As negotiators in the faltering Doha Round Negotiations had been focusing on actual drafts only in the areas of agriculture and industrial goods, having the regulations on fisheries subsidies in a text represented a clear step forward. Any agreement on fisheries subsidies is still contingent on the overall results, with agriculture and industrial goods being the major areas of contention.[594]

The Chair's text (Attachment II), on the basis of the bottom-up approach, reflects the core elements, including a list of prohibitions as a backbone of new regulations and general exceptions to these prohibitions,[595] with complementary regulations guarding against circumvention and taking account of the future evo-

Key Aspects of Article III of the Fisheries Subsidies Annex" (19 May 2008); *WTO* Doc. No. TN/RL/W/226/Rev.5, "Communication from Barbados, Cuba, Dominica, Dominican Republic, El Salvador, Fiji, Honduras, Jamaica, Mauritius, Nicaragua, Papua New Guinea, St. Lucia, St. Vincent & the Grenadines, and Tonga to the Negotiating Group on Rules, Small, Vulnerable Economies (SVEs)-Statement on Key Aspects of Article III of the Fisheries Subsidies Annex" (22 September 2008), para. 4.

590 *UNEP*, *supra* note 41, at 5.

591 *WTO* Doc. No. TN/RL/W/213, "Draft Consolidated Chair Texts of the AD and SCM Agreements" (30 November 2007).

592 *International Centre for Trade and Sustainable Development*, "Fisheries Subsidies Text Provides a Good Starting Point, Delegates Say", Bridges Trade BioRes, Vol. 7, No. 22 (18 December 2007).

593 *WTO* Doc. No. TN/RL/W/235, "Communication from Australia, New Zealand and the United States to the Negotiating Group on Rules, Fisheries Subsidies" (21 July 2008), para. 6.

594 *International Centre for Trade and Sustainable Development*, "Draft Texts Facing Delay, as WTO Contemplates End-2008 for Doha Accord", Bridges Weekly Trade News Digest, Vol. 11, No. 40 (21 November 2007).

595 Articles I and II of the proposed Annex VIII of the Chair's text, *WTO* Doc. No. TN/RL/W/213 (30 November 2007).

lution of fisheries subsidies policy and practice.[596] It also covers S&D treatment, giving policy flexibility to developing country Members to meet their development needs, taking into account sustainability criteria, effective measures of transparency and enforcement, and technical assistance for developing country Members, as well as possible roles for the FAO and other organizations.[597] Further details of the Chair's text on fisheries subsidies regulations are analyzed in Chapter 3.

In late 2008, the Chairman of the Negotiating Group on Rules further issued a conceptual "roadmap" for further discussions of fisheries subsidies regulations. The roadmap identifies the key issues that the Negotiating Group on Rules needs to address in order to reconcile participants' different approaches to regulating subsidies which contribute to overcapacity and overfishing and to formulate appropriate and effective S&D provisions that reflect the interests and concerns of developing country Members.[598]

The final decision of the new regulations principally relies on the decisions taken by consensus among all Members.[599] It should also be noted that the WTO negotiations are a "single undertaking", which means results must be achieved in all areas of the negotiations, not only in those regarding fisheries subsidies, and must be applicable to all Members.[600] Although progress has been made concerning fisheries subsidies regulations, the overall result still depends on all areas of the negotiations.

XI. Conclusion

The discussions in the CTE and the negotiations launched after the Doha Ministerial Conference in the Negotiating Group on Rules have significantly advanced the fisheries subsidies issue on the WTO agenda.

The mandates of the Doha Ministerial Declaration have been considered to be a "win-win" outcome for trade liberalization, fisheries conservation and sustainable development, although at an early stage it was doubted whether these mandates required launching negotiations on new regulations specifically for fisheries sub-

[596] Such as Articles I.2 and IV of the proposed Annex VIII of the Chair's text, *WTO* Doc. No. TN/RL/W/213 (30 November 2007).

[597] *WTO* Doc. No. TN/RL/W/235 (21 July 2008), para. 8

[598] *WTO* Doc. No. TN/RL/W/236, "New Draft Consolidated Chair Texts of the AD and SCM Agreements" (19 December 2008).

[599] Article IX of the Agreement Establishing the World Trade Organization.

[600] *Alice L. Mattice*, *supra* note 5, at 586; *WTO* Doc. No. WT/MIN(01)/DEC/1 (20 November 2001), para. 47 of the Doha Ministerial Declaration states that "with the exception of the improvements and clarifications of the Dispute Settlement Understanding, the conduct, conclusion and entry into force of the outcome of the negotiations shall be treated as parts of a single undertaking. However, agreements reached at an early stage may be implemented on a provisional or a definitive basis. Early agreements shall be taken into account in assessing the overall balance of the negotiations."

sidies in the Negotiating Group on Rules.[601] The negotiations in the WTO moved from arguments on whether there was a need to improve fisheries subsidies regulations under the current SCM Agreement to whether a top-down or a bottom-up approach should be adopted and finally to discussions on sub-categories of fisheries subsidies and other technical provisions.

In terms of the structure of fisheries subsidies regulations, the Members supporting different positions could be divided into two groups. Proposed texts by Brazil[602], New Zealand[603] and the United States[604] were based on the top-down approach consisting of broad prohibition of subsidies along with a "negative listing" of permitted subsidies. Proposals from European Communities[605], Norway[606], Japan, Korea and Taiwan[607] supported the bottom-up approach consisting of a "positive list" of prohibited subsidies.

The negotiations culminated with the publication of the legal text proposed by the Chairman of the Negotiating Group on Rules (Chair's text) in November 2007. In the following Chapter we look at how effective the Chair's text is in bringing together the different positions of the Members and to what extent it achieves the directives of the mandates in the Ministerial Declarations.

601 *WTO* Doc. No. TN/RL/W/11 (2 July 2002).
602 *WTO* Doc. No. TN/RL/GEN/79/Rev.4 (13 March 2007).
603 *WTO* Doc. No. TN/RL/GEN/100 (3 March 2006).
604 *WTO* Doc. No. TN/RL/GEN/145 (22 March 2007).
605 *WTO* Doc. No. TN/RL/GEN/134 (24 April 2006).
606 *WTO* Doc. No. TN/RL/GEN/144 (26 January 2007).
607 *WTO* Doc. No. TN/RL/GEN/114/Rev.1 (2 June 2006).

Chapter 3: Analysis of the Proposed Fisheries Subsidies Regulations by the Chairman of the WTO Negotiating Group on Rules

I. Introduction

In Chapter 1, we looked at the current regulations applicable to fisheries subsidies under international law regimes and identified the need for fisheries subsidies reform. In Chapter 2, we followed the relevant negotiations within the WTO to understand the arguments and concerns of the WTO Members which culminated with the legal draft of fisheries subsidies regulations presented by the Chairman of the WTO Negotiating Group on Rules in November 2007 (Chair's text).[608] The proposed regulations represent the outcome of the efforts that the WTO and its Members have made in the Doha Round Negotiations initiated in 2001. The Chair's text (Attachment II) attempts to take into account the necessary elements for achieving the goals of trade liberalization, fisheries conservation and sustainable development in the fisheries sector. In this Chapter, we examine whether the proposed regulations provide an adequate solution for the issues arising from fisheries subsidies.

According to the mandates of the Doha Ministerial Declaration and the Hong Kong Ministerial Declaration, the new regulations on fisheries subsidies should encompass the following elements: (1) clarifying and improving the existing SCM Agreement; (2) enhancing the mutual supportiveness of trade and the environment; (3) prohibiting subsidies which cause overfishing and overcapacity; (4) taking into account the special needs of developing countries; and (5) improving transparency and enforceability. Moreover, they should also solve the major conflicts between the negotiating Members, by including S&D treatment of developing countries, the criteria and benchmarks designed to prevent overfishing and overcapacity, as well as the means to achieve transparency and enforceability.

Moreover, many intergovernmental and non-governmental organizations, e.g. UNEP, WWF,[609] ICTSD[610] and OCEANA,[611] have long cooperated with the WTO

---

[608] The proposed Annex VIII to the SCM Agreement of the Chair's text, *WTO* Doc. No. TN/RL/W/213 (30 November 2007).

[609] The World Wide Fund for Nature or World Wildlife Fund (WWF) was established in 1961. Its mission is to stop the degradation of the planet's natural environment

C.-J. Chen, *Fisheries Subsidies under International Law*, Hamburg Studies on Maritime Affairs 20, DOI 10.1007/978-3-642-15693-9_4, © Springer-Verlag Berlin Heidelberg 2010

on environmental issues, e.g. sustainability criteria in the Chair's text.[612] Some of these organizations have gained observer status and advisory functions assisting in the development of WTO law and international law, and have provided fora for the exchange of information.[613] The extent to which their suggestions and proposals are incorporated into the Chair's text is also investigated.

In addition, the fundamental and structural issues of the Chair's text and its classification of prohibited and non-prohibited fisheries subsidies are examined as well as three major issues raised by developing country Members: S&D treatment, small-scale fisheries and access-related subsidies. The provisions on fisheries management systems which are the prerequisites for granting fisheries subsidies are also evaluated. Moreover, provisions on the interaction with other institutional mechanisms are analyzed and compared with other existing WTO agreements to see if these can ensure more effective implementation of the proposed fisheries subsidies regulations.

II. Structure and Scope of the Chair's Text

A. Adoption of the Bottom-up Approach

In the early stages of WTO negotiations before the Hong Kong Ministerial Conference in 2005, the discussion focused on the structure of fisheries subsidies regulations. The choice was between a top-down approach or a bottom-up approach, based on whether there should be a broad ban on fisheries subsidies or not.

---

and to build a future in which humans live in harmony with nature, by conserving the world's biodiversity, ensuring that the use of renewable natural resources is sustainable and promoting the reduction of pollution and wasteful consumption. See further information available on-line at <www.panda.org>.

610 The International Centre for Trade and Sustainable Development (ICTSD), an independent non-profit and non-governmental organisation, was established in Geneva in September 1996 to contribute to a better understanding of development and environmental concerns in the context of international trade. See further information available on-line at <http://ictsd.org/>.

611 OCEANA, founded in 2001, is the largest non-governmental organization focused solely on ocean conservation. See further information available on-line at <http://na.oceana.org/>.

612 Since 2008, these organizations have formed the informal framework for discussing the fisheries subsidies regulations. This framework has confirmed the interests of diverse stakeholders in achieving WTO rules that make a real contribution to sustainable fisheries.

613 Scholars have long recognized the important role that both intergovernmental and non-intergovernmental organizations play in the international law-making process. *Rüdiger Wolfrum and Nele Matz*, "Conflicts in International Environmental Law" (Berlin: Springer, 2003), at 204-205; *Malgosia Fitzmaurice and Olufemi Elias*, "Contemporary Issues in the Law of Treaties" (Utrecht: Eleven International Publishing, 2005), at 55-67.

After the Hong Kong Ministerial Conference, the focus of the discussion then turned to the sub-categories of fisheries subsidies and the issue of structural approaches was not discussed by the Members. The Chair's proposed regulations basically choose the bottom-up approach. In view of this, the design of sub-categories and the benchmarks set as the preconditions for authorizing fisheries subsidies become important in order to enforce these regulations effectively and to avoid their circumvention.

As the Chair's draft broadly utilizes the existing fisheries data and norms, these fishery-related norms should be read from a perspective of the fisheries instruments, in particular the FAO Code of Conduct, as it covers a broad range of fishing activities and practices. This is consistent with the concept that trade law should "not be read in clinical isolation from international law".[614]

B. The Scope of the Fishing Industry

Although fisheries subsidies are not defined explicitly in the Chair's text, the elements in Article 1 of the SCM Agreement are still required for a subsidy to the fishing industry to exist. Moreover, it is important to determine the scope of the "fishing industry". The Chair's text covers the shipbuilding, catching, landing and processing sectors. However, in order to manage fisheries effectively, the current fisheries regulations at national, regional and global levels tend to cover the activities from the ship to the shop. For example, the Common Fisheries Policy of the European Union covers the conservation, management and exploitation of living aquatic resources, aquaculture, and the processing and marketing of fishery and aquaculture products.[615] Under the Code of Conduct, the fishing industry includes the shipbuilding, catching, landing, processing, marketing, transporting and selling sectors.

614 *WTO* Doc. WT/DS2/AB/R, "Report of the Appellate Body, Appellate Body-United States, Standards for Reformulated and Conventional Gasoline- AB-1996-1" (29 April 1996); *Gabrielle Marceau*, "A Call for Coherence in International Law: Praises for the Prohibition against "Clinical Isolation" in WTO Dispute Settlement", Journal of World Trade, Vol. 33, No. 5, pp. 87-152 (1999) (arguing in favour of incorporating non-WTO law in WTO DSU decisions). Similar view in *Joost Pauwelyn*, "The Role of Public International Law in the WTO: How Far Can We Go?", American Journal of International Law, Vol. 95, pp. 535-578 (2001), at 535; *Michael Lennard*, "Navigating by the Stars: Interpreting the WTO Agreement", Journal of International Economic Law, Vol. 5, pp. 17-89 (2002).

615 Article 1.1 of Council Regulation (EC) No 2371/2002 of 20 December 2002 on the conservation and sustainable exploitation of fisheries resources under the Common Fisheries Policy, OJ L 358, 31.12.2002, pp. 59–80.

C. Chair's Text Limits Fishing Activities to Marine Wild Capture Fishing

The Chair's text applies only to marine wild capture fishing, leaving out some important components of the fisheries industry. Two such components have been noted, including aquaculture and inland fisheries.

Aquaculture is one of the components which have been taken into account in the Code of Conduct.[616] New Zealand proposed to cover aquaculture fisheries,[617] because there can be some overlap in the activities associated with aquaculture and those with marine wild capture fishing, as wild fish may be caught specifically for use as a feedstock for aquaculture and juvenile wild fish may be trapped and then raised in a partly controlled environment.[618] However, during the negotiations, no other Members supported this proposal. As subsidized aquaculture does not directly affect wild fish stocks, the Chair's text excludes aquaculture.

With respect to inland fishing, the overfishing of inland waters has been considered as a neglected crisis. During the negotiations, most Members also intended to exclude inland fishing from the new regulations. Although overfishing leads to numerous changes in inland fish stocks,[619] the threats to freshwater fisheries and associated biodiversity have received little attention. Moreover, there are fish species migrating between inland waters and the sea or ocean, such as anadromous, catadromous and amphidromous fish. Subsidies to inland fisheries may affect trade and the environment in similar ways as subsidies to marine capture fisheries.

D. Actionable or Non-actionable?

The Chair's text provides a list of prohibited fisheries subsidies and general exceptions to these prohibitions,[620] in contrast to the classification under the general

---

616 Article 9 of the Code of Conduct.

617 *WTO* Doc. No. TN/RL/GEN/54 (1 July 2005), at 5.

618 *WTO* Doc. No. TN/RL/W/218, "Communication from New Zealand to the Negotiating Group on Rules, WTO Disciplines on Fisheries Subsidies: Elements of the Chair's Draft" (21 February 2008), para. 7.

619 Examples of the overfishing of inland waters are that several fish species in the Mekong River (Giant Catfish, River Catfish, Giant Carp and the Giant stingray) are endangered, as are Chinese paddlefish and Yangtze sturgeon in the Yangtze River in China, lake sturgeon in the Great Lakes in the United States and Murray cod in the Murray River in Australia. *J. David Allan, Robin Abell, Zeb Hogan, Carmen Revenga, Brad W. Taylor, Robin L. Welcomme, and Kirk Winemiller*, "Overfishing of Inland *Waters*", BioScience, Vol. 55, No. 12, pp. 1041-1051 (2005); *WWF*, "Threat of Over-fishing in the Mekong", available on-line at <www.panda.org/about_our_earth/about_freshwater/freshwater_problems/river_decline/10_rivers_risk/mekong_lancang/mekong_threats> (last visited on 31 July 2009).

620 Articles I and II of the proposed Annex VIII to the SCM Agreement of the Chair's text, *WTO* Doc. No. TN/RL/W/213 (30 November 2007).

subsidies provisions of the SCM Agreement. The subsidies programmes may be classified as prohibited, actionable or non-actionable subsidies under the general provisions. However, if they fall under the scope of fisheries subsidies regulations, they will only be classified as prohibited or non-prohibited. During the negotiations, the idea of actionable fisheries subsidies was supported by some Members, e.g. the United States and New Zealand, Norway and Indonesia.[621] However, the Chair's text does not explicitly address whether subsidies under the provisions of general exceptions and S&D treatment are still actionable or not.

It would be questionable if non-prohibited fisheries subsidies are not actionable. According to the current SCM Agreement, imposing countervailing measures against the subsidized products is one remedy that the importing countries can apply. Taking into consideration the fact that non-prohibited fisheries subsidies can have negative impact on trade, the rights of importing countries to impose countervailing measures should not be denied. In order to maintain the consistency of law application and enforcement, the exceptions to the prohibitions and S&D treatment provided to developing country Members should be deemed actionable.

III. Sub-categorizations of Fisheries Subsidies

A. Prohibited Fisheries Subsidies and Exceptions

Article I of the Chair's text provides a list of prohibited fisheries subsidies, including subsidies to reduce capital costs and operating costs of fishing or service vessels, subsidies the benefits of which are conferred on the transfer of fishing or service vessels to third countries,[622] subsidies for port infrastructure, income support, price support, subsidies for access to foreign countries' waters, subsidies benefiting IUU fishing (Article I.1) and subsidies affecting fish stocks in an unequivocally overfished condition (Article I.2). Most fisheries subsidies with negative impact on trade and the environment are prohibited.

Article II of the Chair's text provides a list of general exceptions to the prohibited fisheries subsidies, such as when the subsidies have the objective of relief from natural disasters (Article I.1 and footnote 77), to comply with safety standards (Article II(a)), to meet the fisheries management requirements (Article II(b)), to permanently reduce personnel, fishing vessels and fishing capacity in the fishing industry (Article II(c) and (d)) to make user-specific allocations (Article

621 *WTO* Doc. No. TN/RL/W/169 (13 December 2004), *WTO* Doc. No. TN/RL/GEN/127 (24 April 2006), *WTO* Doc. No. TN/RL/GEN/145 (22 March 2007) of the United States; *WTO* Doc. No. TN/RL/GEN/141 (6 June 2006) of New Zealand; *WTO* Doc. No. TN/RL/GEN/144 (26 January 2007) of Norway; *WTO* Doc. No. TN/RL/GEN/150/Rev.1 (10 September 2007) of Indonesia.

622 It is because transferring capacity to third countries does not ultimately reduce overall fishing capacity.

II(e)). It takes into account concerns about public policies and subsidies programmes which may reduce fisheries capacity.[623]

In order to ensure the health of fish stocks, minimum criteria for providing the exceptions to prohibited fisheries subsidies are established.[624] The minimum criteria such as effective fisheries management systems (Article V) are the preconditions for the use of permitted fisheries subsidies based on Articles II and III (S&D treatment). Details of these minimum criteria are analyzed later (Chapter 3.V).

However, most subsidies listed in Article II are not intended to support Members' domestic fish production but to contribute to the promotion of sound fisheries practices or to have other beneficial social functions, e.g. safety, not linked to fishing capacity. It is considered that there is no logical link between Articles II and V.[625]

In the following section, we look at the provisions in Articles I and II which need more clarification. Access-related subsidies will be discussed in the section on S&D treatment, since it is more related to the development dimension.

B. Issues with Prohibited Fisheries Subsidies

1. Subsidies to Fisheries Infrastructure

Fisheries infrastructure consists of port, processing and distribution facilities. Subsidies to fisheries infrastructure account for a very high percentage of all subsidies to the fisheries sector and relieve the fishing industry of a substantial cost.[626] In the Chair's text,[627] subsidies in respect of, or in the form of, port infrastructure or other physical port facilities exclusively or predominantly for activities related to marine wild capture fishing, i.e. fish landing facilities, fish storage facilities, and in- or near-port fish processing facilities, should be prohibited. It does not cover subsidies to fish distribution facilities.

Nevertheless, port facilities generally have high capital costs and low marginal operating costs. This provision does not distinguish between these two types of costs which have different short and long-term impacts on trade and the environment. It could be interpreted that this provision intends to prohibit subsidies for all costs of infrastructure.

---

623 However, some of the objectives of these exceptions can also be achieved by other public policies. For instance, to meet the safety standards and the requirements of fisheries management regimes, mandatory rules are the primary measures for achieving these objectives and may be more effective than providing subsidies.

624 Article V of the proposed Annex VIII to the SCM Agreement of the Chair's text, *WTO* Doc. No. TN/RL/W/213 (30 November 2007).

625 *WTO* Doc. No. TN/RL/GEN/159, "Communication from the Republic of Korea and the Separate Customs Territory of Taiwan, Penghu, Kinmen and Matsu, Relation between Article I and Article V of the Chair's Text" (4 June 2008), para. 12.

626 *R. Sumaila and D. Pauly, supra* note 1, at 23.

627 Article I.1(d) of the proposed Annex VIII to the SCM Agreement of the Chair's text, *WTO* Doc. No. TN/RL/W/213 (30 November 2007).

Furthermore, it is important to distinguish between fisheries infrastructure and general infrastructure, since government support to general infrastructure is not a subsidy.[628] Government support to infrastructure with the objective of benefiting the fishing industry is not general infrastructure and may fall under the scope of the new fisheries subsidies regulations.

2. Subsidies Which Support IUU Fishing

In Chapter 1, the issues of IUU fishing and IPOA-IUU were discussed. The IPOA-IUU takes into consideration the fact that fisheries subsidies may lead to IUU fishing.[629] The Chair's text incorporates the definition of IUU fishing from IPOA-IUU,[630] and prohibits subsidizing any vessel engaged in IUU fishing.[631] It further provides that any Members shall be free to bring to the attention of the SCM Committee information from pertinent RFMOs as to any apparent IUU fishing.[632] These provisions are seen as an example of the interaction between the trade and fisheries legal regimes. To determine whether the subsidized vessels are engaged in IUU fishing, the assessment of their compliance with relevant rules of RFMOs would be considered.

3. Subsidies Which Support Fishing of Stocks in "Unequivocally Overfished Condition"

The Chair's text provides that subsidies to any fishing vessel or activity affecting fish stocks that are in an "unequivocally overfished condition" should be prohibited.[633] This has been considered as an essential "environmental backstop."[634] The determination of this condition would depend on the assessment of fish stocks. However, it provides too little guidance in interpreting and determining the term "unequivocally overfished condition." This may need more clarification to avoid misinterpretation.

It is proposed to adopt the norms or terms which are commonly used by fisheries experts. For instance, the FAO classifies fish stocks as overexploited, depleted and recovering (recovering from depletion) stocks, fully exploited stocks, moder-

---

628 Article 1.1(a)(1)(iii) of the SCM Agreement.

629 See *supra* Chapter 1.III.

630 Footnote 81 of the proposed Annex VIII to the SCM Agreement of the Chair's text, *WTO* Doc. No. TN/RL/W/213 (30 November 2007).

631 *Ibid.*, Article I.1(h).

632 *Ibid.*, Article VI.6.

633 *Ibid.*, Article I.2.

634 *WTO* Doc. No. TN/RL/W/128, "Communication from New Zealand to the Negotiating Group on Rules, WTO Disciplines on Fisheries Subsidies: Elements of the Chair's Draft" (21 February 2008).

ately exploited stocks and underexploited stocks, depending on the rate of exploitation of fish stocks.[635]

Moreover, it should also take into account the technical distinction between the terms "overfishing" and "overfished." The former refers to an unsustainable catch rate and the latter to the depleted biomass of a stock.[636] From the perspective of managing fisheries using a precautionary approach, the term "overfishing" seems more appropriate than the term "overfished" in this provision.

C. Issues with General Exceptions to Prohibited Fisheries Subsidies

1. Provision for Vessel Decommissioning Programmes

Many major fishing States have used vessel decommissioning over the past three decades in order to reduce overcapacity in their fishing fleets.[637] Under ideal circumstances, programmes to reduce capacity by retiring vessels or licenses could make a major contribution to capacity reduction worldwide. Nonetheless, this has proved difficult in practice. Subsidies for vessel decommissioning programmes present two major problems: the fact that the decommissioning subsidies tend to be used to replace the decommissioned vessels with newer vessels, which could have more capacity; and a moral hazard problem where incentives are built into such programmes in such a way that the industry will always expect to be bailed out.[638] Hence, effective safeguards need to be in place when designing decommissioning or license retirement programmes in order to avoid altered incentives to enter the industry or to invest in modernization or the purchase of new vessels.

In the Chair's text, subsidies for vessel decommissioning are considered as the exception to the prohibited fisheries subsidies contingent on certain conditions[639]: that (1) the vessels concerned are scrapped or permanently and effectively prevented from being used for fishing anywhere in the world; (2) the fish harvesting rights associated with such vessels are permanently revoked and may not be reassigned; (3) the owners of such vessels and the holders of such fish harvesting rights are required to relinquish any claim associated with such vessels and rights; and (4) the fisheries management system in place includes management control measures and enforcement mechanisms designed to prevent overfishing in the

---

[635] It is based on the rate of exploitation which the resource stock is drawn below or above the size that would support the long term maximum potential yield of the fishery.

[636] *WTO* Doc. No. TN/RL/W/218 (21 February 2008), para. 13.

[637] Such as Canada, Korea, Spain, Taiwan, the United Kingdom and the United States.

[638] *UNEP*, "Meeting Report, UNEP Informal Expert Consultation on Fisheries Subsidies, 16th July 2003, Geneva" (Geneva: UNEP, 2003), at 4.

[639] Article II(d) of the proposed Annex VIII to the SCM Agreement of the Chair's text, *WTO* Doc. No. TN/RL/W/213 (30 November 2007).

targeted fishery.[640] The provision limits itself to preventing overfishing in the "targeted fishery" only.

2. Provision for Governments' Allocations of Fishing Rights

The Chair's text lays down that it is not prohibited for governments to make user-specific allocations to individuals and groups under limited access privileges and other exclusive quota programmes.[641] The term "user-specific allocations to individuals and groups" should be distinguished from the requirement of "specificity" under Article 2 of the SCM Agreement. Allocation refers both to a share and the process of sharing.[642] It is a part of fisheries management measures, and, therefore, not prohibited.

D. Subsidies to Research and Development and Fisheries Management Services?

A large portion of government support is for research and development (R&D), management and enforcement.[643] Under international fisheries instruments, governments should take measures to conduct fisheries research, management and enforcement.[644] These government interventions may be considered as subsidies. During the negotiations, Members proposed not to prohibit this type of subsidy.[645] However, the Chair's text does not determine whether these constitute subsidies and whether these should be prohibited.

---

640 During the negotiations, other stricter contingent conditions were also suggested, such as (1) preventing enterprises or individuals receiving decommissioning subsidies from investing in other fishing vessels or rights; (2) requiring that decommissioning subsidies lead to demonstrable capacity reductions; (3) using burden shifting devices; and (4) establishing time limits to the decommissioning programme. *WTO* Doc. No. TN/RL/W/218 (21 February 2008), para.16.

641 Article II(e) of the proposed Annex VIII to the SCM Agreement of the Chair's text, *WTO* Doc. No. TN/RL/W/213 (30 November 2007).

642 *FAO* Fisheries Glossary, *supra* note 45. Allocations are (1) a share, a portion, of the allowable catch, effort or area attributed to individuals or groups; and (2) the process of distributing shares or rights among selected recipients, based on historical, cultural or socio-economic criteria.

643 OECD Member countries, for instance, spend one-third of their government financial transfers on fisheries management services in order to ensure sustainable fish stocks and protect the aquatic ecosystem. These management services usually comprise three functions, which are administering the existing management system, adjusting management settings within this system and recommending amendments or additions to this system. *Ola Flaaten and Paul Wallis*, *supra* note 17.

644 E.g. Articles 6, 7, 8 and 12 of the Code of Conduct.

645 E.g. *WTO* Doc. No. TN/RL/GEN/70 (14 October 2005); *WTO* Doc. No. TN/RL/W/196 (22 November 2005); *WTO* Doc. No. TN/RL/GEN/114 (21 April 2006).

There are also some technical obstacles to regulating these subsidies, since it is difficult to put an amount on the value of these services. Governments providing a factor input at below the market price may constitute a subsidy. Nonetheless, there is no "market" for fisheries management services and R&D and the comparison between the market price and the cost of these government interventions is not available. The determination of the existence of subsidies is therefore difficult.

There is still an urgent need to regulate these government interventions, since they can still lead to a certain amount of trade distortion and, in addition, proper regulations can also avoid circumvention.[646] Even though these interventions have not been proven as environmentally harmful, charging the fishing industries that get the benefits from these services may further improve the overall efficiency of management.[647]

It may be difficult and also inappropriate to completely prohibit subsidies to R&D and management services. Therefore, the approach to this dilemma is to allow only the governments which operate robust fisheries management systems to provide subsidies to R&D and management services. Considering their impact on trade, these subsidies should remain actionable.

IV. Considerations for Developing Country Members

A. The Importance of Fisheries to Developing Countries

Fisheries play a fundamental environmental, social and developmental role in developing countries. Fisheries can provide livelihood and employment, increase export earnings, ensure food security, contribute social integration and advancement, and support the multi-functionality of coastal areas of developing countries. Around 30 million people derive their income directly from fishing activities and about 95 percent of that employment is located in the developing world. These countries are responsible for about half of total world exports of fish.[648] With respect to this development dimension, the IPOA-Capacity recognizes the importance of fisheries to developing countries and the need to enhance their ability to develop their own fisheries.[649] It also encourages States to support not only the transfer of scientific and technical information on relevant issues but also pertinent

646 Permitting subsidies for R&D without a certain degree of regulations may open a loophole, as is the case of the research exception to the moratorium on a whaling ban, which is abused by Japan.

647 *FAO*, *supra* note 34, at 94.

648 Developing countries accounted for forty-nine percent of world fishery commodities exported in 2002, up from forty-six percent in 1992. *Stephania Vannuccini*, "Overview of Fish Production, Utilization, Consumption, & Trade" (Rome: FAO, 2004), at 2.

649 Para. 10 of the IPOA-Capacity, also stating that the implementation of the IPOA-Capacity should be based on the Code of Conduct, in particular Article 5, which provides for the special requirements of developing countries.

assistance, training, institutional strengthening, finance, technology, etc., to developing countries.[650]

When regulating fisheries subsidies, the issues associated with developing countries should be taken into account, in particular with regard to the S&D provisions, small-scale fisheries and fisheries access payments from developed countries to developing countries. These factors are reviewed in the following section.

B. Concerns with Special and Differential Treatment Provisions

1. General Concepts of Special and Differential Treatment

The S&D provisions are based on the concept of sustainable development in the WTO. The achievement of sustainable development is not an exception to WTO rules, but rather a fundamental and institutional objective of the multilateral trading system which takes into account the different situations and needs of developing country Members.[651] The WTO's constitutional legal instrument, the Marrakesh Agreement establishing the World Trade Organization (WTO Agreement), and other subsequent WTO legal instruments also emphasize the concern for sustainable development which is part of the Preamble to the WTO Agreement.[652]

A set of multilateral trade rules, the 145 S&D provisions in all WTO agreements,[653] have been crafted to meet these concepts. On the basis of these pro-

---

[650] Paras. 42 and 43 of the IPOA-Capacity.

[651] *UNEP*, "Promoting Development and Sustainability in Fisheries Subsidies Disciplines: An Informal Dialogue on Select Technical Issues, International Environment House, Geneva, 30 June 2005, Chair's Summary" (Geneva: UNEP, 2005), para. 7; *WTO* Doc. No. TN/RL/W/184, "Communication from New Zealand to the Negotiating Group on Rules, Promoting Development and Sustainability in Fisheries Subsidies Disciplines: an Informal Dialogue on Select Technical Issues" (18 July 2005), para. 7.

[652] *WTO* Doc. No. WT/DS58/AB/R, "WTO Appellate Body, United States–Import Prohibition of Certain Shrimp and Shrimp Products (AB-1998-4)" (12 October 1998), para. 129, acknowledging and recognizing the objective of sustainable development in the Preamble to the WTO Agreement. Although statements contained in the preamble to an international instrument are usually considered as not having any binding effect on States which are parties to the instrument, Article 31(2) of the 1969 Vienna Convention on the Law of Treaties states that the preamble constitutes part of the context in which the terms of the international instrument are to be read and interpreted.

[653] The 145 S&D provisions can be classified into six types, including (i) provisions aimed at increasing the trade opportunities of developing country Members; (ii) provisions under which WTO Members should safeguard the interests of developing country Members; (iii) flexibility of commitments, and of action, and the use of policy instruments; (iv) transitional time periods; (v) technical assistance; and (vi) provisions relating to least-developed country Members. *WTO* Doc. No. WT/COMTD/W/77/Rev.1, "Implementation of Special and Differential Treatment Provisions in WTO Agreement and Decisions" (21 September 2001), para. 3.

visions, developing country Members should be able to meet their development needs and to safeguard their policy space and options for adopting and implementing trade, economic and development policies.

However, the ineffectiveness of current S&D provisions has attracted the attention of developing country Members. These Members consider that they hardly benefit from these provisions and that the focus of current S&D treatment has shifted from addressing the problem of promoting economic development to assisting developing country Members to implement their multilateral trade commitments more effectively.[654]

2. Specific Concepts of Special and Differential Treatment in Fisheries Subsidies Negotiations and Regulations

Because of the strategic importance of the fisheries sector to developing country Members, the issues of sustainable development and S&D provisions have become extraordinarily important in fisheries subsidies negotiations and regulations. Current negotiations of S&D provisions in the context of fisheries subsidies regulations have been more effective, as they have been kept separate from broader systemic efforts at S&D reform and considered "parallel" to the fisheries subsidies negotiations.[655] This signals a clear departure from the standard "rule first, exceptions later" approach.[656] Therefore, policy space and flexibility are provided to developing country Members and meet the requirements they proposed during the negotiations.[657]

---

654 There are also concerns that the S&D provisions are not legally enforceable and that there is no mechanism to ensure effective implementation. These are more related to the general reform of S&D provisions under the WTO framework. *WTO* Doc. No. WT/GC/W/442, "Proposal for a Framework Agreement on Special and Differential Treatment, Communication from Cuba, Dominican Republic, Honduras, India, Indonesia, Kenya, Malaysia, Pakistan, Sri Lanka, Tanzania, Uganda and Zimbabwe" (19 September 2001), paras. 7 and 9.

655 *UNEP*, *supra* note 651, paras. 7 and 12(a); *WTO* Doc. No. TN/RL/W/184 (18 July 2005), paras. 7 and 12(a).

656 *WWF*, "Fishing Subsidies: Issues for ACP Countries" (Washington, D.C. and Gland: WWF, 2005), at 2.

657 The developing country Members have also specifically proposed the following illustrative, non-exhaustive list of instruments under S&D provisions: subsidies for infrastructure development, the prevention and control of disease, scientific research and training, and the retraining of fishermen (*WTO* Doc. No. TN/RL/W/9 (20 June 2002), para. 3.; *WTO* Doc. No. TN/RL/GEN/57/Rev.2 (13 September 2005), para. 16 (iv)); subsidies or fiscal incentives for domestication and fisheries development (*WTO* Doc. No. TN/R/W/136 (14 July 2003); *WTO* Doc. No. TN/RL/GEN/57/Rev.2 (13 September 2005)); support for the development of small-scale fisheries, provided that the fisheries resources accessible to small-scale fishermen are not threatened by the fishing activity (*WTO* Doc. No. TN/RL/GEN/57/Rev.2 (13 September 2005), para. 16 (ii)); payments received from other governments for fisheries access to the EEZ of the developing countries (*WTO*

Giving policy space and flexibility in fisheries subsidies regulations to developing country Members attracted the attention of the participants in an informal workshop in 2005 sponsored by UNEP. The preparatory paper for this workshop analyzes the concepts of policy space and flexibility in fisheries subsidies regulations from the following perspectives.[658]

From the perspective of market access, the regulations should be designed to enable developing country Members to take advantage of possible increased market-access opportunities in fish trade while at the same time ensuring that their fisheries are managed in a sustainable manner. This would be particularly important for the Members who have not yet developed their fishing industry to a level commensurate with their economic needs.

From the perspective of sustainable development, the regulations should be designed to support fishing activities with a view to promoting sustainable development-oriented policy objectives, such as poverty alleviation, the promotion of food security, the sustainable utilization of resources, the organization of small-scale fishermen in cooperatives, the improvement of processing and distribution infrastructures, etc.

From the perspective of fisheries conservation and management, the regulations should be designed to conserve, manage and develop the fisheries resources in the waters of developing country Members and on the high seas. This could include measures which may limit access to specified fish stocks by fishermen, which impose certain landing, administrative, technical or other requirements on fishermen, and which are against IUU. They also include positive measures that WTO Members should provide, in a permanent, sustainable and adequate manner, technical cooperation and financial assistance to developing country Members seeking

Doc. No. TN/RL/W/176 (31 March 2005), para. 24(i)(2); *WTO* Doc. No. TN/R/W/136 (14 July 2003), at 3) or to its quotas or any other quantitative limits established by a RFMO (*WTO* Doc. No. TN/RL/GEN/79 (16 November 2005), para. 5.1(c)); development assistance to developing coastal states (*WTO* Doc. No. TN/RL/GEN/57 (7 July 2005); *WTO* Doc. No. TN/RL/GEN/57/Rev.2 (13 September 2005)); assistance to disadvantaged regions within the territory of a developing country pursuant to a general framework of regional development in the sense of Article 8.2(b) of the SCM Agreement (*WTO* Doc. No. TN/RL/W/176 (31 March 2005), para. 24(i)(3); *WTO* Doc. No. TN/RL/GEN/79 (16 November 2005), para. 5.1 (ii)(d)); emergency relief and adjustment to small-scale fishermen suffering significant loss of income as a result of reductions in fishing caused by conservation measures or unforeseeable natural disasters (*WTO* Doc. No. TN/RL/GEN/79 (16 November 2005), para. 21(ii)(b)); subsidies which increase fishing capacity or effort (*WTO* Doc. No. TN/RL/GEN/79 (16 November 2005)); and fuel, bait or ice supplied for fishing activities (*WTO* Doc. No. TN/RL/W/176 (31 March 2005); *WTO* Doc. No. TN/RL/GEN/56 (4 July 2005); *WTO* Doc. No. TN/RL/GEN/79 (16 November 2005)).

658 *Vincente Paolo B. Yu III and Darlan Fonseca-Marti*, "Reflecting Sustainable Development and Special and Differential Treatment for Developing Countries in the Context of New WTO Fisheries Subsidies Rules: An Issue and Options Paper" (Geneva: UNEP, 2005), at 18.

to put in place regimes of effective and sustainable fisheries conservation and management within their waters.

Moreover, providing policy space and flexibility should not create a "*carte blanche*". Minimum criteria in the S&D provisions should be included to avoid distorting trade liberalization and to prevent developing country Members from causing overcapacity or overfishing through their subsidies programmes.

3. Incorporating the Development Dimension into New Regulations

Since the WTO already has the experience of Article 27 of the SCM Agreement and other S&D provisions in other WTO agreements and of dealing with the discussion of general S&D reform, translating these concepts into the fisheries subsidies regulations needs to take into account the issues described in the following sections, i.e. how to incorporate them into the structure of new regulations and how to involve them in different technical provisions.

a. Structural Provisions

Several options have been discussed in the preparatory paper of the UNEP workshop as follows.[659] They are neither mutually exclusive nor exhaustive, so a combination of these options can be envisaged.

First, it should be possible to determine exactly what kind of fisheries-related government transfers relevant to developing country Members would fall into the existing definition of "subsidy."[660]

Second, another option is through the establishment of a prior authorization requirement for qualifying programmes. A developing country Member should seek prior approval from the SCM Committee before actually implementing the programmes. A set of minimum requirements that a requesting Member has to meet should be established.

Third, another option would be a positive and exhaustive list of subsidies that developing country Members would be authorized to apply. The policy objectives of these subsidies should be taken into account when drafting the list. This option is easier to implement and manage, but it would result in a considerable negotiating burden on developing country Members.

Fourth, another option is to adopt a "*de minimis*" amount of support within which developing country Members can freely maintain fisheries subsidies programmes. Setting a level of aggregate amount of support can help to minimize the negative impact on trade and the environment when providing policy spaces and flexibility to developing country Members.

---

659 *Ibid.*, at 21-27.

660 For instance, developing country Members suggested that several types of programmes should not be defined as subsidies, e.g. government-to-government access payments (*WTO* Doc. No. TN/R/W/136 (14 July 2003)) and public investment in fishery infrastructure (*WTO* Doc. No. TN/RL/GEN/57 (7 July 2005)).

Fifth, WTO Members can also consider crafting a list of minimum criteria or conditions for qualifying programmes that would have to be met by developing country Members to access S&D-related flexibility.

b. Technical Provisions

Technical provisions are essential for forming a complete set of S&D provisions and for maintaining the interests of developing country Members under these provisions. Based on the functions and types of the existing S&D provisions in all WTO agreements,[661] the technical provisions of S&D treatment in fisheries subsidies regulations can be identified as follows:[662]

First, technical assistance and capacity building are essential for creating and utilizing reliable scientific information and for effectively implementing the regulations. In the fisheries regime, the Code of Conduct recognizes the special requirements for developing countries by providing them with financial and technical assistance to implement the Code of Conduct.[663] Within the WTO framework, although the existing SCM Agreement does not contain any provision on technical assistance, S&D provisions under other WTO agreements do.[664] Developing country Members should be provided with substantial, long-term and effective technical and financial assistance for the development and implementation of these fisheries subsidies regulations, in particular to meet the requirements for providing fisheries subsidies under the S&D provisions.

Second, a transition mechanism, e.g. time extensions, to allow developing country Members to gradually move out of S&D treatment towards assuming and implementing more stringent regulations is fundamental to the WTO agreements.[665] This flexibility of arrangement allows the conclusion of a number of

---

661 *WTO* Doc. No. WT/COMTD/W/77/Rev.1 (21 September 2001).

662 *Vincente Paolo B. Yu III and Darlan Fonseca-Marti*, *supra* note 658, at 28-29.

663 Article 5 of the Code of Conduct.

664 See *inter alia* Article 9.1 of the SPS Agreement; Articles 11 and 12 of the TBT Agreement; Article 20.3 of the Implementation of GATT Article VII; Article 67 of the TRIPS Agreement; Article 27.2 of DSU. These articles refer to the desirability of developed country Members and international institutions to provide technical assistance to developing and least developed country Members. The main objective of such assistance is the strengthening of their institutional capacity in a way which would enable them to meet the obligations they have assumed under the WTO agreements. In most cases, the relevant articles call for the assistance to be provided upon request by the developing or least-developed country Members and on terms and conditions appropriate to the countries involved. *Constantine Michalopoulos*, "The Role of Special and Differential Treatment for Developing Countries in GATT and the World Trade Organization" (Washington D.C., World Bank, 2004), at 17.

665 The transition mechanism is important and takes place in various forms. For example, the SCM Agreement and the Agreement on Agriculture permit developing country Members to continue to subsidize exports for a period of time in a variety of ways prohibited for other Members. The TRIPS Agreement allows developing country Members to implement their commitments for a transition period of 5 years. The Agreement on Trade-Related Investment Measures (TRIMs) allows de-

agreements on a multilateral basis, as happened in the Uruguay Round Negotiations.[666] Whereas the existing SCM provisions offering transition periods stipulate a specific timeframe,[667] a new S&D transition period for fisheries subsidies regulations could be based on certain criteria to determine exactly when the transition period ends. Minimum criteria could include, *inter alia*: reaching an agreed level of economic development or reaching a state of fisheries resources beyond which further extraction would lead to overexploitation. It can solve the problem of the transition periods, i.e. how much time is enough.[668] It can also avoid the problem that a number of transition periods in other WTO agreements have expired with no option for extension.

Third, the development dimension is not necessarily appropriate and should not be applied to all developing country Members equally. Different levels of development achieved by Members require different sets of policies or obligations to achieve economic growth. The SCM Agreement also provides different treatment of developing country Members and least-developed country Members.[669] In the case of fisheries subsidies, it has been proposed to differentiate between developing country Members with different levels of fisheries economies.[670] Developing country Members with major fishing industries cannot be put into the same category as a small island State concerning the possible impacts of fisheries subsidies programmes. The absolute scale of fishing conducted by a country is a relevant consideration, independent of its development level. Therefore, a simple list or a neutral formula that looks at the state of fishing development rather than the overall development level can be useful in achieving the necessary results.

In addition, the dispute settlement mechanism[671], as well as the imposition of countervailing measures should respect the policy space and flexibility given to developing country Members.[672] Also, to reduce the burden for developing country Members, the data and information that they should report to fulfil the notification requirements could also be simplified. It is important that the benefits of providing fisheries subsidies to developing country Members authorized under S&D provisions do not go to waste.

---

veloping country Members the flexibility to implement the TRIMs Agreement temporarily in conjunction with Article XVIII: B and C.

666 *Constantine Michalopoulos*, *supra* note 664, at 21.

667 Articles 27.2(b), 27.3, 27.4, 27.5, 27.6, 27.11 and 27.14 of the SCM Agreement.

668 *Alexander Keck and Patrick Low*, "Special and Differential Treatment in the WTO: Why, When and How?" (Geneva: WTO, 2004), at 23.

669 Article 27.2 of the SCM Agreement.

670 *WWF*, *supra* note 656, at 4.

671 This may relate to general DSU reform. Further understandings see *William J. Davey*, "Reforming WTO Dispute Settlement" (Illinois Public Law and Legal Theory Research Paper Series, Research Paper No. 04-01, January 29, 2004).

672 For example, Articles 27.10 and 27.15 of the SCM Agreement provide different requirements and procedures for imposing countervailing duties against subsidized products from developing country Members in favour of these Members.

4. Analysis of Special and Differential Treatment Provisions

a. General Structure

With a view to incorporating the development dimension in the new regulations, the Chair's text envisages several of the above-mentioned structural provisions. For example, government-to-government access fees and investment in general infrastructure are exempted from the scope of these regulations (Footnote 80 and Article I.1(d)). It also provides a positive and exhaustive list of subsidies that developing country Members would be authorized to apply (Article III). The fisheries management system of the subsidizing developing country Members are subject to peer review prior to the granting of the subsidy (Article V.1). Each Member should also notify to the SCM Committee in advance of its implementation of any measure for which that Member invokes the provisions of Article III.2 (Article VI.1).

b. Treating Least-Developed and Developing Country Members Differently

The Chair's text provides least-developed and developing country Members with different opportunities for development.

It does not forbid least-developed country Members to provide fisheries subsidies which are prohibited under Article I of the Chair's text (Article III.1). However, this provision is not based specifically on the different levels of fisheries economies of developing countries, but a more general foundation is used to distinguish these countries.

It also provides certain policy space and flexibility for developing country Members. If a developing country Member operates a fisheries management system, three categories of fishing vessels can benefit from these provisions: inshore fishing vessels; decked vessels not longer than ten meters or undecked vessels of any length; and fishing vessels that are used exclusively for specific target stocks within their EEZs.[673] These Members are allowed to give all subsidies which are prohibited under Article I of the Chair's text to their inshore fishing vessels (Article III.2(a)). They can grant subsidies to fisheries infrastructure, income support and price support (Article III.2(b)(1)). They can also grant subsidies to capital and operating costs for their decked vessels not longer than ten meters or undecked vessels (Article III.2(b)(2)). They can also grant subsidies to capital costs to their decked vessels longer than ten meters, provided that these vessels are used exclusively within their EEZs and subject to other contingencies (Article III.2(b)(3)).

---

[673] *WTO* Doc. No. TN/RL/GEN/155, "Submission by India and Indonesia to the Negotiating Group on Rules, Need for Effective Special and Differential Treatment for Developing Country Members in the Proposed Fisheries Subsidies Text" (22 April 2008); *WTO* Doc. No. TN/RL/GEN/155/Rev.1, "Submission by India, Indonesia and China to the Negotiating Group on Rules, Need for Effective Special and Differential Treatment for Developing Country Members in the Proposed Fisheries Subsidies Text" (19 May 2008), at 8.

Access-related subsidies are not prohibited if they are provided to the fisheries which are within the EEZ of a developing country Member (Article III.3). The next sections (Chapter 3.IV.C and D) deal with the S&D provisions on the sub-categories of fisheries subsidies that developing country Members can provide, including small-scale fisheries and access-related subsidies.

c. Preconditions for Special and Differential Treatment

S&D treatment should be granted only when a fisheries management system with regular science-based stock assessment and capacity and effort management measures is in place within the jurisdiction of the subsidizing Member. This requirement is helpful in avoiding negative effects when providing policy space and flexibility to developing country Members.

Concerning the ability of developing country Members to enforce fisheries management regimes effectively, different obligations to meet these criteria have been taken into account. The Chair's text proposes that developing country Members should be free to meet regional management standards, rather than use a national basis.[674] In this case, the developing country Members, especially small, vulnerable economies (SVEs), can enforce effective fisheries management systems with the assistance of relevant regional organizations.

More details about the requirements of fisheries management systems are discussed in the next Section (Chapter 3.V).

C. Other Technical Provisions

The inability to enforce fisheries management cannot be an excuse for avoiding fisheries management for developing country Members; instead, it highlights the fact that more technical assistance should be provided to these Members.[675] The Chair's text states that Members shall establish a mechanism for and facilitate the provision of technical assistance bilaterally and/or through the appropriate international organizations.[676] This provision is a good starting point for technical assistance to developing country Members.[677]

---

674 Footnote 84 of the proposed Annex VIII to the SCM Agreement of the Chair's text, *WTO* Doc. No. TN/RL/W/213 (30 November 2007).

675 *WTO* Doc. No. TN/RL/W/234, "Communication from Argentina, Chile, Colombia, Ecuador, Mexico and Peru, Statement on the Negotiations on Fisheries Subsidies" (17 July 2008), para. 13; *WTO* Doc. No. TN/RL/W/218 (21 February 2008), paras. 21 and 22.

676 Article III.4 of the proposed Annex VIII to the SCM Agreement of the Chair's text, *WTO* Doc. No. TN/RL/W/213 (30 November 2007).

677 However, some developing country Members still considered that a more effective and operational structure is still required and that this provision needs to state more precisely the method of providing technical assistance and the need for effective and timely assistance to be provided to these Members in complying with the new requirements. They also suggested establishing a sub-committee under the SCM

Similar provisions also exist in the TBT Agreement.[678] The TBT Agreement requires Members to provide technical assistance and includes the possibility of it being provided multilaterally. Although the limitation of the TBT Committee's role is not required in the TBT provisions, it is considered that the TBT Committee could and should be involved more directly in granting technical assistance.[679] However, the TBT Committee decided that technical assistance should continue to be provided on a bilateral basis between Members.[680] The Chair's text uses this experience and provides technical assistance on a bilateral basis and further refers to efforts through international organizations.

The Chair's text also requires more responsibilities from Members to provide technical assistance than the SPS Agreement does. The SPS Agreement does not establish a legally binding obligation to provide assistance and simply states that Members "agree to facilitate" the provision of technical assistance to other Members.[681] Members "may" decide to provide assistance based on their morality.[682]

However, the Chair's text does not require the developing country Members to phase out the subsidies provided under the S&D provisions. Given that the existing SCM Agreement requires developing country Members to phase out export subsidies "in a positive manner" over a certain period of time,[683] the Chair's text does not use this principle in the existing SCM Agreement.

D. Concerns with the Provisions for Small-scale Fisheries

1. The Nature of Small-scale Fisheries

The sectoral importance of small-scale fisheries and artisanal fisheries[684] is significant for developing countries in various aspects, e.g. poverty alleviation, food

---

Committee to deal with issues on technical assistance and support programmes, in particular fisheries management systems and measures, and to coordinate the requests from developing country Members as well as monitor subsequent enforcement. *WTO* Doc. No. TN/RL/GEN/158, "Communication from the ACP and SVEs Groups to the Negotiating Group on Rules, Drafting Proposal on Issues Relating to Article III.4 ("Special and Differential Treatment of Developing Country Members") of the Fisheries Subsidies Annex to the SCM Agreement as Proposed by the Chair in TN/RL/W/213" (22 May 2008), paras. 4-5.

678 Article 11 of the TBT Agreement.

679 *Markus Krajewski*, "Article 11 TBT", in *Rüdiger Wolfrum, Peter-Tobias Stoll and Anja Seibert-Fohr* (eds), "WTO-Technical Barriers and SPS Measures", pp. 315-326 (Leiden: Martinus Nijhoff Publishers, 2007), at 322-323.

680 *WTO* Doc. No. G/TBT/W/26, "Technical Assistance" (14 May 1996), para. 1.

681 Article 9.1 of the SPS Agreement.

682 *Anja Seibert-Fohr*, "Article 9 SPS", in *Rüdiger Wolfrum, Peter-Tobias Stoll and Anja Seibert-Fohr* (eds), *supra* note 679, pp. 495-502, at 497.

683 Article 27.4 of the SCM Agreement.

684 Small-scale fisheries and artisanal fisheries are used synonymously in most publications. They are also used interchangeably in this study.

security, employment, community and social development, income and preservation of fishing cultures and lifestyles.[685] The Code of Conduct provides the legal basis for these fisheries. It specifically refers to the importance of these fisheries as providers of food, employment and income.[686] These fisheries should not be marginalized and their contribution to national economies and food security is recognized and valued.

The small-scale fisheries and artisanal fisheries are relative terms and encompass a wide variety of fishery types. It is better to describe this sector based on the range of characteristics instead of formulating a universally applicable definition for a sector as dynamic and diverse as small-scale fisheries and artisanal fisheries.[687]

Small-scale fisheries are from English origin with a technological foundation, while artisanal fisheries are from Latin origin with a socio-economic foundation. These terms imply the use of relatively small-scale fishing gear and a small vessel.

---

685 Small-scale fisheries and artisanal fisheries comprise 90 percent of all fishing jobs worldwide, approximately 45 percent of the world's fisheries and nearly a quarter of the world catch. *David K. Schorr*, "Artisanal Fishing: Promoting Poverty Reduction and Community Development through New WTO Rules on Fisheries Subsidies: An Issue and Options Paper" (Geneva: UNEP, 2005), at 1; *FAO* Doc. No. FIDI/C853, "Marine Fisheries and the Law of the Sea: A Decade of Change, Special Chapter (Revised) of the State of Food and Agriculture 1992" (Rome: FAO, 1993), at 44-45; *FAO* Doc. FAO Fisheries Technical Paper No. 481, at 10-34; *FAO* Doc. FAO Technical Guidelines for Responsible Fisheries No. 10, "Increasing the Contribution of Small-Scale Fisheries to Poverty Alleviation and Food Security" (Rome: FAO, 2005).

686 Articles 6.18, 7.2.2 and 12.12 of the Code of Conduct. However, the Code of Conduct ignores the involvement of small-scale fishermen and small-scale fisheries organizations in the fisheries policy-making process (Articles 6.13 and 6.16 of the Code of Conduct). This may result from poor representation of small-scale fishermen, low levels of educational status in fishing communities and lack of recognition of the importance of small-scale fisheries. Moreover, there is a need for a provision in international fisheries instruments linking small-scale fisheries and poverty alleviation. Although the Code of Conduct refers to the contribution of small-scale fisheries to food security (Articles 2, 6.2, and 6.18 and Annex 2 of the Code of Conduct), it seldom mentions their contribution to poverty alleviation. Given that the Code of Conduct was developed prior to international fisheries declarations and commitments on poverty alleviation, the provisions in the Code of Conduct were certainly not developed with such issues in mind. The Code of Conduct, therefore, should be interpreted and applied as these fisheries documents evolved and should be seen in relation to recent commitments on poverty alleviation (Article 3.2 of the Code of Conduct).

687 In the process of compiling information on the characteristics of small-scale fisheries, the WTO Secretariat categorized the various elements to describe these characteristics, e.g. the description of activity, operator(s), economic orientation, location of activity, nature of activity and attributes of vessels and gear. *WTO* Doc. No. TN/RL/W/197, "Note by the Secretariat to the Negotiating Group on Rules, Definitions Related to Artisanal, Small-Scale and Subsistence Fishing" (24 November 2005); *FAO* Doc. FAO Fisheries Technical Paper No. 481, at 1.

They may also have the connotation of low levels of technology[688] and low capital investment per fisherman, although that may not always be the case.[689] They have also been considered as labour-intensive, with low productivity and supplying local and domestic markets, with family to small-enterprise employment, low yield rates and typically subject to traditional community management arrangements. They usually make short fishing trips, close to shore, and exist in severely impoverished fishing communities which are significant in human, economic and environmental terms.[690] In practice, the characteristics vary between countries, e.g. from gleaning or a one-man canoe in poor developing countries to trawlers over twenty meters, seiners, or long-liners in developed countries.[691]

2. Subsidies to Small-scale Fisheries

In order to finance poverty alleviation and food security in small fisheries communities, subsidizing these sectors has been considered by many governments as a financial measure with a view to meeting the need for income support and social welfare.[692] As with general fisheries subsidies, subsidies to small-scale fisheries also exist in a wide variety of forms.[693]

The use of these subsidies can also result in negative impact on trade and the environment, even though the size of these fisheries tends to be small and these fisheries tend to be cleaner than many industrialized fisheries. Their impact is usually insignificant on a global scale. The negative impact results from the fact that small-scale fishery products are increasingly oriented towards international markets; traditional near-shore small-scale fleets sometimes compete with foreign or export-oriented industrial fleets; small-scale fishing activities are increasingly expanding to high seas fisheries where foreign or export-oriented fleets may be active; and even a fishery that appears commercially isolated may be biologically linked to fisheries of international relevance.[694] These subsidies are considered appropriate if they enhance or diversify livelihoods without leading to increased fishing capacity or trade and production distortions, and if they are used to facilitate a structural change and/or used to assist the poor with the move towards re-

---

688 E.g. using undecked, owner-operated vessels equipped with non-automatic retrieval gear.

689 *FAO* Fisheries Glossary, *supra* note 45.

690 *FAO* Doc. FAO Fisheries Report No. 735, "Report of the Second Session of the Working Party on Small-scale Fisheries. Bangkok, Thailand, 18-21 November 2003" (Rome: FAO, 2004), at 21.

691 *FAO* Fisheries Glossary, *supra* note 45.

692 *FAO* Doc. FAO Fisheries Report No. 749, at 5.

693 E.g. direct cash transfers, subsidized loans and tax deferrals, vessels and gear modernization (including motorization), landing and processing infrastructure (port facilities, refrigeration, roads/transport), export, fuel, other inputs (e.g., ice), training and capital (cheap money).

694 *David K. Schorr*, *supra* note 685, para. 1.16(c).

sponsible fishing.[695] Reforming these subsidies should also take into consideration the different effects of the policies[696] and the importance of other social policies on these fishing communities in order to achieve sustainability.[697] Due to their negative impact, governments should be very careful when providing these subsidies and know that subsidization is not the only way to achieve their policy objectives, e.g. poverty alleviation or food security of the small fisheries communities.

3. Considerations for Provisions on Small-scale Fisheries

Although subsidies to small-scale fisheries were not the intended focus in the WTO negotiations, the question of how to regulate subsidies to these fisheries has been intensely discussed. These regulations should take into consideration both the pressing need for human development and the reality of sustainability challenges.[698] During the negotiations, WTO Members have proposed to exclude these subsidies from the definition of fisheries subsidies,[699] giving them the S&D treatment[700] or categorizing them as non-actionable subsidies.[701] The current negotiations and the Chair's text tend to concentrate on the scope of these fisheries and to what extent the S&D treatment should be applied to these subsidies.

When drafting provisions on these fisheries, the motives for subsidizing the sector should be considered. Subsidies to small-scale fisheries usually aim at pov-

---

695 *FAO* Doc. FAO Fisheries Technical Paper No. 481, at 84.

696 *Ibid.*, at 72; *FAO* Doc. FAO Technical Guidelines for Responsible Fisheries No. 10, at 46; *FAO, supra* note 34, at 71-72. For example, reducing overall overcapacity in small-scale fisheries by reducing the total number of fish nets may not be particularly relevant and may unnecessarily impact poor fishermen. Controlling subsidies for operating costs, e.g. fuel, is viewed as the limiting factor in small-scale fisheries and may be an important entry point for managing fishing effort. Removing all subsidies for the acquisition of capital assets or investments may discourage the growth of the fishing effort. Reducing or removing subsidies on production inputs may lead to the use of smaller boats and engines, reduce expenditure on fuel and increase expenditure on labour. In the long term, it should increase profits, create more employment and income for poor fishermen and reduce debt.

697 *WTO* Doc. No. TN/RL/W/207, "Communication from New Zealand to the Negotiating Group on Rules, Promoting Development and Sustainability in Fisheries Subsidies Disciplines: An Informal Dialogue on Select Technical Issues" (2 April 2007), para. 38; *UNEP and WWF*, "Disciplining Fisheries Subsidies: Incorporating Sustainability at the WTO & Beyond, 1-2 March 2007-Geneva, Switzerland, Chair's Summary" (Geneva: UNEP and WWF, 2007), para. 38, stating that achieving sustainability in these fisheries may rely on factors other than improved fisheries management or subsidization, such as coastal zone management, literacy, reduction of HIV/AIDS, conflict resolution, etc.

698 *UNEP, supra* note 651, para. 3; *WTO* Doc. No. TN/RL/W/184, para. 3.

699 *WTO* Doc. No. TN/RL/W/136 (14 July 2003), at 3.

700 *WTO* Doc. No. TN/RL/W/160 (8 June 2004), at 3-4; *WTO* Doc. No. TN/RL/W/172 (22 February 2005), paras. 15-16.

701 *WTO* Doc. No. TN/RL/GEN/79 (16 November 2005), at 2-3.

erty alleviation, food security, community and social development, improving sustainable fisheries management and preserving fishing cultures and lifestyles. However, the preservation of fishing cultures and lifestyles should not be adopted as a legitimate goal for the relaxation of fisheries subsidies regulations. Only if the subsidies focus on the goals of poverty alleviation, food security and development, may these fall within the scope of S&D treatment. To avoid the creation of a large loophole, a narrow definition should be created which is based on the policy motives underlying the subsidies to small-scale fisheries.[702] It should target situations where poverty or underdevelopment is prevalent.[703]

Moreover, in order to ensure that subsidies to these fisheries do not contribute to production distortion and fisheries depletion, minimum criteria and technical provisions used for S&D treatment should also be considered. However, due to poverty, geographical location, traditional social organization, and isolation from centralized markets, it is particularly difficult to manage small-scale fisheries through data-intensive, command and control techniques. To attain minimum criteria and science-based management techniques can be very expensive for some small-scale fisheries. Modern techniques and science-based fisheries management may not be appropriate to small-scale fisheries.

4. Analysis of Provisions on Small-scale Fisheries

a. Leaving out Small-scale Fisheries in Developed Country Members

The Chair's text provides S&D treatment only to small-scale fisheries in developing country Members. It made a decision that S&D treatment or the exception to prohibited fisheries subsidies is not granted to small-scale fisheries in developed country Members. The reaction from the developed world is that, for example, Canada considers that the issue of small-scale fisheries is relevant for both developed and developing country Members.[704] In view of the fact that small-scale fisheries in developed country Members are not provided with the policy space, it proposes to allow developed country Members to provide "*de minimis*" subsidies.[705]

Even so, not providing developed country Members with the opportunity to subsidize their small-scale fisheries is appropriate for the following reasons.

---

702 *UNEP*, *supra* note 651, paras. 4-6; *WTO* Doc. No. TN/RL/W/184 (18 July 2005), paras. 4-6.

703 *David K. Schorr*, *supra* note 685, para. 4.2, illustrating the situations are poverty and/or subsistence economic patterns; very small vessels and/or vessels with small or no engines; low levels of technological development and high labour-insensitivity; and fishing very close to shore.

704 *WTO* Doc. No. TN/RL/GEN/156, "Communication from Canada to the Negotiating Group on Rules, Fisheries Subsidies-*De Minimis* Exemption" (2 May 2008), para. 2.

705 *Ibid.*, para. 3.

First, the current SCM Agreement tends to create more policy space for subsidies in developing country Members than in developed country Members, based on the assumption that subsidies in developing country Members are less likely to cause trade distortions than those in developed country Members.

Second, even though small-scale fisheries may also exist in developed country Members, subsidies to these fisheries can only be deemed appropriate if they have the policy objectives of poverty alleviation, food security and development. These are not usually the objectives of subsidies programmes of developed country Members.

b. Providing Special and Differential Treatment to Small-scale Fisheries in Developing Country Members

Based on the S&D provisions in the Chair's text, developing country Members are allowed to subsidize their small-scale fisheries, provided that these fishing activities are on an individual basis, the catch is consumed by fishermen and their families and does not go beyond a small profit, and there is no major employer-employee relationship.[706] Subsidies to capital and operational costs can also be provided to fishing vessels not longer than ten meters overall or undecked vessels.[707] These small-scale fisheries are regulated based on their substantial characteristics. The conditions set in these provisions for small-scale fisheries are relatively restrictive.

Criteria of fisheries management are required to be implemented in these fisheries for them to enjoy S&D treatment. In view of the difficulty in implementing modern techniques and science-based fisheries management in these fisheries, making use of indigenous fisheries management institutions and measures is also accepted.[708] However, there are concerns over whether the conditions and criteria as drafted are sufficient to ensure that any new capacity built with subsidies does not go beyond a sustainable level in relation to the targeted fish stocks[709] or for the whole marine ecosystem.

Nevertheless, some improvements need to be taken into account. Apart from some other minor definitional clarifications, such as the scope of "small profit" or the use of "indigenous fisheries management", the major argument is related to using the vessel length as a parameter. Using the vessel length as a parameter for calibrating these regulations is controversial. It may lead to ineffective enforcement, legal circumvention and the introduction of a loophole into the regulations, in particular when Members during the negotiations seek opt-outs in order to sub-

---

706 Article III.2(a) of the proposed Annex VIII to the SCM Agreement of the Chair's text, *WTO* Doc. No. TN/RL/W/213 (30 November 2007).

707 *Ibid.*, Article III.2(b)(2).

708 *Ibid.*, Article III.2(a). Indigenous fisheries, used especially by Australia, are fisheries undertaken by peoples native to a land or region, e.g. aboriginals and Torres Strait Islanders. *FAO* Fisheries Glossary, *supra* note 45.

709 *WTO* Doc. No. TN/RL/W/232, "Working Document from the Chairman to the Negotiating Group on Rules" (28 May 2008), at C-35 and C-36.

sidize their fishing vessels.[710] On the other hand, it has also been considered as an anti-development limit.[711] During the negotiations, Members have suggested increasing the proposed vessel length, as small-scale fisheries in many countries have a vessel size of 20-25 meters.[712] However, in that case, industrial vessels and distant-water fishing would be included.[713] In short, using the vessel length as a criterion lacks a basis in sound policy. It is also inappropriate to apply ten meters as a parameter to all developing country Members with different types and development of fishing activities. These provisions may need to take into consideration the real situation of fishing industries in developing country Members.

E. Concerns with Provisions on Fisheries Access Agreements

1. The Nature of Fisheries Access Agreements

Fisheries access agreements provide fishing opportunities for distant water fleets (DWFs) to fish outside their own country's waters. The distant water fishing nations (DWFNs), e.g. the EU, Japan, Korea, Taiwan and the United States, pay remuneration to coastal developing countries for their DWFs. These payments to coastal developing countries constitute a significant source of income for coastal developing countries.[714] For instance, the EU agreement with Mauritania amounts to EUR 86 million per year and provides 25 percent of the government's budgetary receipts. The coastal developing countries can also generate income in their ports from activities after the fish is caught in their waters such as canneries, lining and processing facilities.

Access payments also form significant fisheries budgets in the DWFNs. However, the transfers of payments between governments and the further transfers of fishing rights to the fishing industries of the DWFNs based on these fisheries access agreements may constitute subsidies. How to regulate access-related subsidies has emerged as a sensitive topic within the WTO negotiations.[715] The dependency of coastal developing countries on these agreements should be taken into account.

---

710 *WWF*, "Small Boats, Big Problems" (Gland: WWF, 2008).

711 *WTO* Doc. No. TN/RL/W/218 (21 February 2008), para. 29.

712 *WTO* Doc. No. TN/RL/W/232 (28 May 2008), at C-34 and C-35; *WTO* Doc. No. TN/RL/W/226/Rev.5 (22 September 2008), para. 5, the SVEs refer to 25 metres, taking into account the size of the small-scale fishing vessels used in their waters; *WTO* Doc. No. TN/RL/GEN/155/Rev.1 (19 May 2008), at 5, illustrating that the restriction of ten meters would render most motorized vessels and many unpowered vessels ineligible to benefit from this exception, so it is proposed to raise it to 24 metres.

713 *WTO* Doc. No. TN/RL/W/218 (21 February 2008), para. 29.

714 *UNEP*, *supra* note 287, at 17; *Roman Grynberg*, supra note 285.

715 *Marcos A. Orellana*, "EEZ Fisheries Access Agreements and the WTO Subsidies Agreement: Legal Analysis and Options for Improved Disciplines" (Geneva: UNEP, 2007), at 4.

2. Legal Basis of Fisheries Access Agreements

The UNCLOS provides the legal basis for fisheries access agreements. Under the UNCLOS, coastal States retain sovereign rights over the natural resources in their EEZs. The UNCLOS also qualifies these sovereign rights in important ways.[716] The coastal State is required to determine the allowable catch, i.e. TAC, of the living resources in its EEZ, to promote the objective of optimum utilization of the living resources in its EEZ and to determine its capacity to harvest the living resources in its EEZ.[717] Where the coastal State does not have the capacity to harvest the entire allowable catch, it shall, through agreements or other arrangements, give other States access to the surplus. However, the coastal State cannot be compelled to allow foreign access, even if it fails to determine an allowable catch or its harvesting capacity. Nor can the coastal State be compelled to provide access, after declaring a surplus, if it fails to allocate the whole, or a part, of the surplus to any other State.[718]

The UNCLOS allows the coastal State considerable discretion in dealing with foreign vessels to harvest the surplus by permitting discrimination among different States.[719] The coastal State is ultimately sovereign in deciding to whom it grants access.[720]

The coastal State is not exempt from ensuring the sustainability of the living resources in its EEZ by granting access to other States' vessels. Nationals of other States fishing in the EEZ of the coastal State have an obligation to comply with the coastal State's laws and regulations.[721] The range of issues which may be regulated under the laws and regulations of the coastal State, and, for that matter, the contents of an access agreement include the licensing of fishermen, fishing vessels and equipment; terms and conditions relating to joint ventures or other cooperative arrangements; and requirements for the training of personnel and the transfer of fisheries technology.[722] The licensing conditions include payment of fees and other forms of remuneration, which, in the case of developing coastal States, may consist of adequate compensation in the field of financing, equipment

716 Part V of the UNCLOS.

717 Articles 61 and 62 of the UNCLOS.

718 *William T. Burke*, "The New International Law of Fisheries: UNCLOS 1982 and Beyond" (Oxford: Clarendon Press, 1994), at 43-69.

719 Article 62.3 of the UNCLOS.

720 Although UNCLOS refers specifically to land-locked States (Article 69) and geographically disadvantaged States (Article 70) that have been displaced by the enclosure movement and, thus, are worthy of extra production, it does not establish any hierarchy among the States. *Charlotte de Fontaubert and Indrani Lutchman*, "Achieving Sustainable Fisheries, Implementing the New International Legal Regime" (Gland, Switzerland and Cambridge: the World Conservation Union, 2003), at 8-9.

721 Article 62.4 of the UNCLOS.

722 *Roman Grynberg and Martin Tsamenyi*, "Fisheries Subsidies, the WTO and the Pacific Island Tuna Fisheries", Journal of World Trade, Vol. 32, No. 6, pp. 127-145 (1998), at 138.

and technology relating to the fishing industry. Based on these, the coastal State has considerable flexibility in the choice of the financial, technical and related terms of an access agreement or arrangement between foreign States. These provisions allow the coastal State to seek and obtain forms of remuneration. It is legitimate for the terms of a fishery joint venture agreement to provide tax exemptions or relief to the foreign venture. It is also equally lawful for the coastal State to receive payment in respect of foreign access to its EEZ in various forms, such as a lump-sum payment or development assistance.

3. Issues of Fisheries Access Agreements

In theory, the form of fisheries access agreements is supposed to reflect the mutual benefit for both coastal States and DWFNs. In practice, the terms and conditions set out in these agreements have not always favoured the coastal States. Some agreements have been used to export excess vessel capacity from the waters of depleted fisheries in developed countries, without due regard for trade and environmental consequences abroad.[723] In addition, fisheries access agreements usually lack transparency.

The impact of fisheries access agreements on trade can be observed from different aspects. First, the fisheries access payments under these agreements may constitute a form of fisheries subsidies if the cost of the agreement is not passed on to the fishing industry and the fleets do not pay back the access fees to their governments in full. Second, the impact on trade is particularly acute when DWFs enter national waters under these agreements, outrivaling the local fishermen and overexploiting the coastal countries' resources in the absence of adequate management and enforcement procedures by both DWFNs and coastal States. Third, concerning market access, some developed countries allow imports from countries with which they have access agreements but not from those not under this umbrella.[724] It may be considered as a restriction of market access. Although the Code of Conduct lays down that States should not make market access conditional on access to fisheries resources in order to promote responsible international fisheries trade,[725] the situation has not improved.

Moreover, the problems of overexploited fisheries are exacerbated by fisheries access agreements. In some regions, such as West Africa and the South Pacific, fishing by DWFs under access agreements makes up the vast majority of fishing in their EEZs. These agreements are usually not based on a comprehensive fisheries management plan and the amount of access fees often do not reflect the value

723 *WWF*, *supra* note 656, at 3; *Béatrice Gorez*, "Experiences with Subsidies and Fisheries Management: the Case of EU-ACP Fisheries Access Agreements" (Geneva: UNEP, 2004); *Niki Sporrong and Kate Bevins*, "Fisheries Agreements with Third Countries-Is the EU Moving towards Sustainable Development?" (London: Institute for European Environmental Policy, 2003), at 1.

724 *UNEP*, *supra* note 638, at 3.

725 Article 11.2.7 of the Code of Conduct.

of the catch nor does the revenue contribute to the development of the local fishing industry.[726] These payments have resulted in overcapacity of DWFs by making it more economically viable for them to fish in distant waters.[727]

Nonetheless, restricting fisheries access agreements is not deemed to be politically feasible, because many developing countries depend on access payments for their national income; these countries have a right to conclude access agreements under the UNCLOS; and there is considerable political pressure from developed countries to have access agreements. Therefore, fisheries access agreements should be properly designed to ensure sustainable fisheries management and to avoid the negative impact which might arise from overexploitation.[728] For instance, the level of fishing allowed under access agreements needs to be determined by sound science and the precautionary approach, rather than by the amount of financial compensation paid and the terms of access agreements should be transparent to all interested stakeholders to ensure sustainable fisheries management and enforcement, as well as fairness in dealing with all interested parties.[729]

4. Analysis of Provisions on Access-related Payments

a. Exempt Government-to-government Payments from the Regulations

During the negotiations, there has been universal consensus that new regulations should not threaten government-to-government access payments flowing between DWFNs and coastal States. According to the Chair's text, government-to-government payments for fishery access are not considered as subsidies.[730] The reliance of coastal States on access payments is respected and reflected in this provision.

b. Prohibition of Access-related Subsidies

Subsidies arising from the further transfer of access rights by the DWFN government to its fishing industry are prohibited.[731] However, the Chair's text does not address the question of how to value the amount of this type of subsidy. Various methods for valuing this type of subsidy have been suggested. One method is the

726 *Stephen Mbithi Mwikya*, "Fisheries Access Agreements: Trade and Development Issues" (Geneva: ICTSD, 2006).

727 *Ibid.*, in addition to overcapacity, problems associated with access agreements also include under-reporting; targeting of endangered species; and the difficulty faced by developing and least developed countries in enforcing standards of fisheries management.

728 *Ibid.*

729 *UNEP*, *supra* note 39, at 5; *WWF*, *supra* note 217, at 8.

730 Footnote 80 of the proposed Annex VIII to the SCM Agreement of the Chair's text, *WTO* Doc. No. TN/RL/W/213 (30 November 2007).

731 *Ibid.*, Article I.1(g).

extent to which access fees paid by the DWFN are not repaid to the DWFN government by its industry. The other method is the difference between the commercial value of the access enjoyed by the private fleet and the amount it paid to its government in return for the securing of that access. The latter method is based on the argument that government-to-government payments for access privileges or their amounts are insignificant relative to the valuation of subsidies.[732]

c. Exception to Prohibition as Special and Differential Treatment

The S&D provisions for developing country Members in the Chair's text provide that subsidies arising from the further transfer of access rights by the DWFN government are not prohibited, provided that the fishery in question is within the EEZ of a developing country Member and that the agreement is made public and contains the provisions designed to prevent overfishing based on international fisheries instruments, including the Fish Stocks Agreement, Compliance Agreement, Code of Conduct, technical guidelines and IPOAs, and in particular science-based stock assessments.[733] This provision takes into account the importance of access agreements for responsible fisheries management. Access agreements containing provisions for supporting responsible fisheries deserve a conditional exemption from prohibited fisheries subsidies.

However, most fisheries access agreements are signed between developed and developing country Members, as developed country Members purchase the fisheries rights from developing country Members and then transfer these rights to their own fishing industries. This transfer is considered as prohibited fisheries subsidies in normal cases.[734] Nevertheless, it is not prohibited in cases where S&D treatment applies, with the end result being that subsidies which benefit the fishing industries in developed country Members are non-prohibited. This is not the objective of providing S&D treatment of developing country Members.

d. Transparency of Fisheries Access Agreements

The Chair's text provides for S&D treatment of access-related subsidies, if the fisheries access agreement is made public. It further requires that each Member that is party to a fisheries access agreement shall publish that agreement and shall notify to the SCM Committee.[735] The terms on which a payer Member transfers these fishing rights shall be notified to the SCM Committee by the payer Mem-

---

[732] *UNEP*, "Development and Sustainability in the WTO Fishery Subsidies Negotiations: Issues and Alternatives, Chair's Summary" (Geneva: UNEP, 2006), paras. 10-13; *WTO* Doc. No. TN/RL/W/206, "Development and Sustainability in the WTO Fishery Subsidies Negotiations: Issues and Alternatives" (31 May 2006), paras. 10-13.

[733] Article III.3 of the proposed Annex VIII to the SCM Agreement of the Chair's text, *WTO* Doc. No. TN/RL/W/213 (30 November 2007).

[734] *Ibid.*, Article I.1(g).

[735] *Ibid.*, Article VI.2.

ber.[736] If the terms are not notified, these shall be presumed to give rise to subsidies. The burden of proof shifts to the payer Member, since it has to demonstrate that no such subsidies have arisen.[737] A system for disclosing these agreements or cooperation with other organizations can help to enforce these provisions better.

V. Criteria Required for Providing Fisheries Subsidies

A. Minimum Criteria

In the process of drafting the new regulations, minimum criteria have been taken into account in the WTO negotiations and the research of other agencies. Certain criteria should be met in order to eliminate the negative impact of subsidies on fisheries conservation. Based on the analysis of the UNEP and WWF,[738] these minimum criteria can be set in the areas of fish stock, fishing capacity and fisheries management. Each one of these is indispensable. These criteria reflect the requirements under current international fisheries instruments for responsible fisheries. When these criteria are coordinated, the potential for fisheries subsidies to cause harm is significantly lower. These criteria, i.e. stock-related, capacity-related and management-related criteria, are described in the next sections.

1. Stock-related Criteria

Stock-related criteria require that the affected stocks be at well below sustainable levels of exploitation. This means fish stocks in the waters of the Members which intend to provide subsidies should not be in an overexploited, depleted or recovering status, i.e. "patently at risk."[739] Under the major international fisheries instruments,[740] States are responsible for assessing and maintaining their fish

---

736 *Ibid.*, Article VI.3.

737 *Ibid.*, Article VIII.3.

738 *David K. Schorr and John F. Caddy*, "Sustainability Criteria for Fisheries Subsidies, Options for the WTO and Beyond" (Geneva: UNEP and WWF, 2007).

739 *WTO* Doc. No. TN/RL/GEN/79 (16 November 2005), Brazil suggested that a fishery could be considered "patently at risk" if its status of exploitation is "not known or uncertain", "overexploited", "depleted", or "recovering" according to the FAO or by a competent regional or international authority having jurisdiction over the fishery.

740 The major instruments establishing international norms for responsible fisheries require governments to assess their fish stocks and to maintain them at levels consistent with long-term sustainability, including Article 61 of the UNCLOS, Article 7 and *esp.* Articles 7.2 and 7.4 of the Code of Conduct, and Articles 5(b), 5(d), 6.3(d), 10(d), and 14, as well as Paras. 2 and 7 of Annex II of the Fish Stocks Agreement.

stocks. Stock-related criteria are based on the availability of data and information on fish stocks required in these instruments. Evidence of fish depletion is considered as an important factor weighing against the use of effort- or capacity-enhancing subsidies.

According to an FAO statistic, 80 percent of reported global marine catches come from stocks for which the available stock-assessment information makes possible the computation of an estimate of the state of fish exploitation.[741] At the national level, the data is most frequently collected by governments or government institutes, sometimes with the involvement of non-governmental actors, e.g. academic institutes or private consultants. At the international level, some RFMOs sponsor fisheries assessments, while other intergovernmental bodies are dedicated exclusively to developing fisheries-related data and/or advice.[742]

However, access to reliable data and information on fish stocks is still sometimes problematic, due to the expense and the lack of budgetary and human resources, particularly in developing countries and small-scale fisheries. Therefore, in some fisheries, management techniques have been developed on the basis of scant data. If these are accompanied by a precautionary approach, they can be considered appropriate and acceptable, although these are not the optimal and permanent solution.

Moreover, effort- or capacity-enhancing subsidies obviously should not be employed to expand or maintain fishing beyond optimal levels of fish exploitation. Such optimal levels can be defined as maximum sustainable yield (MSY).[743] Proposals in the WTO negotiations have also included MSY as a measure of stock health in setting conditions for fisheries subsidies.[744] However, where multi-species fisheries and the impact of small species on the whole food chain and the marine ecosystem are involved, simple reliance on MSY of one species is not sufficient.[745]

2. Capacity-related Criteria

Capacity as defined in Chapter 1 should be used as one of the components of minimum criteria. Under the major international fisheries instruments,[746] States

[741] *FAO* Doc. FAO Fisheries Technical Paper No. 457, "Review of the State of World Marine Fishery Resources" (Rome: FAO, 2005), at 6, explaining that it is 441 stock or species groups out of 584 stock and species groups.

[742] *David K. Schorr and John F. Caddy*, *supra* note 738, at 7-8.

[743] See *supra* Chapter 1 for the definition of MSY.

[744] *WTO* Doc. No. TN/RL/W/21 (15 August 2002); *WTO* Doc. No. TN/RL/GEN/145 (22 March 2007); *WTO* Doc. No. TN/RL/W/154 (26 April 2004); *WTO* Doc. No. TN/RL/GEN/138/Rev.1 (26 January 2007); *WTO* Doc. No. TN/RL/W/176 (31 March 2005).

[745] *David K. Schorr and John F. Caddy*, *supra* note 738, at 9, considering that MSY is a risky upper limit rather than the best target for sustainable fishing yields.

[746] Article 5(h) of the Fish Stock Agreement; Articles 6.3 and 7.4 of the Code of Conduct; IPOA-Capacity.

are responsible for managing their fishing capacity. Capacity-related criteria require that the affected fleets should be well below sustainable levels of capacity before a subsidy is allowed or for a subsidy to exist continuously.

Due to the uncertainties of and rapid changes in market forces and environmental fluctuations, fisheries with a high capacity are often difficult to manage. Where capacity-enhancing subsidies are involved, a fishery that is approaching full capacity or is not substantially under-capacity faces the risk of overrunning sustainable limits.[747] The reasons include (i) the difficulty of knowing reliably and precisely how much capacity is appropriate or how much capacity actually exists in a fishery; (ii) the continuous trend in fisheries to implement technological advances for more effective capacity, often without much visible change in the configuration or number of licenses of a fleet; (iii) the frequent practice of replacing old licensed vessels with vessels of higher efficiency; (iv) the difficulty of effectively controlling capacity growth in many fisheries, especially in fisheries where illegal fishing is a significant factor; (v) the often significant and unpredictable impact of exogenous causes of fishing mortality,[748] including both natural ecosystem cycles and anthropogenic threats such as pollution and climate change; (vi) the lifespan of fishing vessels that, with regular refitting, may continue to operate for up to 40 years or more, resulting in the subsidy decision having long-term consequences.[749]

Designing capacity-related criteria should be in accordance with the input-based and output-based measures as well as a precautionary approach. The measure of capacity is based on two basic approaches, input-based and output-based.[750] Input-based measures look at the factors used to harvest fish, e.g. the number of vessels active in a fishery or the level of effort they apply, days at sea, number of traps deployed, etc. Output-based measures describe capacity in terms of potential levels of production, in quantities of fish. While input-based measures are often found in the vocabulary of fisheries regulators, output-based measures may make more intuitive sense to the layperson. They are compatible and complementary; so fisheries subsidies regulations should adopt this dual-based approach to measure capacity. Moreover, assuming that effective fishing capacity normally increases by approximately two to four percent per year as a result of improved technology and fishing techniques, there is a need to consider this factor and adopt a precautionary approach to capacity management and to fisheries subsidies policies.[751]

---

747 *WTO* Doc. No. TR/RL/W/207 (2 April 2007), para. 24; *UNEP and WWF*, *supra* note 697, para. 24.

748 *FAO* Fisheries Glossary, *supra* note 45. Fishing mortality is often expressed as a rate that indicates the percentage of the population caught in a year.

749 *David K. Schorr and John F. Caddy*, *supra* note 738, at 15.

750 *Ibid.*, at 14-15.

751 *WTO* Doc. No. TR/RL/W/207 (2 April 2007), paras. 22 and 25; *UNEP and WWF*, *supra* note 697 paras. 22 and 25.

3. Management-related Criteria

Management-related criteria require that the affected fisheries be subject to effective fisheries management. In the absence of effective management, under-exploited and under-capacity fisheries could result in overfishing and fish depletion. Unlike stock-related and capacity-related criteria, management-related criteria are unquantifiable. The design of management-related criteria focuses on how to assess the management systems of Members. There is no international obligation for governments to assess the quality of their fisheries management systems.

Two agencies have made considerable progress on the assessment of fisheries management systems.[752]

First, the FAO has made substantial efforts to develop instruments for assessing the adequacy of management, including a 1996 checklist for management issues associated with the implementation of the Code of Conduct[753] and guidelines adopted in 2005 for the eco-labelling of fish products.[754]

Second, the Marine Stewardship Council (MSC),[755] a globally focused institution, also developed a guideline to evaluate regularly and formally the regimes of fisheries management.

With these instruments, it is possible to establish universally acknowledged criteria of minimum adequate management for all fisheries. These criteria include data-based stock assessment; fishery capacity assessment; science-based limits on

---

752 *David K. Schorr and John F. Caddy*, *supra* note 738, at 20.

753 *FAO* Doc. FAO Fisheries Circular No. 917 FRIM/C917, "A Checklist for Fisheries Resource Management Issues Seen from the Perspective of the FAO Code of Conduct for Responsible Fisheries" (Rome: FAO, 1996). This checklist is a suggested system of scoring which assists those concerned with fisheries management in evaluating the adherence of a particular fishery or fishery management system to the provisions of the Code of Conduct and for monitoring progress in this respect. This document focuses particularly on Article 7 of the Code of Conduct, which deals with fisheries management *sensu strictu* but extracts from other Articles those clauses that have immediate relevance to the proper management of living aquatic resources.

754 *FAO*, "Guidelines for the Ecolabelling of Fish and Fishery Products from Marine Capture Fisheries" (Rome: FAO, 2005). The Guidelines are voluntary and applicable to ecolabelling schemes that are designed to certify and promote labels for products from well-managed marine capture fisheries and focus on issues related to the sustainable use of fisheries resources. The Guidelines refer to principles, general considerations, terms and definitions, minimum substantive requirements and criteria, and procedural and institutional aspects of the ecolabelling of fish and fishery products from marine capture fisheries.

755 The Marine Stewardship Council (MSC) is a nongovernmental organization, launched by a partnership of Unilever and the WWF. It sets standards for responsible fishery and marine ecosystem practices, and offers a label to qualifying companies. It is the world's leading certification and ecolabelling program for sustainable seafood. See further information available on-line at <www.msc.org>.

catch, capacity or fishing effort; basic monitoring and control; cooperative management of trans-boundary or migratory stocks.[756]

With respect to this checklist and the guidelines, a three-tiered approach, using the simpler and more broadly applicable criteria, can be established.

The first tier requires Members that intend to subsidize to use the basic regulatory elements of a responsible management regime, i.e. assessment, control and enforcement, recognized by international fisheries instruments. The rudiments of good management should include science-based assessments of fish stocks and fishing fleets; appropriate regulatory limits on fishing activities and fishing capacity; and the surveillance and enforcement of those limits.[757]

The second tier requires Members that intend to subsidize to establish fisheries management regimes which include certain key elements of a monitoring, control and surveillance (MCS) administrative infrastructure. Examples are the maintenance of public vessel registry information, fishing-license regimes, catch documentation and on-board observers. Concerning public vessel registry information, various international instruments[758] establish a clear norm requiring every government to maintain a registry or record of vessels authorized to fish under its flag and to cooperate in the sharing and harmonization of registry information.[759] Fishing-license regimes, as a complement to vessel registration, require that all vessels active in a fishery be formally authorized to fish and that public records of those authorizations be maintained. Maintaining catch records is the minimum level of data necessary for all stock assessment. However, catch-documentation systems have not yet been subject to the same degree of international harmonization and cooperation as those for vessel registries. Some efforts are underway at both the global and regional levels.[760] On-board observers could also be a required element of catch-documentation systems.

The third tier is to employ a set of simplified benchmarks to help make qualitative judgments about the basic health of the fishery and its management regime.[761]

---

756 *WWF*, *supra* note 221, at 8, adding that where such elements of management are not in place, the subsidies to these "patently undermanaged" fisheries should be suspected.

757 *Ibid.*, at 19-21.

758 Article 94.2(a) of the UNCLOS; Article IV of the Compliance Agreement; Article 8.2.1 of the Code of Conduct; Para. 17 of the IPOA-Capacity.

759 Based on this norm, the FAO administers the High Seas Vessel Authorization Records (HSVAR) and Comprehensive Record of Fishing Vessels (Global Record). The EU also administers the international EQUASIS system as part of its vessel-safety programme.

760 On the global level, relevant efforts are underway, including a new international consortium for the sharing of fisheries data, called the Fishery Resources Monitoring System (FIRMS), and the FAO Strategy for Improving Information on Status and Trends of Capture Fisheries. On the regional level, there are relevant RFMOs and other international cooperative instruments, which can be exemplified with the catch-documentation programme for toothfish set up by the CCAMLR.

761 *David K. Schorr and John F. Caddy*, *supra* note 738, at 27-28.

The UNEP together with the WWF have been developing the benchmarks for rapid overall evaluations.[762]

Moreover, whenever subsidies affect shared or multi-national fish stocks, international cooperation should be established. The criteria for these fish stocks need to be strengthened. For instance, the MCS infrastructure on the high seas poses significant logistic obstacles, because their implementation on the high seas may depend on the use of satellite tracking systems for effective surveillance.[763]

B. Analysis of the Chair's Text

1. Effective Fisheries Management Systems as Criteria

Based on this analysis, the Chair's text sets out these stock-related, capacity-related and management-related criteria and requires effective fisheries management systems as the preconditions for exceptions to prohibited fisheries subsidies and the S&D treatment of developing country Members.[764] These measures focus on the management of subsidized fisheries. They draw on international norms and standards emanating from international fisheries instruments, especially the Code of Conduct, which requires fisheries to be managed to achieve long-term sustainability through the application of three fundamental elements of fisheries management: assessment of fish stocks and fleet capacity; limitation of fishing and fishing capacity through regulatory controls; and surveillance and enforcement of regulatory limits. Articles IV and V of the Chair's text refer to these elements, but give more weight to the first two.

Article IV adopts the general principle on the use of subsidies. It requires that "no Member shall cause, through the use of any subsidy, depletion of or harm to, or creation of overcapacity in respect of, (a) straddling or highly migratory fish stocks whose range extends into the EEZ of another Member; or (b) stocks in which another Member has identifiable fishing interests."[765] It also lays down the method for determining this requirement and states that "the existence of such situations shall be determined taking into account available pertinent information, including from other relevant international organizations."[766] The international organizations here are taken to be the FAO and RFMOs, since they collect, compile and access the relevant information at the global and regional levels. The information includes the status of the fisheries management system of the subsidizing Member.[767] Moreover, the Chair's text emphasizes that any subsidy referred to in these regulations "shall be attributed to the Member conferring it,

---

[762] *Ibid.*, at 48-49.

[763] *Ibid.*, at 25-27.

[764] Article V of the proposed Annex VIII to the SCM Agreement of the Chair's text, *WTO* Doc. No. TN/RL/W/213 (30 November 2007).

[765] *Ibid.*, first part of Article IV.1.

[766] *Ibid.*, second part of Article IV.1.

[767] *Ibid.*, third part of Article IV.1.

regardless of the flag(s) of the vessel(s) involved or the application of rules of origin to the fish involved."[768] It avoids the problems of jurisdictional zones of UNCLOS and reflects the trend of application across these zones that has been led by the Code of Conduct.[769]

Article V further sets up the requirements for appropriate fisheries management systems. It requires that "any Member granting or maintaining any subsidy as referred to in Article II or Article III.2(b) shall operate a fisheries management system regulating marine wild capture fishing within its jurisdiction, designed to prevent overfishing."[770] This management system shall be based on "internationally-recognized best practice for fisheries management and conservation" and shall include regular science-based stock assessment and capacity and management measures. Prior to authorizing the granting of the subsidy, the fisheries management system of the subsidizing Member is subject to peer review by the FAO.[771]

Using effective fisheries management systems as a precondition for exceptions to prohibited fisheries subsidies and S&D treatment is an example of interaction between two regimes.

2. "Internationally Recognized Best Practice of Fisheries Management"

Article V also states what should be considered effective fisheries management systems. However, more clarification or more discussion between Members is needed in order to reach a consensus.

It requires that a fisheries management system "shall be based on internationally-recognized best practices for fisheries management and conservation as reflected in the relevant provisions of international instruments aimed at ensuring the sustainable use and conservation of marine species, such as, *inter alia*, the Fish Stocks Agreement, the Code of Conduct, the Compliance Agreement, technical guidelines and plans of action (including criteria and precautionary reference points) for the implementation of these instruments, or other related or successor instruments."[772]

Best practices are reflected in a non-exhaustive list of five international fisheries instruments: (1) the Fish Stocks Agreement, (2) the Code of Conduct, (3) the Compliance Agreement, (4) FAO's technical guidelines and (5) FAO's international plans of action (IPOAs). As discussed in Chapter 1, there are international

768 *Ibid.*, Article IV.2.

769 The Code of Conduct has an extensive scope and is applicable across the jurisdictional zones of UNCLOS.

770 First part of Article V.1 of the proposed Annex VIII to the SCM Agreement of the Chair's text, *WTO* Doc. No. TN/RL/W/213 (30 November 2007).

771 *Ibid.*, sixth part of Article V.1.

772 *Ibid.*, second part of Article V.1 and third part of Article IV.1.

fisheries instruments other than those illustrated above, in particular the UNCLOS, so the list should be considered non-exhaustive.

Among these instruments, the Fish Stock Agreement and the Compliance Agreement are binding, while the others are voluntary. In addition to the Compliance Agreement, which was adopted by the FAO Conference, there are also others developed under the FAO framework: the Code of Conduct adopted by the FAO Conference[773]; the IPOAs adopted by the FAO Committee on Fisheries (COFI)[774]; and the technical guidelines elaborated under the auspices of the FAO Secretariat.[775] The negotiations of the Code of Conduct and its supporting IPOAs have been both political and technical in character, as technical specialist input played a secondary role to the political objectives of the negotiators.[776] Technical guidelines provide detailed guidance on how to implement the Code of Conduct for States or for regional or sub-regional fisheries bodies or for the actors in the fisheries sector. These guidelines are flexible, since they can be revised at any time as new developments occur.[777] This set of instruments developed by the FAO has a wide scope and contains provisions which are based on strong technical inputs, e.g. precautionary approach, and those which have a normative effect, e.g. port state control. Some of them have received wide recognition in a number of international fora[778] and acquired certain legitimacy in international law.[779]

773 The FAO Conference is the supreme governing body of the FAO that meets in regular session every two years. Its main functions are to determine the policies of the Organization, approve the Programme of Work and Budget and make recommendations to Members and international organizations.

774 The Committee on Fisheries (COFI), a subsidiary body of the FAO Council, was established by the FAO Conference at its Thirteenth Session in 1965. The Committee currently constitutes the only global inter-governmental forum where major international fisheries and aquaculture problems and issues are examined and recommendations addressed to governments, regional fishery bodies, nongovernmental organizations, fishworkers, the FAO and the international community, periodically on a world-wide basis. COFI has also been used as a forum in which global agreements and non-binding instruments have been negotiated.

775 Since 1995, the FAO Fisheries Department has been publishing wide-ranging guideline documentation to assist those concerned with the implementation of the recommendations of the Code of Conduct. Some of the Technical Guidelines for Responsible Fisheries target issues important to both aquaculture and capture fisheries: for example, those dealing with the precautionary approach and species introductions, food safety, fish utilization and trade.

776 *William Edeson*, "The Role of Technical Bodies", in *Rüdiger Wolfrum and Volker Röben* (eds), *supra* note 85, at 89-90. The Code of Conduct is a mixture of specialist technical and political input. Its general principles were formulated initially as a secretariat draft, revised by an informal working group of experts, further revised by the FAO Secretariat, considered by a technical consultation and by the COFI, and then approved by the FAO Conference. See further information in *William Edeson*, "The Code of Conduct for Responsible Fisheries: An Introduction", International Journal of Marine and Coastal Law, Vol. 11, pp. 233-238 (1996).

777 *Ibid.*, at 85.

778 Para. 31 of the WSSD Plan of Implementation, *supra* note 94.

779 *William Edeson*, *supra* note 776, at 89-90.

Moreover, since the provisions in the Chair's text refer only to the system within the jurisdiction of the subsidizing Member, when international fisheries are involved,[780] the existing rules of RFMOs should also be subject to requirements equivalent to those imposed on domestic fisheries.[781]

3. Incorporating Fisheries Instruments into the WTO Regulations

There is concern regarding whether incorporating international fisheries instruments into the binding WTO systems makes them binding for the WTO Members. This is a rather crucial question, since not all WTO Members are signatories to these agreements, e.g. the Fish Stock Agreement and the Compliance Agreement. The status of the WTO Members and Observers in these fisheries agreements is shown in Attachment III. Some of these instruments are voluntary, e.g. the Code of Conduct, the technical guidelines and the plans of action. It is the phenomenon of "rule referencing" or the creation of rules on the basis of provisions in an international treaty instrument.[782] It makes reference by means of "incorporating" other binding or non-binding rules or standards which exist in another treaty instrument or have been developed by a formal or informal institution or body outside the WTO.[783]

The current WTO agreements also make use of this kind of "rule referencing" as a basis for incorporating international standards, guidelines and recommendations into the WTO framework. The TBT Agreement distinguishes between a standard and a regulation, as the former is voluntary and the latter is mandatory.[784]

---

780 International fisheries refer to highly migratory fish stocks and straddling fish stocks.

781 *WTO* Doc. No. TN/RL/W/218 (21 February 2008), para. 19, although the weakness of many RFMO regimes is questionable.

782 "Rule referencing" is not exclusive in the WTO framework. In the law of the sea regime, the UNCLOS also refer to the relevant international rules and standards developed by or through the competent international organization, i.e. International Maritime Organization (IMO). Its function has been considered by scholars as to make certain international practices and norms "obligatory" for all Member States regardless of whether particular States are parties to a treaty entailing these norms or not. Rules and standards of nonbinding instruments such as the Code of Conduct qualify as references if they are widely accepted. *Rüdiger Wolfrum*, "IMO Interface with the Law of the Sea Convention", in *Myron H. Nordquist and John Norton Moore* (eds), "Current Maritime Issues and the International Maritime Organization", pp. 223-236 (The Hague: Kluwer Law International, 1999), at 231; *Rüdiger Wolfrum, Volker Röben and Fred Morrison*, "Preservation of the Marine Environment", in *Fred Morrison and Rüdiger Wolfrum* (eds), "International, Regional and National Environmental Law", pp. 225-283 (The Hague: Kluwer Law International, 2000), at 225-233.

783 *Mary E. Footer*, "An Institutional and Normative Analysis of the World Trade Organization" (Leiden, Koninklijke Brill NV: 2006), at 320-321.

784 Para. 1 of Annex 1 to the TBT Agreement defines a regulation as that "document which lays down product characteristics or their related processes and production

This definition of "standard" is relatively narrow. In the case of the Chair's text, internationally-recognized best practices for fisheries management are considered to be the standards established in the fisheries instruments which are mostly developed by the FAO and some of which are non-mandatory but have been considered widely accepted. The discussion about international standards is not necessary here to refer to this definition under the TBT Agreement.[785]

The WTO agreements do not actually prevent the adoption of standards developed outside the context of this international treaty regime. They rely on international standard-setting bodies to determine whether WTO Members can be exempt from disciplines or whether WTO Members have fulfilled their obligations under other regimes. Examples of rule-referencing in the WTO agreements include the provisions in the TBT and SPS Agreements.

The importance of international standards and international conformity assessment systems is enshrined in the TBT Agreement. The preamble to the TBT Agreement also recognizes this importance for the following reasons: to improve efficiency of production; to facilitate the conduct of international trade; and to contribute to the transfer of technology from developed to developing countries.[786] The TBT Agreement directs governments to use international standards as a basis for their technical regulations except when such standards "would be an ineffective or inappropriate means for the fulfilment of the legitimate objectives pursued, for instance because of fundamental climatic or geographical factors or fundamental technological problems."[787] When a national technical regulation has a legitimate objective and is in accordance with relevant international standards, it shall be "rebuttably presumed" not to create an unnecessary obstacle to trade and therefore violate the TBT Agreement.[788] However, these standards may be decisive in a WTO dispute even if they were not intended to be binding, as the EC-Sardines case shows.[789]

methods, including the applicable administrative provisions, with which compliance is *mandatory*." Para. 2 defines a standard as that "document approved by a recognized body, that provides, for common and repeated use, rules, guidelines or characteristics for products or related processes and production methods, with which compliance is *not mandatory*. It may also include or deal exclusively with terminology, symbols, packaging, marking or labelling requirements as they apply to a product, process or production method" (emphasis added).

785 Similar interpretation is also adopted by scholars when discussing "international standards" without following the TBT definitions. *Steve Charnovitz*, "International Standards and the WTO", The George Washington University Law School, Public Law and Legal Theory Working Paper No. 133 (2005).

786 *Ludivine Tamiotti*, "Article 2 TBT", in *Rüdiger Wolfrum, Peter-Tobias Stoll and Anja Seibert-Fohr* (eds), *supra* note 679, pp. 210-234, at 221.

787 Article 2.4 of the TBT Agreement.

788 Article 2.5 of the TBT Agreement. It is a provision of the burden of proof. See further information in *Ludivine Tamiotti*, *supra* note 786, at 226.

789 In the EC-Sardines case, the Appellate Body had to determine whether Codex Stan 94 was a "relevant international standard" which had been used "as a basis for" the EC technical regulation within the meaning of Article 2.4 of the TBT Agreement and whether the "relevant international standard" needs to be adopted by consen-

The SPS Agreement directs Members to base their sanitary and phytosanitary measures (SPS measures) on "international standards, guidelines or recommendations."[790] It further provides that SPS measures conforming to international standards shall be "presumed" to be consistent with the relevant provisions of the SPS Agreement and the GATT.[791] The conforming measures are presumed to be necessary to protect human, animal or plant life or health. However, it should be noted that the WTO Appellate Body stated that these SPS provisions should not be read "as requiring Members to harmonize their SPS measures by conforming those measures with international standards, guidelines and recommendations" because to do so would be "to vest such international standards, guidelines and recommendations with obligatory force and effect."[792] In other words, this incorporation by reference cannot "transform those standards, guidelines and recommendations into binding norms."[793] These international standards, nonetheless, can still have significant influence on the international harmonization of food safety standards, since products applying these standards are presumed to have met the requirement of the SPS Agreement.[794] The SPS cases have also shown that fully incorporating international standards into national SPS measures is the only way of escaping the obligation of risk assessment and international standards have been vested with a new form of *de facto* effect.[795]

In the same way, incorporating by reference the fisheries instruments in fisheries subsidies regulations, either on a binding or voluntary basis, may not necessarily transform them into binding provisions. The fisheries instruments could be considered as the guidelines on which effective fisheries management systems are based or as the international standards and criteria for determining the effectiveness of these systems. During dispute settlements, the requirements under these fisheries instruments can be decisive. WTO Members which are not parties to these fisheries instruments still need to comply with their requirements. In the case of developing country Members that have difficulty in adopting these standards, the need for technical assistance is critical.

In order to reduce the opposition to rule-referencing by the WTO Members who are not parties to these fisheries instruments nor FAO Member Nations, reference can be made to other WTO agreements which contain a commitment of WTO Members to assist developing countries so as to promote the use of international standards. Since these standards have a substantial impact on Members'

sus. *WTO* Doc. WT/DS231/AB/R, "Report of the Appellate Body, European Communities-Trade Description of Sardines" (26 September 2002).

790 Article 3.1 of the SPS Agreement.

791 Article 3.2 of the SPS Agreement.

792 *WTO* Doc. No. WT/DS26/AB/R, WT/DS48/AB/R, "Report of the Appellate Body, EC Measures Concerning Meat and Meat Products (Hormones)" (16 January 1998), para. 165.

793 *Ibid.*

794 *Rüdiger Wolfrum*, "Introduction", in *Rüdiger Wolfrum and Volker Röben* (eds), *supra* note 85, at 6.

795 *Oliver Landwehr*, "Article 3 SPS", in *Rüdiger Wolfrum, Peter-Tobias Stoll and Anja Seibert-Fohr* (eds), *supra* note 679, pp. 412-427, at 421-422.

ability to develop their policies, all Members should be able to contribute to the standard-setting process. The TBT Agreement calls for assistance to developing country Members in establishing national standardizing bodies and participating in international standardizing bodies.[796] It also calls for assistance to these Members in establishing the institutional and legal framework that they need to participate in international or regional systems for conformity assessment.[797] S&D provisions of the TBT Agreement also contain provisions aimed at improving the participation of developing country Members in international standardizing bodies.[798] The SPS Agreement similarly provides that WTO Members should encourage and facilitate the active participation of developing country Members in the relevant international organizations.[799] In cases of rule-referencing in the fisheries subsidies regulations, the WTO and its Members should assist and encourage WTO Members who are not parties to some of the fisheries instruments nor FAO Member Nations to actively comply with the requirements of these instruments and to participate in these organizations. Although Article III.4 of the Chair's text provides a good start on technical assistance to developing country Members, it focuses on assisting them in complying with the requirements of the fisheries subsidies regulations. It does not have the same degree of encouragement that the TBT and SPS Agreements do.

4. Illustrating Elements in the Fisheries Management Systems

Concerning the management measures, Article V provides that the fisheries management system shall "include regular science-based stock assessment, as well as capacity- and effort-management measures, including harvesting licences or fees; vessel registries; establishment and allocation of fishing rights, or allocation of exclusive quotas to vessels, individuals and/or groups, and related enforcement mechanisms; species-specific quotas, seasons and other stock-management measures; vessel monitoring which could include electronic tracking and on-board observers; systems for reporting in a timely and reliable manner to the competent national authorities and relevant international organizations data on effort, catch and discards in sufficient detail to allow sound analysis; and research and other measures related to conservation and stock maintenance and replenishment."[800] It illustrates various management measures and can also be seemed correspond to the first- and second- tier approaches of management-related criteria promoted by the UNEP and WWF. It further requires that "the Member shall adopt and implement pertinent domestic legislation and administrative or judicial enforcement mechanisms." This requirement is intended to correct the frequently occurring

[796] Article 11.2 of the TBT Agreement.
[797] Article 11.6 of the TBT Agreement.
[798] Articles 12.5 and 12.6 of the TBT Agreement.
[799] Article 10.4 of the SPS Agreement.
[800] The third part of Article V.1 of the proposed Annex VIII to the SCM Agreement of the Chair's text, *WTO* Doc. No. TN/RL/W/213 (30 November 2007).

situation that WTO Members tend to adopt management systems on paper without adequately implementing or enforcing them.[801]

Since the fisheries management measures are broad, diverse and developing, the measures listed in this provision should be deemed non-exhaustive. Moreover, the requirement of effective fisheries management systems should focus on the result to be achieved, i.e. that a subsidy shall not result in overfishing, rather than on prescribing each measure that may be employed to reach this goal.[802]

5. Setting the Enquiry Points

In order to improve the transparency of the sector, the Chair's text also requires that each Member maintains an enquiry point to answer all reasonable enquiries concerning its fisheries management system, including measures in place to address fishing capacity and fishing effort, and the biological status of the fisheries in question.[803] The enquiry point is the single contact point for enabling other Members or other interested parties to easily obtain information about the fisheries management systems of subsidizing Members. Similar provisions can also be found under the SPS Agreement.[804] This establishment enables Members to directly contact the agency responsible for any given function of another Member.[805]

VI. Establishment of Institutional Mechanisms

A. The Need of Institutional Mechanisms

Establishment of institutional mechanisms is deemed necessary to enforce fisheries subsidies regulations and dispute settlement.[806] In this section, we will look at

---

801 *Margaret A. Young*, "Fragmentation or Interaction: the WTO, Fisheries Subsidies and International Law", World Trade Review, Vol. 8, No. 4, pp.477-515 (2009), at 501.

802 *WTO* Doc. No. TN/RL/W/231, "Communication from Norway to the Negotiating Group on Rules, Drafting Proposal on Issues Relating to Article V ("Fisheries Management") of the Fisheries Subsidies Annex to the SCM Agreement as Proposed by the Chair in TN/RL/213" (24 April 2008), paras. 11 and 12.

803 Article V.2 of the proposed Annex VIII to the SCM Agreement of the Chair's text, *WTO* Doc. No. TN/RL/W/213 (30 November 2007).

804 Paras. 3 and 4 of Annex B of the SPS Agreement. The scope of a Member's obligation under these provisions was under scrutiny in the Australia-Salmon case. *WTO* Doc. WT/DS18/RW, "Report of the Panel, Australia-Measures Affecting Importation of Salmon-Recourse to Article 21.5 by Canada" (18 February 2000), paras. 7.15 and 8.107.

805 *Markus Böckenförde*, "Article 7 and Annex B SPS", in *Rüdiger Wolfrum, Peter-Tobias Stoll and Anja Seibert-Fohr* (eds), *supra* note 679, pp. 476-487, at 481-482.

806 *UNEP*, *supra* note 651, para. 11(c); *WTO* Doc. No. TN/RL/W/184 (18 July 2005), para. 11(c).

the reasons why this is necessary for evaluating whether stock-related, capacity-related and management-related criteria are being observed by the recognized international fisheries organizations with the technical competence and fisheries expertise to perform the assessments.

Also, the WTO, as a trade organization, should not be held responsible as the global enforcer of good fisheries management policies or the global investigator of effective fisheries management systems.[807] Therefore, the institutional competence of the WTO must be respected when the dispute concerning fisheries subsidies comes before the WTO.

Furthermore, in order to bridge the gap between voluntary instruments and binding regulations, a strong institutional mechanism is required. It has been proposed to incorporate the voluntary international fisheries instruments, e.g. the Code of Conduct and IPOAs, into the binding WTO framework. Since some WTO Members did not participate in the development of these international fisheries instruments, when drafting fisheries subsidies regulations, the only way of resolving this problem would be to build a more concrete link between the WTO and other competent international organizations. It may provide the WTO Members with more opportunities to participate in the decision makings regarding the international fisheries instruments and more inclination to respect the decisions.

B. Options for the Establishment of Institutional Mechanisms

How the WTO can make use of external institutional or individual experts during its settlement of disputes concerning fisheries subsidies and what kind of legal effects can be given to the decisions made in this framework should be decided in fisheries subsidies regulations. The UNEP and WWF proposed several methods for establishing this mechanism.[808] These methods are summarized as follows.

The first method is to urge the WTO dispute panel and parties to consult experts. The establishment of this link is simple and does not involve a considerable change to the WTO framework. However, it may lead to the arguments between WTO adjudicators and experts and the uncertainties in disputes and processes.

The second method is to create a body wholly under WTO auspices, e.g. a permanent group of fisheries experts (PGFE) which can provide expert advice to the dispute panel. The PGFE as proposed by the WWF can be comprised of fisheries experts from the FAO, UNEP, RFMOs and other nongovernmental organizations.

---

807 *Seung Wha Chang*, "WTO Disciplines on Fisheries Subsidies: A Historic Step Towards Sustainability?", Journal of International Economic Law, Vol. 6, No. 4, pp. 879-921 (2003).

808 *David K. Schorr*, "Healthy Fisheries, Sustainable Trade: Crafting New Rules on Fishing Subsidies in the World Trade Organization" (Washington, D.C. and Gland: WWF, 2004), at 103-106; *David K. Schorr and John F. Caddy*, *supra* note 738, at 38-39.

A similar example of making use of a Permanent Group of Experts (PGE) already exists in the SCM Agreement.[809]

The third method is to make it obligatory for dispute panels or Members to consult relevant external organizations by establishing formal links with these organizations or giving them authority over the implementation of WTO rules. This method can outsource factual judgments made by these organizations. However, it needs to clarify the capability of these organizations to respond to the consultative process and the legal weight of external organizations in the course of disputes. This method is not new within the WTO framework, since links built between the GATT/WTO and other international organizations have already been established, as the following examples demonstrate:

(1) GATT 1994: The GATT directs the Contracting Parties to seek cooperation with the International Monetary Fund (IMF).[810] The GATT Contracting Parties shall consult fully with the IMF regarding the problems of monetary reserves, balance of payments or foreign exchange arrangements.[811] The Contracting Parties shall accept the decision of the IMF as a legal fact which is binding on them.
(2) Agreement on Implementation of Article VII of GATT 1994: Based on the Agreement on Implementation of Article VII of the General Agreement on Tariffs and Trade (Tokyo Round Customs Valuation Code), a tight working relationship between the GATT and World Customs Organization (WCO)[812] was established.[813] The Technical Committee on Customs Valuation under the WCO, established in 1980, has actively provided the WTO with advisory opinions on customs valuation for many years.

809 Articles 4.5 and 24 of the SCM Agreement.

810 Article XV.1 of the GATT. The IMF is an international organization of 185 member countries. It was established to promote international monetary cooperation, exchange stability, and orderly exchange arrangements; to foster economic growth and high levels of employment; and to provide temporary financial assistances to countries to help ease balance-of-payment adjustment. See further information available on-line at <www.imf.org/external/index.htm>.

811 Article XV.2 of the GATT.

812 The World Customs Organization (WCO) is the only intergovernmental organization exclusively focused on customs matters. With its worldwide membership, the WCO is recognized as the voice of the global customs community. It is particularly noted for its work in areas covering the development of global standards, the simplification and harmonization of customs procedures, trade supply chain security, the facilitation of international trade, the enhancement of customs enforcement and compliance activities, anti-counterfeiting and piracy initiatives, public-private partnerships, integrity promotion, and sustainable global customs capacity building programmes. The WCO also maintains the international Harmonized System (HS) goods nomenclature, and administers the technical aspects of the WTO agreements on Customs Valuation and Rules of Origin. See further information available online at <www.wcoomd.org/home.htm>.

813 Article 18.2 of the Tokyo Round Customs Valuation Code. The WCO is the "working name" of the Customs Cooperation Council which is referred to in this Article.

(3) SPS Agreement: According to the SPS Agreement, the WTO recognizes the authority of the Codex Alimentarius Commission (CAC)[814], the International Office of Epizootics (OIE)[815], and the Secretariat of the International Plant Protection Convention (IPPC)[816] to set international standards within the field of sanitary and phytosanitary protection.[817] Members are required to play a full part in these organizations.[818]

(4) TBT Agreement: The TBT Agreement directs governments to play a full part in the preparation by international standardizing bodies of international standards for products.[819] The TBT Committee has engaged in many activities to promote international standard-setting and compliance with TBT rules. Unlike the SPS Agreement, which includes a direct reference to three international standardizing bodies, the TBT Agreement does not contain a precise definition of what an international standardizing body is.[820] Several standard-setting organizations have made contributions to the TBT Agreement.[821]

The fourth method is to establish formal relationships with existing external fisheries organizations, e.g. the FAO or RFMOs, through memorandums of understanding (MOUs) to identify the role they may play in advising the WTO on facts within the competence of these organizations. A MOU can create a standing body in cooperation with these organizations or establish ad hoc bodies to liaise explicitly between the WTO and these organizations. An example is the MOU be-

---

814 The Codex Alimentarius Commission (CAC) was created in 1963 by the FAO and World Health Organization (WHO) to develop food standards, guidelines and related texts, such as codes of practice under the Joint FAO/WHO Food Standards Programme. The main purposes of this programme are protecting the health of consumers, ensuring fair trade practices in the food trade and promoting the coordination of all food standards work undertaken by international governmental and non-governmental organizations. See further information available on-line at <www.codexalimentarius.net/web/index_en.jsp>.

815 The International Office of Epizootics (OIE) is the intergovernmental organization responsible for animal health. As of April 2009, it had a total of 174 Member Countries and Territories. See further information available on-line at <www.oie.int/eng/en_index.htm>.

816 The International Plant Protection Convention (IPPC) is the international treaty relating to plant health. As of July 2009, it had 172 Member governments. See further information available on-line at <www.ippc.int/IPP/En/default.jsp>.

817 Para. 3 in Annex A of the SPS Agreement.

818 Article 3.4 of the SPS Agreement.

819 Article 2.6 of the TBT Agreement.

820 Para. 4 of Annex 1 of the TBT Agreement only provides the definition of an "international body or system" as a body or system whose membership is open to the relevant bodies of at least all Members.

821 E.g. the FAO, OECD, OIE, CAC, International Telecommunications Union (ITU), International Organization of Legal Metrology (OIML), International Electrotechnical Commission (IEC) and International Organization for Standardization (ISO). Among these organizations, the latter two are not intergovernmental organizations. There have been concerns that the procedures used to develop international standards may lack the full participation of developing countries.

tween the Convention on International Trade in Endangered Species of Wild Fauna and Flora (CITES) and the FAO in 2006.[822] It strengthens the processes in the CITES and FAO for scientific evaluation concerning commercially exploited aquatic species and improves communication between fisheries agencies and CITES authorities.[823] This method is the best way of building up a strong institutional mechanism. However, it needs a new round of international negotiations.

The most feasible and suitable institutional mechanism of the methods described above would be to adopt the second and third methods in parallel, because examples already exist within the WTO framework and it should not increase the burden on international negotiations. The responsibilities of these international fisheries organizations and/or expert individuals are to make findings of fact or other judgements in the context of WTO adjudications. In order to ensure legal consistency and certainty, the legal effect of these findings made by the institutional mechanism should be legislated. The controversy over cases can be reduced in the future. The findings can be binding on the WTO panels and not only have a purely advisory function. The professional and technical assessment or decisions made by these organizations or experts should be accepted by the WTO and not be open to challenge by Members in any WTO forum, including dispute settlement.[824]

C. Analysis of Provisions on Institutional Mechanisms

The Chair's text incorporates the concepts of institutional mechanisms into two areas of its provisions, i.e. enforcement of the criteria required for providing fisheries subsidies and dispute settlement.

---

822 The Convention on International Trade in Endangered Species of Wild Fauna and Flora (CITES) is an international agreement between governments, aimed at ensuring that international trade in specimens of wild animals and plants does not threaten their survival. See further information available on-line at <www.cites.org>. In terms of structure, the FAO and CITES have entered into a MOU under which an expert panel convened by the FAO provides CITES members with non-binding advice concerning proposals for imposing trade controls on marine species that are considered at risk of extinction. The CITES-FAO panels evaluate proposed CITES listings in accordance with a set of criteria that were previously developed by the FAO and politically agreed by CITES members. Based on FAO recommendations, CITES members then vote on the listing proposals at a CITES Conference of the Parties (COPs). Under the CITES-FAO process, FAO expert panels provide technical advice to CITES, but CITES then takes decisions under its own authority. Moreover, the CITES-FAO panel must decide whether trade is a threat to the survival of a given marine species, and consider cases every two years. *WTO* Doc. No. TN/RL/W/218 (21 February 2008), paras. 23-25.

823 *FAO* Doc. FAO Fisheries Report. No. 748, "Report of the FAO Ad Hoc Expert Advisory Panel for the Assessment of Proposals to Amend Appendices I and II of CITES Concerning Commercially-exploited Aquatic Species" (Rome: FAO, 2004).

824 *Vincente Paolo B. Yu III and Darlan Fonseca-Marti*, *supra* note 658, at 21-23.

1. Institutional Mechanisms in Enforcing Fisheries Subsidies Regulations

a. "Peer Review" in the FAO

With regard to the establishment of institutional mechanisms for administering fisheries subsidies regulations, the Chair's text contains "peer review" mechanisms involving the FAO or other recognized and competent international organizations to carry out the assessment of fish stocks, fishing capacity and fisheries management systems. This arrangement is consistent with the mission, expertise and experience of the FAO. The FAO is also aware of its potential review role in the new regulations.[825]

"Peer review" mechanisms are adopted in two instances in the Chair's text. Under the S&D provisions, subsidies for capital costs are not prohibited for fishing vessels which are longer than ten meters, provided that they are used in the EEZs of developing country Members and that targeted stocks have been subject to prior scientific status assessment conducted in accordance with relevant international standards and peer review in the FAO.[826] Another provision states that the assessment of the affected fish stocks and fishing capacity and the fisheries management systems of the subsidizing Members are subject to peer review prior to the granting of the subsidy.[827]

b. Issues with Dissimilar Memberships between the WTO and FAO

If a WTO Member is not a FAO Member Nation, the peer review shall take place in another recognized and competent international organization.[828] The WTO Members that are not FAO Member Nations are Brunei Darussalam, Singapore and Taiwan (see Attachment III).[829] The latter is a major fishing nation. RFMOs may play an important role in this case.[830] RFMOs are the real enforcer for managing

---

825 *FAO* Doc. No. COFI:FT/XI/2008/3, "Committee on Fisheries, Sub-Committee on Fish Trade, Eleventh Session, Bremen, Germany, 2-6 June 2008, Status and Important Recent Events Concerning International Trade in Fishery Products" (Rome: FAO, 2008), paras. 40-41.

826 Article III.2(b)(3) of the proposed Annex VIII to the SCM Agreement of the Chair's text, *WTO* Doc. No. TN/RL/W/213 (30 November 2007).

827 *Ibid.*, Article V.1.

828 *Ibid.*, footnote 83.

829 There are also FAO Member Nations which are not WTO Members.

830 In the case of Taiwan, the RFMO which can be referred to is the Western and Central Pacific Fisheries Commission (WCPFC). The WCPFC was established by the Convention for the Conservation and Management of Highly Migratory Fish Stocks in the Western and Central Pacific Ocean (WCPF Convention), which entered into force on 19 June 2004. The Convention was concluded after six years of negotiation which commenced in 1994. The period between the conclusion of the Convention and its entry into force was taken up by a series of Preparatory Conferences that laid the foundations for the Commission to commence its work. Taiwan

fish stocks on the high seas and fish stocks which migrate through the waters of different countries.[831] Although RFMOs have been unable to manage fisheries effectively,[832] it should not be an obstacle for the WTO to make reference to RFMOs. The problem of the RFMOs' performance should be resolved in general RFMO reform.[833] Technical or financial assistance through other higher level international organizations should help RFMOs fulfil their tasks effectively. Taking into account the importance of RFMOs in fisheries management, a stronger link between the WTO and RFMOs should be established.

Taiwan has objected to the peer review in the FAO, because it is not a FAO Member Nation. However, with its participation in the WTO as a full Member, Taiwan has faced the challenges of dissimilar memberships between the WTO and international standard-setting bodies. Most of the international standard-setting bodies discussed above are not open to Taiwan,[834] even though it is illustrious for its industrialization. It has been suggested that the WTO should take action to promote Taiwan's effective participation in these organizations.[835] Reference is made to the relevant provisions in the TBT and SPS Agreements[836]: WTO Members which are not Members Nations of the FAO or RFMOs and developing country Members which do not actively participate in these organizations should be encouraged and supported to participate in the relevant fisheries organizations, i.e. the

---

is one of the Members. See further information available on-line at <www.wcpfc.int/>.

831 The role of RFMOs in managing fisheries subsidies has been emphasized by Asian scholars. *Michael Sheng-ti Gau*, "Asia Perspectives on Fishery Subsidy Issues and Linkages with Environment", Asian Journal of the WTO and International Health Law & Policy, Vol. 1, pp. 189 *et seq* (2006).

832 Scholars have considered that RFMOs have been unable to manage fisheries effectively due to lack of compliance with international instruments, lack of enforcement capability, lack of political will to engage effectively in multilateral cooperation, etc. *Peter G. Davies and Catherine Redgwell*, "The International Legal Regulation of Straddling Fish Stocks", British Yearbook of International Law, Vol. 67, pp. 199-274 (1996), at 207-210. *M J Peterson*, "International Fisheries Management", in *Peter Haas, Robert Keohane and Marc Levy* (eds), "Institutions for the Earth: Sources of Effective International Environmental Protection", pp. 249-305 (Cambridge: MIT Press, 1993).

833 *Michael Lodge*, "Managing International Fisheries: Improving Fisheries Governance by Strengthening Regional Fisheries Management Organizations" (London: The Royal Institute of International Affairs, 2007). It is suggested that RFMO reform be considered in the context of wider discussions about the global governance of fisheries, which include new strategies for managing and conserving biodiversity and a new paradigm for allocating fishing rights.

834 In particular the CAC, IEC and ISO.

835 *Steve Charnovitz*, "Taiwan's WTO Membership and Its International Implications", Asian Journal of the WTO and International Health Law & Policy, Vol. 1, pp. 401-431 (2006).

836 Article 10.4 of the SPS Agreement and Articles 11.2 and 11.6 of the TBT Agreement.

FAO and RFMOs, in order to improve the effectiveness of fisheries subsidies regulations.

Moreover, strengthening the role of the SCM Committee can also help resolve this problem to a certain extent. If the peer review is going to be carried out by the FAO, the SCM Committee should participate in it so as to scrutinize this process in the FAO activities and address the concerns of non-FAO Members. However, the Chair's text tends to limit the focus of the tasks for the SCM Committee to collecting and compiling notifications from Members.[837] In comparison, the SPS Agreement requires the SPS Committee to monitor the process of international harmonization and coordinate efforts with relevant international organizations[838] and to secure from these organizations the best available scientific and technical advice for the administration of the SPS Agreement.[839] The SPS Committee may invite these organizations to examine specific matters with respect to a particular standard and the reason for a Member not using a standard.[840] If more interaction between the FAO and SCM Committee can be established in the provisions, it can provide more opportunities for inter-regime learning and understanding. The decision of peer review might also earn more respect from WTO Members.

2. Institutional Mechanisms in Dispute Settlement

The Chair's text makes a distinction between two procedures for dispute settlement based on whether disputes are concerned with prohibited fisheries subsidies or not. For disputes about prohibited fisheries subsidies, the procedure under Article 4 of the SCM Agreement shall apply.[841] When the dispute panel has been established, it may request the assistance of the Permanent Group of Experts (PGE) with regard to whether the measure in question is a prohibited subsidy or not. The PGE's conclusions on this issue shall be accepted by the panel without modification.[842] The PGE is composed of five independent persons, highly qualified in the fields of subsidies and trade relations. The experts are elected by the SCM Committee and one of them is replaced every year.[843] The decisions made by the SCM Committee have been political. The membership of the PGE does not vary on a case-by-case basis. The function of the PGE needs to be strengthened. It is a problem that the current SCM Agreement faces and it needs to be addressed at a more general level. For disputes other than those about prohibited fisheries sub-

---

837 Articles V and VI of the proposed Annex VIII to the SCM Agreement of the Chair's text, *WTO* Doc. No. TN/RL/W/213 (30 November 2007).

838 Article 3.5 of the SPS Agreement.

839 Article 12.3 of the SPS Agreement.

840 Articles 12.4 and 12.6 of the SPS Agreement.

841 Article VIII.1 of the proposed Annex VIII to the SCM Agreement of the Chair's text, *WTO* Doc. No. TN/RL/W/213 (30 November 2007), referring to Article 4 of the SCM Agreement.

842 Article 4.5 of the SCM Agreement.

843 Article 24.3 of the SCM Agreement.

sidies, the procedure under Article 30 of the SCM Agreement shall apply.[844] The dispute panel is constituted on the basis of the DSU.

If a dispute raises scientific or technical questions related to fisheries, the Chair's text provides the opportunities for the dispute panel to establish an advisory technical fisheries expert group or consult recognized and competent international organizations at the request of either party to the dispute or on its own initiative. These fisheries experts are chosen by the panel in consultation with the parties.[845] This provision gives the dispute panel the discretion to decide how to solve scientific and technical questions related to fisheries.

A Similar provision can be found under the SPS Agreement. When a dispute involves "scientific or technical issues", a dispute panel should seek advice from experts chosen by the panel in consultation with the parties. It may establish an advisory technical experts group or consult the relevant international organizations.[846] The function of the experts is to help the panel to understand and evaluate the evidence submitted and the arguments raised by the parties.[847] Under this provision, the dispute panel has no legal obligation to seek expert advice or information, but has the discretionary competence to decide which scientific experts to appoint and the procedures for appointment. In one WTO case, the panel decided to hear from individual experts rather than to establish an expert review group.[848] In another case, the panel gave each party the right to nominate one scientific expert,[849] though in other cases it did not.[850] The application of this provision exposes the uncertainty about the role of international organizations in dispute settlement.[851] To balance the role of international standards or organizations, the SPS Agreement emphasizes that nothing in the SPS Agreement shall impair the rights of Members under other international agreements to resort to the good offices or dispute settlement mechanisms of these agreements.[852] It confirms

---

844 Article VIII.1 of the proposed Annex VIII to the SCM Agreement of the Chair's text, *WTO* Doc. No. TN/RL/W/213 (30 November 2007), referring to Article 4 of the SCM Agreement.

845 *Ibid.*, Article VIII.4.

846 Article 11.2 of the SPS Agreement.

847 *WTO* Doc. WT/DS76/AB/R, "Report of the Appellate Body, Japan-Measures Affecting Agricultural Products" (22 February 1999), paras. 126 and 129.

848 *WTO* Doc. WT/DS48/R/CAN, "Report of the Panel, EC Measures Concerning Meat and Meat Products (Hormones), Complaint by Canada" (18 August 1997), para. 8.7; *WTO* Doc. WT/DS26/R/USA, "Report of the Panel, EC Measures Concerning Meat and Meat Products (Hormones), Complaint by the United States" (18 August 1997), para. 8.7.

849 *WTO* Doc. WT/DS26/R/USA, para. 8.8.

850 *WTO* Doc. WT/DS18/RW, "Report of the Panel, Australia-Measures Affecting Importation of Salmon-Recourse to Article 21.5 by Canada" (18 February 2000), paras. 6.2-6.3; *WTO* Doc. WT/DS76/R, "Report of the Panel, Japan-Measures Affecting Agricultural Products" (27 October 1998), para. 6.3.

851 *Margaret A. Young*, *supra* note 801, at 506.

852 Article 11.3 of the SPS Agreement.

the right of governments to use other dispute settlement procedures in the SPS area.[853] A similar provision is adopted in the Chair's text.[854]

The Chair's text reflects some of the methods for establishing the institutional mechanism proposed by the UNEP and WWF. However, it is rather moderate as its provisions are still restricted to a similar range of the current WTO agreements. It does not expand the role of fisheries experts, e.g. the proposed PGFE, to include more structural inter-regime enforcement. The possible reason for this arrangement would be to balance the adoption of international standards, even though a more robust role of fisheries experts in dispute settlements may help to resolve scientific and technical questions better.

VII. Provisions on Notifications and Surveillance

The issues of transparency and enforcement are fundamental to the ultimate effectiveness of fisheries subsidies regulations; in particular, poor transparency is endemic to fisheries subsidies programmes. Reporting mechanisms and assistance in implementation are both important for managing compliance with international agreements.[855] A strong notification system with appropriate technical assistance for developing country Members would be the best approach to dealing with this concern in fisheries subsidies cases. Moreover, in order to improve the surveillance and administration of Member's policies for fisheries subsidies, a trade policy review mechanism (TPRM)[856] under the WTO to regularly evaluate these policies is also necessary.[857]

In analyzing the provisions on notifications and surveillance in the Chair's text, several clarifications should be made.

The first issue is what the legal consequences are if governments fail to notify. The notification provisions under the current SCM Agreement have no legal consequences if Members fail to notify. The Chair's text requires Members to notify to the SCM Committee in advance of its implementation of any measure for which the Member invokes the provisions of general exceptions to prohibited

853 At the regional level, NAFTA can be an example chosen by Members to deal with SPS-related matters. Some international standard-setting organizations, e.g. the IPPC, also have their own procedures for settling differences between Members. *Frank Schorkopf*, "Article 11 SPS", in *Rüdiger Wolfrum, Peter-Tobias Stoll and Anja Seibert-Fohr* (eds), *supra* note 679, pp. 513-523, at 523.

854 Article VIII.5 of the proposed Annex VIII to the SCM Agreement of the Chair's text, *WTO* Doc. No. TN/RL/W/213 (30 November 2007).

855 *Rüdiger Wolfrum*, "Means of Ensuring Compliance with and Enforcement of International Law", Recueil des Cours de l'Académie de droit international de La Haye *272*, pp. 10 *et seq* (1998).

856 See information about the TPRM on-line at <www.wto.org/english/tratop_e/tpr_e/tp_int_e.htm> (last visited on 31 October 2009).

857 *UNEP*, "Fisheries Subsidies: a Critical Issue for Trade and Sustainable Development at the WTO, an Introductory Guide" (Geneva: UNEP, 2008), at 14.

fisheries subsidies or S&D provisions.[858] A subsidy that has not been notified is presumed to be prohibited. It is for the subsidizing Member to demonstrate that the subsidy in question is not prohibited.[859]

The second issue is what kind of data and information is sufficiently precise to enable assessment and evaluation. Both economic and environmental impacts should be taken into consideration in the notification requirements. The notifications should enable the assessment of the state of fish stocks, the identification of the causal relationship and the actual quantitative impact of fisheries subsidies programmes on the environmental condition of the fish stocks assessed. In order to ensure the quality of the data and information, the provisions can require the submission of an information sheet or notification form to facilitate the notification system. The design of the information sheet and notification form should take into account the criteria on fish stocks, fishing capacity and fisheries management. In this case, the WTO can ask for the assistance of or refer to the expertise of fisheries organizations to establish the criteria. With regard to the difficulty of developing country Members in providing science-based data, a simpler sheet or form can be established or technical assistance provided.

VIII. Conclusion

Based on the efforts of the WTO and its Members during the negotiations in the past few years, the Chair's text represents a substantial step in the WTO negotiations on fisheries subsidies. It reflects the mandates of the Ministerial Declarations and incorporates suggestions and proposals from other relevant international organizations. These organizations have, through research and informal meetings with the WTO, promoted a deeper involvement by the WTO in fisheries conservation.

Since the Chair's text does not adopt the top-down approach as its structure, the provisions for sub-categories are fundamentally important and need to be more detailed and precise. Although certain norms in the provisions need to be clarified, the provisions for prohibited fisheries subsidies and the exceptions to these prohibitions reflect the major concerns of Members about various types of fisheries subsidies expressed during the negotiations.

The Chair's text also takes into account the importance of fisheries to developing country Members and adopts S&D provisions to provide the developing country Members with policy space and flexibility along with sustainability criteria. It also provides for technical assistance to developing country Members.

While providing policy space and flexibility to subsidize, the Chair's text also sets the minimum criteria for the fisheries management systems required to avoid the negative impact of fisheries subsidies on fisheries conservation. It incorporates the fisheries management instruments from the FAO and other inter-governmental

858 Article VI.1 of the proposed Annex VIII to the SCM Agreement of the Chair's text, *WTO* Doc. No. TN/RL/W/213 (30 November 2007).

859 *Ibid.*, Article VIII.2.

organizations into the WTO framework, which demonstrates a willingness to interact with other legal regimes. These instruments are considered as the international standards with which the subsidizing Members must comply. These can be decisive during the dispute settlement and therefore may be *de facto* binding on Members. In order to enforce the minimum criteria provisions, the Chair's text establishes an institutional mechanism between the WTO and FAO which requires stock-related, capacity-related and management-related criteria subject to peer review in the FAO.

Other WTO agreements already contain similar provisions on rule-referencing and the involvement of international standard-setting bodies, in particular the TBT and SPS Agreements. The incorporation of the fisheries management instruments from organizations with fisheries expertise in the Chair's text does not go beyond the scope which already exists in similar agreements.

The Chair's text reconciles the positions of Members and assists in developing the required consensus needed to approve the legal text. This will be the legal basis for regulating fisheries subsidies at the global level.

Chapter 4: Regulations of Fisheries Subsidies under the European Union Regime and Comparison with the Fisheries Subsidies Regulations in the WTO Chair's Text

I. Introduction

The European Union (EU) has played an important role in global fishing activities. It faces the problems of overfishing and overcapacity of fishing fleets like other countries in the rest of the world. Although it has implemented measures to improve the situation, these problems remain to a large degree unresolved.

The European fishing industries receive subsidies from two sources: State aid provided by the Member States and structural assistance provided by the EU. The amount of fisheries subsidies in the EU is the second largest among the OECD countries after Japan. Subsidies are considered as a contributing factor to the overcapacity of the European fishing fleets.[860]

The EU, as a major trade player and Member of the WTO,[861] is required to comply with WTO rules. In the WTO negotiations on fisheries subsidies regulations, the EU has presented proposals on how to regulate fisheries subsidies as detailed in Chapter 2.[862] In order for the EU to play a more influential role in the WTO negotiations, the EU could share its current internal policies and experience on fisheries subsidies and capacity management issues with other Members, similar to a submission in 2005 in which the EU shared its experience on enforcement and implementation of its fisheries subsidies regulations.[863] In addition, in view of the fact that the EU has one of the most mature and sophisticated fisheries subsidies regimes, the WTO could benefit significantly from EU experience on the sub-

---

860 *European Commission*, "Commission Working Paper: Reflections on Further Reform of the Common Fisheries Policy" (Brussels: European Commission, 2008), at 5.

861 *Supra* note 223.

862 *WTO* Doc. No. TN/RL/W/82 (23 April 2003); *WTO* Doc. No. TN/RL/W/178 (11 April 2005); *WTO* Doc. No. TN/RL/GEN/39 (12 May 2005); *WTO* Doc. No. TN/RL/GEN/134 (24 April 2006).

863 *WTO* Doc. No. TN/RL/W/178 (11 April 2005).

C.-J. Chen, *Fisheries Subsidies under International Law*, Hamburg Studies on Maritime Affairs 20, DOI 10.1007/978-3-642-15693-9_5, © Springer-Verlag Berlin Heidelberg 2010

categories of fisheries subsidies and fisheries management systems, and in particular with reference to the effectiveness of these regulations.

This Chapter looks into European fisheries resources and its fisheries policies and analyzes the regulations pertaining to State aid and structural assistance provided to the European fishing industries. A comparison of EU regulations with the proposed fisheries subsidies regulations in the WTO Chair's text is made in order to identify potential problems that the EU may have in integrating its existing regulations with the new WTO rules when these come into effect.

II. The State of Fishing Industries and Fisheries Resources in the European Union

A. The European Union as a Major Fish Producer, Catcher and Importer

The EU is the second largest world producer of fish after China.[864] In spite of the fact that the EU produces and catches a large share of global fish products, the fish produced and caught by the European fishermen is mostly for local consumption within the EU. The EU is the world's largest net importer of fish products and its dependency on imports for its fish supply continues to increase. It also plays a major role as an exporter of high-value fish products. In 2006, the net imports to the EU amounted to approximately four million tonnes and had a value of approximately EUR 14,000 million.[865]

B. Overfished State of Fish Stocks in the European Waters

The EU's total production of fish products has decreased compared with previous years. For example, the production in 2005 was approximately 17 percent less than in 1993.[866] Also, the catch in 2005 was 22 percent less than the catch in

864 *Eurostat*, "Facts and Figures on the CFP, Basic Data on the Common Fisheries Policy" (Luxembourg: Office of Official Publications of the European Communities, 2006), at 1.

865 Fish products here refer to as both fish and aquaculture products. *Eurostat*, "Fishery Statistics Data 1990-2006" (Luxembourg: Office of Official Publications of the European Communities, 2007), at 48-49.

866 *Ibid.*, at 18-19; *Eurostat*, *supra* note 864, at 1-2. In 2005, the EU-27 produced 6.9 million tonnes of fish products which accounted for four percent of total global fish products. The largest producers within the EU by volume are Denmark and Spain, whose catches account for one third of the EU's total catches. The catch of the EU-27 accounted for six percent of the world total in 2005 and amounted to 5.6 million tonnes. The EU is also the third biggest world fisheries catcher after China and Peru. In 2004, the fish landed in EU ports amounted to approximately EUR 6.2 billion.

1993, while the total world catch increased by eight percent over the same period of time.[867] The depletion of commercially important fish stocks has led to a declining trend in catches in the EU. A recent EU report states that 88 percent of fish stocks in the EU waters are overfished.[868] Despite substantial efforts, e.g. structural policies for fishing industries and fleets, there has been no overall improvement in the state of fish stocks since 2003.[869] Overfishing has led to smaller stock size and reduced harvesting opportunities.

C. Overcapacity of the European Fishing Fleets

The fundamental feature of the European fishing fleets has long been its "chronic overcapacity."[870] In 1995, the capacity of the European fishing fleets was estimated to be forty percent above the level which would ensure a sustainable exploitation of living aquatic resources.[871] This sizable overcapacity in the EU results in part from excessive subsidization, ineffective controls, technological advances and insufficient political will to introduce effective instruments to adjust fleet capacity and neutralise incentives to overfishing.[872]

Over the past ten years, the EU's efforts to reduce the capacity of fishing fleets have managed to reduce the capacity of the European fishing fleets at a steady yearly rate of approximately two percent in terms of number, 1.5 percent in terms of tonnage and two percent in terms of engine power. Despite the enlargement of the EU in 2004 and 2007, the number of vessels in 2008 was slightly less than 87,000, which was 17,000 less than in 1995.[873] The EU fishing fleets continued to decline in 2008 and will probably continue to do so in the future.[874] However, recent EU statistics show that the European fishing fleets are still exerting unsustainable pressure on the fish stocks,[875] and that the overcapacity in most European fishing fleets in most fishing fleet segments continues to exist.[876] The efforts

867 *Eurostat*, *supra* note 865, at 23.

868 *European Commission*, No. IP/08/828, "Commission: Policy Statement Proposes Major Changes in Fisheries Management Regime for 2009" (Brussels: European Commission, 2008).

869 *Ibid.*

870 *European Commission*, "Factsheets on the New CFP-2003-Why did we need a new fisheries policy?", available on-line at <http://ec.europa.eu/fisheries/publications/factsheets/facts/2003/01_en.pdf> (last visited on 28 February 2009).

871 *European Commission*, "Report of the Group of Independent Experts to Advise the European Commission on the Fourth Generation of Multi-annual Guidance Programmes" (Brussels: European Commission, 1996).

872 *European Commission*, *supra* note 860, at 5.

873 *Eurostat*, *supra* note 865, at 52-55.

874 *Eurostat*, "Statistics in Focus, Agriculture and Fisheries" (Luxembourg: Office of Official Publications of the European Communities, 2009), at 1.

875 *European Commission*, *supra* note 860, at 4.

876 *Indrani Lutchman, Sophie des Clers and Koen Van den Bossche*, "Overcapacity-What Overcapacity? An Evaluation of Member States Reporting on Efforts to

to decrease the capacity of the European fishing fleets over the past few years have not been sufficient enough to reach a sustainable level.

D. Subsidies to the European Fishing Industries

Subsidies to the fishing industries by the EU and its Member States have played a major role in the viability of these industries. State aid paid by the governments of Member States in 2002 accounted for five percent of the total value of landed fish. Subsidies that the European fishing industries received from both the EU and the governments of its Member States amounted to eleven percent of the total value of landed fish.[877] Reform of these subsidies is considered important for securing capacity reduction, stock recovery and sustainable fisheries.[878] The following measures have been considered useful for addressing the issue of overcapacity, including subsidizing fishing capacity reduction programmes and eliminating subsidies for vessel modernisation or for operating costs, e.g. fuel.[879]

III. Common Fisheries Policy as the European Fisheries Management Instrument

The Common Fisheries Policy (CFP), based on a common organization of the markets,[880] is the EU's instrument for the management of fisheries and aquaculture. The CFP was developed in the 1970s and established in 1983. It has since then been reviewed every ten years. The latest reform was agreed in 2002 and will be up for review at the latest in 2012.

A. The 2002 Reform of Common Fisheries Policy

Due to the lack of success with previous policies, the 2002 CFP reform had the following objectives: to conserve fish stocks against overfishing, protect the ma-

Achieve a Sustainable Balance between Capacity and Fishing Opportunities in 2007" (London: Institute for European Environmental Policy, 2009).

877 *WTO*, "World Trade Report 2006, Exploring the Links between Subsidies, Trade and the WTO" (Geneva: WTO, 2006).

878 *WWF*, "Putting an End to Fishing in the Dark? WWF's European Marine Programme's Response to the ETI Green Paper-Part III" (Brussels: WWF European Policy Office, 2006), at 1.

879 *WWF*, "A Leading Role for the EU in Combating Illegal, Unreported and Unregulated Fishing" (Brussels: WWF European Policy Office, 2007), at 4.

880 The common organization of the market in fisheries and aquaculture products was set up in the European Union in order to create a common market in fish products inside the Union that would match production to demand for the benefit of producers and consumers.

rine environment, ensure the economic viability of the European fishermen, provide good quality food to consumers at reasonable prices, and ensure the sustainable development of fishing activities from environmental, economic and social perspectives. It also aimed to implement progressively an ecosystem-based approach to fisheries management and to improve the basis of the decision-making process through sound and transparent scientific advice and the increased participation of stakeholders. Coherence with other EU policies such as environmental and development policies was an important element of this reform, as were accountability and effectiveness. This CFP reform also introduced a long-term approach to fisheries management, involving the establishment of multi-annual plans for recovering fish stocks outside safe biological limits and for managing other fish stocks.

Another key component of the CFP is the negotiation and implementation of bilateral fisheries agreements between the EU and third countries which provide the EU fishing fleets with access to surplus fisheries resources in the waters of these countries. In the early 2000's, one-fifth of the European fishing vessels were fishing under the bilateral EU-ACP fisheries agreements.[881] With the reform of the CFP in 2002, these agreements have been transformed. The fisheries access arrangements with a financial contribution have become fisheries partnership agreements (FPAs) which represent genuine partnerships for sustainable development and responsible fisheries. The FPAs align access arrangements more closely with development policy. The idea of FPAs is to build partnerships and to help third countries put in place their own fisheries policies to pursue economic development while protecting fish resources.[882] The EU has concluded 21 FPAs (as in Attachment V) with third countries, mainly developing countries in Africa and in the Pacific, with financial contribution for access to their fishing zones. The EU has also executed fisheries agreements not involving financial compensation with Faeroe Islands, Iceland and Norway. These agreements contain the means to exploit their own resources and usually take the form of a straightforward exchange of quotas.

B. Outcome of the 2002 Reform of Common Fisheries Policy

The CFP reform in 2002 has not achieved the desired objectives. Although some progress has been made in reducing excessive capacity, it is unclear if the reductions have been sufficient to offset technology creep and it is also unclear

---

881 *Béatrice Gorez*, *supra* note 723. Based on the Lomé Agreement and the subsequent Cotonou Agreement between the ACP countries and the EU, fishing firms within the EU gained access to ACP waters in return for the EU allowing preferential access of the foreign partner's fish products to the EU markets.

882 About the Common Fisheries Policy, Bilateral Fisheries Partnership Agreements between the EC and Third Countries, further information available on-line at <http://ec.europa.eu/fisheries/cfp/external_relations/bilateral_agreements_en.htm> (last visited on 31 August 2009).

whether a sustainable level will be attained any time soon. As far as improving the economic viability of the fishing industries is concerned, the outcome is uncertain.[883]

The EU itself frequently highlights the failings of the CFP. The European Commission has noted that "excessive fishing pressure has eroded away the present and future productivity of the fish stocks" and that "the result is poor economic efficiency, high environmental impact, high fuel burn and low contribution of European fisheries to food supply" and initiated a review of the current CFP in 2008.[884] The Commission identified "five structural failings" of the CFP as a deep-rooted problem of the system: fleet overcapacity; imprecise policy objectives resulting in insufficient guidance for decisions and implementation; a decision-making system that encourages a short-term focus; a framework that does not give sufficient responsibility to the industry; lack of political will to ensure compliance and poor compliance by the industry.[885]

C. Outlook for the 2012 Reform of Common Fisheries Policy

Based on the results of the CFP reform in 2002, the Commission launched a public debate in 2009 on the way that EU fisheries were managed and released the "Green Paper on a Reform of the Common Fisheries Policy"[886] outlining the state of Europe's fisheries in order to prepare for the next reform in 2012. The Commission proposed to prioritise the recovery and long-term health of fish stocks rather than short-term economic targets and recommended the transition to smaller and more efficient fishing fleets.[887] In order to achieve these objectives, more radical changes need to be made to the CFP reform in 2012, including a reduction in excessive fishing fleet overcapacity to match available fisheries resources; healthy marine ecosystems as a pre-requisite for economically viable fisheries; clear and binding management principles and objectives at EU level, more delegation of implementing powers from the Council to the Commission, Member States and/or regional management bodies; and a shift of responsibilities to fishermen, rewarding those who follow the rules.[888] As the public debate is still going on, the possibility of additional changes being made to the 2012 CFP reform still exists.

---

883 *Michael Sissenwine and David Symes*, "Reflections on the Common Fisheries Policy, Report to the General Directorate for Fisheries and Maritime Affairs of the European Commission" (Brussels: Greenpeace European Unit, 2007), at 23.

884 *European Commission*, "Commission Working Document, Reflections on Further Reform of the Common Fisheries Policy" (Brussels: European Commission, 2008).

885 *European Commission,* No. COM(2009)163 Final, "Green Paper, Reform of the Common Fisheries Policy" (Brussels: Commission of the European Communities, 2009), at 8.

886 *Ibid.*

887 *Ibid.*, at 14-22.

888 *Greenpeace*, "Reform of the EU's Common Fisheries Policy, Commission Green Paper on the Reform of the Common Fisheries Policy (21 April 2009)" (Brussels: Greenpeace European Unit, 2009), at 1.

IV. Regulations on Fisheries Subsidies in the European Union

Subsidies to the EU fishing industries are granted at the Member State and the EU levels; as such, the following sections look into these two types of assistance for the fisheries sector.

A. State Aid to the Fisheries Sector in the European Union

1. State Aid Control

To ensure that government interventions do not distort competition and intra-Community trade, the control of State aid has been incorporated in the EU rules. State aid is defined as an advantage in any form whatsoever conferred by national public authorities on a selective basis to undertakings for the production of certain goods. Based on this definition, subsidies granted to individual consumers on a non-discriminatory basis and general measures open to all enterprises are not covered by State aid control under the EC. Although State aid is generally prohibited, government interventions are in some circumstances necessary for a well-functioning and equitable economy. Therefore, a certain amount of policy freedom has been allowed through a series of legislative acts that provide for a number of exemptions. A system of rules to monitor and assess State aid has also been established.

Four Directorate-Generals (DGs) are responsible for the execution of effective State aid control with sector-specific services, namely Agriculture,[889] Coal, Fisheries[890] and Transport,[891] while the DG for Competition deals with all other sectors. For fisheries, the DG for Maritime Affairs and Fisheries is responsible for dealing with State aid provided to the fisheries and aquaculture sector.

2. State Aid Control to the Fisheries and Aquaculture Sector

a. Legal Basis

Aid granted by Member States to the fisheries and aquaculture sector is governed by the State aid rules laid down in Articles 87 to 89 of the Treaty establishing the European Community (the EC Treaty).[892] This is the legal foundation for Council

---

889 Aid to the production, processing and marketing of agricultural products.

890 Aid to the production, processing and marketing of fisheries and aquaculture products.

891 Aid to companies in the road, rail, inland waterway, sea and air transport sectors.

892 Council Regulation (EC) No 104/2000 of 17 December 1999 on the common organisation of the markets in fishery and aquaculture products, OJ L 17, 21.1.2000, pp. 21-52.

regulations on State aid. However, State aid co-financed by the European Fisheries Fund (EFF)[893] and temporary specific aid granted to combat economic crises fall under the special regime of the EFF[894] and are exempted from these rules.

Article 87 of the EC Treaty[895] contains the substantive rules governing State aid, namely the general principle that State aid is incompatible with the common market, as well as a list of possible exemption conditions. In order to clarify how to apply the exemption clauses, a number of interpretative frameworks and guidelines have been adopted by the Commission, such as the Community framework for State aid for R&D and the Community guidelines on State aid for environ-

---

893 Article 7(2) of Council Regulation (EC) No 1198/2006 on the European Fisheries Fund, OJ L 223, 15.8.2006, pp. 1-44, provides that Articles 87, 88 and 89 of the EC Treaty shall not apply to financial contributions from Member States to operations co-financed by the EFF and provided as part of an operational programme. Article 53 of Council Regulation (EC) No 1998/2006 provides more details on contributions from the EFF.

894 Article 4(1) of Council Regulation (EC) No 744/2008 instituting a temporary specific action aiming to promote the restructuring of the European Community fishing fleet affected by the economic crisis, OJ L 202, 31.7.2008, pp. 1-8, provides that without prejudice to paragraph 2 of this Article, Articles 87, 88 and 89 of the Treaty shall not apply to aid granted by Member States, pursuant to and in conformity with this Regulation within the scope of Article 36 of the Treaty.

895 Article 87 of the Treaty establishing the European Community, OJ C 325, 24.12.2002, p. 67, provides that 1. [s]ave as otherwise provided in this Treaty, any aid granted by a Member State or through State resources in any form whatsoever which distorts or threatens to distort competition by favouring certain undertakings or the production of certain goods shall, in so far as it affects trade between Member States, be incompatible with the common market. 2. The following shall be compatible with the common market: (a) aid having a social character, granted to individual consumers, provided that such aid is granted without discrimination related to the origin of the products concerned; (b) aid to make good the damage caused by natural disasters or exceptional occurrences; (c) aid granted to the economy of certain areas of the Federal Republic of Germany affected by the division of Germany, in so far as such aid is required in order to compensate for the economic disadvantages caused by that division. 3. The following may be considered to be compatible with the common market: (a) aid to promote the economic development of areas where the standard of living is abnormally low or where there is serious underemployment; (b) aid to promote the execution of an important project of common European interest or to remedy a serious disturbance in the economy of a Member State; (c) aid to facilitate the development of certain economic activities or of certain economic areas, where such aid does not adversely affect trading conditions to an extent contrary to the common interest; (d) aid to promote culture and heritage conservation where such aid does not affect trading conditions and competition in the Community to an extent that is contrary to the common interest; (e) such other categories of aid as may be specified by decision of the Council acting by a qualified majority on a proposal from the Commission.

mental protection. They ensure a consistent application of State aid rules across all Member States and sectors of the industry.[896]

To enforce Article 87, the basic procedural rules are set out under Articles 88[897] and 89[898] of the EC Treaty. Member States are to notify the Commission of any plan to grant aid and to implement aid only after the Commission's approval. The Commission should be notified of State aid in accordance with detailed provisions that have been complemented by the procedural regulation,[899] the implementing regulation[900] and the enabling regulation.[901]

---

[896] *European Commission*, "EU Competition Policy and the Consumer" (Brussels: European Commission, 2004), at 19.

[897] Article 88 of the Treaty establishing the European Community provides that 1. [t]he Commission shall, in cooperation with Member States, keep under constant review all systems of aid existing in those States. It shall propose to the latter any appropriate measures required by the progressive development or by the functioning of the common market. 2. If, after giving notice to the parties concerned to submit their comments, the Commission finds that aid granted by a State or through State resources is not compatible with the common market having regard to Article 87, or that such aid is being misused, it shall decide that the State concerned shall abolish or alter such aid within a period of time to be determined by the Commission. If the State concerned does not comply with this decision within the prescribed time, the Commission or any other interested State may, in derogation from the provisions of Articles 226 and 227, refer the matter directly to the Court of Justice. On application by a Member State, the Council may, acting unanimously, decide that aid which that State is granting or intends to grant shall be considered to be compatible with the common market, in derogation from the provisions of Article 87 or from the regulations provided for in Article 89, if such a decision is justified by exceptional circumstances. If, as regards the aid in question, the Commission has already initiated the procedure provided for in the first subparagraph of this paragraph, the fact that the State concerned has made its application to the Council shall have the effect of suspending that procedure until the Council has made its attitude known. If, however, the Council has not made its attitude known within three months of the said application being made, the Commission shall give its decision on the case. 3. The Commission shall be informed, in sufficient time to enable it to submit its comments, of any plans to grant or alter aid. If it considers that any such plan is not compatible with the common market having regard to Article 87, it shall without delay initiate the procedure provided for in paragraph 2. The Member State concerned shall not put its proposed measures into effect until this procedure has resulted in a final decision.

[898] Article 89 of the Treaty establishing the European Community provides that [t]he Council, acting by a qualified majority on a proposal from the Commission and after consulting the European Parliament, may make any appropriate regulations for the application of Articles 87 and 88 and may in particular determine the conditions in which Article 88(3) shall apply and the categories of aid exempted from this procedure.

[899] Council Regulation (EC) No 659/1999 of 22 March 1999 laying down detailed rules for the application of Article 93 of the EC Treaty, OJ L 83, 27.3.1999, pp. 1–9.

b. Guidelines

State aid to fisheries and aquaculture is assessed by the Commission in line with the *Guidelines for the examination of State aid to fisheries and aquaculture* (Guidelines). The Commission first adopted the Guidelines for the examination of State aid to the fisheries sector in 1985,[902] not long after the establishment of a Community system for the conservation and management of fisheries resources in 1983.[903] The European Court of Justice stated that the Guidelines adopted by the Commission are binding.[904] Neither the Commission nor a Member State can release itself from the obligations set out in the Guidelines.[905]

According to the most recent Guidelines adopted in 2008,[906] State aid is any measure entailing a financial advantage in any form whatsoever funded directly or indirectly from the budgets of public authorities (national, regional, provincial, departmental or local) or from other State resources. Examples are capital transfers, reduced-interest loans, interest subsidies, certain State holdings in the capital of undertakings, aid financed by special levies or parafiscal charges, aid granted in the form of State securities against bank loans, the reduction of or exemption from charges or taxes, including accelerated depreciation and the reduction of social contributions.[907] These Guidelines apply to the entire fisheries sector and concern the exploitation of aquatic resources and aquaculture together with the means of production, processing and marketing of the resultant products, but excluding recreation and sport fishing which do not result in the sale of fishery products.[908]

---

900 Commission Regulation (EC) No 794/2004 of 21 April 2004 implementing Council Regulation (EC) No 659/1999 laying down detailed rules for the application of Article 93 of the EC Treaty, OJ L 140, 30.4.2004, pp. 1-134.

901 Council Regulation (EC) No 994/98 of 7 May 1998 on the application of Articles 92 and 93 of the Treaty establishing the European Community to certain categories of horizontal State aid, OJ L 142, 14.5.1998, pp. 1-4.

902 Guidelines for the examination of State aid to fisheries and aquaculture, OJ 1985 C 268, pp. 2 *et seq.*

903 Council Regulation (EEC) No 170/83 of 25 January 1983 establishing a Community system for the conservation and management of fisheries resources.

904 Judgment of the Court of 15 October 1996. Case C-311/94. IJssel-Vliet Combinatie BV v Minister van Economische Zaken, para. 40; Judgment of the Court (Fifth Chamber) of 24 March 1993. Case C-313/90. Comité International de la Rayonne et des Fibres Synthétiques (CIRFS) and others Commission of the European Communities, paras. 34-36; Judgment of the Court (Fifth Chamber) of 5 October 2000. Case C-288/96. Federal Republic of Germany v Commission of the European Communities, paras. 62 and 64.

905 *Michel Morin*, "State Aid to the Fisheries Sector", in *Michael Sánchez Rydelski* "The EC State Aid Regime: Distortive Effects of State Aid on Competition and Trade", pp. 501-510 (London: Cameron May, 2006), at 505.

906 Guidelines for the examination of State aid to fisheries and aquaculture, OJ C 84, 3.4.2008, pp. 10-16.

907 Para. 1.4 of Guidelines for the examination of State aid to fisheries and aquaculture.

908 Para. 1.1 of Guidelines for the examination of State aid to fisheries and aquaculture.

For the application of these Guidelines, fishery products mean both products caught at sea or in inland waters.[909]

Based on the Guidelines, several types of aid may be compatible with the common market, including aid covered by a block exemption regulation, aid for investment on board fishing vessels, aid to make good damage caused by natural disasters, exceptional occurrences or specific adverse climatic events, tax relief and labour related costs concerning European fishing vessels operating outside Community waters, aid financed through parafiscal charges, aid for marketing of fishery products from the outermost regions and aid for fishing fleets in the outermost regions.[910]

Operating aid is considered incompatible with the common market.[911] Operating aid is that which increases the business liquidity of the recipient or is calculated on the quantity produced or marketed, or on product prices, and which has the effect of reducing the recipient's production costs or improving the recipient's income. Only if the aid clearly and firmly contributes to the objectives of the CFP is it considered compatible.[912]

Moreover, in order to be compatible with the common market, State aid must contain an incentive effect on the part of the beneficiary.[913] Therefore, aid which is granted for operations that the beneficiary has already started to implement as well as aid for activities in which the beneficiary would have engaged under normal market conditions are not considered to have the incentive effect and are therefore incompatible with the common market.

State aid to the fisheries and aquaculture sector should also be consistent with the CFP as well as with the EU structural policies.[914] It should also be consistent with the Competition Policy. The EU's control over Competition Policy gives it the power to rule on mergers, takeovers, cartels and the use of state aid. The objective of Competition Policy is to prevent distortion of competition in the internal market.

---

[909] Para. 1.2 of Guidelines for the examination of State aid to fisheries and aquaculture.

[910] Paras. 4.1-4.8 of Guidelines for the examination of State aid to fisheries and aquaculture.

[911] Judgment of the Court (Fifth Chamber) of 5 October 2000. - Federal Republic of Germany v Commission of the European Communities. - State aid - Operating aid - Guidelines in the fisheries sector - Article 92(1) and (3)(c) of the EC Treaty (now, after amendment, Article 87(1) and (3)(c) EC) - Rights of the defence - Statement of reasons. - Case C-288/96, paras. 49, 77, 78 and 90.

[912] Para. 3.4 of Guidelines for the examination of State aid to fisheries and aquaculture.

[913] Para. 3.3 of Guidelines for the examination of State aid to fisheries and aquaculture.

[914] Paras. 3.1 and 3.2 of Guidelines for the examination of State aid to fisheries and aquaculture.

c. Exemptions from the Prior Notification Requirements

On the basis of Article 89 of the EC Treaty, the Commission has adopted a number of legal instruments which exempt certain aid from the notification requirement under Article 88(3) of the EC Treaty. Those regarding fisheries are as follows:

(1) Block Exemption Regulation for Fisheries

Aid to small and medium-sized enterprises (SMEs) is considered compatible with the common market and not subject to the notification requirement of Article 88(3) of the EC Treaty.[915] A set of provisions was established to regulate State aid to SMEs in 2001.[916] However, these provisions on State aid to SMEs did not apply to activities linked to the production, processing or marketing of fishery and aquaculture products.[917]

Later, the Commission adopted a new block exemption regulation for fisheries in 2004,[918] which was designed to apply until the end of 2006 and was later prolonged until the Commission adopted another new regulation in 2008.[919] The Commission has gained considerable experience in applying Articles 87 and 88 of the EC Treaty in numerous decisions to SMEs in the production, processing and marketing of fisheries products and has also stated its policy, most recently in the Guidelines for the examination of State aid to fisheries and aquaculture.[920] Based on this experience, this regulation exempts State aid to SMEs[921] in fisheries from the requirement of prior notification on condition that they comply with the relevant provisions established under the European Fisheries Fund and provided that they do not exceed the threshold of a total amount of EUR 1 million per beneficiary per year or a total amount of eligible costs per project of EUR 2 million.[922]

---

915 Article 1.1(a) of Council Regulation (EC) No 994/98.

916 Commission Regulation (EC) No 70/2001 of 12 January 2001 on the application of Articles 87 and 88 of the EC Treaty to State aid to small and medium-sized enterprises, OJ L 10, 13.1.2001, pp. 33-42.

917 Para. 7 of the preamble to Commission Regulation (EC) No 70/2001.

918 Commission Regulation (EC) No 1595/2004 of 8 September 2004 on the application of Article 87 and 88 of Treaty to State aid to small and medium-sized enterprises active in the production, processing and marketing of fisheries products, OJ L 291, 14.9.2004, pp. 3-11.

919 Commission Regulation (EC) No 736/2008 of 22 July 2008 on the application of Article 87 and 88 of Treaty to State aid to small and medium-sized enterprises active in the production, processing and marketing of fisheries products, OJ L 201, 30.7.2008, pp. 16-28.

920 Para. 3 of the preamble to Commission Regulation (EC) No 736/2008.

921 Para. 16 of the preamble to Commission Regulation (EC) No 736/2008 defines the SMEs as those in Article 1 of Annex 1 of Commission Regulation (EC) No 70/ 2001: enterprises which have fewer than 250 employees and have either an annual turnover not exceeding EUR 40 million or total assets not exceeding EUR 27 million.

922 Article 1(3) of Commission Regulation (EC) No 736/2008.

(2) *De Minimis* Aid in the Fisheries Sector

Aid measures of a limited amount shall be deemed as *de minimis* and not required to meet all the criteria of Article 87(1) of the EC Treaty and shall be exempt from the notification requirement of Article 88(3) of the EC Treaty.[923]

A specific "*de minimis*" regulation for aid to undertakings in the fisheries sector not exceeding EUR 30,000 per beneficiary over any three-year period may be deemed not to affect trade between Member States and/or not to distort or threaten to distort competition, provided that the cumulative sum of all aid granted in the Member State concerned remains below 2.5 percent of the turnover of its fisheries sector.[924] As the method of calculation is also important for the enforcement of these regulations, more detailed rules have been established.[925] Member States should apply precise calculations uniformly for the purpose of transparency, equal treatment and effective monitoring, as well as the correct application of the *de minimis* ceiling.[926]

B. *Structural Assistance to the Fisheries Sector in the European Union*

1. Structural Policy in the Fisheries Sector

In order to adapt and manage the development of structures in a targeted sector, the EU develops structural policies. The term "structures" here means the equipment required to produce goods and the organization of the production process.

The objective of these structural policies is to strengthen economic and social cohesion between the regions. Therefore, various funds to channel financial assistance to the areas, people and types of enterprises have been established. Currently, there are four structural funds providing financial assistance to resolve structural economic and social problems, namely the European Regional Development Fund (ERDF), the European Social Fund (ESF), the European Agri-

---

923 Article 2 of Council Regulation (EC) No 994/98; Article 3(1) of Commission Regulation (EC) No 875/2007 of 24 July 2007 on the application of Article 87 and 88 of the EC Treaty to *de minimis* aid in the fisheries sector and amending Regulation (EC) No 1860/2004, OJ L 193, 25.7.2007, pp. 6-12.

924 Article 3 and Para. 6 of the preamble to Commission Regulation (EC) No 875/ 2007. In the previous regulation, the ceiling is set at EUR 3,000 per beneficiary over any period of three years, where the total amount of such aid granted to all enterprises over three years remains below a ceiling to be set by the Commission at around 0.3% of the annual fisheries output. Article 3 of Commission Regulation (EC) No 1860/2004 of 6 October 2004 on the application of Articles 87 and 88 of the EC Treaty to *de minimis* aid in the agriculture and fisheries sectors, OJ L 325, 28.10.2004, pp. 4-9.

925 Article 3(7) of Commission Regulation (EC) No 875/2007.

926 Paras. 14 and 15 of the preamble to Commission Regulation (EC) No 875/2007.

cultural Guarantee Fund (EAGF), the European Agricultural Fund for Rural Development (EAFRD),[927] and the European Fisheries Fund (EFF).[928]

Providing structural assistance in the fisheries and aquaculture sector has been part of the role of the EU's structural funds. For the fishing industries, the objective is to protect fisheries resources and the marine environment to guarantee sustainable fisheries, while ensuring the economic and social development of coastal areas where fishing is a major component of economic activities. The general principle was that these public funds should not contribute to increasing fishing capacity.[929]

2. Structural Assistance between 1971 and 1993

Between the years 1971 and 1993, the European fisheries structural policy was financed by the European Agriculture Guidance and Guarantee Fund (EAGGF).[930] However, the first comprehensive fisheries structural programme, known as Multi-Annual Guidance Programmes (MAGPs), was not adopted until 1983. The MAGPs were generally five-to six-year programmes administered by the Commission with the purpose of restructuring the European fishing fleets. The programmes adjusted the amount of fishing effort to a level that would ensure a long-term balance between fishing activities and resources by the main segments of the fleet, e.g., trawlers, netters.[931] This adjustment was needed to ensure the survival of a sector which was seriously under threat from the overexploitation of fisheries resources and which therefore had to be restructured.

MAGP I ran from 1984 until the end of 1986. It included targets for fleet capacity to be achieved by the end of 1986. However, in most cases the aim was merely to balance investments with removals in order to maintain overall capacity

---

927 Replacing the European Agriculture Guidance and Guarantee Fund (EAGGF), the European Agricultural Guarantee Fund (EAGF) and the European Agricultural Fund for Rural Development (EAFRD) were created by Council Regulation (EC) No 1290/2005 of 21 June 2005 on the financing of the common agricultural policy, OJ L 209, 11.8.2005, pp. 1–25.

928 With regard to the Common Fisheries Policy, the Role of Structural Policy and the European Fisheries Fund, further information is available on-line at <http://ec.europa.eu/fisheries/cfp/structural_policy_overview_en.htm> (last visited on 15 October 2009).

929 *Clare Coffey and David Baldock*, "Reforming European Union Fisheries Subsidies – A Briefing Paper", in *WWF*, "Fishing in the Dark, A Symposium on Access to Environmental Information and Government Accountability in Fishing Subsidy Programmes, 28-29 November 2000, Brussels, Belgium" (Washington, D.C. and Gland: WWF, 2004), at 15-16.

930 Council Regulation (EEC) No 2141/70 of October 20 1970 laying down a common structural policy for the fishing industry, OJ L 236, 27.10.1970, which is replaced by Council Regulation (EEC) No 101/76 of 19 January 1976 laying down a common structural policy for the fishing industry, OJ L 20, 28.01.1976.

931 *OECD*, Glossary of Statistical Terms, available on-line at <http://stats.oecd.org/glossary/index.htm> (last visited on 31 October 2009).

at or slightly below the 1982-1983 level. MAGP II ran from 1987 until the end of 1991. Objectives were assigned to each national fleet. This represented overall reductions of three percent in tonnage and two percent in engine power compared to the objectives which should have been achieved by the end of 1986 under the previous MAGP. MAGP III ran from 1992 until the end of 1996. Its objective was an average ten percent reduction in vessel capacity. MAGP IV ran from 1997 until the end of 2001. It called for reductions in fishing effort of 30 percent on stocks in danger of collapse and of 20 percent on overfished stocks. After 1993, these MAGPs were financed under the Financial Instrument for Fisheries Guidance, which is now discussed.

3. Structural Assistance between 1994 and 2006

In 1993, as part of a general reform of European structural funds, all common fisheries structural measures were integrated into the overall funding system under a single Financial Instrument for Fisheries Guidance (FIFG).[932] Each FIFG ran for six years. The most recent one ran from 2000 to 2006 with ab overall budget allocation of EUR 4.1 billion. It included funds allocated to the new Member States which joined the EU in 2004.[933]

The FIFG was intended to help the industry strengthen competitiveness and respond to the challenge of present-day world economic conditions; to guarantee the environmentally sustainable and economically viable exploitation of fisheries resources; to improve market supply and increase the value of fish and aquaculture products through processing; to preserve fishing in regions where there are few economic alternatives; and to provide European consumers with a wide range of quality fish products.[934] It gave more responsibilities to the Member States for achieving a better balance between their fleet capacity and available resources.

The structural measures provided under the FIFG included the adjustment of fishing effort,[935] fleet renewal and modernisation of fishing vessels,[936] improvement of small-scale inshore fishing,[937] and inland fishing conditions, protection and development of aquatic resources, fishing port facilities, development of

---

[932] Council Regulation (EEC) No 2080/93 of 20 July 1993 laying down provisions for implementing Regulation (EEC) No 2052/88 as regards the financial instrument of fisheries guidance, OJ L 193, 31.7.1993, pp. 1-4.

[933] *Eurostat*, *supra* note 864, at 5.

[934] Article 1.2 of Council Regulation (EC) No 1263/1999 of 21 June 1999 on the Financial Instrument for Fisheries Guidance, OJ L 161, 26.6.1999, pp. 54-56; *European Commission*, "Financial Instrument for Fisheries Guidance, Instructions for Use" (Luxembourg: Office for Official Publications of the European Communities, 2002), at 6.

[935] Article 7 of Council Regulation (EC) No 2792/1999 of 17 December 1999 laying down the detailed rules and arrangements regarding Community structural assistance in the fisheries sector, OJ L 337, 30.12.1999, pp.10-35.

[936] Article 9 of Council Regulation (EC) No 2792/1999.

[937] Article 11 of Council Regulation (EC) No 2792/1999.

aquaculture, processing and marketing of fish and aquaculture products, measures to identify and promote new market outlets, social measures accompanying restructuring,[938] measures by groups within the trade and temporary cessation of activities.[939]

The FIFG was seen as a positive result of the EU's commitment towards the fishing industry.[940] Between the years 1994 and 2005, the FIFG co-financed the withdrawal from operation of vessels in eight Member States fishing on the Baltic Sea.[941] The result was a net capacity reduction which was considered an improvement in the state of the resources or at least the halting of further degradation.[942]

Even though the FIFG was a big improvement over its predecessors, it did not fail to escape criticism. First, it was criticized for failing to control real growth in the catching capacity of all European fishing fleets.[943] Second, there was a lack of coordination between structural policy and other elements of the CFP. Funding fleet renewal and modernizing fishing vessels under the FIFG was in conflict with the goal of the CFP to reduce marine overfishing actively. Despite calls to eliminate renewal and modernization grants as part of the FIFG reform, it continued offering funding for such projects. It also represented the apparent internal contradictions of a policy that simultaneously provided aid for both increasing and decreasing fleet capacity, e.g. aid for vessel withdrawals and aid for new vessel construction.[944] Third, the FIFG programmes generally ran behind targets in terms of commitments and even more in terms of actual spending. Only few programmes were close to target or above target. There were many reasons for the relatively slow implementation of FIFG programmes. The lower-than-expected progress resulted from the late start of the programmes and other administrative issues, e.g. cumbersome application processes, slow payments, lack of administrative resources and occasional problems with the availability of State co-financing funds. Moreover, a number of deeper systemic factors appeared to be responsible for this.

---

938 Article 12 of Council Regulation (EC) No 2792/1999.

939 Articles 15 and 16 of Council Regulation (EC) No 2792/1999.

940 *European Commission, supra* note 934, at 43.

941 The eight Member States include Germany, Denmark, Sweden, Finland, Poland, Lithuania, Latvia and Estonia.

942 *Jan Horbowy and Emil Kuzebski*, "Impact of the EU Structural Funds on the Fleet and Fish Resources in the Baltic Fisheries Sector" (Gdynia: WWF Poland Sea Fisheries Institute, 2006), at 85. The total tonnage of the vessels withdrawn under the FIFG amounted to 58 thousand GT, while the FIFG supported construction of vessels with a total tonnage of 25 thousand GT. Therefore, the net balance of the reduction of the fleet capacity equalled 33 thousand GT, which is more or less equivalent to the size of the whole Polish Baltic fleet at the end of 2004.

943 *Aaron Hatcher*, "Subsidies for European Fishing Fleets: the European Community's Structural Policy for Fisheries 1971-1999", Marine Policy, Vol. 24, pp. 129-140 (2000), at 138-139.

944 *Ibid.*

The uncertain economic prospects for the fisheries sector and the fragmentation of the industry tended to reduce the take-up of the programmes.[945]

4. European Fisheries Fund

a. The Nature of the European Fisheries Fund

Within the EU, France, Spain, Italy, Greece and Portugal, plus Estonia and Poland, were the "pro-subsidies" Member States, while Britain, Germany, Sweden, the Netherlands and Belgium objected to the expansion of fisheries subsidies.[946] The wrestling between the two groups shaped the final version of the European Fisheries Fund (EFF) regulations.

The EFF, which replaced the FIFG as of January 2007, was designed to secure a sustainable European fishing and aquaculture industry. It runs for seven years from 2007 to 2013 with a total budget of around EUR 3.8 billion.

The EFF is the financial instrument for the fisheries structural policy and the financial component of the CFP. Based on its five priority axes,[947] the EFF contributes to the steps that have been taken since the CFP reform in order to reduce pressure on fish stocks and ensures sustainable social and economic conditions for the sector. It supports the fishing industry as it adapts its fleet to make it more competitive and promotes measures to protect and enhance the environment. It also helps fisheries communities most affected by the resulting changes to diversify their economic base and to work towards the regeneration of severely depleted fish stocks. Support is also provided for measures ensuring that the industry continues to have access to the skilled labour force it requires. Funding is available for all sectors of the industry, from sea and inland fisheries, aquaculture business and producer organizations to the processing and marketing sectors. It also fosters the sustainable development of fisheries areas.[948] The EFF also provides technical assistance to promote innovative approaches and practices for simple and transparent implementation.

These reflect EFF's task of facilitating the implementation of measures adopted under the CFP reform to secure economic, environmental and social sustainability in fisheries.

---

945 *London Economics*, "A Synthesis of the Mid-term Evaluations of the FIFG 2000-2006, Report to European Commission-Directorate General for Fisheries" (2004).

946 *R. Sumaila & D. Pauly*, *supra* note 1, at 28; *Clare Coffey,* "Fisheries Subsidies, Will the EU Turn Its Back on the 2002 Reforms?" (Brussels: WWF European Policy Office, 2006), at 5.

947 Title IV of Council Regulation (EC) No 1198/2006. The five priority axes of the EFF are: (1) the adjustment of Community fishing fleets to available resources; (2) aquaculture, inland fishing, processing and marketing of fishery and aquaculture products; (3) measures of common interest; (4) sustainable development of fisheries areas; and (5) technical assistance to facilitate the delivery of EFF aid.

948 Article 4 of Council Regulation (EC) No 1198/2006.

b. Comparison of the European Fisheries Fund

Several characteristics and improvements of the EFF can be identified when compared with its predecessor, the FIFG.[949]

(1) A Comprehensive Policy

The EFF is better at targeting the objectives of the reformed CFP and integrating other EU policies, e.g. the environment and employment.

Unlike the FIFG, the EFF emphasizes the environmental dimension of sustainable fisheries through various measures. The EFF finances several measures to protect marine resources and the environment and to counter the degradation of the marine ecosystem. The EFF also promotes more selective and environmentally-friendly fishing methods.

Furthermore, support for inland fishing and environmentally-friendly aquaculture has been given more emphasis. The EFF supports organic aquaculture, encourages fishing farms and finances measures for the protection of aquatic fauna and flora. It also tries to resolve the challenges of environmental degradation in fisheries regions.

The economic and social needs of the people employed in this industry are also taken into consideration. Member States can establish their strategy with regard to preserving human resources and securing sustainable employment in the sector. Aid to upgrade professional skills and to improve working conditions and safety is available for all persons employed in the fisheries sector, be it on board vessels, within aquaculture and processing units, fishing ports or landing sites. Moreover, the necessary adjustment of the fishing fleet is accompanied by a set of social and economic measures, including non-renewable compensation for the permanent or temporary cessation of activities, aid for the diversification of fishermen's activities, early retirement or re-direction to other activities.[950] The local strategies for the sustainable development of fisheries areas to be funded by the EFF are driven by the objective of improving the quality of life and maintaining the economic and social prosperity of the areas concerned.

(2) A Unified Assistance Programme

The rules and mechanisms for delivering assistance are simplified under the EFF. FIFG support for the fisheries sector was split up between different programmes of each Member State. A single EFF programme per Member State makes it possible to concentrate on support and to maximize the effectiveness of measures.

The allocation of EFF assistance is based on the decisions and priorities of Member States.[951] The EFF requires Member States to draw up a National Strate-

---

949 Council Regulation (EC) No 1263/1999 of 21 June 1999 on the Financial Instrument for Fisheries guidance, OJ L 161, 26.6.1999, pp. 54-56.

950 Article 27 of Council Regulation (EC) No 1198/2006.

951 Rules are set in Council Regulation (EC) No 1198/2006 and Commission Regulation (EC) No 498/2007 of 26 March 2007 laying down detailed rules for the im-

gic Plan (NSP) for the entire fisheries sector and on all relevant aspects of the CFP[952]. The NSP presents an overall strategic vision of each Member State with regard to the medium-term development policy of the fisheries and aquaculture sector.[953] Drafting the NSP helps the Member State to identify its priorities, targets and public financial resources better for attaining policy objectives.

Based on its NSP, each Member State sets up an operational programme to be co-financed by the EFF for the whole programming period from 2007 to 2013. In the operational programmes, they describe and justify their choice of priorities and set specific targets for each one. The operational programme contains a financing plan with a breakdown of the budget expenditures by category and by year for the whole programming period. The operational programme is subject to approval by the Commission which checks whether every operational programme is consistent with the objectives of the CFP and other EU policies and priorities.[954] The contribution from the EFF to the total public expenditures set out in the operational programme shall be subject to the following ceilings: 75 percent of the public expenditure co-financed by the EFF in regions eligible under the Convergence objective[955] and 50 percent in regions not eligible under the Convergence objective.[956]

c. Temporary Specific Action to Deal with the Economic Crisis

Following the drastic increase in fuel prices in 2008, an impending need to take additional measures aimed at a more rapid adaptation of the European fishing fleet to the existing situation was taken into consideration by the Commission.[957] A specific Community action, as a special regime under the EFF, was then designed to provide exceptional and temporary support for fishermen and fishing enterprises affected by the economic crisis induced by the substantial increase in oil prices.[958] Public aid to this sector, addressing both the immediate situation of economic and social hardship, may be granted until the end of 2010.[959] Major measures can be summarized as follows:

---

plementation of Council Regulation (EC) No 1198/2006 on the European Fisheries Fund, OJ L 120, 10.5.2007, pp.1-80.

952 Para. 17 of the preamble to Council Regulation (EC) No 1198/2006.

953 Article 15 of Council Regulation (EC) No 1198/2006.

954 Article 17 of Council Regulation (EC) No 1198/2006.

955 Article 3(n) of Council Regulation (EC) No 1198/2006 defines the Convergence objective as the objective of the action for the least developed Member States and regions according to Council Regulation (EC) No 1083/2006 of 11 July 2006 laying down the general provisions on the European Regional Development Fund, the European Social Fund and the Cohesion Fund and repealing Regulation (EC) No 1260/1999.

956 Article 53.3 of Council Regulation (EC) No 1198/2006.

957 Para. 3 of the preamble to Council Regulation (EC) No 744/2008.

958 Article 1(1) of Council Regulation (EC) No 744/2008.

959 Article 5 of Council Regulation (EC) No 744/2008.

(1) Financing temporary cessation of fishing activities

In order to allow Member States and fishing enterprises to elaborate the necessary restructuring and adaptation initiatives, these temporary measures provide Member States with the opportunities of financing the temporary cessation of fishing vessels for a maximum period of three months. This measure may finance crew costs and fixed costs of vessels.[960]

(2) Investments in fuel-efficiency equipment

The temporary measures include financing for equipment, gear or engine replacement, including auxiliary motors. These measures may significantly improve energy efficiency on board fishing vessels, reduce emissions and contribute to the fight against climate change.[961]

(3) Socio-economic compensation

Under normal circumstances, the EFF grants assistance for early retirement only to fishermen.[962] Under the temporary regime, early retirement is expanded to include workers in all fishery-related activities.[963]

(4) Pilot projects

The temporary measures may finance pilot projects to test technical improvements aimed at reducing energy consumption for vessels, engines, equipment or gear and at reducing emissions and fighting against climate change.[964]

(5) Other actions

The temporary measures also provide financial assistance to vessel owners seeking expertise in relation to energy audits and expert advice on the development of restructuring and modernisation plans.[965]

To ensure the long-term viability of the fishing sector, Fleet Adaptation Schemes have been introduced to allow Member States to reduce capacity and to increase fleet profitability.[966] Member States adopting this scheme are allowed to implement partial decommissioning measures.[967] As part of these measures, vessel owners withdrawing one or more of their vessels from the fleet are allowed to re-use part of the capacity withdrawn for a new smaller and less energy consuming

960 Article 6 of Council Regulation (EC) No 744/2008.
961 Article 7 of Council Regulation (EC) No 744/2008.
962 Article 27 of Council Regulation (EC) No 1198/2006.
963 Article 8 of Council Regulation (EC) No 744/2008.
964 Article 10 of Council Regulation (EC) No 744/2008.
965 Article 9(1) of Council Regulation (EC) No 744/2008.
966 Article 12 of Council Regulation (EC) No 744/2008.
967 Chapter IV, Articles 17-19 of Council Regulation (EC) No 744/2008.

vessel. In such cases, funds should be made available only for the part of the capacity which is permanently withdrawn.[968]

These temporary measures are to be implemented by the Member States in the context of their operational programmes under the EFF. The percentage of EU co-financing under the EFF for the measures covered by this initiative is increased to 95 percent, in view of the urgency of the situation and the need for immediate action by all Member States.[969]

These temporary measures with short term objectives may seem contradictory to the CFP reform which has a long term perspective. However, these measures are essential for helping the fishing industry tackle the difficulties resulting from the economic crisis. The temporary measures, as a special and exceptional regime, do not supersede the principles set in the EFF and the CFP.

d. Challenges of the European Fisheries Fund

Even though the EFF has been more progressive than its predecessor, the FIFG, it still faces some challenges as follows:

(1) The Need for More Appropriate Budget Allocations

The budget allocations of the EFF during the first two years of operation did not indicate any direct links between specific recovery plans and fleet adaptation measures.[970] Member States allocated funds to fleet modernisation instead of assistance for fisheries conservation.[971] In the future, the EFF budget should be allocated so as to ensure the balance between fish mortality, fishing effort and fleet capacity.[972]

(2) The Need for More Compliance with the CFP Reform in 2002

Provisions for several types of EFF assistance do not comply with the objectives of the CFP reform in 2002 and need to be carefully implemented in order to meet these objectives.[973] Examples are provisions on assistance for fleet modernisation and investment and assistance for the construction or acquisition of new vessels.

First, regarding assistance for fleet modernisation and investment, reintroducing funding for engines under the EFF provision does not seem to comply with the

968 Para. 16 of the preamble to Council Regulation (EC) No 744/2008.

969 Article 20 of Council Regulation (EC) No 744/2008.

970 *Indrani Lutchman, Chris Grieve, Sophie des Clers, and Elizabeth de Santo*, "Towards a Reform of the Common Fisheries Policy in 2012-a CFP Health Check" (London: Institute for European Environmental Policy, 2009), at 42.

971 *Ibid.*, at 46.

972 *Ibid.*, at 46-47; *WWF*, "Proposal for a Council Regulation for the European Fisheries Fund COM(2004) 497" (Brussels: WWF European Policy Office, 2006).

973 *Clare Coffey, supra* note 946, at 9-11; Council Regulation (EC) No 2371/2002 of 20 December 2002 on the conservation and sustainable exploitation of fisheries resources under the Common Fisheries Policy, OJ L 358, 31.12.2002, pp. 59–80.

CFP reform of 2002.[974] Vessels equipped with more economical engines may have incentives to increase their fishing effort to catch fish. Therefore, when applying EFF assistance to investment in the improvement of "energy efficiency and selectivity" of fishing vessels, there should be a threshold to limit the ability of the vessels to catch fish.

Second, regarding assistance for the construction of new vessels,[975] the CFP provision requires a certain amount of capacity reduction when public aid is provided for fleet renewal. However, the EFF provision provides assistance to young fishermen to acquire vessels for socio-economic concerns without taking into account capacity reduction. When EFF assistance is granted, the objective of the CFP to reduce capacity should be a requirement.

V. Comparison between the EU Regime and the Proposed WTO Regulations

A. The Effect of the WTO Agreements on the European Union Regime

As outlined in Chapter 1, the current SCM agreement, with its focus on controlling subsidies which incentivize exports or cause injury to the domestic market of

[974] The comparison between the provisions of the CFP reform in 2002 and the EFF regulations is as follows: The CFP provision, Article 11(5) of Council Regulation (EC) No 2371/2002, states that "on fishing vessels of five years of age or more, modernisation over the main deck to improve safety on board, working conditions, hygiene and product quality may increase the tonnage of the vessel, provided that such modernisation does not increase the ability of the vessel to catch fish." The EFF provisions, Articles 25(1) and 25(2) of Council Regulation (EC) No 1198/2006, provides that "the EFF may contribute to the financing of equipment and the modernisation of fishing vessels of five years of age or more only under the conditions of this Article and in accordance with the provisions of Chapter III of Regulation (EC) 2371/2002. Such investments may concern improvements for safety on board, working conditions, hygiene, product quality, *energy efficiency and selectivity*, provided that it does not increase the ability of the vessels to catch fish."

[975] The comparison between the provisions of the CFP reform in 2002 and the EFF regulations is as follows: The CFP provision, Article 13(2) of Council Regulation (EC) No 2371/2002, states that "from1 January 2003 until 31 December 2004 each Member State which chooses to enter into new public aid commitments for fleet renewal after 31 December 2002 shall achieve a reduction in the overall capacity of its fleet of 3 percent for the whole period in comparison to the reference levels referred to in Article 12." The EFF provision, Article 27(1) of Council Regulation (EC) No 1198/2006, states that "the EFF may contribute to individual premiums to fishers younger than 40 years who can demonstrate that they have worked at least five years as fishers or have equivalent professional training and who acquire for the first time part or total ownership of a fishing vessel of less than 24 metres in overall length which is equipped to go fishing at sea and is between 5 to 30 years old."

another WTO Member, targets mainly manufacturing industries and fails to address the particular characteristics of fisheries subsidies. The reason for this is that most subsidies are given by the biggest consumers of fish, which are in most instances net importers of fish, and as a result, these countries have no real need to subsidize fish exports and thus no negative impact on the domestic markets of other Members. In 2006, the EU imported almost five times as much as it exported in terms of value.[976] Another effect not targeted in the SCM agreement is the deprivation of the productive capacity of other fleets in common fishing areas. The proposed regulations by the WTO seek to address these issues.

The EU has been a WTO Member since 1 January 1995. The EU is a WTO Member in its own right as are each of its 27 Member States — making 28 WTO Members altogether. While the Member States coordinate their position in Brussels and Geneva, the European Commission alone speaks for the EU and its Member States at almost all WTO meetings and in almost all WTO affairs.[977] The WTO requires its Members to ensure that their laws, regulations and administrative procedures conform with the obligations contracted under the WTO agreements.[978] Under Article 300(7) of the EC Treaty, the EC agrees to comply with international agreements. EU law and WTO law are increasingly linked with each other.[979] However, the European Court of Justice (ECJ) in *Portugal v Council* made it clear that WTO law as such does not have direct effect in the Community legal system,[980] and the Court of First Instance found that "the reference to the concept of "subsidy" within the meaning of the WTO Agreement on Subsidies and Countervailing Measures has no relevance whatsoever to the classification of the measure in question as State aid within the meaning of Community law."[981] Even though the ECJ has been reluctant to accept a direct effect on its internal laws, scholars have suggested that EU law should be consistent "as much and as far as possible" with the EU's obligations to the WTO.[982]

Concerning fisheries subsidies regulations, the new regulations with their emphasis on the control of fishing capacity, environmental protection and sustainable

976 *Eurostat, supra* note 865, at 44-50.

977 Member Information, the European Union and the WTO, available on-line at <www.wto.org/english/thewto_e/countries_e/european_communities_e.htm> (last visited 31 October 2009).

978 Article 16.4 of the WTO Agreement.

979 *Luca Rubini*, "The International Context of EC State Aid Law and Policy: The Regulation of Subsidies in the WTO", in *Andrea Biondi, Piet Eeckhout, James Flynn* (eds), "The Law of State Aid in the European Union", pp. 149-188 (New York: Oxford University Press: 2004), at 149-150.

980 Judgment of the Court of 23 November 1999. Case C-149/96. Portuguese Republic V Council of the European Union, para. 32.

981 Judgement of the Court of First Instance of 29 September 2000. Case T-55/99. Confederación Española de Transporte de Mercancías V Commission of the European Communities.

982 *Piet Eeckhout*, "Judicial Enforcement of WTO Law in the European Union-Some Further Reflections", Journal of International Economic Law, Vol. 5, No. 1 (2002), pp. 91-110, at 91.

development are similar to those laid out in the CFP reform. In the following section, the EU measures are compared to the proposed WTO regulations (the Chair's text) to see to what extent, if any, the EU will need to adjust its policies to conform with the new regulations.

B. Provisions of Structural Assistance

This issue lies in how the type of the EFF assistance would fall under the scope of prohibited fisheries subsidies and the exceptions to these prohibitions under the Chair's text. If they do not fall under the scope of the proposed fisheries subsidies regulations, the general provisions of the SCM Agreement apply. Based on the comparison in Attachment IV, the results can be summarized as follows.

First, where the types of EFF assistance are considered prohibited according to the Chair's text, the future European fund and policy may need to be adjusted to conform with the new regulations. Some types of assistance that would be prohibited are most investment on board fishing vessels and selectivity, except for safety on board (Article 25), certain types of socio-economic compensation for the management of the Community fishing fleet (Article 27), investments in processing activities (Articles 34.1 and 37(h)), certain investments in fisheries infrastructure (Article 39), modifications for the reassignment of fishing vessels (Article 42), supporting small fisheries and tourism-related infrastructure and services for the benefit of small fisheries communities (Article 44.1(e)), contributing to the running costs (Article 44.1(j) of the Council Regulations (EC) No 1198/2006), etc.

Second, where the types of EFF assistance are considered non-prohibited according to the Chair's text, the future European fund may need to meet the more restrictive conditions for providing these types of assistance as required in the Chair's text. It would be particularly important that the effective fisheries management systems are required as the preconditions for providing non-prohibited fisheries subsidies.[983] The following types of EFF assistance would be the exceptions to prohibited fisheries subsidies: public aid for the permanent cessation of fishing activities (Article 23), financing the redeployment and retraining of fishermen in occupations outside sea fishing; early departure, e.g. early retirement (Article 27.1(a)(c)(d)), measures of common interest, e.g. safety and fisheries management (Articles 37-39), re-establishing the production potential in the fisheries sector when damaged by natural disasters (Article 44.1(g) of the Council Regulations (EC) No 1198/2006), etc.

Third, many types of EFF assistance are outside the scope of the proposed fisheries subsidies regulations. It implies that there are still some types of assistance that the Chair's text still needs to take into account, especially those that may have negative impact on trade and the environment. This is due to the fact that the scope of the EFF regulations is broader, since it has many objectives which are not taken into consideration in the Chair's text, e.g. improving the qual-

[983] Article V of the proposed Annex VIII to the SCM Agreement of the Chair's text, *WTO* Doc. No. TN/RL/W/213 (30 November 2007).

ity of fisheries products and ensuring the stability of the fish market and the living standards of fishing areas. Moreover, some measures under the EFF which provide for protecting fish stocks and areas may instigate action at the WTO level on whether this type of non-actionable/permitted fisheries subsidies can be integrated in the new regulations. These types of EFF assistance include public aid for the temporary cessation of fishing activities (Article 24), financing fishing skills training for young fishermen (Article 27.1(b)), measures of aquaculture, inland fishing and marketing of fishery and aquaculture products (Articles 29-35), measures of common interest, e.g. food safety and quality, product traceability, research and training (Articles 37-41), measures of sustainable development of fishing areas (Articles 44 and 45 of the Council Regulations (EC) No 1198/2006), etc.

C. Bilateral Fisheries Agreements

Access-related subsidies are prohibited in the Chair's text, when these are paid by a government and subsequently given to the industry at either no cost or subsidized cost.[984] However, if the fishery in question is within the EEZ of a developing country Member, these subsidies may be exempted from the prohibition.[985] The types of European fisheries agreements with other countries can be summarized as follows.

Under fisheries agreements involving financial compensation, i.e. FPAs, as described above, the financial contribution from the EU to the contracting countries is to support the sectoral fisheries policy of the contracting countries. This is a government-to-government payment and not considered as a subsidy in the Chair's text.[986]

However, there are questions on the provisions of licence conditions in these FPAs, e.g. fees paid by European fishermen to the EU in order to obtain fishing licenses under these FPAs. The Council of the European Union ensured that terms and detailed arrangements for the granting of fishing licences under the FPAs need to ensure that "the level of fees payable by Community ship-owners for their fishing activities is fair, balanced and non-discriminatory."[987] The method for calculating the amount paid under these provisions is based on the fishing opportunities allowed to the European fleet by establishing the principle of a 65-35 share between the Community budget and the ship-owners.[988] Based on this information, it is still difficult to determine the existence of subsidies and it depends on the study of fish markets to decide whether it may constitute a subsidy.

---

984 *Ibid.*, Article I.1(g).
985 *Ibid.*, Article III.3.
986 *Ibid.*, footnote 80.
987 *Council of the European Union*, 11234/2/04 REV 2 (Press 221), "Press Release 2599th Council Meeting Agriculture and Fisheries" (Brussels, 19 July 2004).
988 *Supra* note 870.

Moreover, even if they constitute subsidies, access-related subsidies are not prohibited provided that the fishery in question is within the EEZ of a developing country Member and that this fisheries agreement is made public and contains provisions designed to manage fisheries.[989] As the FPAs are concluded with the developing countries and contain the provisions regarding measures to ensure fisheries management based on the Code of Conduct, these subsidies appear not to be prohibited. The list of these FPAs and relevant provisions, e.g. amount of financial contribution and licence conditions, is attached in Attachment V.

As to fisheries agreements which do not involve financial compensation, such as exchanging quotas between the EU and a third country and allocating the acquired quota to the European fishermen, these are considered as general exceptions to prohibited fisheries subsidies under the Chair's text.[990]

VI. Conclusion

State aid by Member States and structural assistance by the EU are the two sources of public assistance received by the European fishing industry. These types of assistance are supposed to conform to the CFP objectives and strive to actively reduce excessive overexploitation of fisheries resources. The next reforms of the CFP and EFF should support the principles of reducing the environmental harmfully subsidies and emphasize more vigorously subsidies aimed at fisheries conservation and sustainable development. The new CFP reform should promote and facilitate the restructuring of the European fishing industry, help it improve its long term economic viability and avoid supporting overcapacity. State aid by Member States and structural assistance by the EU should play a more aggressive role in pursuit of these objectives.

Both the WTO and EU can benefit each other with their experience in drafting, enforcing and implementing these regulations. The future fisheries subsidies regulations within the WTO framework should consider incorporating in the draft the types of fisheries subsidies which currently exist in practice and with which the EU has to deal on a regular basis as well as the EU's more detailed procedural regulations and other technical provisions in order to improve transparency. The EU framework, when reforming the CFP of 2012 and designing the fund to succeed the EFF, needs to consider developments in the WTO fisheries subsidies negotiations. In the WTO negotiations, the EU should take a more commanding role and share its internal fisheries subsidies policies, regulations and experience with the WTO Members. It should also promote the establishment of a robust fisheries subsidies policy which supports fisheries conservation and sustainable development. This will assist the WTO framework in establishing a set of more meaningful regulations.

---

989 Article III.3 of the proposed Annex VIII to the SCM Agreement of the Chair's text, *WTO* Doc. No. TN/RL/W/213 (30 November 2007).

990 *Ibid.*, Article II(e).

Conclusion

This study has probed into the magnitude of the fisheries subsidies issue. We have looked at the negative impacts of fisheries subsidies on trade, the environment and sustainable development. These show no signs of abating, because subsidies are continuously fed by a seemingly bottomless source of government funds to the fishing industry, reaching the unprecedented level of approximately 20 percent of the total global revenues of the fisheries sector. This has led to the creation of fleet overcapacity and overfishing, ultimately resulting in the depletion of fish stocks; and if left to run its course uncontrolled, could in the end bring about the extinction of certain species, the destruction of the marine habitat and the devastation of coastal fishing communities whose livelihoods depend on those fisheries. The reason for this state of affairs is that there is no single instrument in international law which can effectively control fisheries subsidies. The instruments that exist at this time are either voluntary in nature or were not designed to target the unique characteristics of fisheries subsidies.

Is the international community in a position to avert this ominous future?

As evidence of the negative impacts of fisheries subsidies mounted, awareness of and concern about this issue increased in the international community. A group of WTO Members finally managed to get the fisheries subsidies issue on the WTO agenda, which resulted in the mandates of the Doha Ministerial Declaration. This led to the complex set of negotiations which culminated with the Chair's text in 2007.

The analysis of the Chair's text shows that it represents the efforts of the WTO, its Members and organizations with environmental concerns at crafting a set of regulations to control the negative impacts of fisheries subsidies. It responds to the mandates of Ministerial Declarations and the concerns of the different stakeholders during the negotiations.

Although some changes could still be made to the Chair's text, such as providing more detailed procedural provisions and clarifying certain terms or providing for the types of fisheries subsidies which positively conserve fisheries resources, the text represents a convincing effort at integrating the issues of trade, the environment and sustainable development. What is needed now is immediate action to approve the Chair's text, legislate and enforce it; and by doing so, ensuring that the health of fish stocks and the livelihoods of fishing communities are preserved.

C.-J. Chen, *Fisheries Subsidies under International Law*, Hamburg Studies on Maritime Affairs 20, DOI 10.1007/978-3-642-15693-9_6, © Springer-Verlag Berlin Heidelberg 2010

Attachments

Attachment I

Categories of Fisheries Subsidies

Table I: FAO Categorization of fisheries subsidies

Category	Examples and/or descriptions
Direct government payments to the fishing industry	Investment grants (e.g. for the purchases of new fishing vessels or safety equipment), vessel-decommissioning payments, fishermen's unemployment insurance, income guarantee schemes, disaster relief payments, direct export incentives, compensation for closed seasons, equity infusions, price support programmes, etc.
Services and indirect financial transfers	Services and indirect financial transfers cover any other active and explicit government intervention which does not involve a direct financial transfer as specified. They can be sub-categorized into:
	(1) Government loans, loan guarantees and insurance: investment loans to fishermen or fishing firms on favourable terms (e.g. loans with lower than market interest rates or longer than usual amortization periods), loan guarantees, special insurance schemes for vessel and gear, provision of bait services, indirect export promotion support, inspection and certification for exports, specialized training, extension, ports and landing site facilities, payments to foreign governments to secure access to fishing grounds, government-funded research and development programmes, international cooperation and negotiations, etc.
	(2) Tax waivers and deferrals: fuel tax exemptions for fishing vessel fuel, sales tax exemptions, investment tax credits, deferred tax programmes, special income tax deductions, etc.

Category	Examples and/or descriptions
Implicit payments to, or charges against the industry	1. These are payments that do not transfer funds to the industry and do not waive or defer payments that normally would be made by the industry to the government. 2. These include programmes that reduce the prices that the industry pays the government for goods at below market prices. Also included are programmes where the government makes payments or incurs costs on behalf of the industry without the payments being made directly to the industry, e.g. payments for fishing rights to foreign nations; fisheries management; fisheries enhancement and gear development.
General programmes that affect fisheries	Tax waivers applicable to all industries, subsidy programmes aimed at industries other than fisheries that may affect fisheries either positively or negatively, and general social programmes that affect the whole society.
Regulations	The examples of import quotas, direct foreign investment restrictions, environmental protection programmes, gear regulations, chemicals and drugs regulations, fisheries management, etc.
Lack of government intervention	1. This category comprises inaction on behalf of the government that allows producers to impose, in the short or long term, certain costs of production on others, e.g. on the environment and natural resources. 2. By definition, these do not imply a direct expenditure by the government (but may represent foregone revenue) and their value to the industry is often implicit. 3. Examples are free access to fishing grounds, lack of pollution control, lack of management measures, non-implementation of existing regulations, etc.

Table II: OECD Categorization of fisheries subsidies

Category	Examples and Descriptions
Direct payments (direct income support)	1. Transfers that increase the income of fishermen or enhance the revenue of the recipients. 2. Payments from government budgets (i.e., financed by taxpayers) directly to fishermen and which do not increase the price to consumers. 3. Payments to fishermen based on the level of catches or sales, vessel ownership, overall fishing income and/or fishermen's historical interest in a fishery or fisheries.
Cost-reducing transfers (indirect income support)	1. Payments from the government to fishermen that reduce the costs of fixed capital or variable inputs. 2. Implemented directly or implicitly through the budget and with no direct impact on market prices.
General services	Transfers that are not received directly by fishermen, but that reduce the costs faced by the sector as a whole, including expenditures on research, management and enforcement.
Market-price support	1. A revenue-enhancing transfer. 2. Transfers from consumers and taxpayers to fishermen arising from policy measures that create a gap between the domestic market prices and the border prices of specific commodities.
Cost recovery	1. The extent to which the government costs of managing fisheries are recovered from the fishing sector. 2. For some countries, cost recovery is a significant feature of their management regimes. New Zealand, Iceland and Australia, for example, recover around 50%, 37% and 24% respectively of the public costs of fisheries research, management and enforcement from the industry.

Attachment II

Fisheries Subsidies Regulations proposed by the Chairman of the WTO Negotiating Group on Rules, *WTO* Doc. No. TN/RL/W/213 (30 November 2007)

ANNEX VIII

FISHERIES SUBSIDIES

Article I

Prohibition of Certain Fisheries Subsidies

I.1Except as provided for in Articles II and III, or in the exceptional case of natural disaster relief[77], the following subsidies within the meaning of paragraph 1 of Article 1, to the extent they are specific within the meaning of paragraph 2 of Article 1, shall be prohibited:

(a) Subsidies the benefits of which are conferred on the acquisition, construction, repair, renewal, renovation, modernization, or any other modification of fishing vessels[78] or service vessels[79], including subsidies to boat building or shipbuilding facilities for these purposes.

(b) Subsidies the benefits of which are conferred on transfer of fishing or service vessels to third countries, including through the creation of joint enterprises with third country partners.

(c) Subsidies the benefits of which are conferred on operating costs of fishing or service vessels (including licence fees or similar charges, fuel,

---

77 Subsidies referred to in this provision shall not be prohibited when limited to the relief of a particular natural disaster, provided that the subsidies are directly related to the effects of that disaster, are limited to the affected geographic area, are time-limited, and in the case of reconstruction subsidies, only restore the affected area, the affected fishery, and/or the affected fleet to its pre-disaster state, up to a sustainable level of fishing capacity as established through a science-based assessment of the post-disaster status of the fishery. Any such subsidies are subject to the provisions of Article VI.

78 For the purposes of this Agreement, the term "fishing vessels" refers to vessels used for marine wild capture fishing and/or on-board processing of the products thereof.

79 For the purposes of this Agreement, the term "service vessels" refers to vessels used to tranship the products of marine wild capture fishing from fishing vessels to on-shore facilities; and vessels used for at-sea refuelling, provisioning and other servicing of fishing vessels.

ice, bait, personnel, social charges, insurance, gear, and at-sea support); or of landing, handling or in- or near-port processing activities for products of marine wild capture fishing; or subsidies to cover operating losses of such vessels or activities.

(d) Subsidies in respect of, or in the form of, port infrastructure or other physical port facilities exclusively or predominantly for activities related to marine wild capture fishing (for example, fish landing facilities, fish storage facilities, and in- or near-port fish processing facilities).

(e) Income support for natural or legal persons engaged in marine wild capture fishing.

(f) Price support for products of marine wild capture fishing.

(g) Subsidies arising from the further transfer, by a payer Member government, of access rights that it has acquired from another Member government to fisheries within the jurisdiction of such other Member.[80]

(h) Subsidies the benefits of which are conferred on any vessel engaged in illegal, unreported or unregulated fishing.[81]

I.2In addition to the prohibitions listed in paragraph 1, any subsidy referred to in paragraphs 1 and 2 of Article 1 the benefits of which are conferred on any fishing vessel or fishing activity affecting fish stocks that are in an unequivocally overfished condition shall be prohibited.

Article II

General Exceptions

Notwithstanding the provisions of Article I, and subject to the provision of Article V:

(a) For the purposes of Article I.1(a), subsidies exclusively for improving fishing or service vessel and crew safety shall not be prohibited, provided that:

---

80 Government-to-government payments for access to marine fisheries shall not be deemed to be subsidies within the meaning of this Agreement.

81 The terms "illegal fishing", "unreported fishing" and "unregulated fishing" shall have the same meaning as in paragraph 3 of the International Plan of Action to Prevent, Deter and Eliminate Illegal Unreported and Unregulated Fishing of the United Nations Food and Agricultural Organization.

(1) such subsidies do not involve new vessel construction or vessel acquisition;

(2) such subsidies do not give rise to any increase in marine wild capture fishing capacity of any fishing or service vessel, on the basis of gross tonnage, volume of fish hold, engine power, or on any other basis, and do not have the effect of maintaining in operation any such vessel that otherwise would be withdrawn; and

(3) the improvements are undertaken to comply with safety standards.

(b) For the purposes of Articles I.1(a) and I.1(c) the following subsidies shall not be prohibited:

subsidies exclusively for: (1) the adoption of gear for selective fishing techniques; (2) the adoption of other techniques aimed at reducing the environmental impact of marine wild capture fishing; (3) compliance with fisheries management regimes aimed at sustainable use and conservation (e.g., devices for Vessel Monitoring Systems); provided that the subsidies do not give rise to any increase in the marine wild capture fishing capacity of any fishing or service vessel, on the basis of gross tonnage, volume of fish hold, engine power, or on any other basis, and do not have the effect of maintaining in operation any such vessel that otherwise would be withdrawn.

(c) For the purposes of Article I.1(c), subsidies to cover personnel costs shall not be interpreted as including:

(1) subsidies exclusively for re-education, retraining or redeployment of fishworkers[82] into occupations unrelated to marine wild capture fishing or directly associated activities; and

(2) subsidies exclusively for early retirement or permanent cessation of employment of fishworkers as a result of government policies to reduce marine wild capture fishing capacity or effort.

(d) Nothing in Article I shall prevent subsidies for vessel decommissioning or capacity reduction programmes, provided that:

---

82 For the purpose of this Agreement, the term "fishworker" shall refer to an individual employed in marine wild capture fishing and/or directly associated activities.

(1) the vessels subject to such programmes are scrapped or otherwise permanently and effectively prevented from being used for fishing anywhere in the world;

(2) the fish harvesting rights associated with such vessels, whether they are permits, licences, fish quotas or any other form of harvesting rights, are permanently revoked and may not be reassigned;

(3) the owners of such vessels, and the holders of such fish harvesting rights, are required to relinquish any claim associated with such vessels and harvesting rights that could qualify such owners and holders for any present or future harvesting rights in such fisheries; and

(4) the fisheries management system in place includes management control measures and enforcement mechanisms designed to prevent overfishing in the targeted fishery. Such fishery-specific measures may include limited entry systems, catch quotas, limits on fishing effort or allocation of exclusive quotas to vessels, individuals and/or groups, such as individual transferable quotas.

(e) Nothing in Article I shall prevent governments from making user-specific allocations to individuals and groups under limited access privileges and other exclusive quota programmes.

Article III

Special and Differential Treatment of Developing Country Members

III.1The prohibition of Article 3.1(c) and Article I shall not apply to least-developed country ("LDC") Members.

III.2For developing country Members other than LDC Members:

(a)Subsidies referred to in Article I.1 shall not be prohibited where they relate exclusively to marine wild capture fishing performed on an inshore basis (i.e., within the territorial waters of the Member) with non-mechanized net-retrieval, provided that (1) the activities are carried out on their own behalf by fishworkers, on an individual basis which may include family members, or organized in associations; (2) the catch is consumed principally by the fishworkers and their families and the activities do not go beyond a small profit trade; and (3) there is no major employer-employee relationship in the activities carried out. Fisheries management measures aimed at ensuring sustainability, such as the measures referred to in Article V, should be implemented in respect of the fisheries in question, adapted as necessary to the particular situation, including by making use of indigenous fisheries management institutions and measures.

(b)In addition, subject to the provisions of Article V:

(1) Subsidies referred to in Articles I.1(d), I.1(e) and I.1(f) shall not be prohibited.

(2) Subsidies referred to in Article I.1(a) and I.1(c) shall not be prohibited provided that they are used exclusively for marine wild capture fishing employing decked vessels not greater than 10 meters or 34 feet in length overall, or undecked vessels of any length.

(3) For fishing and service vessels of such Members other than the vessels referred to in paragraph (b)(2), subsidies referred to in Article I.1(a) shall not be prohibited provided that (i) the vessels are used exclusively for marine wild capture fishing activities of such Members in respect of particular, identified target stocks within their Exclusive Economic Zones ("EEZ"); (ii) those stocks have been subject to prior scientific status assessment conducted in accordance with relevant international standards, aimed at ensuring that the resulting capacity does not exceed a sustainable level; and (iii) that assessment has been subject to peer review in the relevant body of the United Nations Food and Agriculture Organization ("FAO")[83].

III.3Subsidies referred to in Article I.1(g) shall not be prohibited where the fishery in question is within the EEZ of a developing country Member, provided that the agreement pursuant to which the rights have been acquired is made public, and contains provisions designed to prevent overfishing in the area covered by the agreement based on internationally-recognized best practices for fisheries management and conservation as reflected in the relevant provisions of international instruments aimed at ensuring the sustainable use and conservation of marine species, such as, *inter alia*, the *Agreement for the Implementation of the Provisions of the United Nations Convention on the Law of the Sea of 10 December 1982 Relating to the Conservation and Management of Straddling Fish Stocks and Highly Migratory Fish Stocks* ("*Fish Stocks Agreement*"), the *Code of Conduct on Responsible Fisheries of the Food and Agriculture Organization* ("*Code*

[83] If the Member in question is not a member of the FAO, the peer review shall take place in another recognized and competent international organization.

of Conduct"), the *Agreement to Promote Compliance with International Conservation and Management Measures by Fishing Vessels on the High Seas* ("*Compliance Agreement*"), and technical guidelines and plans of action (including criteria and precautionary reference points) for the implementation of these instruments, or other related or successor instruments. These provisions shall include requirements and support for science-based stock assessment before fishing is undertaken pursuant to the agreement and for regular assessments thereafter, for management and control measures, for vessel registries, for reporting of effort, catches and discards to the national authorities of the host Member and to relevant international organizations, and for such other measures as may be appropriate.

III.4Members shall give due regard to the needs of developing country Members in complying with the requirements of this Annex, including the conditions and criteria set forth in this Article and in Article V, and shall establish mechanisms for, and facilitate, the provision of technical assistance in this regard, bilaterally and/or through the appropriate international organizations.

Article IV

General Discipline on the Use of Subsidies

IV.1No Member shall cause, through the use of any subsidy referred to in paragraphs 1 and 2 of Article 1, depletion of or harm to, or creation of overcapacity in respect of, (a) straddling or highly migratory fish stocks whose range extends into the EEZ of another Member; or (b) stocks in which another Member has identifiable fishing interests, including through user-specific quota allocations to individuals and groups under limited access privileges and other exclusive quota programmes. The existence of such situations shall be determined taking into account available pertinent information, including from other relevant international organizations. Such information shall include the status of the subsidizing Member's implementation of internationally-recognized best practices for fisheries management and conservation as reflected in the relevant provisions of international instruments aimed at the sustainable use and conservation of marine species, such as, *inter alia*, the *Fish Stocks Agreement*, the *Code of Conduct*, the *Compliance Agreement*, and technical guidelines and plans of action (including criteria and precautionary reference points) for the implementation of these instruments, or other related or successor instruments.

IV.2Any subsidy referred to in this Annex shall be attributable to the Member conferring it, regardless of the flag(s) of the vessel(s) involved or the application of rules of origin to the fish involved.

Article V

Fisheries Management[84]

V.1Any Member granting or maintaining any subsidy as referred to in Article II or Article III.2(b) shall operate a fisheries management system regulating marine wild capture fishing within its jurisdiction, designed to prevent overfishing. Such management system shall be based on internationally-recognized best practices for fisheries management and conservation as reflected in the relevant provisions of international instruments aimed at ensuring the sustainable use and conservation of marine species, such as, *inter alia*, the *Fish Stocks Agreement*, the *Code of Conduct*, the *Compliance Agreement*, technical guidelines and plans of action (including criteria and precautionary reference points) for the implementation of these instruments, or other related or successor instruments. The system shall include regular science-based stock assessment, as well as capacity and effort management measures, including harvesting licences or fees; vessel registries; establishment and allocation of fishing rights, or allocation of exclusive quotas to vessels, individuals and/or groups, and related enforcement mechanisms; species-specific quotas, seasons and other stock management measures; vessel monitoring which could include electronic tracking and on-board observers; systems for reporting in a timely and reliable manner to the competent national authorities and relevant international organizations data on effort, catch and discards in sufficient detail to allow sound analysis; and research and other measures related to conservation and stock maintenance and replenishment. To this end, the Member shall adopt and implement pertinent domestic legislation and administrative or judicial enforcement mechanisms. It is desirable that such fisheries management systems be based on limited access privileges[85]. Information as to the nature and operation of these systems, including the results of the stock assessments performed, shall be notified to the relevant body of the FAO, where it shall be subject to peer review prior to the granting of the subsidy[86]. References for such legislation and mechanism, including for any modifications thereto, shall be notified to the Committee on Subsidies and Countervailing Measures ("the Committee") pursuant to the provisions of Article VI.4.

V.2Each Member shall maintain an enquiry point to answer all reasonable enquiries from other Members and from interested parties in other Members

---

84 Developing country Members shall be free to implement and operate these management requirements on a regional rather than a national basis provided that all of the requirements are fulfilled in respect of and by each Member in the region.

85 Limited access privileges could include, as appropriate to a given fishery, community-based rights systems, spatial or territorial rights systems, or individual quota systems, including individual transferable quotas.

86 If the Member in question is not a member of the FAO, the notification for peer review shall be to another relevant international organization. The specific information to be notified shall be determined by the relevant body of the FAO or such other organization.

concerning its fisheries management system, including measures in place to address fishing capacity and fishing effort, and the biological status of the fisheries in question. Each Member shall notify to the Committee contact information for this enquiry point.

Article VI

Notifications and Surveillance

VI.1Each Member shall notify to the Committee in advance of its implementation any measure for which that Member invokes the provisions of Article II or Article III.2; except that any subsidy for natural disaster relief[87] shall be notified to the Committee without delay[88]. In addition to the information notified pursuant to Article 25, any such notification shall contain sufficiently precise information to enable other Members to evaluate whether or not the conditions and criteria in the applicable provisions of Article II or Article III.2 are met.

VI.2Each Member that is party to an agreement pursuant to which fishing rights are acquired by a Member government ("payer Member") from another Member government to fisheries within the jurisdiction of such other Member shall publish that agreement, and shall notify to the Committee the publication references for it.

VI.3The terms on which a payer Member transfers fishing rights it has obtained pursuant to an agreement as referred to in paragraph 2 shall be notified to the Committee by the payer Member in respect of each such agreement.

VI.4Each Member shall include in its notifications to the Committee the references for its applicable domestic legislation and for its notifications made to other organizations, as well as for the documents related to the reviews conducted by those organizations, as referred to in Article V.1.

VI.5Other Members shall have the right to request information about the notified subsidies, including about individual cases of subsidization, about notified agreements pursuant to which fishing rights are acquired, and about the stock assessments and management systems notified to other organizations pursuant to Article V.1. Each Member so requested shall provide such information in accordance with the provisions of Article 25.9.

VI.6Any Member shall be free to bring to the attention of the Committee information from pertinent outside sources (including intergovernmental organizations with fisheries management-related activities, regional fisheries

---

87 As provided for in Article I.1 and footnote 77.

88 For the purposes of this provision, "without delay" shall mean not later than the date of entry into force of the programme, or in the case of an ad hoc subsidy, the date of commitment of the subsidy.

management organizations and similar sources) as to any apparent illegal, unreported and unregulated fishing activities.

VI.7Measures notified pursuant to this Article shall be subject to review by the Committee as provided for in Article 26.

Article VII

Transitional Provisions

VII.1Any subsidy programme which has been established within the territory of any Member before the date of entry into force of the results of the DDA and which is inconsistent with Article 3.1(c) and Article I shall be notified to the Committee not later than 90 days, or in the case of a developing country Member 180 days, after the date of entry into force of the results of the DDA.

VII.2Provided that a programme has been notified pursuant to paragraph 1, a Member shall have two years, or in the case of a developing country Member four years, from the date of entry into force of the results of the DDA to bring that programme into conformity with Article 3.1(c) and Article I, during which period the programme shall not be subject to those provisions.

VII.3No Member shall extend the scope of any programme, nor shall a programme be renewed upon its expiry.

Article VIII

Dispute Settlement

VIII.1Where a measure is the subject of dispute settlement claims pursuant to Article 3.1(c) and Article I, the relevant provisions of Article 4 and of this Article shall apply. Article 30 and the relevant provisions of this Article shall apply to disputes arising under other provisions of this Annex.

VIII.2Where a subsidy that has not been notified as required by Article VI.1 is the subject of dispute settlement pursuant to the DSU and Article 4, such subsidy shall be presumed to be prohibited pursuant to Article 3.1(c) and Article I. It shall be for the subsidizing Member to demonstrate that the subsidy in question is not prohibited.

VIII.3Where a further transfer of access rights as referred to in Article I.1(g) is the subject of a dispute arising under this Annex, and the terms of that transfer have not been notified as required by Article VI.3, the transfer shall be presumed to give rise to a subsidy. It shall be for the payer Member to demonstrate that no such subsidy has arisen.

VIII.4Where a dispute arising under this Annex raises scientific or technical questions related to fisheries, the panel should seek advice from fisheries experts chosen by the panel in consultation with the parties. To this end, the panel may, when it deems it appropriate, establish an advisory technical fisheries expert group, or consult recognized and competent international organizations, at the request of either party to the dispute or on its own initiative.

VIII.5Nothing in this Annex shall impair the rights of Members to resort to the good offices or dispute settlement mechanisms of other international organizations or under other international agreements.

Attachment III

Status of WTO Members and Observers and their Membership in Relevant Organizations and Agreements

WTO Members (with years of membership) and Observers		FAO	UNCLOS (in force as from 16 November 1994)		UN Fish Stock Agreement (in force as from 11 December 2001)		FAO Compliance Agreement
			Sign	Ratify/ Access	Sign	Ratify/ Access	Accept
Afghanistan	Observer	X					
Albania	2000	X		2003			2005
Algeria	Observer	X					
Andorra	Observer	X					
Angola	1996	X	1982	1990			2006
Antigua & Barbuda	1995	X	1983	1989			
Argentina	1995	X	1984	1995	1995		1996
Armenia	2003	X		2002			
Australia	1995	X	1982	1994	1995	1999	2004
Austria	1995	X	1982	1995	1996	2003	
Azerbaijan	Observer	X					
Bahamas	Observer	X				1997	
Bahrain, Kingdom of	1995	X	1982	1985			
Bangladesh	1995	X	1982	2001	1995		
Barbados	1995	X	1982	1993		2000	2000
Belarus	Observer	X	1982	2006			
Belgium	1995	X	1984	1998	1996	2003	
Belize	1995	X	1982	1983	1995	2005	2005
Benin	1996	X	1983	1997			1999
Bhutan	Observer	X	1982				
Bolivia	1995	X	1984	1995			
Bosnia & Herzegovina	Observer	X		1994			
Botswana	1995	X	1984	1990			
Brazil	1995	X	1982	1988	1995	2000	2009
Brunei Darussalam	1995		1984	1996			
Bulgaria	1996	X	1982	1996		2006	
Burkina Faso	1995	X	1982	2005	1996		
Burundi	1995	X	1982				
Cambodia	2004	X	1983				
Cameroon	1995	X	1982	1985			
Canada	1995	X	1982	2003	1995	1999	1994
Cape Verde	2008	X	1982	1987			2006
Central African Republic	1995	X	1984				
Chad	1996	X	1982				
Chile	1995	X	1982	1997			2004
China	2001	X	1982	1996	1996		
Colombia	1995	X	1982				

WTO Members (with years of membership) and Observers		FAO	UNCLOS (in force as from 16 November 1994)		UN Fish Stock Agreement (in force as from 11 December 2001)		FAO Compliance Agreement
			Sign	Ratify/ Access	Sign	Ratify/ Access	Accept
Comoros	Observer	X	1984	1994			
Congo	1997	X	1982	2008			
Costa Rica	1995	X	1982	1992		2001	
Côte d'Ivoire	1995	X	1982	1984	1996		
Croatia	2000	X		1995			
Cuba	1995	X	1982	1984			
Cyprus	1995	X	1982	1988		2002	2000
Czech Republic	1995	X	1993	1996		2007	
Democratic Republic of the Congo	1997	X	1983	1989			
Denmark	1995	X	1982	2004	1996	2003	
Djibouti	1995	X	1982	1991			
Dominica	1995	X	1983	1991			
Dominican Republic	1995	X	1982	2009			
Ecuador	1996	X					
Egypt	1995	X	1982	1983	1995		2001
El Salvador	1995	X	1984				
Equatorial Guinea	Observer	X	1984	1997			
Estonia	1999	X		2005		2006	
Ethiopia	Observer	X	1982				
European Communities	1995	X	1984	1998	1996	2003	1996
Fiji	1996	X	1982	1982	1995	1996	
Finland	1995	X	1982	1996	1996	2003	
Former Yugoslav Republic of Macedonia (FYROM)	2003	X		1994			
France	1995	X	1982	1996	1996	2003	
Gabon	1995	X	1982	1998	1996		
The Gambia	1996	X	1982	1984			
Georgia	2000	X		1996			1994
Germany	1995	X		1994	1996	2003	
Ghana	1995	X	1982	1983			2003
Greece	1995	X	1982	1995	1996	2003	
Grenada	1996	X	1982				
Guatemala	1995	X	1983	1997			
Guinea	1995	X	1984	1985		2005	
Guinea Bissau	1995	X	1982	1986	1995		
Guyana	1995	X	1982	1993			
Haiti	1996	X	1982	1996			
Holy See (Vatican)	Observer						
Honduras	1995	X	1982	1993			

WTO Members (with years of membership) and Observers		FAO	UNCLOS (in force as from 16 November 1994)		UN Fish Stock Agreement (in force as from 11 December 2001)		FAO Compliance Agreement
			Sign	Ratify/ Access	Sign	Ratify/ Access	Accept
Hong Kong, China	1995						
Hungary	1995	X	1982	2002		2008	
Iceland	1995	X	1982	1985	1995	1997	
India	1995	X	1982	1995		2003	
Indonesia	1995	X	1982	1986	1995	2009	
Indonesia	1995	X	1982	1986	1995	2009	
Iran	Observer	X	1982			1998	
Iraq	Observer	X	1982	1985			
Ireland	1995	X	1982	1996	1996	2003	
Israel	1995	X			1995		
Italy	1995	X	1984	1995	1996	2003	
Jamaica	1995	X	1982	1983	1995		
Japan	1995	X	1983	1996	1996	2006	2000
Jordan	2000	X		1995			
Kazakhstan	Observer	X					
Kenya	1995	X	1982	1989		2004	
Korea, Republic of	1995	X			1996	2008	2003
Kuwait	1995	X	1982	1986			
Kyrgyz Republic	1998	X					
Lao People's Democratic Republic	Observer	X	1982	1998			
Latvia	1999	X		2004		2007	
Lebanese Republic	Observer	X	1984	1995			
Lesotho	1995	X	1982	2007			
Liberia, Republic of	Observer	X	1982	2008		2005	
Libya	Observer	X	1984				
Liechtenstein	1995		1984				
Lithuania	2001	X		2003		2007	
Luxembourg	1995	X	1984	2000	1996	2003	
Macao, China	1995						
Madagascar	1995	X	1983	2001			1994
Malawi	1995	X	1984				
Malaysia	1995	X	1982	1996			
Maldives	1995	X	1982	2000	1996	1998	
Mali	1995	X	1983	1985			
Malta	1995	X	1982	1993		2001	
Mauritania	1995	X	1982	1996	1995		
Mauritius	1995	X	1982	1994		1997	2003
Mexico	1995	X	1982	1983			1999
Moldova	2001	X		2007			
Mongolia	1997	X	1982	1996			
Montenegro	Observer	X		2006			

WTO Members (with years of membership) and Observers		FAO	UNCLOS (in force as from 16 November 1994)		UN Fish Stock Agreement (in force as from 11 December 2001)		FAO Compliance Agreement
			Sign	Ratify/ Access	Sign	Ratify/ Access	Accept
Morocco	1995	X	1982	2007	1995		2001
Mozambique	1995	X	1982	1997		2008	2009
Myanmar	1995	X	1982	1996			1994
Namibia	1995	X	1982	1983	1996	1998	1998
Nepal	2004	X	1982	1998			
Netherlands	1995	X	1982	1996	1996	2003	
New Zealand	1995	X	1982	1996	1995	2001	2005
Nicaragua	1995	X	1984	2000			
Niger	1996	X	1982				
Nigeria	1995	X	1982	1986		2009	
Norway	1995	X	1982	1996	1995	1996	1994
Oman	2000	X	1983	1989		2008	2008
Pakistan	1995	X	1982	1997	1996		
Panama	1997	X	1982	1996			
Papua New Guinea	1996	X	1982	1997			
Paraguay	1995	X	1982	1986			
Peru	1995	X					2001
Philippines	1995	X	1982	1984			
Poland	1995	X	1982	1998		2006	
Portugal	1995	X	1982	1997	1996	2003	
Qatar	1996	X	1984	2002			
Romania	1995	X	1982	1996		2007	
Russian Federation	Observer	X	1982	1997	1995	1997	
Rwanda	1996	X	1982				
St. Kitts & Nevis	1996	X	1984	1993			1994
St. Lucia	1995	X	1982	1985	1995	1996	2002
St. Vincent & Grenadines	1995	X	1982	1993			
Samoa	Observer	X	1984	1995	1995	1996	
Sao Tomé & Principe	Observer	X	1983	1987			
Saudi Arabia	2005	X	1984	1996			
Senegal	1995	X	1982	1984	1995	1997	2009
Serbia	Observer	X		2001			
Seychelles	Observer	X	1982	1991	1996	1998	2000
Sierra Leone	1995	X	1982	1994			
Singapore	1995		1982	1994			
Slovak Republic	1995	X	1993	1996		2008	
Slovenia	1995	X		1995		2006	
Solomon Islands	1996	X	1982	1997		1997	
South Africa	1995	X	1984	1997		2003	
Spain	1995	X	1984	1997	1996	2003	
Sri Lanka	1995	X	1982	1994	1996	1996	
Sudan	Observer	X	1982	1985			

WTO Members (with years of membership) and Observers		FAO	UNCLOS (in force as from 16 November 1994)		UN Fish Stock Agreement (in force as from 11 December 2001)		FAO Compliance Agreement
			Sign	Ratify/ Access	Sign	Ratify/ Access	Accept
Suriname	1995	X	1982	1998			
Swaziland	1995	X	1984				
Sweden	1995	X	1982	1996	1996	2003	1994
Switzerland	1995	X	1984	2009			
Chinese Taipei	2002						
Tajikistan	Observer	X					
Tanzania	1995	X	1982	1985			1999
Thailand	1995	X	1982				
Togo	1995	X	1982	1985			
Tonga	2007	X		1995	1995	1996	
Trinidad & Tobago	1995	X	1982	1986		2006	
Tunisia	1995	X	1982	1985			
Turkey	1995	X					
Uganda	1995	X	1982	1990	1996		
Ukraine	2008	X	1982	1999	1995	2003	
United Arab Emirates	1996	X	1982				
United Kingdom	1995	X		1997	1995	2001	
United States of America	1995	X			1995	1996	1995
Uruguay	1995	X	1982	1992	1996	1999	1999
Uzbekistan	Observer	X					
Vanuatu	Observer	X	1982	1999	1996		
Venezuela (Bolivarian Republic of)	1995	X					
Viet Nam	2007	X	1982	1994			
Yemen	Observer	X	1982	1987			
Zambia	1995	X	1982	1983			
Zimbabwe	1995	X	1982	1993			

Sources

WTO:
WTO Members and Observers, at <www.wto.org/english/thewto_e/whatis_e/tif_e/org6_e.htm> (last updated 31 October 2009)

UN:
UNCLOS and Fish Stocks Agreement, Participants, at <www.un.org/Depts/los/reference_files/status2008.pdf> (last updated 31 October 2009)

FAO:
FAO Member Nations, at <www.fao.org/legal/member-e.htm> (last updated 31 October 2009)
FAO Compliance Agreement, Participants, at <www.fao.org/legal/treaties/012s-e.htm> (last updated 31 October 2009)

Attachment IV

The Comparison of the Types of the EFF Assistance* (Council Regulations (EC) No 1198/2006) and the WTO Chair's Text of Fisheries Subsidies Regulations (the Proposed Annex VIII to the SCM Agreement, WTO Doc. No. TN/RL/W/213(30 November 2007))

Council Regulation (EC) No 1198/2006 of 27 July 2006 on the EFF		WTO Chair's Text of Fisheries Subsidies Regulations	Assessment and Note: 1.Prohibited fisheries subsidies in the Chair's text. 2.Exceptions to prohibited fisheries subsidies in the Chair's text. 3. Assistance not covered in the Chair's text. General provisions in the SCM Agreement may apply.
Priority axis 1: Measures for the adaptation of the Community fishing fleet			
Article 23	Public aid for permanent cessation of fishing activities	Article II(d)	2
Article 24	Public aid for temporary cessation of fishing activities	N/A	3
Article 25	Investments on board fishing vessels and selectivity		
	Article 25.1 Investments for modernisation of fishing vessels	Article I.1(a)	1
	Article 25.2 Investments to improve safety on board, working conditions, hygiene, product quality, energy efficiency and selectivity	Safety on board: Article II(a) Selectivity: Article II(b) Others: N/A	Safety on board and selectivity: 2 Others: 3

Article 26	Small-scale coastal fishing	N/A	The Chair's text regulates small-scale fisheries by providing S&D treatment for small-scale fisheries in developing country Members; however, the EU and its Member States do not fall under the developing country category.
Article 27	Socio-economic compensation for the management of the Community fishing fleet		
	Article 27.1 (a)(c)(d) Financing the redeployment and retraining of fishermen in occupations outside sea fishing; early departure, e.g. early retirement	Article II(c)	2
	Article 27.1 (b) Financing fishing skills training for young fishermen	N/A	3
	Article 27.1 (e) Financing certain fishermen leaving fishing temporarily	N/A	3
	Article 27.2 Financing younger fishermen to acquire fishing vessels	Article I.1(a)	1
Priority axis 2: Aquaculture, inland fishing, processing and marketing of fishery and aquaculture products		Covers only processing of fishery products.	Assistance to aquaculture, inland fishing, processing of aquaculture products, marketing of fishery and aquaculture products: 3
Article 29	Measures for productive investment in aquaculture	N/A	3
Article 30	Aqua-environmental measures	N/A	3
Article 31	Public health measures	N/A	3
Article 32	Animal health measures	N/A	3
Article 33	Inland fishing	N/A	3
Article 34	Investments in processing and marketing		

	Article 34.1 Investments in processing and marketing of fisheries and aquaculture products	Processing of fisheries products: Article I.1(c)(d) Others: N/A	Processing of fisheries products: 1 Others: 3
	Article 34.3 Supporting lifelong learning	N/A	3
Article 35	Eligible measures in processing and marketing	N/A	3
Priority axis 3: Measures of common interest			
Article 37	Collective actions		
	Article 37(a) Measures which contribute sustainably to the better management or conservation of resources	Article II(b)	2
	Article 37(b) Promoting selective fishing methods or gears and reduction of by-catches	Article II(b)	2
	Article 37(c) Removing lost fishing gear from the sea bed in order to combat ghost fishing	Article II(b)	2
	Article 37(d) Improving working conditions and safety	Article II(a)	2
	Article 37(e) Contributing to the transparency of markets in fisheries and aquaculture products including traceability	N/A	3
	Article 37(f) Improving quality and food safety	N/A	3
	Article 37(g) Develop, restructure or improve aquaculture sites	N/A	3
	Article 37(h) Investments concerning production, processing or marketing equipment and infrastructure including for waste treatment	Production and processing: Article I.1(c) and (d) Marketing: N/A	Production and processing: 1 Marketing: 3
	Article 37(i) Upgrading professional skills, or developing new training methods and tools	N/A	3

	Article 37(j) Promoting partnership between scientists and operators in the fisheries sector	N/A	3
	Article 37(k) Networking and exchange of experience and best practice among organisations promoting equal opportunities between genders and other stakeholders	N/A	3
	Article 37(l) Contributing to the objectives laid down for small-scale coastal fishing	N/A	3
	Article 37(m) Improving management and control of access conditions to fishing areas, in particular through the drawing up of local management plans approved by the competent national authorities	Article II(b)	2
	Article 37(n) Financing the establishment of producer organisations, their restructuring and the implementation of their plans to improve quality	N/A	3
	Article 37(o) Carrying out feasibility studies relating to promotion of partnerships with third countries in the fisheries sector	N/A	3
Article 38	Measures intended to protect and develop aquatic fauna and flora	N/A	3
Article 39	Fishing ports, landing sites and shelters	Article I.1(d)	1
	Article 39.1 Supporting investments in existing public or private fishing ports	Article I.1(d)	1
	Article 39.2(a) Improving the conditions under which fisheries and aquaculture products are landed, processed, stored in the ports and auctioned	Article I.1(d)	1

	Article 39.2(b) The provision of fuel, ice, water and electricity	N/A	3
	Article 39.2(c) Repair equipment and the maintenance of fishing vessels	Article I.1(a)	1
	Article 39.2(d) Construction, modernisation and extension of quays improving safety during landing or loading	Article I.1(d)	1
	Article 39.2(e) Computerised management of fishing activities	Article II(b)	2
	Article 39.2(f) Improving safety and working conditions	Article II(a)	2
	Article 39.2(g) The storage and treatment of waste	Article I.1(d)	1
	Article 39.2(h) Measures to reduce discards	Article II(b)	2
	Article 39.3 Supporting safety related investments for the construction or modernisation of small fishing shelters	N/A	3
Article 40	Development of new markets and promotional campaigns	N/A	3
Article 41	Pilot projects	N/A	3
Article 42	Modifications for the reassignment of fishing vessels	Article I.1(b)	1
Priority axis 4: Sustainable development of fisheries areas			Assistance to fishing areas may still refer to specific fishing industries.
Article 44	Eligible measures		
	Article 44.1(a) Strengthening the competitiveness of fisheries areas	N/A	3

	Article 44.1(b) Restructuring and redirecting economic activities, in particular by promoting eco-tourism, provided that these activities do not result in an increase in fishing effort	N/A	3
	Article 44.1(c) Diversifying activities through the promotion of multiple employment for fishers through the creation of additional jobs outside the fisheries sector	N/A	3
	Article 44.1(d) Adding value to fisheries products	N/A	3
	Article 44.1(e) Supporting small fisheries and tourism related infrastructure and services for the benefit of small fisheries communities	Article I.1(d)	1
	Article 44.1(f) Protecting the environment in fisheries areas to maintain its attractiveness, regenerating and developing coastal hamlets and villages with fisheries activities and protecting and enhancing the natural and architectural heritage	N/A	3
	Article 44.1(g) Re-establishing the production potential in the fisheries sector when damaged by natural or industrial disasters	Damaged by natural disasters: Exception under Article I.1 Damaged by industrial disasters: N/A	Damaged by natural disasters: 2 Damaged by industrial disasters: 3
	Article 44.1(h) Promoting inter-regional and transnational cooperation among groups in fisheries areas, mainly through networking and disseminating best practice	N/A	3

	Article 44.1(i) Acquiring skills and facilitating the preparation and implementation of the local development strategy	N/A	3
	Article 44.1(j) Contributing to the running costs of the groups	Article I.1(c)	1
Article 45	Participation in the sustainable development of fisheries areas	N/A	3
Priority axis 5: technical assistance			
Article 46	Technical assistance	N/A	Technical assistance provided by the EFF to the Member States is not a type of subsidy defined in the SCM Agreement.

* The expression and examples of the types of EFF assistance listed in Council Regulations (EC) No 1198/2006 are non-exhaustive and do not exemplify the assistance that each Member State plans. The types of EFF assistance still depend on how Member States draft their NSPs and operational programmes.

Attachment V

The List of Fisheries Partnership Agreements (FPAs) of the European Union and the Provisions on Licence Conditions

Country with Duration of Protocol**	Type of FPA	EC Annual Contri-ution	Licence Conditions	
			Fee for Ship Owners	Advance Payments
Angola	No protocol in force			
Cape Verde 4 years and 5 months (30.03.2007-31.08.2011)	Tuna	€ 385 000	- € 35 per tonne caught (seiners and longliners) - € 25 per tonne caught (pole and liners)	- Tuna seiners: € 3 950 per year (ref catches: 110 t) - Surface longliners: € 2 900 per year (ref catches: 80 t) - Pole and liners: € 500 per year (ref catches: 16 t)
Comoros 6 years (01.01.2005-31.12.2010)	Tuna	€ 390 000	€ 35 per tonne caught.	- Tuna seiners: € 3 375 per year (ref catches: 96 t) - Surface longliners: € 2 095 per year (ref catches: 59 t)
Côte d'Ivoire 6 years (01.07.2007-30.06.2013)	Tuna	€ 595 000	€ 35 per tonne caught.	- Tuna seiners: € 3 850 per year (ref catches: 110 t) - Surface longliners: € 1 400 per year (ref catches: 40 t)
Gabon 6 years (03.12.2005-02.12.2011)	Tuna	€ 860 000	€ 35 per tonne caught.	- Tuna seiners: € 4 550 per year (ref catches: 130 t) - Surface longliners: € 2 030 per year (ref catches: 58 t)
Gambia	No protocol in force			

Greenland 6 years (01.01.2007-31.12.2012)	Mixed	€ 15 847 244	License Fees: Cod- € 90 per tonne caught; Redfish- € 53 per tonne caught; Greenland Halibut- € 129 per tonne caught; Shrimp- € 80 per tonne caught; Atlantic halibut- € 217 per tonne caught; Capelin- € 5 per tonne caught; Snowcrab- € 120 per tonne caught.	
Guinea 4 years (01.01.2009-31.12.2012)	Tuna	€ 1 050 000 1st year decreasing the following years	- € 35 per tonne caught (seiners) - € 25 per tonne caught (pole and liners)	- Tuna seiners: € 4 025 per year (ref catches: 115 t) - Pole and liners: € 500 per year (ref catches: 20 t)
Guinea-Bissau 4 years (16.06.2007-15.06.2011)	Mixed	€ 7 500 000	- € 35 per tonne caught (seiners and longliners) - € 25 per tonne caught (pole and liners) - Others: Shrimps: 307; fish & cephalopods: 229 €/t/year (increase if biannual or quarterly licences)	- Pole and liners: € 500 per year (ref catches: 20 t) - Longliners and seiners: € 3 150 per year (ref catches: 90 t)
Equatorial Guinea	No protocol in force			
Kiribati 6 years (16.09.2006-15.09.2012)	Tuna	€ 478 400	€ 35 per tonne caught.	- Tuna seiners: € 21 000 per year (ref catches: 600 t) - Surface longliners: € 4 200 per year (ref catches: 120 t)

Madagascar 6 years (01.01.2007-31.12.2012)	Tuna	€ 1 197 000	€ 35 per tonne caught.	- Tuna seiners: € 3 920 per year (ref catches: 112 t) - Surface longliners > 100 GT: € 3 500 per year (ref catches: 100 t) - Surface longliners = or < 100 GT: € 1 680 per year (ref catches: 48 t)
Mauritania 4 years renewable (01.08.2008 -31.07.2012)	Mixed	€ 86 million 1st year decreasing the following years	- € 35 per tonne caught (seiners and longliners) - € 25 per tonne caught (pole and liners) - Others: Vessels fishing for crustaceans: 291 (315); Black hake trawlers: 148 (159); Vessels fishing for demersal species (other than trawlers): 254 (274); Freezer trawler fishing for demersal species: 156 (169); Cephalopods: 349 (377); Spiny lobster: 283 (305); Crab: 283 (305); Non freezer pelagic vessels: 7.2 (7.5) €/t/year (up to in 2011/2012); Pelagic freezer trawlers: 6.2 (8.2) or 6.5 (8.5) €/t/month (up to in 2011/2012).	- Tuna seiners: € 1 750 per year - Pole and line: € 2 500 per year - Surface longliners: € 3 500 per year

Mauritius	No protocol in force since 03.12.2007			
Micronesia 3 years (26.02.2007-25.02.2010)	Tuna	€ 559 000	€ 35 per tonne caught.	- Tuna seiners: € 15 000 per year (ref catches: 428 t) - Surface longliners: € 4 200 per year (ref catches: 120 t)
Morocco 4 years (28.02.2007-27.02.2011)	Mixed	€ 36.1 million	- Tuna: € 25 per tonne caught. - Industrial fishing for pelagic species: € 20 per tonne caught. - Small scale fishing/north, pelagic species: 67; Small scale fishing /north, long-liners: 60; Demersal fishing: 53; Small scale fishing/south: 60 (€/t/trims)	Tuna fishing: € 5 000 per year
Mozambique 5 years (01.01.2007-31.12.2011)	Tuna	€ 900 000	€ 35 per tonne caught.	- Tuna seiners: € 4 200 per year (ref catches: 120 t) - Surface long liners < 250 GT: € 1 680 per year (ref catches: 48 t) - Surface longliners > 250 GT: € 1 400 per year (ref catches: 40 t)

São Tomé and Principe 4 years (01.06.2006-31.05.2010)	Tuna	€ 663 000	€ 35 per tonne caught.	- Seiners: € 5 250 per year (ref catches: 150 t) - Longliners: € 1 925 per year (ref catches: 55 t)
Senegal	No protocol in force since 01.07.2006			
Seychelles 6 years (18.01.2005-17.01.2011)	Tuan	€ 5 355 000	€ 35 per tonne caught.	- Tuna seiners: € 21 000 per year (ref catches: 600 t) - Surface longliners = or < 150 GRT: € 4 200 per year (ref catches: 90 t) - Surface longliners > 150 GRT: € 3 150 per year (ref catches: 120 t)
Solomon Islands 3 years (09.10.2006-08.10.2009)	Tuan	€ 400 000	€ 35 per tonne caught.	- Tuna seiners: € 13 000 per year (ref catches: 371 t) - Surface longliners: € 3 000 per year (ref catches: 80 t)

Source

EU:
Bilateral Fisheries Partnership Agreements between the EC and Third Countries, at http://ec.europa.eu/fisheries/cfp/external_relations/bilateral_agreements_en.htm (last visited on 15 October 2009)

**The specific conditions (technical, financial, type of resources, etc.) of the agreements are laid down in "protocols", each of which runs for a period of several years.

Bibliography

I. Literature

1. Adamantopoulos, Konstantinos and Pereyra-Friedrichsen, Maria J., "EU Anti-Subsidy Law & Practice" (Bembridge: Palladian Law Publishing,2001).
2. Alessandrini, S., "Subsidies, Strategic Trade Policies and the GATT", in Bourgeois, Jacques H. J. (ed), "Subsidies and International Trade, a European Lawyer's Perspective", pp. 5-19 (Bruges: College of Europe, Kluwer Law and Taxation Publishers, 1991).
3. Allan, J. David, Abell, Robin, Hogan, Zeb, Revenga, Carman, Taylor, Brad W., Welcomme, Robin L., and Winemiller, Kirk, "Overfishing of Inland Waters", BioScience, Vol. 55, No. 12, pp. 1041-1051 (2005).
4. Anonymous, "Measuring Assistance to the Fishing Industry: Some Conceptual Issues, Submitted by the Australian Authorities" (Paris: OECD, 2001).
5. Anonymous, "Scope for Market Liberalization in the OECD Fisheries Sector" (Paris: OECD, 2003).
6. Barcelo, John, "Subsidies, Countervailing Duties, and Antidumping after the Tokyo Round", Cornell International Law Journal, Vol. 13, pp. 257 et seq (1980).
7. Benitah, Marc, "The Law of Subsidies under the GATT/WTO System" (The Hague: Kluwer Law International, 2001).
8. Böckenförde, Markus, "Article 7 and Annex B SPS", in Wolfrum, Rüdiger, Stoll, Peter-Tobias and Seibert-Fohr, Anja (eds), "WTO-Technical Barriers and SPS Measures", pp. 476-487 (Leiden: Martinus Nijhoff Publishers, 2007).
9. Burke, William T., "The New International Law of Fisheries: UNCLOS 1982 and Beyond" (Oxford: Clarendon Press, 1994).
10. Chang, Seung Wha, "WTO Disciplines on Fisheries Subsidies: A Historic Step Towards Sustainability?", Journal of International Economic Law, Vol. 6, No. 4, pp. 879-921 (2003).
11. Charnovitz, Steve, "International Standards and the WTO", The George Washington University Law School, Public Law and Legal Theory Working Paper No. 133 (2005).

12. Charnovitz, Steve, "Taiwan's WTO Membership and Its International Implications", Asian Journal of the WTO and International Health Law & Policy, Vol. 1, pp. 401-431 (2006).
13. Churchill, R.R. and Lowe, A.V., "The Law of the Sea" (2ed., Manchester: Manchester University Press, 1988).
14. Coffey, Clare and Baldock, David, "Reforming European Union Fisheries Subsidies – A Briefing Paper", in WWF, "Fishing in the Dark, A Symposium on Access to Environmental Information and Government Accountability in Fishing Subsidy Programmes, 28-29 November 2000, Brussels, Belgium" (Washington, D.C. and Gland: WWF, 2004).
15. Coffey, Clare, "Fisheries Subsidies, Will the EU Turn Its Back on the 2002 Reforms?" (Brussels: WWF European Policy Office, 2006).
16. Council of the European Union, 11234/2/04 REV 2 (Press 221), "Press Release 2599th Council Meeting Agriculture and Fisheries" (Brussels, 19 July 2004).
17. Cox, Anthony and Schmidt, Carl-Christian, "Subsidies in the OECD Fisheries Sector: a Review of Recent Analysis and Future Directions" (Paris: OECD, 2002).
18. Cox, Anthony, "OECD Work on Defining and Measuring Subsidies in Fisheries" (Paris: OECD, 2003).
19. Cox, Anthony, "Overview of Approaches for Assessing Subsidies", in OECD, "Subsidy Reform and Sustainable Development, Economic, Environmental and Social Aspects" (Paris: OECD, 2006), pp. 25-40.
20. Davey, William J., "Reforming WTO Dispute Settlement" (Illinois Public Law and Legal Theory Research Paper Series, Research Paper No. 04-01, January 29, 2004).
21. Davies, Peter G. and Redgwell, Catherine, "The International Legal Regulation of Straddling Fish Stocks", British Yearbook of International Law, Vol. 67, pp. 199-274 (1996).
22. Didier, Pierre, "WTO Trade Instruments in EU Law" (1999).
23. Dostal, Derek J., "Global Fisheries Subsidies: Will the WTO Reel in Effective Regulations?", University Pennsylvania Journal of International Economic Law, Vol. 26, No. 4, pp. 815-839 (2005).
24. Doulman, David J., "A General Overview of some Aspects of Illegal, Unreported and Unregulated Fishing", in FAO Doc. Fisheries Report No. 666, "Report of and Papers Presented at the Expert Consultation on Illegal, Unreported and Unregulated Fishing" (Rome: FAO, 2001).
25. Edeson, William, "The Code of Conduct for Responsible Fisheries: An Introduction", International Journal of Marine and Coastal Law, Vol. 11, pp. 233-238 (1996).
26. Edeson, William, "The Role of Technical Bodies", in Wolfrum, Rüdiger and Röben, Volker (eds), "Developments of International Law in Treaty Making", pp. 63-92 (Berlin: Springer, 2005).
27. Eeckhout, Piet, "Judicial Enforcement of WTO Law in the European Union-Some Further Reflections", Journal of International Economic Law, Vol. 5, No. 1, pp. 91-110 (2002).

28. European Commission, "Commission Working Document, Reflections on Further Reform of the Common Fisheries Policy" (Brussels: European Commission, 2008).
29. European Commission, "EU Competition Policy and the Consumer" (Brussels: European Commission, 2004).
30. European Commission, "Financial Instrument for Fisheries Guidance, Instructions for Use" (Luxembourg: Office for Official Publications of the European Communities, 2002).
31. European Commission, "Report of the Group of Independent Experts to Advise the European Commission on the Fourth Generation of Multiannual Guidance Programmes" (Brussels: European Commission, 1996).
32. European Commission, No. COM(2009)163 Final, "Green Paper, Reform of the Common Fisheries Policy" (Brussels: Commission of the European Communities, 2009).
33. European Commission, No. IP/08/828, "Commission: Policy Statement Proposes Major Changes in Fisheries Management Regime for 2009" (Brussels: European Commission, 2008).
34. Eurostat, "Facts and Figures on the CFP, Basic Data on the Common Fisheries Policy" (Luxembourg: Office of Official Publications of the European Communities, 2006).
35. Eurostat, "Fishery Statistics Data 1990-2006" (Luxembourg: Office of Official Publications of the European Communities, 2007).
36. Eurostat, "Statistics in Focus, Agriculture and Fisheries" (Luxembourg: Office of Official Publications of the European Communities, 2009).
37. FAO, "The State of World Fisheries and Aquaculture 2002" (Rome: FAO, 2002).
38. Fitzmaurice, Malgosia and Elias, Olufemi, "Contemporary Issues in the Law of Treaties" (Utrecht: Eleven International Publishing, 2005).
39. Flaaten, Ola and Wallis, Paul, "Government Financial Transfers to Fishing Industries in OECD Countries" (Paris: OECD, 2000).
40. Fontaubert, Charlotte de and Lutchman, Indrani, "Achieving Sustainable Fisheries, Implementing the New International Legal Regime" (Gland, Switzerland and Cambridge: the World Conservation Union, 2003).
41. Footer, Mary E., "An Institutional and Normative Analysis of the World Trade Organization" (Leiden, Koninklijke Brill NV: 2006).
42. Friedrich, Jürgen, "Legal Challenges of Nonbinding Instruments: The Case of the FAO Code of Conduct for Responsible Fisheries", German Law Journal, Vol. 109, No. 11, pp. 1539-1564 (2008).
43. Garcia, Frank J., "Beyond Special and Differential Treatment", Boston College International and Comparative Law Review, Vol. 27, pp. 291 et seq (2004).
44. Gau, Michael Sheng-ti, "Asia Perspectives on Fishery Subsidy Issues and Linkages with Environment", Asian Journal of the WTO and International Health Law & Policy, Vol. 1, pp. 189 et seq (2006).
45. Gavouneli, Maria, "Functional Jurisdiction in the Law of the Sea" (Leiden: Martinus Nijhoff, 2007).

46. Gorez, Béatrice, "Experiences with Subsidies and Fisheries Management: the Case of EU-ACP Fisheries Access Agreements" (Geneva: UNEP, 2004).
47. Greenpeace, "Reform of the EU's Common Fisheries Policy, Commission Green Paper on the Reform of the Common Fisheries Policy (21 April 2009)" (Brussels: Greenpeace European Unit, 2009).
48. Grynberg, Roman and Remy, Jan Yves, "Small Vulnerable Economy Issues and the WTO", in Mbirimi, Ivan, Chilala, Bridget, and Grynberg, Roman (eds), "From Doha to Cancun: Delivering a Development Round", pp. 269-290 (London: Commonwealth Secretariat, 2003).
49. Grynberg, Roman and Rochester, Natallie, "The Emerging Architecture of a World Trade Organization Fisheries Subsidies Agreement and the Interests of Developing Coastal States", Journal of World Trade, Vol. 39, No. 3, pp. 503-526 (2005).
50. Grynberg, Roman and Tsamenyi, Martin, "Fisheries Subsidies, the WTO and the Pacific Island Tuna Fisheries", Journal of World Trade, Vol. 32, No. 6, pp. 127-145 (1998).
51. Grynberg, Roman, "WTO Fisheries Subsidies Negotiations: Implications for Fisheries Access Arrangements and Sustainable Management", in Mbirimi, Ivan, Chilala, Bridget and Grynberg, Roman (eds), "From Doha to Cancun: Delivering a Development Round", pp. 291-314 (London: Commonwealth Secretariat, 2003).
52. Grynberg, Roman, "WTO Fisheries Subsidies Negotiations: Implication for Fisheries Access Arrangements and Sustainable Management", Marine Policy, Vol. 27, pp. 499-511 (2003).
53. Hatcher, Aaron, "Subsidies for European Fishing Fleets: the European Community's Structural Policy for Fisheries 1971-1999", Marine Policy, Vol. 24, pp. 129-140 (2000).
54. Horbowy, Jan and Kuzebski, Emil, "Impact of the EU Structural Funds on the Fleet and Fish Resources in the Baltic Fisheries Sector" (Gdynia: WWF Poland Sea Fisheries Institute, 2006).
55. Ibsen, Thorir, "Iceland's Proposal about Fisheries Subsidies", in Nordquist, Myron H. and Moore, John Norton (eds), "Current Fisheries Issues and the Food and Agriculture Organization of the United Nations", pp. 459-478 (The Hague: Nijhoff, 2000).
56. Ibsen, Thorir, "Sustainable Fisheries: the Linkages with Trade and Environment", Linkages Journal, Vol. 4., No. 2 (28 May 1999).
57. International Centre for Trade and Sustainable Development, "Draft Texts Facing Delay, as WTO Contemplates End-2008 for Doha Accord", Bridges Weekly Trade News Digest, Vol. 11, No. 40 (21 November 2007).
58. International Centre for Trade and Sustainable Development, "Fisheries Subsidies Text Provides a Good Starting Point, Delegates Say", Bridges Trade BioRes, Vol. 7, No. 22 (18 December 2007).
59. Jackson, John H., "The World Trade System: Law and Policy of International Economic Relations" (2ed., Cambridge: The MIT Press, 1997).

60. Keck, Alexander and Low, Patrick, "Special and Differential Treatment in the WTO: Why, When and How?" (Geneva: WTO, 2004).
61. Krajewski, Markus, "Article 11 TBT", in Wolfrum, Rüdiger, Stoll, Peter-Tobias and Seibert-Fohr, Anja (eds), "WTO-Technical Barriers and SPS Measures", pp. 315-326 (Leiden: Martinus Nijhoff Publishers, 2007).
62. Krasner, Stephen D., "Structural causes and regime consequences: regimes as intervening variables," in Krasner Stephen D. (ed), "International Regimes", pp. 1-22 (United States: Cornell University Press, 1983).
63. Landwehr, Oliver, "Article 3 SPS", in Wolfrum, Rüdiger, Stoll, Peter-Tobias and Seibert-Fohr, Anja (eds), "WTO-Technical Barriers and SPS Measures", pp. 412-427 (Leiden: Martinus Nijhoff Publishers, 2007).
64. Lee, Ryan E., "Dogfight: Criticizing the Agreement on Subsidies and Countervailing Measures amidst the Largest Dispute in World Trade Organization History", North Carolina Journal of International Law and Commercial Regulation, Vol. 32, pp. 115 et seq (2007).
65. Lennard, Michael, "Navigating by the Stars: Interpreting the WTO Agreement", Journal of International Economic Law, Vol. 5, pp. 17-89 (2002).
66. Lodge, Michael, "Managing International Fisheries: Improving Fisheries Governance by Strengthening Regional Fisheries Management Organizations" (London: The Royal Institute of International Affairs, 2007).
67. London Economics, "A Synthesis of the Mid-term Evaluations of the FIFG 2000-2006, Report to European Commission-Directorate General for Fisheries" (2004).
68. Luengo Hernandez de Madrid, Gustavo E., "Regulation of Subsidies and State Aids in WTO and EC Law" (The Hague: Kluwer Law International, 2007).
69. Lutchman, Indrani, Clers, Sophie des and Bossche, Koen Van den, "Overcapacity-What Overcapacity? An Evaluation of Member States Reporting on Efforts to Achieve a Sustainable Balance between Capacity and Fishing Opportunities in 2007" (London: Institute for European Environmental Policy, 2009).
70. Lutchman, Indrani, Grieve, Chris, Clers, Sophie des, and Santo, Elizabeth de, "Towards a Reform of the Common Fisheries Policy in 2012-a CFP Health Check" (London: Institute for European Environmental Policy, 2009).
71. Marceau, Gabrielle, "A Call for Coherence in International Law: Praises for the Prohibition against "Clinical Isolation" in WTO Dispute Settlement", Journal of World Trade, Vol. 33, No. 5, pp. 87-152 (1999).
72. Mattice, Alice L., "The Fisheries Subsidies Negotiations in the World Trade Organization: a "Win-Win" for Trade, the Environment and Sustainable Development", Golden Gate University Law Review, Vol. 34, pp. 573 et seq (2005).

73. Michalopoulos, Constantine, "The Role of Special and Differential Treatment for Developing Countries in GATT and the World Trade Organization" (Washington D.C., World Bank, 2004).
74. Milazzo, Matteo, "Subsidies in World Fisheries: A Reexamination", World Bank Technical Paper No. 406 (Washington, D.C.: World Back, 1998).
75. Moore, Gerald, "The Code of Conduct for Responsible Fisheries", in Hey, Ellen (ed), "Development in International Fisheries Law", pp. 85-105 (The Hague: Kluwer Law International, 1999).
76. Morin, Michel, "State Aid to the Fisheries Sector", in Rydelski, Michael Sánchez "The EC State Aid Regime: Distortive Effects of State Aid on Competition and Trade", pp. 501-510 (London: Cameron May, 2006).
77. Mwikya, Stephen Mbithi, "Fisheries Access Agreements: Trade and Development Issues" (Geneva: ICTSD, 2006).
78. Mwikya, Stephen Mbithi, "Fisheries Access Agreements: Trade and Development Issues" (Geneva: ICTSD, 2006).
79. O'Brien, Robert, "Subsidies Regulation and State Transformation in North America, the GATT and the EU" (New York: St. Martin's Press, 1997).
80. OECD, "Environmental Aspects of Fisheries Subsidies", Background Paper Prepared for the OECD Technical Expert Meeting on Environmentally Harmful Subsidies, Paris, 3-4 November (Paris: OECD, 2003).
81. OECD, "Environmentally Harmful Subsidies: Challenges for Reform" (Paris: OECD, 2005).
82. OECD, "Financial Support to Fisheries, Implications for Sustainable Development" (Paris: OECD, 2006).
83. OECD, "Policy Brief: Subsidies: a Way towards Sustainable Fisheries?" (Paris: OECD, 2005).
84. OECD, "Review of Fisheries and Transition to Responsible Fisheries" (Paris: OECD, 2000).
85. OECD, "Transition to Responsible Fisheries: Economic and Policy Implications" (Paris: OECD, 2000).
86. Orellana, Marcos A., "EEZ Fisheries Access Agreements and the WTO Subsidies Agreement: Legal Analysis and Options for Improved Disciplines" (Geneva: UNEP, 2007).
87. Pauwelyn, Joost, "The Role of Public International Law in the WTO: How Far Can We Go?", American Journal of International Law, Vol. 95, pp. 535-578 (2001).
88. Peterson, M J, "International Fisheries Management", in Haas, Peter, Keohane, Robert and Levy, Marc (eds), "Institutions for the Earth: Sources of Effective International Environmental Protection", pp. 249-305 (Cambridge: MIT Press, 1993).
89. PEW Oceans Commission, "America's Living Oceans: Charting a Course for Sea Change" (Virginia: PEW, 2003).
90. Porter, Gareth, "Fisheries Subsidies and Overfishing: Towards a Structured Discussion" (Geneva: UNEP, 2002).

91. Pradeep Metha, "Trade, Debt and Finance: A Complex Agenda for the WTO", in Mbirimi, Ivan, Chilala, Bridget, and Grynberg, Roman (eds), "From Doha to Cancun: Delivering a Development Round", pp. 315-334 (London: Commonwealth Secretariat, 2003).
92. Price, Tracey M., "Negotiating WTO Fisheries Subsidy Discipline: Can Subsidy Transparency and Classification Provide the Means Towards an End to the Race for Fish?", Tulane Journal of International and Comparative Law, Vol. 13, pp. 141 et seq (2005).
93. Rosenthal, Paul C. and Vermylen, Robert T.C., "Review of Key Substantive Agreements: Panel II E: Antidumping Agreement (AD) and Agreement on Subsidies and Countervailing Measures (SCM): the WTO Antidumping and Subsidies Agreements: Did the United States Achieve Its Objectives During the Uruguay Round?", Law and Policy in International Business, Vol. 31, pp. 871 et seq (2000).
94. Rubini, Luca, "The International Context of EC State Aid Law and Policy: The Regulation of Subsidies in the WTO", in Biondi, Andrea, Eeckhout, Piet and Flynn, James (eds), "The Law of State Aid in the European Union", pp. 149-188 (New York: Oxford University Press: 2004).
95. Schmidt, Carl-Christian, "Globalisation, Industry Structure, Market Power and Impact on Fish Trade, Opportunities and Challenges for Developed (OECD) Countries" (Paris: OECD, 2004).
96. Schorkopf, Frank, "Article 11 SPS", in Wolfrum, Rüdiger, Stoll, Peter-Tobias and Seibert-Fohr, Anja (eds), "WTO-Technical Barriers and SPS Measures", pp. 513-523 (Leiden: Martinus Nijhoff Publishers, 2007).
97. Schorr, David K. and Caddy, John F., "Sustainability Criteria for Fisheries Subsidies, Options for the WTO and Beyond" (Geneva: UNEP and WWF, 2007).
98. Schorr, David K., "Artisanal Fishing: Promoting Poverty Reduction and Community Development through New WTO Rules on Fisheries Subsidies: An Issue and Options Paper" (Geneva: UNEP, 2005).
99. Schorr, David K., "Fisheries Subsidies and the WTO", in Sampson, Gary P. and Chambers, Bradnee (eds), "Trade, Environment and the Millennium", pp. 175-206 (2ed., Tokyo: United Nations University Press, 2002).
100. Schorr, David K., "Healthy Fisheries, Sustainable Trade: Crafting New Rules on Fishing Subsidies in the World Trade Organization" (Washington, D.C. and Gland: WWF, 2004).
101. Schrank, W.E. and Keithly, W.R., Jr., "The Concept of Subsidies", Marine Resource Economics, Vol. XIV, pp. 151 et seq (1999).
102. Seibert-Fohr, Anja, "Article 9 SPS", in Wolfrum, Rüdiger, Stoll, Peter-Tobias and Seibert-Fohr, Anja (eds), "WTO-Technical Barriers and SPS Measures", pp. 495-502 (Leiden: Martinus Nijhoff Publishers, 2007).
103. Sissenwine, Michael and Symes, David, "Reflections on the Common Fisheries Policy, Report to the General Directorate for Fisheries and Maritime Affairs of the European Commission" (Brussels: Greenpeace European Unit, 2007).

104. Skeen, Richard, "Will the WTO Turn Green? The Implications of Injecting Environmental Issues Into the Multilateral Trading System", Georgetown International Environmental Law Review, Vol. 17, pp. 161 et seq (2004).
105. Snape, Richard H., "International Regulation of Subsidies", the World Economy, Vol. 14, pp.139-164 (1991).
106. Sporrong, Niki and Bevins, Kate, "Fisheries Agreements with Third Countries-Is the EU Moving towards Sustainable Development?" (London: Institute for European Environmental Policy, 2003).
107. Steenblik, Ronald P., "Previous Multilateral Efforts to Discipline Subsidies to Natural Resource Based Industries" (Paris: OECD, 1998).
108. Stokke, Olav Schram and Vidas, Davor, "Regulating IUU Fishing or Combating IUU Operations", in OECD Publication, "Fish Piracy Combating Illegal, Unreported and Unregulated Fishing", pp. 19-48 (Paris: OECD, 2004).
109. Sumaila, R. and Pauly, D., "Catching More Bait: A Bottom-up Re-Estimate of Global Fisheries Subsidies" (Vancouver: U. Brit. Columbia Fisheries Centre, 2006).
110. Sumaila, U. R., Alder, J. and Keith, H., "The Cost of Being Apprehended for Fishing Illegally: Empirical Evidence and Policy Implications", in OECD Publication, "Fish Piracy Combating Illegal, Unreported and Unregulated Fishing", pp.201-230 (Paris: OECD, 2004).
111. Sutinen, Jon G., NOAA Technical Memorandum NMFS-NE-158 "A framework for monitoring and assessing socioeconomics and governance of large marine ecosystems" (Massachusetts: National Marine Fisheries Service, 2000).
112. Tallontire, Anne, "Trade Issues Background Paper: The Impact of Subsidies on Trade in Fisheries Products" (Rome: FAO, 2004).
113. Tamiotti, Ludivine, "Article 2 TBT", in Wolfrum, Rüdiger, Stoll, Peter-Tobias and Seibert-Fohr, Anja (eds), "WTO-Technical Barriers and SPS Measures", pp, 210-234 (Leiden: Martinus Nijhoff Publishers, 2007).
114. UN Department of Economic and Social Affairs, Division for Sustainable Development, "Plan of Implementation of the World Summit on Sustainable Development" (2002).
115. UNEP and WWF, "Disciplining Fisheries Subsidies: Incorporating Sustainability at the WTO & Beyond, 1-2 March 2007-Geneva, Switzerland, Chair's Summary" (Geneva: UNEP and WWF, 2007).
116. UNEP, "A UNEP Update, United Nations Environment Programme, Division of Technology, Industry and Economics, Economics and Trade Branch" (Geneva: UNEP, 2004).
117. UNEP, "Analyzing the Resource Impact of Fisheries Subsidies: A Matrix Approach" (Geneva: UNEP, 2004).
118. UNEP, "Chairman's Summary, UNEP Fisheries Subsidies Workshop Geneva, 12 February 2001" (Geneva: UNEP, 2001).

119. UNEP, "Development and Sustainability in the WTO Fishery Subsidies Negotiations: Issues and Alternatives, Chair's Summary" (Geneva: UNEP, 2006).
120. UNEP, "Fisheries Subsidies: a Critical Issue for Trade and Sustainable Development at the WTO, an Introductory Guide" (Geneva: UNEP, 2008).
121. UNEP, "Incorporating Resource Impact into Fisheries Subsidies Disciplines: Issues and Options, a Discussion Paper" (Geneva: UNEP, 2004).
122. UNEP, "Meeting Report, UNEP Informal Expert Consultation on Fisheries Subsidies, 16th July 2003, Geneva" (Geneva: UNEP, 2003).
123. UNEP, "Promoting Development and Sustainability in Fisheries Subsidies Disciplines: An Informal Dialogue on Select Technical Issues, International Environment House, Geneva, 30 June 2005, Chair's Summary" (Geneva: UNEP, 2005).
124. UNEP, "Reflecting Sustainable Development and Special and Differential Treatment for Developing Countries in the Context of New WTO Fisheries Subsidies Rules" (Geneva: UNEP, 2005).
125. UNEP, "UNEP Workshop on Fisheries Subsidies and Sustainable Fisheries Management, Geneva, 26-27 April 2004, Summary of the Chairs" (Geneva: UNEP, 2004).
126. Vannuccini, Stefania, "Overview of Fish Production, Utilization, Consumption and Trade, Based on 2002" (Rome: FAO, 2004).
127. Wolfrum, Rüdiger and Matz, Nele, "Conflicts in International Environmental Law" (Berlin: Springer, 2003).
128. Wolfrum, Rüdiger, "IMO Interface with the Law of the Sea Convention", in Nordquist, Myron H. and Moore, John Norton (eds), "Current Maritime Issues and the International Maritime Organization", pp. 223-236 (The Hague: Kluwer Law International, 1999).
129. Wolfrum, Rüdiger, "Introduction", in Wolfrum, Rüdiger and Röben, Volker (eds), "Developments of International Law in Treaty Making", pp. 1-13 (Berlin: Springer, 2005).
130. Wolfrum, Rüdiger, "Means of Ensuring Compliance with and Enforcement of International Law", Recueil des Cours de l'Académie de droit international de La Haye 272, pp. 10 et seq (1998).
131. Wolfrum, Rüdiger, "The Role of the International Tribunal for the Law of the Sea," in Nordquist, Myron H. and Moore, John Norton (eds), "Current Fisheries Issues and the Food and Agriculture Organization of the United Nations", pp. 369-385 (The Hague: Kluwer Law International, 2000).
132. Wolfrum, Rüdiger, Röben, Volker and Morrison, Fred, "Preservation of the Marine Environment", in Morrison, Fred and Wolfrum, Rüdiger (eds), "International, Regional and National Environmental Law", pp. 225-283 (The Hague: Kluwer Law International, 2000).
133. WWF, "A Leading Role for the EU in Combating Illegal, Unreported and Unregulated Fishing" (Brussels: WWF European Policy Office, 2007).

134. WWF, "Fishing Subsidies: Issues for ACP Countries" (Washington, D.C. and Gland: WWF, 2005).
135. WWF, "Hard Facts, Hidden Problems: A review of Current Data on Fishing Subsidies" (Washington, D.C. and Gland: WWF, 2001).
136. WWF, "Proposal for a Council Regulation for the European Fisheries Fund COM(2004) 497" (Brussels: WWF European Policy Office, 2006).
137. WWF, "Putting an End to Fishing in the Dark? WWF's European Marine Programme's Response to the ETI Green Paper-Part III" (Brussels: WWF European Policy Office, 2006).
138. WWF, "Small Boats, Big Problems" (Gland: WWF, 2008).
139. WWF, "Turning the Tide on Fishing Subsidies, Can the World Trade Organization Play a Positive Role?" (Washington, D.C. and Gland: WWF, 2002).
140. WWF, "What's the Catch?" (Washington, D.C. and Gland: WWF, 2005).
141. Young, Margaret A., "Fragmentation or Interaction: the WTO, Fisheries Subsidies and International Law", World Trade Review, Vol. 8, No. 4, pp.477-515 (2009).
142. Yu, Vincente Paolo B., III and Fonseca-Marti, Darlan, "Reflecting Sustainable Development and Special and Differential Treatment for Developing Countries in the Context of New WTO Fisheries Subsidies Rules: An Issue and Options Paper" (Geneva: UNEP, 2005)

II. Documents

EU

143. Commission Regulation (EC) No 1595/2004 of 8 September 2004 on the application of Article 87 and 88 of Treaty to State aid to small and medium-sized enterprises active in the production, processing and marketing of fisheries products, OJ L 291, 14.9.2004, pp. 3-11.
144. Commission Regulation (EC) No 1860/2004 of 6 October 2004 on the application of Articles 87 and 88 of the EC Treaty to *de minimis* aid in the agriculture and fisheries sectors, OJ L 325, 28.10.2004, pp. 4-9.
145. Commission Regulation (EC) No 498/2007 of 26 March 2007 laying down detailed rules for the implementation of Council Regulation (EC) No 1198/2006 on the European Fisheries Fund, OJ L 120, 10.5.2007, pp.1-80.
146. Commission Regulation (EC) No 70/2001 of 12 January 2001 on the application of Articles 87 and 88 of the EC Treaty to State aid to small and medium-sized enterprises, OJ L 10, 13.1.2001, pp. 33-42.
147. Commission Regulation (EC) No 736/2008 of 22 July 2008 on the application of Article 87 and 88 of Treaty to State aid to small and medium-sized enterprises active in the production, processing and marketing of fisheries products, OJ L 201, 30.7.2008, pp. 16-28.

148. Commission Regulation (EC) No 794/2004 of 21 April 2004 implementing Council Regulation (EC) No 659/1999 laying down detailed rules for the application of Article 93 of the EC Treaty, OJ L 140, 30.4.2004, pp. 1-134.
149. Commission Regulation (EC) No 875/2007 of 24 July 2007 on the application of Article 87 and 88 of the EC Treaty to *de minimis* aid in the fisheries sector and amending Regulation (EC) No 1860/2004, OJ L 193, 25.7.2007, pp. 6-12.
150. Council Regulation (EC) No 104/2000 of 17 December 1999 on the common organisation of the markets in fishery and aquaculture products, OJ L 17, 21.1.2000, pp. 21-52.
151. Council Regulation (EC) No 1198/2006 on the European Fisheries Fund, OJ L 223, 15.8.2006, pp. 1-44.
152. Council Regulation (EC) No 1263/1999 of 21 June 1999 on the Financial Instrument for Fisheries Guidance, OJ L 161, 26.6.1999, pp. 54-56.
153. Council Regulation (EC) No 1263/1999 of 21 June 1999 on the Financial Instrument for Fisheries Guidance, OJ L 161, 26.6.1999, pp. 54-56.
154. Council Regulation (EC) No 1290/2005 of 21 June 2005 on the financing of the common agricultural policy, OJ L 209, 11.8.2005, pp. 1–25.
155. Council Regulation (EC) No 2371/2002 of 20 December 2002 on the conservation and sustainable exploitation of fisheries resources under the Common Fisheries Policy, OJ L 358, 31.12.2002, pp. 59–80.
156. Council Regulation (EC) No 2792/1999 of 17 December 1999 laying down the detailed rules and arrangements regarding Community structural assistance in the fisheries sector, OJ L 337, 30.12.1999, pp.10-35.
157. Council Regulation (EC) No 659/1999 of 22 March 1999 laying down detailed rules for the application of Article 93 of the EC Treaty, OJ L 83, 27.3.1999, pp. 1–9.
158. Council Regulation (EC) No 744/2008 instituting a temporary specific action aiming to promote the restructuring of the European Community fishing fleet affected by the economic crisis, OJ L 202, 31.7.2008, pp. 1-8.
159. Council Regulation (EC) No 994/98 of 7 May 1998 on the application of Articles 92 and 93 of the Treaty establishing the European Community to certain categories of horizontal State aid, OJ L 142, 14.5.1998, pp. 1-4.
160. Council Regulation (EEC) No 101/76 of 19 January 1976 laying down a common structural policy for the fishing industry, OJ L 20, 28.01.1976.
161. Council Regulation (EEC) No 170/83 of 25 January 1983 establishing a Community system for the conservation and management of fisheries resources.
162. Council Regulation (EEC) No 2080/93 of 20 July 1993 laying down provisions for implementing Regulation (EEC) No 2052/88 as regards the financial instrument of fisheries guidance, OJ L 193, 31.7.1993, pp. 1-4.

163. Council Regulation (EEC) No 2141/70 of October 20 1970 laying down a common structural policy for the fishing industry, OJ L 236, 27.10.1970.
164. Guideline for the examination of State aid to fisheries and aquaculture, OJ C 84, 3.4.2008, pp. 10-16.
165. Guidelines for the examination of State aid to fisheries and aquaculture, OJ 1985 C 268, pp. 2 *et seq.*
166. Judgment of the Court (Fifth Chamber) of 24 March 1993. Case C-313/90. Comité International de la Rayonne et des Fibres Synthétiques (CIRFS) and others Commission of the European Communities.
167. Judgment of the Court (Fifth Chamber) of 5 October 2000. Case C-288/96. Federal Republic of Germany v Commission of the European Communities.
168. Judgment of the Court of 15 October 1996. Case C-311/94. IJssel-Vliet Combinatie BV v Minister van Economische Zaken.
169. Judgment of the Court of 23 November 1999. Case C-149/96. Portuguese Republic V Council of the European Union.
170. Judgment of the Court of First Instance of 29 September 2000. Case T-55/99. Confederación Española de Transporte de Mercancías V Commission of the European Communities.
171. Treaty establishing the European Community, OJ C 325, 24.12.2002, pp. 1-184.

FAO

172. FAO Doc. COFI:FT/VII/2000/5, "Item 7.1 of the Provisional Agenda, Committee on Fisheries, Sub-Committee on Fish Trade, Seventh Session, Bremen, Germany, 22-25 March 2000, Implementation of World Trade Organization Agreements and Multilateral Trade Negotiations: Agreements on the Application of Sanitary and Phytosanitary Measures, Technical Barriers to Trade and on Subsidies and Countervailing Measures" (Rome: FAO, 2000).
173. FAO Doc. COFI:FT/VII/2000/6, "Item 7.2 of the Provisional Agenda, Committee on Fisheries, Sub-Committee on Fish Trade, Seventh Session, Bremen, Germany, 22-25 March 2000, Implementation of World Trade Organization Agreements and Multilateral Trade Negotiations: Ongoing Multilateral Trade Negotiations and FAO Training Programme" (Rome: FAO, 2000).
174. FAO Doc. FAO Fisheries Circular No. 917 FRIM/C917, "A Checklist for Fisheries Resource Management Issues Seen from the Perspective of the FAO Code of Conduct for Responsible Fisheries" (Rome: FAO, 1996).
175. FAO Doc. FAO Fisheries Report No. 484, "Report of the Technical Consultation on High Sea Fishing" (Rome: FAO, 1992).
176. FAO Doc. FAO Fisheries Report No. 519 "Guidelines for responsible management of fisheries. Report of the Expert Consultation on Guide-

lines for Responsible Fisheries Management, Wellington, New Zealand, 23-27 January 1995" (Rome: FAO, 1995).
177. FAO Doc. FAO Fisheries Report No. 638, "Report of the Expert Consultation on Economic Incentives and Responsible Fisheries - Rome, 28 November-1 December 2000" (Rome: FAO, 2000).
178. FAO Doc. FAO Fisheries Report No. 702, Report of the Twenty-fifth Session of the Committee on Fisheries, Rome, 24-28 February 2003, (Rome: FAO, 2003).
179. FAO Doc. FAO Fisheries Report No. 722, "Report of the Expert Consultation on Fishing Vessels Operating under Open Registries and Their Impact on Illegal, Unreported and Unregulated Fishing" (Rome: FAO, 2004).
180. FAO Doc. FAO Fisheries Report No. 735, "Report of the Second Session of the Working Party on Small-scale Fisheries. Bangkok, Thailand, 18-21 November 2003" (Rome: FAO, 2004).
181. FAO Doc. FAO Fisheries Report No. 752, "Report of the Technical Consultation on the Use of Subsidies in the Fisheries Sector" (Rome: FAO, 2004).
182. FAO Doc. FAO Fisheries Technical Paper No. 437, "Introducing Fisheries Subsidies" (Rome: FAO, 2003).
183. FAO Doc. FAO Fisheries Technical Paper No. 438, "Guide for Identifying, Assessing and Reporting on Subsidies in the Fisheries Sector" (Rome: FAO, 2004).
184. FAO Doc. FAO Fisheries Technical Paper No. 457, "Review of the State of World Marine Fishery Resources" (Rome: FAO, 2005).
185. FAO Doc. FAO Technical Guidelines for Responsible Fisheries No. 10, "Increasing the Contribution of Small-Scale Fisheries to Poverty Alleviation and Food Security" (Rome: FAO, 2005).
186. FAO Doc. No. COFI/2003/8, "Conclusions and Recommendations of the FAO Expert Consultation on Identifying, Assessing and Reporting on Subsidies in the Fishing Industry" (Rome: FAO, 2003).
187. FAO Doc. No. COFI:FT/XI/2008/3, "Committee on Fisheries, Sub-Committee on Fish Trade, Eleventh Session, Bremen, Germany, 2-6 June 2008, Status and Important Recent Events Concerning International Trade in Fishery Products" (Rome: FAO, 2008).
188. FAO Doc. No. FIDI/C853, "Marine Fisheries and the Law of the Sea: A Decade of Change, Special Chapter (Revised) of the State of Food and Agriculture 1992" (Rome: FAO, 1993).
189. FAO, "Guidelines for the Ecolabelling of Fish and Fishery Products from Marine Capture Fisheries" (Rome: FAO, 2005).
190. FAO, "International Plan of Action for Reducing Incidental Catch of Seabirds in Longline Fisheries. International Plan of Action for the Conservation and Management of Sharks. International Plan of Action for the Management of Fishing Capacity" (Rome: FAO, 1999).
191. FAO, "International Plan of Action to Prevent, Deter and Eliminate Illegal, Unreported and Unregulated Fishing" (Rome: FAO, 2001).

OECD

192. OECD Doc. No. AGR/FI(93)11/REV1, "Economic Assistance to the Fishing Industry Observations and Finding" (Paris: OECD, 1993).
193. OECD Doc. No. Env/EPOC/GSP/BIO(2003)2/FINAL, "Perverse Incentives in Biodiversity Loss" (Paris: OECD, 2003).

UN

194. UN Doc. No. A/CN.4/L.682 and Corr.1, "Analytical Study finalized by the Chairman" (13 April 2006).
195. UN Doc. No. A/CN.4/L.702, "Report of the Study Group, Fragmentation of International Law: Difficulties arising from the Diversification and Expansion of International Law: Conclusions" (18 July 2006).
196. UN Doc. No. A/RES/42/187, "Report of the World Commission on Environment and Development" (11 December 1987).
197. UN Doc. No. A/RES/S-19/2, "Resolution Adopted by the General Assembly" (19 September 1997).

WTO

198. WTO Doc. No. G/SCM/39, "Procedures for Extensions under Article 27.4 for Certain Developing Country Members" (20 November 2001)
199. WTO Doc. No. G/SCM/W/421, "Communication from the European Community to the Committee on Subsidies and Countervailing Measures, Frequency of Article 25 Subsidy Notifications" (30 March 1999).
200. WTO Doc. No. PRESS/TE/033, "Trade and Environment Bulletin: CTE Holds Information Session with MEAs and Addresses the Relationship between the WTO and MEAs, the Export of Domestically Prohibited Good, the TRIPs Agreement and Fisheries Subsidies" (10 July 2000).
201. WTO Doc. No. PRESS/TE/034, "Trade and Environment Bulletin: CTE Holds MEA Information Session and Discusses WTO-MEA Relationships, Services and the Environment, Relations with IGOs and NGOs, Fisheries subsidies and Liberalizing Environmental Services" (31 October 2000).
202. WTO Doc. No. PRESS/TE/036, "Trade and Environment Bulletin: UNEP and MEAs Participate in CTE Information Session on Compliance and Dispute Settlement. CTE Discussions WTO-MEA Relationship, Domestically Prohibited Goods, Biodiversity Convention and TRIPS Agreement, ECO-labelling, and Fisheries Subsidies Reform" (6 July 2001).
203. WTO Doc. No. PRESS/TE/038, "Trade and Environment Bulletin: WTO Committee on Trade and Environment Focuses on Market Access Issues, Fisheries Subsidies, Technical Cooperation and Capacity Building, and Its Mandate to Identify and Debate the Environmental and Developmental Aspects of WTO Negotiations (4 April 2002).
204. WTO Doc. No. TN/MA/W/15/Add.1, "Communication from Japan to the Negotiating Group on Market Access, Market Access for Non-agri-

cultural Products: Addendum-Japanese Proposal on Sustainable Development and the Trade of Forest and Fishery Products" (6 January 2003).
205. WTO Doc. No. TN/RL/21, "Report by the Chairman to the Trade Negotiations Committee to the Negotiating Group on Rules, Negotiating Group on Rules" (27 July 2007).
206. WTO Doc. No. TN/RL/9, "Negotiating Group on Rules, Report by the Chairman to the Trade Negotiations" (25 June 2004).
207. WTO Doc. No. TN/RL/GEN/100, "Paper from New Zealand to the Negotiating Group on Rules, Fisheries Subsidies Framework for Disciplines" (3 March 2006).
208. WTO Doc. No. TN/RL/GEN/114, "Communication from Japan; the Republic of Korea; and the Separate Customs Territory of Taiwan, Penghu, Kinmen and Matsu to the Negotiating Group on Rules, Fisheries Subsidies Framework for Disciplines" (21 April 2006).
209. WTO Doc. No. TN/RL/GEN/114/Rev.1, "Communication from Japan; the Republic of Korea; and the Separate Customs Territory of Taiwan, Penghu, Kinmen and Matsu to the Negotiating Group on Rules, Fisheries Subsidies Framework for Disciplines, Revised" (2 June 2006).
210. WTO Doc. No. TN/RL/GEN/114/Rev.2, "Communication from Japan; the Republic of Korea; and the Separate Customs Territory of Taiwan, Penghu, Kinmen and Matsu to the Negotiating Group on Rules, Fisheries Subsidies: Framework for Disciplines" (5 June 2007).
211. WTO Doc. No. TN/RL/GEN/127, "Communication from the United States to the Negotiating Group on Rules, Fisheries Subsidies" (24 April 2006).
212. WTO Doc. No. TN/RL/GEN/134, "Submission from the European Communities to the Negotiating Group on Rules, Fisheries Subsidies" (24 April 2006).
213. WTO Doc. No. TN/RL/GEN/138, "Paper from Argentina to the Negotiating Group on Rules, Fisheries Subsidies: Special and Differential Treatment" (1 June 2006).
214. WTO Doc. No. TN/RL/GEN/138/Rev.1, "Paper from Argentina to the Negotiating Group on Rules, Fisheries Subsidies: Special and Differential Treatment, Revision" (26 January 2007).
215. WTO Doc. No. TN/RL/GEN/141, "Paper from New Zealand to the Negotiating Group on Rules, Fisheries Subsidies Exhaustive List of Non-Prohibited Fisheries Subsidies" (6 June 2006).
216. WTO Doc. No. TN/RL/GEN/144, "Proposal by Norway to the Negotiating Group on Rules, Fisheries Subsidies" (26 January 2007).
217. WTO Doc. No. TN/RL/GEN/145, "Proposal from the United States to the Negotiating Group on Rules, Fisheries Subsidies: Proposed New Disciplines" (22 March 2007).
218. WTO Doc. No. TN/RL/GEN/150, "Proposal from the Republic of Indonesia to the Negotiating Group on Rules, Fisheries Subsidies: Proposed New Disciplines" (2 July 2007).

219. WTO Doc. No. TN/RL/GEN/150/Rev.1, "Revised Proposal from the Republic of Indonesia to the Negotiating Group on Rules, Fisheries Subsidies: Proposed New Disciplines" (10 September 2007).
220. WTO Doc. No. TN/RL/GEN/151, "Proposal from Argentina and Brazil to the Negotiating Group on Rules, Special and Differential Treatment" (17 September 2007).
221. WTO Doc. No. TN/RL/GEN/151/Rev.1, "Paper from Argentina and Brazil to the Negotiating Group on Rules, Fisheries Subsidies: Special and Differential Treatment and Fishery Adverse Effects, Revision" (26 November 2007).
222. WTO Doc. No. TN/RL/GEN/155, "Submission by India and Indonesia to the Negotiating Group on Rules, Need for Effective Special and Differential Treatment for Developing Country Members in the Proposed Fisheries Subsidies Text" (22 April 2008).
223. WTO Doc. No. TN/RL/GEN/155/Rev.1, "Submission by India, Indonesia and China to the Negotiating Group on Rules, Need for Effective Special and Differential Treatment for Developing Country Members in the Proposed Fisheries Subsidies Text" (19 May 2008).
224. WTO Doc. No. TN/RL/GEN/156, "Communication from Canada to the Negotiating Group on Rules, Fisheries Subsidies-De Minimis Exemption" (2 May 2008).
225. WTO Doc. No. TN/RL/GEN/158, "Communication from the ACP and SVEs Groups to the Negotiating Group on Rules, Drafting Proposal on Issues Relating to Article III.4 ("Special and Differential Treatment of Developing Country Members") of the Fisheries Subsidies Annex to the SCM Agreement as Proposed by the Chair in TN/RL/W/213" (22 May 2008).
226. WTO Doc. No. TN/RL/GEN/159, "Communication from the Republic of Korea and the Separate Customs Territory of Taiwan, Penghu, Kinmen and Matsu, Relation between Article I and Article V of the Chair's Text" (4 June 2008).
227. WTO Doc. No. TN/RL/GEN/36, "Paper from New Zealand to the Negotiating Group on Rules, Fisheries Subsidies to Management Services" (23 March 2005).
228. WTO Doc. No. TN/RL/GEN/39, "Paper from the European Communities to the Negotiating Group on Rules, Paper on Fisheries" (12 May 2005).
229. WTO Doc. No. TN/RL/GEN/41, "Communication from the United States to the Negotiating Group on Rules, Fisheries Subsidies: Programmes for Decommissioning of Vessels and Licence Retirement" (13 May 2005).
230. WTO Doc. No. TN/RL/GEN/47, "Paper from Japan to the Negotiating Group on Rules, IUU Fishing and Fisheries Subsidies" (10 June 2005).
231. WTO Doc. No. TN/RL/GEN/54, "Submission from Australia, Ecuador and New Zealand to the Negotiating Group on Rules, Contribution to the

Discussion on the Framework for Disciplines on Fisheries Subsidies-Aquaculture" (1 July 2005).
232. WTO Doc. No. TN/RL/GEN/56, "Paper from Brazil to the Negotiating Group on Rules, Contribution to the Discussion on the Framework for Disciplines on Fisheries Subsidies" (4 July 2005).
233. WTO Doc. No. TN/RL/GEN/57, "Paper from Fiji, Papua New Guinea and the Solomon Islands to the Negotiating Group on Rules, WTO Fisheries Subsidies Disciplines Architecture on Fisheries Subsidies Disciplines" (7 July 2005).
234. WTO Doc. No. TN/RL/GEN/57/Rev.1, "Paper from Fiji, Jamaica, Papua New Guinea, and the Solomon Islands to the Negotiating Group on Rules, WTO Fisheries Subsidies Disciplines Architecture on Fisheries Subsidies Disciplines" (4 August 2005).
235. WTO Doc. No. TN/RL/GEN/57/Rev.2, "Paper from Antigua and Barbuda, Barbados, Dominican Republic, Fiji, Grenada, Guyana, Jamaica, Papua New Guinea, St, Kitts and Nevis, St. Lucia, Solomon Islands, and Trinidad and Tobago to the Negotiating Group on Rules, WTO Fisheries Subsidies Disciplines Architecture on Fisheries Subsidies Disciplines" (13 September 2005).
236. WTO Doc. No. TN/RL/GEN/70, "Paper from New Zealand to the Negotiating Group on Rules, Subsidies to Fisheries Infrastructure" (14 October 2005).
237. WTO Doc. No. TN/RL/GEN/79, "Paper from Brazil to the Negotiating Group on Rules, Further Contribution to the Discussion on the Framework for Disciplines on Fisheries Subsidies" (16 November 2005).
238. WTO Doc. No. TN/RL/GEN/79/Rev.1, "Paper from Brazil to the Negotiating Group on Rules, Possible Disciplines on Fisheries Subsidies, Revision" (21 February 2006).
239. WTO Doc. No. TN/RL/GEN/79/Rev.2, "Paper from Brazil to the Negotiating Group on Rules, Possible Disciplines on Fisheries Subsidies, Revision" (21 April 2006).
240. WTO Doc. No. TN/RL/GEN/79/Rev.3, "Paper from Brazil to the Negotiating Group on Rules, Possible Disciplines on Fisheries Subsidies, Revision" (2 June 2006).
241. WTO Doc. No. TN/RL/GEN/79/Rev.4, "Paper from Brazil to the Negotiating Group on Rules, Possible Disciplines on Fisheries Subsidies, Revision" (13 March 2007).
242. WTO Doc. No. TN/RL/GEN/92, "Paper from the Republic of Korea to the Negotiating Group on Rules, Fisheries Subsidies: Small-Scale Fisheries" (18 November 2005).
243. WTO Doc. No. TN/RL/W/11, "Japan's Basic Position on the Fisheries Subsidies Issue to the Negotiating Group on Rules" (2 July 2002).
244. WTO Doc. No. TN/RL/W/115, "Communication from Chile to the Negotiating Group on Rules, Possible Approaches to Improved Disciplines on Fisheries Subsidies" (10 June 2003).

245. WTO Doc. No. TN/RL/W/12, "Submission from New Zealand to the Negotiating Group on Rules, Fisheries Subsidies: Limitations of Existing Subsidy Disciplines" (4 July 20002).
246. WTO Doc. No. TN/RL/W/128, "Communication from New Zealand to the Negotiating Group on Rules, WTO Disciplines on Fisheries Subsidies: Elements of the Chair's Draft" (21 February 2008).
247. WTO Doc. No. TN/RL/W/136, "Fisheries Subsidies, submitted by Antigua and Barbuda, Belize, Fuji Islands, Guyana, the Maldives, Papua New Guinea, Solomon Islands, St. Kitts and Nevis to the Negotiating Group on Rules" (14 July 2003).
248. WTO Doc. No. TN/RL/W/154, "Communication from New Zealand to the Negotiating Group on Rules, Fisheries Subsidies: Overcapacity and Overexploitation" (26 April 2004).
249. WTO Doc. No. TN/RL/W/159, "Communication from Japan to the Negotiating Group on Rules, Fisheries Subsidies: Proposed Structure of the Discussion" (7 June 2004).
250. WTO Doc. No. TN/RL/W/160, "Questions and Comments from Korea on New Zealand's Communication on Fisheries Subsidies (TN/RL/W/154) to the Negotiating Group on Rules" (8 June 2004).
251. WTO Doc. No. TN/RL/W/161, "Communication from New Zealand, Fisheries Subsidies: UNEP Workshop on Fisheries Subsidies and Sustainable Fisheries Management" (8 June 2004).
252. WTO Doc. No. TN/RL/W/164, "Paper by Japan to the Negotiating Group on Rules, Proposal on Fisheries Subsidies" (27 September 2004).
253. WTO Doc. No. TN/RL/W/166, "Communication from Argentina, Chile, Ecuador, New Zealand, Philippines, Peru to the Negotiating Group on Rules, Fisheries Subsidies" (2 November 2004).
254. WTO Doc. No. TN/RL/W/169, "Communication from the United States to the Negotiating Group on Rules, Additional Views on the Structure of the Fisheries Subsidies Negotiations" (13 December 2004).
255. WTO Doc. No. TN/RL/W/17, "Korea's Views on the Doha Development Agenda Discussions on Fisheries Subsidies to the Negotiating Group on Rules" (2 October 2002).
256. WTO Doc. No. TN/RL/W/172, "Communication from Japan; the Republic of Korea; and the Separate Customs Territory of Taiwan, Penghu, Kinmen and Matsu to the Negotiating Group on Rules, Contribution to the Discussion on the Framework for the Disciplines on the Fisheries Subsidies" (22 February 2005).
257. WTO Doc. No. TN/RL/W/176, "Paper from Brazil to the Negotiating Group on Rules, Contribution to the Discussion on the Framework for Disciplines on Fisheries Subsidies" (31 March 2005).
258. WTO Doc. No. TN/RL/W/178, "Paper from the European Communities to the Negotiating Group on Rules, Fisheries Subsidies" (11 April 2005).
259. WTO Doc. No. TN/RL/W/184, "Communication from New Zealand to the Negotiating Group on Rules, Promoting Development and Sustain-

ability in Fisheries Subsidies Disciplines: an Informal Dialogue on Select Technical Issues" (18 July 2005).
260. WTO Doc. No. TN/RL/W/196, "Paper from Brazil; Chile; Colombia; Ecuador; Iceland; New Zealand; Pakistan; Peru and the United States to the Negotiating Group on Rules, Fisheries Subsidies" (22 November 2005).
261. WTO Doc. No. TN/RL/W/197, "Note by the Secretariat to the Negotiating Group on Rules, Definitions Related to Artisanal, Small-Scale and Subsistence Fishing" (24 November 2005).
262. WTO Doc. No. TN/RL/W/201, "Paper from Japan to the Negotiating Group on Rules, Fisheries Subsidies, Subsidies for Vessel Construction and Modification" (6 March 2006).
263. WTO Doc. No. TN/RL/W/202, "Communication from the Separate Customs Territory of Taiwan, Penghu, Kinmen and Matsu to the Negotiating Group on Rules, Fisheries Subsidies for Social Security and Welfare" (6 March 2006).
264. WTO Doc. No. TN/RL/W/203, "Submission by India to the Negotiating Group on Rules, Small-scale, Artisanal Fisheries" (6 March 2006).
265. WTO Doc. No. TN/RL/W/206, "Development and Sustainability in the WTO Fishery Subsidies Negotiations: Issues and Alternatives" (31 May 2006).
266. WTO Doc. No. TN/RL/W/207, "Communication from New Zealand to the Negotiating Group on Rules, Promoting Development and Sustainability in Fisheries Subsidies Disciplines: An Informal Dialogue on Select Technical Issues" (2 April 2007).
267. WTO Doc. No. TN/RL/W/209, "Communication from the ACP Group to the Negotiating Group on Rules, Access Fees in Fisheries Subsidies Negotiations" (5 June 2007).
268. WTO Doc. No. TN/RL/W/21, "Communication from the United States to the Negotiating Group on Rules, Adverse Trade and Conservation Effects of Fisheries Subsidies" (15 October 2002).
269. WTO Doc. No. TN/RL/W/210, "Communication from Barbados, Cuba, Dominican Republic, El Salvador, Fiji, Guyana, Honduras, Mauritius, Nicaragua, Papua New Guinea, and Solomon Islands to the Negotiating Group on Rules, S&DT in the Fisheries Subsidies Negotiations: Views of the Small, Vulnerable Economies (SVEs)" (6 June 2007).
270. WTO Doc. No. TN/RL/W/210/Rev.1, "Communication from Antigua and Barbuda, Barbados, Cuba, Dominican Republic, El Salvador, Fiji, Guyana, Honduras, Mauritius, Nicaragua, Papua New Guinea, and Solomon Islands to the Negotiating Group on Rules, S&DT in the Fisheries Subsidies Negotiations: Views of the Small, Vulnerable Economies (SVEs)" (18 June 2007).
271. WTO Doc. No. TN/RL/W/210/Rev.2, "Communication from Antigua and Barbuda, Barbados, Cuba, Dominican Republic, El Salvador, Fiji, Guyana, Honduras, Jamaica, Mauritius, Nicaragua, Papua New Guinea, and Solomon Islands to the Negotiating Group on Rules, S&DT in the

Fisheries Subsidies Negotiations: Views of the Small, Vulnerable Economies (SVEs)" (22 June 2007).

272. WTO Doc. No. TN/RL/W/211, "Paper from Argentina to the Negotiating Group on Rules, Fisheries Subsidies: Continuation of Work on Special and Differential Treatment" (19 June 2007).

273. WTO Doc. No. TN/RL/W/212, "Paper from Brazil to the Negotiating Group on Rules, Fisheries Subsidies: "Fisheries Adverse Effects" and "S&D" Treatment" (29 June 2007).

274. WTO Doc. No. TN/RL/W/213, "Draft Consolidated Chair Texts of the AD and SCM Agreements" (30 November 2007).

275. WTO Doc. No. TN/RL/W/217, "Communication from India and the ACP Group to the Negotiating Group on Rules, Joint Statement on Treatment of Artisanal and Small-scale Fisheries in Fisheries Subsidies Negotiations" (15 February 2008).

276. WTO Doc. No. TN/RL/W/218, "Communication from New Zealand to the Negotiating Group on Rules, WTO Disciplines on Fisheries Subsidies: Elements of the Chair's Draft" (21 February 2008).

277. WTO Doc. No. TN/RL/W/226, "Communication from Barbados, Cuba, El Salvador, Fiji, Honduras, Mauritius, Papua New Guinea and Tonga to the Negotiating Group on Rules, Small, Vulnerable Economies (SVEs)-Statement on Key Aspects of Article III of the Fisheries Subsidies Annex" (20 March 2008).

278. WTO Doc. No. TN/RL/W/226/Rev.1, "Communication from Barbados, Cuba, Dominican Republic, El Salvador, Fiji, Honduras, Mauritius, Papua New Guinea and Tonga to the Negotiating Group on Rules, Small, Vulnerable Economies (SVEs)-Statement on Key Aspects of Article III of the Fisheries Subsidies Annex" (31 March 2008).

279. WTO Doc. No. TN/RL/W/226/Rev.2, "Communication from Barbados, Cuba, Dominican Republic, El Salvador, Fiji, Honduras, Mauritius, Papua New Guinea, St. Vincent & the Grenadines, and Tonga to the Negotiating Group on Rules, Small, Vulnerable Economies (SVEs)-Statement on Key Aspects of Article III of the Fisheries Subsidies Annex" (24 April 2008).

280. WTO Doc. No. TN/RL/W/226/Rev.3, "Communication from Barbados, Cuba, Dominican Republic, El Salvador, Fiji, Honduras, Jamaica, Mauritius, Papua New Guinea, St. Vincent & the Grenadines, and Tonga to the Negotiating Group on Rules, Small, Vulnerable Economies (SVEs)-Statement on Key Aspects of Article III of the Fisheries Subsidies Annex" (13 May 2008).

281. WTO Doc. No. TN/RL/W/226/Rev.4, "Communication from Barbados, Cuba, Dominican Republic, El Salvador, Fiji, Honduras, Jamaica, Mauritius, Papua New Guinea, St. Lucia, St. Vincent & the Grenadines, and Tonga to the Negotiating Group on Rules, Small, Vulnerable Economies (SVEs)-Statement on Key Aspects of Article III of the Fisheries Subsidies Annex" (19 May 2008).

282. WTO Doc. No. TN/RL/W/226/Rev.5, "Communication from Barbados, Cuba, Dominica, Dominican Republic, El Salvador, Fiji, Honduras, Jamaica, Mauritius, Nicaragua, Papua New Guinea, St. Lucia, St. Vincent & the Grenadines, and Tonga to the Negotiating Group on Rules, Small, Vulnerable Economies (SVEs)-Statement on Key Aspects of Article III of the Fisheries Subsidies Annex" (22 September 2008).
283. WTO Doc. No. TN/RL/W/231, "Communication from Norway to the Negotiating Group on Rules, Drafting Proposal on Issues Relating to Article V ("Fisheries Management") of the Fisheries Subsidies Annex to the SCM Agreement as Proposed by the Chair in TN/RL/213" (24 April 2008).
284. WTO Doc. No. TN/RL/W/232, "Working Document from the Chairman to the Negotiating Group on Rules" (28 May 2008).
285. WTO Doc. No. TN/RL/W/234, "Communication from Argentina, Chile, Colombia, Ecuador, Mexico and Peru, Statement on the Negotiations on Fisheries Subsidies" (17 July 2008).
286. WTO Doc. No. TN/RL/W/235, "Communication from Australia, New Zealand and the United States to the Negotiating Group on Rules, Fisheries Subsidies" (21 July 2008).
287. WTO Doc. No. TN/RL/W/236, "New Draft Consolidated Chair Texts of the AD and SCM Agreements" (19 December 2008).
288. WTO Doc. No. TN/RL/W/3, "Submission from Australia, Chile, Ecuador, Iceland, New Zealand, Peru, Philippines and the United States to the Negotiating Group on Rules, the Doha Mandate to Address Fisheries Subsidies: Issues" (24 April 2002).
289. WTO Doc. No. TN/RL/W/52, "Japan's Contribution to Discussion on Fisheries Subsidies Issue to the Negotiating Group on Rules" (6 February 2003).
290. WTO Doc. No. TN/RL/W/52, "Japan's Contribution to Discussion on Fisheries Subsidies Issue to the Negotiating Group on Rules" (6 February 2003).
291. WTO Doc. No. TN/RL/W/58, "Submission from Argentina, Chile, Iceland, New Zealand, Norway and Peru to the Negotiating Group on Rules, Subsidies in the Fisheries Sector: Possible Categorizations" (10 February 2003).
292. WTO Doc. No. TN/RL/W/77, "Communication from the United States to the Negotiating Group on Rules, Possible Approaches to Improved Disciplines on Fisheries Subsidies" (19 March 2003).
293. WTO Doc. No. TN/RL/W/82, "Submission of the European Communities to the Negotiating Group on Rules, Fisheries Subsidies" (23 April 2003).
294. WTO Doc. No. TN/RL/W/84, "Questions from Japan Concerning Papers on the Fisheries Subsidies Issue to the Negotiating Group on Rules" (30 April 2003).

295. WTO Doc. No. TN/RL/W/88, "Comments from the People's Republic of China on the United States Proposal on Fisheries Subsidies (TN/RL/W788) to the Negotiating Group on Rules" (1 May 2003).
296. WTO Doc. No. TN/RL/W/9, "Proposal from the People's Republic of China on Fisheries Subsidies to the Negotiating Group on Rules" (20 June 2002).
297. WTO Doc. No. TN/RL/W/97, "Korea's Comments on the Submission from the United States (TN/RL/W/77)" (5 May 2003).
298. WTO Doc. No. WT/COMTD/W/77/Rev.1, "Implementation of Special and Differential Treatment Provisions in WTO Agreement and Decisions" (21 September 2001).
299. WTO Doc. No. WT/CTE/W/103, "Submission by Iceland to the Committee on Trade and Environment, the Icelandic Fisheries Management System: a Market-Driven Sustainable Fisheries Regime" (25 January 1999).
300. WTO Doc. No. WT/CTE/W/105, "Submission by Australia to the Committee on Trade and Environment, Trade Liberalization and the Environment: A positive Agenda for Trade Reform" (2 February 1999).
301. WTO Doc. No. WT/CTE/W/111, "Submission by Iceland to the Committee on Trade and Environment, On the Environmental Impact of Fisheries Subsidies" (11 March 1999).
302. WTO Doc. No. WT/CTE/W/121, "Submission by New Zealand to the Committee on Trade and Environment, Benefits of Eliminating Trade Distorting and Environmentally Damaging Subsidies in the Fisheries Sector" (28 June 1999).
303. WTO Doc. No. WT/CTE/W/132, "Communication from Iceland to the Committee on Trade and Environment, Fisheries Subsidies and the Environment" (21 February 2000).
304. WTO Doc. No. WT/CTE/W/134, "Communication from New Zealand to the Committee on Trade and Environment, Subsidies in the Fisheries Sector: Update on Recent Work Conducted by New Zealand" (24 February 2000).
305. WTO Doc. No. WT/CTE/W/149, "Communication from the CBD Secretariat to the Committee on Trade and Environment, Response of the Executive Secretary of the Convention on Biological Diversity (CBD) to the Chair of the CTE" (28 June 2000).
306. WTO Doc. No. WT/CTE/W/154, "Communication from the United States to the Committee on Trade and Environment, Environmentally-Harmful and Trade-Distorting Subsidies in Fisheries" (4 July 2000).
307. WTO Doc. No. WT/CTE/W/167, "Note by the Secretariat to the Committee on Trade and Environment, Environmental Benefits of Removing Restrictions and Distortions: the Fisheries Sector-Item 6 of the Work Programme" (16 October 2000).
308. WTO Doc. No. WT/CTE/W/167/Add.1, "Note by the Secretariat to the Committee on Trade and Environment, Environmental Benefits of Re-

moving Restrictions and Distortions: the Fisheries Sector-Item 6 of the Work Programme" (19 June 2001).

309. WTO Doc. No. WT/CTE/W/173, "Submission by Japan to the Committee on Trade and Environment, Japan's Basic Position on the Fishery Subsidy Issue, Item 6" (23 October 2000).
310. WTO Doc. No. WT/CTE/W/175, "Communication from Korea to the Committee on Trade and Environment, Utilization of Subsidies and their Positive Role in the Fisheries Sector" (24 October 2000).
311. WTO Doc. No. WT/CTE/W/187, "Communication from UNEP to the Committee on Trade and Environment, UNEP Fisheries Subsidies Workshop, Chairman's Summary" (15 March 2001).
312. WTO Doc. No. WT/CTE/W/189, "Communication from the FAO to the Committee on Trade and Environment, Update of FAO Activities Related to Fisheries, Report of the Expert Consultation on Economic Incentives and Responsible Fisheries, 28 November-1 December 2000" (18 June 2001).
313. WTO Doc. No. WT/CTE/W/204, "Submission from New Zealand on Paragraph 32(i) of the Doha Declaration to the Committee on Trade and Environment, Fisheries Subsidies" (19 March 2002).
314. WTO Doc. No. WT/CTE/W/226, "Submission by Japan to the Committee on Trade and Environment, Analysis on the Relationship between Fisheries Subsidies and Over-Exploitation of Fisheries Resources" (24 April 2003).
315. WTO Doc. No. WT/CTE/W/236, "Contribution by UNEP, UNEP Workshop on Fisheries Subsidies and Sustainable Fisheries Management, Geneva, 26-27 April 2004, Summary of the Chair" (17 June 2004).
316. WTO Doc. No. WT/CTE/W/46, "Note by the Secretariat to the Committee on Trade and Environment, Provisions of the Multilateral Trading System with Respect to Transparency of Trade Measures Used for Environmental Purposes and Environmental Measures and Requirements Which Have Significant Trade Effects" (29 April 1997).
317. WTO Doc. No. WT/CTE/W/51, "Submission by the United States to the Committee on Trade and Environment, Environmental and Trade Benefits of Removing Subsidies in the Fisheries Sector" (19 May 1997).
318. WTO Doc. No. WT/CTE/W/67, "Note by the Secretariat to the Committee on Trade and Environment, Environmental Benefits of Removing Trade Restrictions and Distortions" (7 November 1997).
319. WTO Doc. No. WT/CTE/W/80, "Note by the Secretariat to the Committee on Trade and Environment, GATT/WTO Rules on Subsidies and Aids Granted in the Fishing Industry" (9 March 1998).
320. WTO Doc. No. WT/CTE/W/80/Add.1, "Note by the Secretariat to the Committee on Trade and Environment, GATT/WTO Rules on Subsidies and Aids Granted in the Fishing Industry, Addendum" (21 September 1999).
321. WTO Doc. No. WT/CTE/W/80/Add.2, "Note by the Secretariat to the Committee on Trade and Environment, GATT/WTO Rules on Subsidies

and Aids Granted in the Fishing Industry, Update of Notifications under the SCM Agreement, Addendum" (1 June 2001).
322. WTO Doc. No. WT/DS22/AB/R, "Report of the Appellate Body, Brazil-Measures Affecting Desiccated Coconut" (21 February 1997).
323. WTO Doc. No. WT/DS22/R, "Report of the Panel, Brazil-Measures Affecting Desiccated Coconut" (17 October 1996).
324. WTO Doc. No. WT/DS26/AB/R, WT/DS48/AB/R, "Report of the Appellate Body, EC Measures Concerning Meat and Meat Products (Hormones)" (16 January 1998).
325. WTO Doc. No. WT/DS316/1, "Request of Consultations by the United States, European Communities & Certain Member States-Measures Affecting Trade in Large Civil Aircraft" (12 October 2004).
326. WTO Doc. No. WT/DS317/1 "Request for Consultations by the European Communities, United States-Measures Affecting Trade in Large Civil Aircraft" (12 October 2004).
327. WTO Doc. No. WT/DS58/AB/R, "WTO Appellate Body, United States – Import Prohibition of Certain Shrimp and Shrimp Products (AB-1998-4)" (12 October 1998).
328. WTO Doc. No. WT/DS70/AB/RW, "Report of the Appellate Body, Canada-Measures Affecting the Export of Civilian Aircraft" (21 July 2000).
329. WTO Doc. No. WT/GC/W/221, "Communication from Japan to the General Council, Preparations for the 1999 Ministerial Conference: Negotiations on Forestry and Fishery Products" (28 June 1999).
330. WTO Doc. No. WT/GC/W/229, "Communication from Iceland to the General Council, Preparations for the 1999 Ministerial Conference: Fisheries Subsidies" (6 July 1999).
331. WTO Doc. No. WT/GC/W/292, "Communication from New Zealand to the General Council, Preparations for the 1999 Ministerial Conference: Elimination of Trade Distorting and Environmentally Damaging Subsidies in the Fisheries Sector" (5 August 1999).
332. WTO Doc. No. WT/GC/W/303, "Communication from Australia, Iceland, New Zealand, Norway, Peru, Philippines and United States to the General Council, Preparations for the 1999 Ministerial Conference: Fisheries Subsidies" (6 August 1999).
333. WTO Doc. No. WT/GC/W/442, "Proposal for a Framework Agreement on Special and Differential Treatment, Communication from Cuba, Dominican Republic, Honduras, India, Indonesia, Kenya, Malaysia, Pakistan, Sri Lanka, Tanzania, Uganda and Zimbabwe" (19 September 2001).
334. WTO Doc. No. WT/MIN(01)/17, "Implementation-Related Issues and Concerns, Ministerial Conference, Fourth Session, Doha, 9-14 November 2001" (20 November 2001).
335. WTO Doc. No. WT/MIN(01)/DEC/1, "WTO Doha Ministerial Declaration" (20 November 2001).

336. WTO Doc. WT/DS18/RW, "Report of the Panel, Australia-Measures Affecting Importation of Salmon-Recourse to Article 21.5 by Canada" (18 February 2000).
337. WTO Doc. WT/DS2/AB/R, "Report of the Appellate Body, Appellate Body-United States, Standards for Reformulated and Conventional Gasoline- AB-1996-1" (29 April 1996).
338. WTO Doc. WT/DS231/AB/R, "Report of the Appellate Body, European Communities-Trade Description of Sardines" (26 September 2002).
339. WTO Doc. WT/DS26/R/USA, "Report of the Panel, EC Measures Concerning Meat and Meat Products (Hormones), Complaint by the United States" (18 August 1997).
340. WTO Doc. WT/DS48/R/CAN, "Report of the Panel, EC Measures Concerning Meat and Meat Products (Hormones), Complaint by Canada" (18 August 1997).
341. WTO Doc. WT/DS76/AB/R, "Report of the Appellate Body, Japan-Measures Affecting Agricultural Products" (22 February 1999).
342. WTO Doc. WT/DS76/R, "Report of the Panel, Japan-Measures Affecting Agricultural Products" (27 October 1998).
343. WTO News–General Council, "General Council Supports Suspension of Trade Talks, Task Force Submits "Aid for Trade" Recommendations" (July 27-28, 2006).
344. WTO, "World Trade Report 2006, Exploring the Links between Subsidies, trade and the WTO" (Geneva: WTO, 2006).
345. WTO, "WTO Annual Report 1997" (Geneva: WTO, 1997).

III. Selected Internet Resources

1. Convention on Biological Diversity, <www.cbd.int>
2. European Union, <http://ec.europa.eu>
3. Food and Agriculture Organization of the United Nations, <www.fao.org>
4. Food and Agriculture Organization of the United Nations, Fisheries Glossary, <www.fao.org/fi/glossary/default.asp>
5. Organisation for Economic Co-operation and Development, <www.oecd.org>
6. Organisation for Economic Co-operation and Development, Glossary of Statistical Terms, <http://stats.oecd.org/glossary/index.htm>
7. World Trade Organization, <www.wto.org>

Index

About the International Max Planck Research School for Maritime Affairs at the University of Hamburg

The International Max Planck Research School for Maritime Affairs at the University of Hamburg was established by the Max Planck Society for the Advancement of Science, in co-operation with the Max Planck Institute for Foreign Private Law and Private International Law (Hamburg), the Max Planck Institute for Comparative Foreign Public Law and International Law (Heidelberg), the Max Planck Institute for Meteorology (Hamburg) and the University of Hamburg. The School's research is focused on the legal, economic, and geophysical aspects of the use, protection, and organization of the oceans. Its researchers work in the fields of law, economics, and natural sciences. The School provides extensive research capacities as well as its own teaching curriculum. Currently, the School has 17 Directors who determine the general work of the School, act as supervisors for dissertations, elect applicants for the School's PhD-grants, and are the editors of this book series:

Prof. Dr. Dr. h.c. Jürgen Basedow is Director of the Max Planck Institute for Foreign Private Law and Private International Law; *Prof. Dr. Peter Ehlers* is the Director of the German Federal Maritime and Hydrographic Agency; *Prof. Dr. Robert Freitag* is Professor at the Law Faculty of the University of Hamburg; *Prof. Dr. Dr. h.c. Hartmut Graßl* is Director emeritus of the Max Planck Institute for Meteorology; *Prof. Dr. Lars Kaleschke* is Junior Professor at the Institute of Oceanography of the University of Hamburg; *Prof. Dr. Hans-Joachim Koch* is Managing Director of the Seminar of Environmental Law at the University of Hamburg; *Prof. Dr. Doris König* is Professor at the Bucerius Law School; *Prof. Dr. Rainer Lagoni* is Director emeritus of the Institute of Maritime Law and the Law of the Sea at the University of Hamburg; *PD Dr. Gerhard Lammel* is Senior Scientist at the Max Planck Institute for Meteorology; *Prof. Dr. Ulrich Magnus* is Managing Director of the Seminar of Foreign Law and Private International Law at the University of Hamburg; *Prof. Dr. Peter Mankowski* is Director of the Seminar of Foreign and Private International Law at the University of Hamburg; *Prof. Dr. Marian Paschke* is Managing Director of the Institute of Maritime Law and the Law of the Sea at the University of Hamburg; *PD Dr. Thomas Pohlmann* is Senior Scientist at the Centre for Marine and Climate Research and Member of the Institute of Oceanography at the University of Hamburg; *Dr. Uwe Schneider* is Assistant Professor at the Research Unit Sustainability and Global Change of the University of Hamburg; *Prof. Dr. Jürgen Sündermann* is Director emeritus of the Centre for Marine and Climate Research at the University of Hamburg;

Prof. Dr. Rüdiger Wolfrum is Director at the Max Planck Institute for Comparative Foreign Public Law and International Law and a judge at the International Tribunal for the Law of the Sea; *Prof. Dr. Wilfried Zahel* is Professor emeritus at the Centre for Marine and Climate Research of the University of Hamburg.

At present, *Prof. Dr. Dr. h.c. Jürgen Basedow* and *Prof. Dr. Ulrich Magnus* serve as speakers of the Research School.

MIX
Papier aus verantwortungsvollen Quellen
Paper from responsible sources
FSC® C105338

If you have any concerns about our products,
you can contact us on
ProductSafety@springernature.com

In case Publisher is established outside the EU,
the EU authorized representative is:
Springer Nature Customer Service Center GmbH
Europaplatz 3, 69115 Heidelberg, Germany

Printed by Libri Plureos GmbH
in Hamburg, Germany